lonely planet

Discover

Contents ➤

Great Britain

Throughout this book, we use these icons to highlight special recommendations:

 The Best...
Lists for everything from bars to wildlife – to make sure you don't miss out

 Don't Miss
A must-see – don't go home until you've been there

 **Local Knowledge** Local experts reveal their top picks and secret highlights

 Detour
Special places a little off the beaten track

 If you like...
Lesser-known alternatives to world-famous attractions

These icons help you quickly identify reviews in the text and on the map:

 Sights

 Eating

 Drinking

 Sleeping

 Information

This edition written and researched by

David Else

David Atkinson, Oliver Berry, Joe Bindloss, Fionn Davenport, Marc Di Duca, Belinda Dixon, Peter Dragicevich, Etain O'Carroll, Andy Symington, Neil Wilson

Contents

Contents

On the Road

This Is Great Britain

Icons – Britain is full of them: the Tower of London, Edinburgh Castle, Buckingham Palace, Manchester United, The Beatles. And alongside these big names, Britain boasts many more delights that'll soon become your own personal favourites.

Britain's astounding variety is a major reason to travel here. In cities such as Bath and York, the streets buzz day and night, with tempting shops and restaurants, and some of the finest museums in the world. Next day, you're deep in the Cotswolds countryside, climbing mountains in Snowdonia, enjoying the coast at Brighton or sailing across to the Isle of Skye.

A journey through Britain is a journey through history. You can walk beside the ancient megaliths of Stonehenge, stroll around the masterpiece of Canterbury Cathedral or explore the ancient colleges of Oxford and Cambridge. Then fast forward to the future and you're admiring 21st-century architecture in Manchester or the space-age domes of Cornwall's Eden Project.

Britain boasts a rich and complex culture, but it's familiar to many visitors. This is all thanks to a vast catalogue of British film and TV exports. The same applies when it comes to communication; this is home turf for the English language, so many visitors don't need to carry a phrasebook. Of course Wales and Scotland have their own languages, but everyone speaks English too.

Finally, travel in Britain is a breeze. Granted, it may not be totally effortless, but it's easy compared with many other parts of the world. Although the locals may grumble (in fact, it's a national pastime) public transport is pretty good, and a train ride through the British landscape can be a highlight in itself. For drivers road distances are short, and in this compact country you're never far from the next scenic town, the next welcoming pub, the next national park or the next impressive castle on your hit-list of highlights.

> 66
> A journey through Britain is a journey through history
> 99

Walkers on the Pembrokeshire Coast (p264)

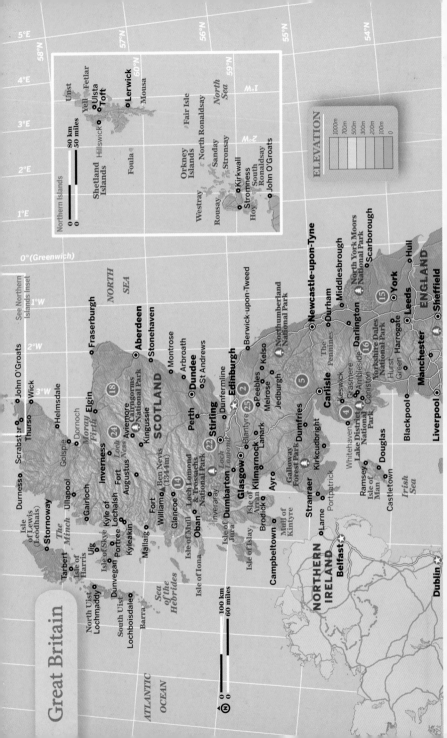

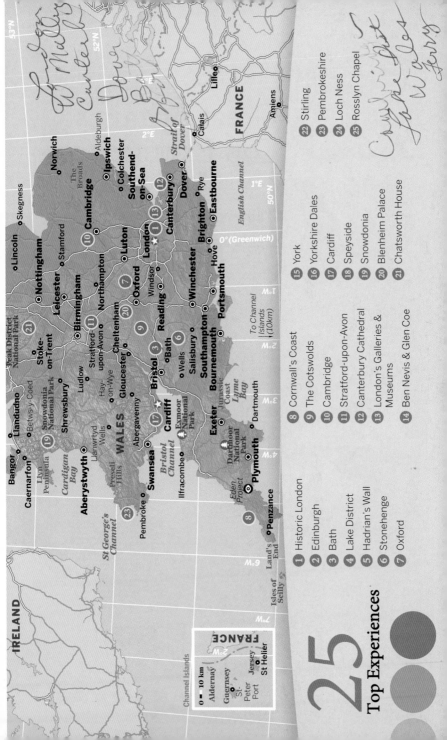

25 Top Experiences

1. Historic London
2. Edinburgh
3. Bath
4. Lake District
5. Hadrian's Wall
6. Stonehenge
7. Oxford
8. Cornwall's Coast
9. The Cotswolds
10. Cambridge
11. Stratford-upon-Avon
12. Canterbury Cathedral
13. London's Galleries & Museums
14. Ben Nevis & Glen Coe
15. York
16. Yorkshire Dales
17. Cardiff
18. Speyside
19. Snowdonia
20. Blenheim Palace
21. Chatsworth House
22. Stirling
23. Pembrokeshire
24. Loch Ness
25. Rosslyn Chapel

25 Great Britain's Top Experiences

Historic London

London's (p51) visible history stretches across almost 2000 years, from the ancient remains of Roman walls in the oldest parts of the metropolis to the space-age designs of skyscrapers in the City financial district and new millennium projects such as the London Eye. In between the very old and very new, other eras have bequeathed Britain's capital with some of the world's best-known and most instantly recognisable buildings – the Tower of London, St Paul's Cathedral, Tower Bridge – along with other iconic structures like the Southbank Centre and the great maritime monuments of Greenwich.

Tower Bridge with Wendy Taylor's *Timepiece* sculpture in the foreground

② Edinburgh

Edinburgh (p294) is a city of many moods, famous for its festivals and especially lively in the summer. Visit in spring to see the castle silhouetted against a blue sky, with a yellow haze of daffodils misting the slopes below the esplanade. In winter, frost snags the spires of the Old Town in the morning, and the city's dark lanes are more mysterious than ever, with rain on the cobblestones and a warm glow beckoning from the window of a pub. Princes Street Gardens

Bath

Britain can boast many great cities, but Bath (p181) stands out as the belle of the ball. Thanks to natural hot water bubbling to the surface, the Romans built a health resort here. The waters were rediscovered in the 18th century and Bath became *the* place to see and be seen by British high society. Today, the stunning Georgian architecture of grand town houses, sweeping crescents and Palladian mansions (not to mention Roman remains, a beautiful cathedral and cutting-edge 21st-century spa), mean Bath demands your undivided attention.

Great Bath, Roman Baths complex

The Best...
Monuments

NELSON'S COLUMN
In the centre of Trafalgar Sq (p69), commemorating Nelson's landmark victory.

HOUSES OF PARLIAMENT & THE TOWER OF BIG BEN
The seat of British political power for centuries and the nation's best-known landmark. (p64)

NATIONAL WALLACE MONUMENT
A Gothic tower dedicated to the Scottish freedom fighter William Wallace. (p320)

SCOTT MONUMENT
A decorated spire in Edinburgh built in memory of writer Sir Walter Scott. (p299)

THE MONUMENT
Raised by the surviving populace after London's Great Fire of 1666. (p77)

The Best...
Museums

BRITISH MUSEUM
Vast collections from the ancient world. (p84)

VICTORIA & ALBERT MUSEUM
The cultural equivalent of the nation's attic. (p80)

IMPERIAL WAR MUSEUM NORTH
Manchester branch of the famous London museum. (p227)

INTERNATIONAL SLAVERY MUSEUM
Clear and uncompromising exhibition in Liverpool. (p222)

NATIONAL MUSEUM OF SCOTLAND
A trove full of Scottish treasures. (p298)

KELVINGROVE MUSEUM
Glasgow's favourite eclectic and eccentric gem. (p312)

DAVID TOMLINSON / LONELY PLANET IMAGES ©

Lake District

4

William Wordsworth and his Romantic friends were the first to champion the charms of the Lake District (p233) and it's not hard to see what stirred them. With high mountains, razor-edged ridges, deep valleys – plus, of course, lakes – this craggy corner of northern England is still considered by many to be the spiritual home of British hiking. So put on your boots, head for the hills or stroll along the lake shores, and drink in the views. Inspiration is sure to follow.

ANDREW MARSHALL & LEANNE WALKER / LONELY PLANET IMAGES ©

Hadrian's Wall

5

Hadrian's Wall (p241) is one of Britain's most dramatic Roman ruins, its procession of forts, garrisons, towers and milecastles marching across a wild and lonely landscape on the borderlands between England and Scotland. Almost 2000 years ago, this barrier marked the northernmost edge of the Roman Empire. To the south was the civilised world of underfloor heating, bathhouses and orderly taxpaying; to the north the unruly land of the marauding Celts.

Stonehenge

Mysterious Stonehenge (p178) is Britain's most iconic ancient site, drawing people for more than 5000 years. And we still don't know quite why it was built. Most visitors get to gaze at the 50-ton megaliths from behind the perimeter fence, but with enough planning you can book a tour and get even closer. In the slanting sunlight, away from the crowds, it's an ethereal place – a visit here is an experience that certainly stays with you.

Oxford

Brilliant minds and venerable institutions – and not a little money – have made the university in Oxford (p134) famous across the globe. The beautiful college buildings, archaic traditions and stunning architecture have changed little over the centuries, leaving the city centre much as former alumni Einstein or Tolkien would have found it. This is still a world of cobbled lanes and hushed quads where gowned cyclists and dusty academics roam.

Cornwall's Coast

Cornwall (p191) boasts many miles of scenic coastline with rugged cliffs, sparkling bays and some of the loveliest sandy beaches in all England, favoured by everyone from bucket-and-spade families to beach-bronzed surfers. Add to this the charming seaside towns like St Ives and the landmark of St Michael's Mount, and you'll see why this is one of the most popular holiday spots in the country. Visit in early spring or late autumn and you might even have the sands to yourself.

Fishing village, Cornwall coast

The Best...
Hiking

LAKE DISTRICT
Follow Wordsworth's footsteps among England's highest peaks. (p233)

SNOWDONIA
Rugged mountains in North Wales. (p276)

PEAK DISTRICT
High moorland plateaus and lush tranquil valleys. (p154)

YORKSHIRE DALES
Perfect hikes and strolls in a green and pleasant land. (p217)

THE TROSSACHS
High peaks and deep glens offer some serious hiking country. (p321)

BEN NEVIS
Britain's highest summit and popular goal for visiting hikers. (p344)

The Cotswolds

A rolling landscape of hills and valleys, dotted with glorious villages, old mansions, thatched cottages and atmospheric churches – that's the Cotswolds (p141). The medieval wool trade brought wealth to the area and left it with a glut of beautiful buildings – all built with local honey-coloured stone and glowing contentedly whenever the sun shines. This is the place to come if you've ever craved exposed beams, dreamed of English-rose wallpaper or lusted after a cream tea.

Lavender field in the Cotswolds

The Best...
Nightlife

LONDON
With all its clubs, bars and theatres, you'll never be bored in the capital. (p96 and p97)

LIVERPOOL
The Beatles kicked things off at the Cavern Club; today's city continues the legacy. (p226)

CARDIFF
City clubs, waterfront bars and restaurants, plus a live music scene that punches above its weight. (p261)

EDINBURGH
The speciality here is welcoming pubs with local jazz or folk bands. (p309)

Cambridge

10

Along with Oxford, the eternal rival, Cambridge (p116) is one of Britain's most famous university towns. The ancient colleges that make up the university are marvels of architecture and include the show-stopping Gothic masterpiece of King's College Chapel, as well as historic Trinity College and Caius College. After seeing the sights, relax in the Backs, the leafy lawns that run down to the river behind the colleges, enjoy a picnic and watch the country's academic elite drift by on punts and rowing boats. Or hire a boat and join them.

Stratford-upon-Avon

11

The pretty market town of Stratford-upon-Avon (p145) just happens to be the birthplace of Britain's best-known literary figure, and also where he shuffled off this mortal coil, and so today its tight knot of Tudor streets form a living street-map of Shakespeare's life and times. Huge crowds of theatre lovers and would-be thespians congregate here to visit the five historic houses owned by Shakespeare and his relatives, with a respectful detour to the old stone church where the Bard was laid to rest.

Half-timbered houses, Stratford-upon-Avon

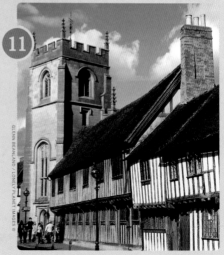

GLENN BEANLAND / LONELY PLANET IMAGES ©

12

Canterbury Cathedral

Few other English cathedrals come close to Canterbury (p109), top temple of the Anglican Church and a place of worship for over 15 centuries. Its intricate tower dominates the skyline, its grandeur unsurpassed by later structures. At its heart lies a 12th-century crime scene, the spot where Archbishop Thomas Becket was put to the sword – an epoch-making event that launched a million pilgrimages and still pulls in the crowds. A lone candle mourns the gruesome deed, the pink sandstone before it smoothed by 800 years' worth of devout kneeling.

13

London's Galleries & Museums

Institutions great and small, wise and wonderful – the city of London (p64) has them all. The range is vast: generalist collections (the British Museum, Victoria & Albert), specific themes (Imperial War Museum, Natural History Museum), famous and recognisable (National Portrait Gallery), and the oddball and intriguing (Tate Modern). You could spend weeks without even scratching the surface.

Tate Modern at night

Ben Nevis & Glen Coe

The allure of Scotland's natural features is strong. Ben Nevis (p344) is Britain's highest mountain, and every year around 100,000 people set off to reach the summit, though rocky paths and fickle weather mean not all reach the top. The reward for those that do is a truly magnificent view (cloud permitting) and a great sense of achievement. Real enthusiasts can warm up with a hike in nearby Glen Coe (p341), the county's most famous glen and a combination of those two essential qualities of the Highland landscape – dramatic scenery and deep history. View from Ben Nevis

The Best...
Castles

WINDSOR CASTLE
The largest and oldest occupied fortress in the world, and the Queen's weekend retreat. (p106)

WARWICK CASTLE
Preserved enough to be impressive; ruined enough to be romantic. (p149)

CAERNARFON CASTLE
Military stronghold, seat of government, royal palace and Welsh icon. (p273)

CONWY CASTLE
Stunning medieval fortress, symbolic of English power in Wales. (p272)

EDINBURGH CASTLE
The focal point of the Scottish capital. (p294)

STIRLING CASTLE
Perched on a volcanic crag, with stunning views. (p317)

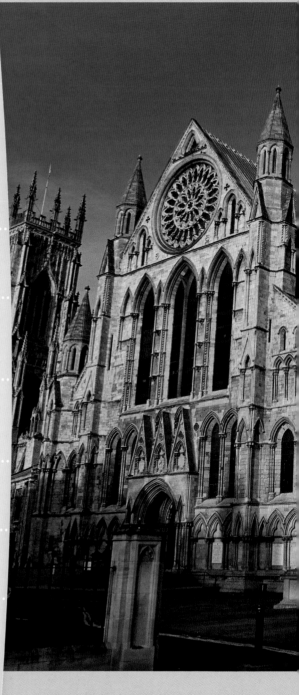

The Best...
Cathedrals

ST PAUL'S CATHEDRAL
A symbol of London for centuries, still a feature of the city skyline. (p78)

YORK MINSTER
One of the largest medieval cathedrals in Europe, especially renowned for its windows. (p214)

CANTERBURY CATHEDRAL
The mother ship of the Anglican Church, still attracting visitors in their thousands. (p109)

ST DAVID'S CATHEDRAL
An ancient place of worship in Britain's smallest city. (p265)

LIVERPOOL'S CATHEDRALS
Classics of 19th- and 20th-century architecture. (p221)

GLASGOW CATHEDRAL
Shining example of Gothic architecture. (p312)

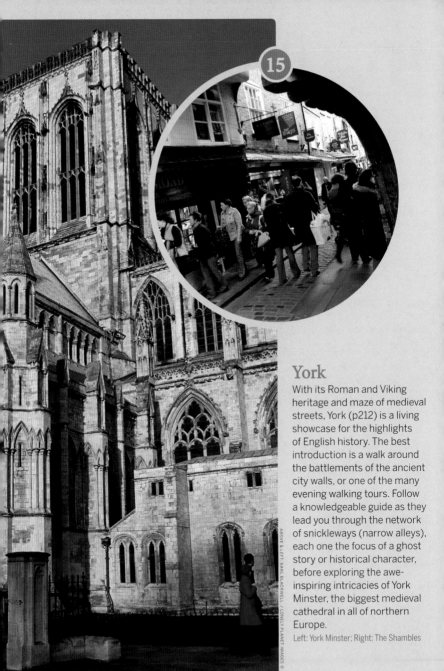

15

York

With its Roman and Viking heritage and maze of medieval streets, York (p212) is a living showcase for the highlights of English history. The best introduction is a walk around the battlements of the ancient city walls, or one of the many evening walking tours. Follow a knowledgeable guide as they lead you through the network of snickleways (narrow alleys), each one the focus of a ghost story or historical character, before exploring the awe-inspiring intricacies of York Minster, the biggest medieval cathedral in all of northern Europe.

Left: York Minster; Right: The Shambles

ABOVE & LEFT: KARL BLACKWELL / LONELY PLANET IMAGES ©

Yorkshire Dales

This national park (p217) is characterised by a distinctive landscape of high moorland, stepped skylines and flat-topped hills rising above green valley floors – patchworked with walls and ancient stone barns, and remote settlements where sheep and cattle still graze on village greens. Across the countryside are historic market towns and hardy villages such as Skipton and Malham, which make excellent bases for exploring this quintessential northern English landscape.

Cardiff

Exuberant Cardiff (p258), has emerged as one of Britain's leading urban centres, entering the new millennium with vigour and confidence, and flexing new-found architectural muscles. From the historic castle to the stunning range of buildings on the ultra-modern waterfront; from the Victorian shopping arcades to the gigantic rugby stadium that is the pulsating heart of the city on match days – Cardiff has a buzz that reverberates through the streets.
Cardiff Castle

Speyside

Scotland's national drink is whisky (note, there's no 'e') – from the Gaelic *uisge bagh*, meaning 'water of life' – and has been distilled here for more than 500 years. Today, Dufftown (p324) and surrounding Speyside – the valley of the silvery River Spey – is a major whisky-making centre, with several distilleries producing many famous varieties. Some distilleries offer a guided tour, rounded off with a tasting session. Sampling a dram or two of the local specialities is a great way to explore this region.

Whisky distillery, Speyside

The Best...
Stately Homes

BLENHEIM PALACE
A monumental baroque fantasy and one of Britain's greatest stately homes. (p144)

CASTLE HOWARD
Another stunning baroque edifice, best known as the setting for *Brideshead Revisited*. (p213)

CULZEAN CASTLE
Most impressive of Scotland's great stately homes, perched dramatically on the edge of cliffs. (p315)

CHATSWORTH HOUSE
The quintessential stately home; a treasure trove of heirlooms and works of art. (p158)

Snowdonia

19

The rugged northwest corner of Wales has rocky mountain peaks, glacier-hewn valleys, sinuous ridges, and sparkling lakes and rivers. Protected as Snowdonia National Park (p276), the most popular area is around Snowdon – Wales' highest peak – where many people hike to the top, and many more take the cog railway to the spectacular visitor centre perched just below the summit. Around the base of the mountain are charm-infused villages with cosy hotels and welcoming pubs.

Climber in Snowdonia

The Best...
Shopping

LONDON
Everything from world-brand megastores to back-street markets. (p99)

HAY-ON-WYE
The self-proclaimed secondhand-book capital of the world. (p267)

CARDIFF
Victorian-era arcades branch off the main street, lined with speciality shops. (p261)

EDINBURGH
Stock up on kilts along the Royal Mile, or go down the cobbled alleys for fashion, music and crafts. (p310)

BRIGHTON
The Lanes has boutiques; nearby North Laine has essentials like Elvis outfits and monocycles. (p115)

Blenheim Palace

20

One of the country's greatest stately homes, Blenheim Palace (p144) is a monumental baroque fantasy designed by Sir John Vanbrugh and now a Unesco World Heritage Site. Inside, the house is stuffed with statues, tapestries, ostentatious furniture and giant oil paintings in elaborate gilt frames. Other attractions include the Churchill Exhibition, dedicated to the life, work and writings of WWII hero Sir Winston Churchill, who was born at Blenheim in 1874. Around the house are lavish gardens and vast parklands, some landscaped by 'Capability' Brown.

Chatsworth House

The sumptuous Chatsworth House (p158) has been occupied by the earls and dukes of Devonshire for centuries. Famous visitors include Mary, Queen of Scots, who was imprisoned here on the orders of Elizabeth I in 1569. Chatsworth was altered over the years, and the current building has a Georgian feel, dating back to 1820. The lavish apartments and mural-painted state-rooms are packed with paintings and priceless furniture.

Stirling

For centuries Stirling (p316) sat astride the route taken by English armies invading from the south. Its crag-top castle commanded a crossing of the River Forth – site of a famous victory for Scots freedom-fighter William Wallace in 1297 – and was a favourite residence of kings James IV and James V. Today Stirling Castle (above) is as much of a must-see as Edinburgh, along with the streets and walls of the Old Town and the nearby National Wallace Monument.

Pembrokeshire

Perched at the tip of wild and wonderful West Wales, Pembrokeshire (p264) boasts one of Britain's most beautiful and dramatic stretches of coast, with sheer cliffs, natural arches, blowholes, sea stacks and a wonderful hinterland of tranquil villages and secret waterways. It's a landscape of Norman castles, Iron Age hill forts, holy wells and Celtic saints – including the nation's patron, St David – and the remnants of an even older people that left behind intriguing stone circles.

Coastal view, Pembrokeshire

The Best...
Galleries

TATE BRITAIN
The best-known gallery in London, full to the brim with the finest works. (p80)

TATE MODERN
London's other Tate focuses on modern art in all its wonderful permutations. (p79)

TATE LIVERPOOL
Sometimes dubbed 'Tate of the North', it has 20th-century artists plus touring exhibitions from the London mothership. (p222)

NATIONAL GALLERY OF SCOTLAND
An important collection of European works and the best place to see well-known Scottish paintings. (p299)

Loch Ness

In a land rich in legends, there are few that match the international reach of 'Nessie' the Loch Ness Monster, a mythical beast or prehistoric appearance, known the world over from Texas to Tokyo. While the monster legend may attract you to Loch Ness (p340) in the first place, once you've arrived you'll soon realise that it's a hauntingly beautiful place, rich in historic sites, such as Urquhart Castle, and close to some of Scotland's finest Highland scenery.

Urquhart Castle ruins on the edge of Loch Ness

The Best...
Ruined Abbeys

FOUNTAINS ABBEY
Extensive ruins set in landscaped water-gardens – one of the most beautiful sites in Britain. (p219)

TINTERN ABBEY
Riverside ruins that inspired generations of poets and artists. (p263)

ST ANDREWS CATHEDRAL
Not technically an abbey, but still impressive remains of one of Britain's most magnificent medieval buildings. (p322)

GLASTONBURY ABBEY
The legendary burial place of King Arthur and Queen Guinevere. (p189)

25

Rosslyn Chapel

This beautiful 15th-century chapel (p303) on the outskirts of Edinburgh shot to international stardom thanks to its role in Dan Brown's *The Da Vinci Code* and the subsequent Hollywood movie. Its ornate and elaborate carvings are most unusual for the period, and include flowers, vines, angels and biblical figures, as well as the pagan 'Green Man' and other images associated with Freemasonry and the Knights Templar. Conspiracy theories aside, it's a stunning place to visit.

Great Britain's
Top Itineraries

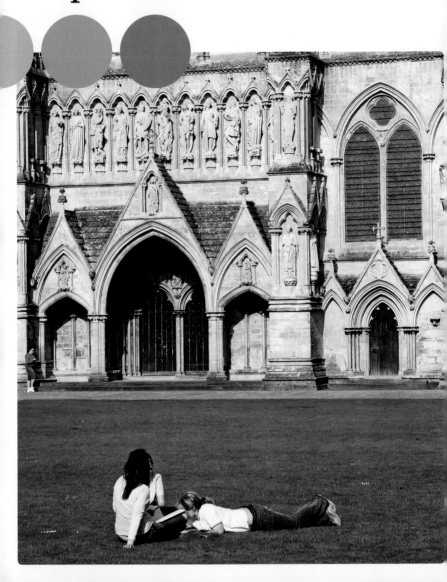

London to Salisbury
Absolute Classics

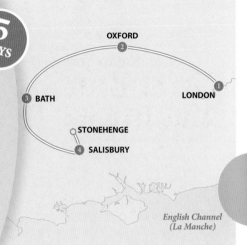

5 DAYS

If time is tight you'll have to make the most of every moment, so we've stripped down this trip to include Britain's absolute essentials.

OXFORD

BATH

LONDON

STONEHENGE

SALISBURY

English Channel (La Manche)

① London (p51)

With so many sights in the capital, you'll have to plan your time with military precision. Try to tick off **Trafalgar Square** plus **Buckingham Palace** and **Westminster Abbey** followed by the **Houses of Parliament** and the tower of **Big Ben**. Other must-sees are the **Tower of London** and **Tower Bridge**. In the evening, take in the city's skyline from the **London Eye**.

LONDON ➡ OXFORD

🚆 **One hour** From London's Paddington station. 🚗 **90 minutes** (traffic permitting) From central London to Oxford on the M40 motorway.

② Oxford (p134)

Elegant **Oxford** is one of England's most famous university towns, with a wealth of historic traditions and stunning architecture. The university consists of many separate colleges, with **Christ Church College** and **Magdalen College** among the best to visit. Just outside Oxford is the fabulous mansion of **Blenheim Palace**.

OXFORD ➡ BATH

🚆 **75-90 minutes** Frequent trains from Oxford requiring a change at Didcot. 🚗 **Two hours** On the scenic (but slower) roads through the Cotswolds; **90 minutes** Via main highways A34 and M4.

③ Bath (p181)

The beautiful city of Bath is renowned for its grand streets of Georgian architecture, especially the **Royal Crescent**. Other highlights include awesome **Bath Abbey**. Don't forget, of course, the **Roman Baths** that give the city its name.

BATH ➡ SALISBURY

🚆 **One hour** Frequent trains from Bath Spa train station. 🚗 **One hour** Follow the main road (A36), detouring slightly via Stonehenge (p178).

④ Salisbury (p175)

Salisbury is most famous for the magnificent **Salisbury Cathedral**, especially its graceful spire, the tallest in England. Other sights include the medieval **Cathedral Close**, a tranquil enclave surrounded by beautiful houses. If you didn't detour on your way here, a half-day excursion to **Stonehenge** from Salisbury is easy to arrange.

Salisbury Cathedral (p177)

33

London to York
Eastern Promise

This trip takes you up the eastern side of England, to visit historic cities and two of the country's finest stately homes.

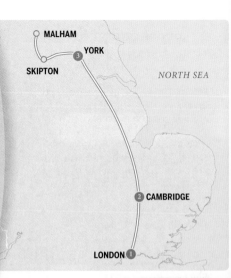

MALHAM

YORK

SKIPTON

NORTH SEA

CAMBRIDGE

LONDON

1 London (p51)

With only five days in total to play with, that means just one or two days in London, so cherry-picking is essential. Highlights to tick off include **Trafalgar Square** and maybe the **National Gallery**, the **Tower of London**, and a view of the Thames at **Tower Bridge**. Add a visit to **St Paul's Cathedral**, followed by a stroll along the **South Bank** via the works of art at **Tate Modern**, and a birds-eye view of the city's skyline from the **London Eye**. On your second day, take a river boat down the Thames to the maritime splendour of **Greenwich** – where you can also stand in two hemispheres – or hop on a train for a day trip out to **Windsor Castle** and the nearby historic exclusive school of **Eton**.

LONDON ⟳ CAMBRIDGE

🚃 **1¼ hours** From London Kings Cross or Liverpool St stations to Cambridge. 🚗 **1½ hours** Once you've escaped London traffic, it's an easy drive to Cambridge on the M11.

2 Cambridge (p116)

The beautiful city of Cambridge is awash with elegant architecture and landmark buildings. Most famous are the historic university colleges, including **Trinity College**, **Corpus Christi College** and **Gonville & Caius College**. And don't miss the truly awe-inspiring **Kings College Chapel**, renowned for its intricate fan-vaulted ceiling and lofty stained-glass windows. After seeing the sights, relax in the **Backs**, tranquil lawns behind the colleges leading down to the river – often the most enduring image of Cambridge for visitors. Across the shimmering waters are graceful bridges including the **Mathematical Bridge** and the Venice-inspired **Bridge of Sighs**.

CAMBRIDGE ⟳ YORK

🚃 **2½ hours** Regular trains; change at Peterborough. 🚗 **Three hours** A combination of the A1 and M1 major routes. If time allows branch off the motorway near Derby to visit Chatsworth House (p158).

3 York (p212)

It's easy to spend a full day in the graceful city of York. Famous highlights include the medieval streets known as the **Shambles**, the remarkably intact **city walls** and the spectacular cathedral of **York Minster**, while the city's Viking heritage is celebrated at the **Jorvik** exhibition. If you still have a day in hand, head out west from York into the green valleys of the **Yorkshire Dales**, stopping in the town of **Skipton** or the village of **Malham**. Or take a tour to nearby **Castle Howard**, one of the finest stately homes in the north of England.

Punting in Cambridge (p116)

PHOTOGRAPHER: MAX PAOLI & RUTH EASTHAM / LONELY PLANET IMAGES ©

10 DAYS

London to Edinburgh
Northern Exposure

This itinerary leads you through central and northern England, then crosses the border into Scotland, where highlights include two of the country's finest castles.

STIRLING CASTLE ○ ─ 6 EDINBURGH

NORTH SEA

HADRIAN'S WALL 5

IRISH SEA

4 YORK

STRATFORD-UPON-AVON 3

OXFORD 2

1 LONDON

① London (p51)

On the first couple of days, orientate yourself by visiting London's key sites, such as **Trafalgar Square** and **Buckingham Palace**, followed by **Westminster Abbey** and **St Paul's Cathedral**. On your second or third day, take in the **Tower of London** then head down the river to explore **Greenwich**.

LONDON ➲ OXFORD

🚃 **One hour** From London's Paddington Station direct to Oxford. 🚗 **90 minutes** (traffic permitting) From central London to Oxford on the M40.

② Oxford (p134)

The city of Oxford is one of England's most famous university towns. While here, be sure to visit **Christ Church College** and **Magdalen College**, and take a trip just outside Oxford to the fabulous mansion and park of **Blenheim Palace**.

OXFORD ➲ STRATFORD-UPON-AVON

🚃 **1½ hours** From Oxford to Stratford by train requires a change at Banbury. 🚌 **Two hours** Direct bus service. 🚗 **One hour** Various scenic routes through the Cotswolds.

③ Stratford-upon-Avon (p145)

Key sights here include the house where it all (probably) began, **Shakespeare's Birthplace** and **Anne Hathaway's Cottage**. Leave time enough to visit **Holy Trinity Church** and, if you're overnighting here, take in a play at the **Royal Shakespeare Theatre**.

STRATFORD-UPON-AVON ➲ YORK

🚃 **Four hours** A bit of a long haul; change at Leamington and Birmingham. 🚗 **Three hours** Drive via Birmingham and the M1 and A1 highways.

④ York (p212)

You can enjoy a full day in the graceful city of York. Famous highlights include the rickety old streets of the **Shambles**, the remarkably intact **city walls** and the spectacular might of **York Minster** – one of the largest medieval cathedrals in Europe.

YORK ➲ HADRIAN'S WALL

🚃 **2½ hours** Scenic rail journey via a change at Newcastle. 🚗 **Two hours** Aim north up the A1; turn west near Newcastle to reach Haltwhistle.

⑤ Hadrian's Wall (p241)

The 2000-year-old remains of **Hadrian's Wall** are one of Britain's most revealing and dramatic Roman sites. Base yourself in **Haltwhistle** and go out to explore the forts of **Housesteads** and **Vindolanda**.

HADRIAN'S WALL ➲ EDINBURGH

🚃 **2½ hours** Go to Newcastle, change, then it's a spectacular journey north. 🚗 **2½ hours** Direct via Newcastle and the A1, or a scenic cross-country route.

⑥ Edinburgh (p294)

Scotland's capital city is awash with sights, including **Edinburgh Castle** and the **Palace of Holyroodhouse**, as well as the **Royal Yacht Britannia**. With another day in hand, take a tour out to nearby **Stirling Castle**.

A section of Hadrian's Wall (p241)

10 DAYS

London to St Ives
Southern Belles

This trip leads through some of the most beautiful cities in southern England, including four of the country's outstanding medieval cathedrals.

① London (p51)

Most journeys through Britain start or end in London and this one is no exception. Take a day or two to enjoy the key sites, such as **Buckingham Palace** and **Westminster Abbey** plus the **Houses of Parliament** and tower of **Big Ben**. Other highlights include the **Tower of London** and **Tower Bridge**. If time allows, take a day trip to **Windsor Castle**.

LONDON ➡ WINCHESTER

🚃 **One hour** It's an easy train ride from London Waterloo to Winchester. 🚗 **1½ hours** London traffic is heavy but usually clearer on the M3.

② Winchester (p172)

The ancient capital of England is famous for its connections to legendary King Alfred and for the immense **Winchester Cathedral** that dominates the centre of town; relatively plain on the outside, the interior is awe-inspiring.

WINCHESTER ➡ SALISBURY

🚃 **1¼ hours** The journey by train requires a change at Southampton. 🚗 **45 minutes** It's an easy drive via the A30.

③ Salisbury (p175)

Visit Salisbury's magnificent **Salisbury Cathedral**. The spire of this medieval monument is the tallest in England. Other sights in Salisbury include the impressive **Cathedral Close**.

SALISBURY ➡ BATH

🚃 **One hour** Easy direct train ride. 🚗 **1½ hours** It's an easy drive, except the last few miles; Bath traffic is always bad. Detour via Stonehenge (p175).

④ Bath (p181)

The grand streets of Bath are filled with Georgian architecture, especially the **Royal Crescent**. Other highlights of this beautiful city include the cathedral of **Bath Abbey**, and the **Roman Baths** that give the city its name.

BATH ➡ PLYMOUTH

🚃 **Three hours** Regular trains; change at Bristol. 🚗 **Three hours** Direct via the M4 and M5, or a scenic cross-country route via Wells (p187).

⑤ Plymouth (p191)

Not on everyone's radar, but Plymouth is where the Pilgrim Fathers' *Mayflower* set sail for America in 1620. Today, the **Mayflower Steps** mark the point of departure. About 150 years later, Captain James Cook cast off from the same place to search for a southern continent.

PLYMOUTH ➡ ST IVES

🚃 **2¼ hours** Change at St Erth; it's a scenic branchline from St Erth to St Ives. 🚗 **Two hours** Via the A38 and A30; there are frequent traffic jams in holiday periods.

⑥ St Ives (p195)

To relax after your tour, head for the delightful coast town of St Ives. The beaches attract surfers and holiday-makers, while the sea light attracts artists. Galleries abound, including **Tate St Ives** and the **Barbara Hepworth Museum**.

Crypt, Winchester Cathedral (p174)

London to Edinburgh
The Full Monty

One trip, three countries. This grand tour takes in the very best of England, Scotland and Wales – the three constituent nations that make Britain truly Great.

London (p51)

Take a day or two to enjoy the key sites, such as **Buckingham Palace** and **Westminster Abbey**. Another high point is a visit to the **Tower of London** and nearby **Tower Bridge**. If time allows, take a day trip to **Canterbury Cathedral** and **Leeds Castle**, two of the most spectacular buildings in southeast England.

LONDON ○ SALISBURY

🚃 **1½ hours** Frequent trains from London Waterloo to Salisbury. 🚗 **Two hours** Leaving London is slow, then go via the M3 and A303. Detour via Winchester (p172).

② Salisbury (p175)

Salisbury is most famous for magnificent **Salisbury Cathedral**, whose graceful spire is the tallest in England. Other sights include the impressive **Cathedral Close**.

SALISBURY ○ BATH

🚃 **One hour** Easy direct train ride. 🚗 **1½ hours** It's an easy drive, except the last few miles; Bath traffic is always bad. Detour via Stonehenge (p178).

Bath (p181)

The **Royal Crescent** is a highlight among Bath's grand streets of Georgian architecture, while other attractions include **Bath Abbey** and the **Roman Baths**.

BATH ○ OXFORD

🚃 **75–90 minutes** Frequent trains from Bath to Oxford; change at Didcot. 🚗 **Two hours** On the scenic (but slower) roads through the Cotswolds; 1½ hours via the main highways M4 and A34. If time allows, detour first to Cardiff (p258).

④ Oxford (p134)

Key sights in this famous university town include **Christ Church College** and **Magdalen College**. If time allows, take a tour from Oxford to the fabulous mansion of **Blenheim Palace**.

OXFORD ○ CHESTER

🚃 **Three hours** Long train ride, requiring changes at Birmingham and Crewe. 🚗 **Two hours** Via M40 and M6; not all so scenic. Detour via Stratford-upon-Avon (p145).

Sheep crossing, Lake District
PHOTOGRAPHER: SHANNON NACE / LONELY PLANET IMAGES ©

7 **Lake District** (p233)

This scenic part of England has high mountains, deep valleys and beautiful lakes such as **Windermere**. Literary fans visit **Grasmere**, home to poet William Wordsworth. Hikers should head for the hills or stroll along the lake shores.

LAKE DISTRICT ○ EDINBURGH

🚃 **2½ hours** Go to Oxenholme, change, then take the mainline service direct to Edinburgh. 🚗 **2½ hours** North on the M6, then via the M74 and M8 to Edinburgh.

8 **Edinburgh** (p294)

Scotland's capital city is awash with spectacular buildings, so you'll need at least a day here to see the key features, such as **Edinburgh Castle** and the **Palace of Holyroodhouse**, as well as the **Royal Yacht Britannia**. If you have another day to spare, end your tour with a trip to stunning **Stirling Castle**.

5 **Chester** (p230)

Chester is home to several outstanding features from English history: the medieval **city walls**, Tudor and Victorian buildings around the **Rows**; and the famous **Chester Cathedral** built of local pink-red sandstone.

CHESTER ○ LIVERPOOL

🚃 **45 minutes** Easy local hop by train. 🚗 **One hour** If time allows, detour first into North Wales to see the mountains of Snowdonia (p276).

6 **Liverpool** (p219)

Liverpool is still mainly associated with The Beatles, with museums, hotels and shops devoted to the Fab Four – even a replica **Cavern Club**. Meanwhile, down on the revitalised **Victoria & Albert Waterfront**, the city is rediscovering and celebrating its (gritty in parts) maritime heritage.

LIVERPOOL ○ LAKE DISTRICT

🚃 **Two hours** Liverpool Lime Street Station to Windermere; change at Preston and/or Oxenholme. 🚗 **1½ hours** Varied drive, on M6 then A591.

Great Britain Month by Month

Top Events

Edinburgh Festivals August

Glyndebourne
Late May–August

Trooping the Colour
Mid-June

Glastonbury Festival
Late June

Braemar Gathering
September

January

Celtic Connections
Glasgow plays host to a celebration of Celtic music, dance and culture, with participants from all over the globe. www.celticconnections.com

February

Jorvik Viking Festival
The ancient Viking capital of York becomes home once again to invaders, with the intriguing addition of longship races. www.jorvik-viking-centre.co.uk/viking-festival

March

University Boat Race
Annual race down the River Thames in London between the rowing teams from Cambridge and Oxford universities, an event that's been an institution since 1856.

April

Grand National
On the first Saturday of the month, half the country has a flutter on the highlight of the three-day horse race meeting at Aintree – a steeplechase with a testing course and notoriously high jumps. www.grand-national-world.co.uk

Beltane
Thousands of revellers climb Edinburgh's Calton Hill for this modern revival of a pagan fire festival marking the end of winter. www.beltane.org

Tug of war at the Braemar Gathering
PHOTOGRAPHER: JONATHAN SMITH / LONELY PLANET IMAGES ©

Spirit of Speyside

Based in Dufftown, a Scottish festival of whisky, food and music, with five days of art, cooking, distillery tours and outdoor activities. www.spiritofspeyside.com

 # May

FA Cup Final

The highlight of the football season, culminating in this heady spectacle at Wembley Stadium, home of English footy. p386

Brighton Festival

The lively three-week arts fest takes over the streets of buzzy southcoast resort Brighton. www.brightonfestival.org

Chelsea Flower Show

The Royal Horticultural Society flower show at Chelsea is the highlight of the gardener's year. www.rhs.org.uk/Shows-Events

Hay Festival

Brings an intellectual influx to book-town Hay-on-Wye. www.hayfestival.com/wales

Glyndebourne

Open-air festival of opera in the pastoral surroundings of Glyndebourne House, East Sussex. www.glyndebourne.com

 # June

Cotswolds Olimpicks

Welly-wanging, pole-climbing and shin-kicking are the key disciplines at this traditional Gloucestershire sports day, held every year since 1612. www.olimpickgames.co.uk

Trooping the Colour

Military bands and bearskin-clad grenadiers march down London's Whitehall in this martial pageant to mark the monarch's birthday. www.trooping-the-colour.co.uk

Wimbledon Tennis

Wimbledon attracts all the big names, while crowds cheer or eat tons of strawberries and cream. p389

Glastonbury Festival

One of the country's favourite pop and rock gatherings, invariably muddy and still a rite of passage for British teens. p189

Meltdown Festival

London's Southbank Centre hands over the curatorial reins to a legend of contemporary music (the likes of David Bowie, Morrissey or Patti Smith) to create a program of concerts, talks and films. meltdown.southbankcentre.co.uk

Royal Regatta

Boats take to the water for Henley's upper-crust river regatta. www.hrr.co.uk

Pride

Highlight of the gay and lesbian calendar, a technicolour street parade heads through London's West End. www.pridelondon.org

Glasgow Festivals

The music and arts **West End Festival** (www.westendfestival.co.uk); the **International Jazz Festival** (www.jazzfest.co.uk); and the **Glasgow Mela** (www2.see glasgow.com/glasgowmela), celebrating the city's Asian community.

 # July

Great Yorkshire Show

Harrogate plays host to one of Britain's largest county shows. Expect Yorkshire grit, Yorkshire tykes, Yorkshire puddings, Yorkshire beef... www.greatyorkshireshow.co.uk

T in the Park

World-class acts since 1994 ensure this major music festival is Scotland's answer to Glastonbury. www.tinthepark.com

International Musical Eisteddfod

A week-long festival of international folk music at Llangollen, with an eclectic fringe and big-name evening concerts. p269

 Cowes Week

The country's biggest yachting spectacular on the choppy seas around the Isle of Wight. www.aamcowesweek.co.uk

 Womad

Roots and world music take centre stage at this festival in a country park in the south Cotswolds. www.womad.org

 Big Green Gathering

The UK's biggest ecofestival, showcasing everything from solar panels to compost toilets. www.big-green-gathering.com

 Truck

Indie music festival in Oxfordshire, known for its eclectic acts. www.thisistruck.com

 # August

 Edinburgh Festivals

Most famous are the **International Festival and Fringe** (www.edinburgh festivals.co.uk) and **Military Tattoo** (www.edintattoo.co.uk).

 Notting Hill Carnival

A multicultural Caribbean-style street carnival in the London district of Notting Hill. www.thenottinghillcarnival.com

 Reading Festival

Venerable rock and pop festival, still a good bet for big-name bands. www.readingfestival.com

 Leeds Festival

Reading's northern sister. Same weekend, same line-up, with bands shuttling between the two. www.leedsfestival.com

 National Eisteddfod of Wales

The largest celebration of native Welsh culture, steeped in history, pageantry and pomp. p269

 Brecon Jazz Festival

One of Europe's leading jazz festivals, in the charming Mid-Wales town of Brecon. www.hayfestival.com/breconjazz

 # September

 Abergavenny Food Festival

The mother of all epicurean festivals and the champion of Wales' burgeoning food scene. www.abergavenny foodfestival.com

Braemar Gathering

The biggest and most famous Highland Games in the Scottish calendar, traditionally attended by members of the royal family. p320

 # October

 Horse of the Year Show

The country's major indoor horse event, with dressage, show-jumping and other equine activities, at the NEC arena near Birmingham. www.hoys.co.uk

 Dylan Thomas Festival

A celebration of the Welsh laureate's work with readings, events and talks in Swansea. www.dylanthomas.com

 # November

 Guy Fawkes Night

Also called Bonfire Night, 5 November sees fireworks to remember the failed attempt to blow up parliament way back in 1605. www.bonfirenight.net

 Remembrance Day

Red poppies are worn and wreaths are laid in towns and cities around the country on 11 November in commemoration of fallen military personnel. www.poppy.org.uk

 # December

 New Year Celebrations

The last night of December sees fireworks and street parties in town squares across the region, as Brits gather to herald in the New Year.

Far left: Costumed participant at the Notting Hill Carnival
Left: Performance at the Edinburgh Festival

What's New

For this new edition of Discover Great Britain, our authors hunted down the fresh, the transformed, the hot and the happening. Here are a few of our favourites. For up-to-the-minute recommendations, see lonelyplanet.com/great-britain.

1 DARWIN CENTRE, NATURAL HISTORY MUSEUM, LONDON

The latest feature at the Natural History Museum is the striking new home for the Darwin Centre, where you catch a lift to the top of the 'Cocoon' and watch the biologists at work. (p81)

2 ASHMOLEAN MUSEUM, OXFORD

Britain's oldest public museum re-opened in late 2009 after a massive £61 million redevelopment; it's now lauded as one of the finest museums in the world. (p135)

3 HOTEL MISSONI, EDINBURGH

The Italian fashion house turns to luxury hotels, comes to Scotland and instantly establishes a style icon in the heart of the city. (p307)

4 AGATHA CHRISTIE'S GREENWAY, DEVON

The famous crime writer's riverside holiday home is opened to visitors. You can wander between rooms much as she left them, admire the books in her library and even the piles of hats in the lobby. (p191)

5 HAFOD ERYRI, MOUNT SNOWDON

Located just below Snowdon's summit, this striking piece of architecture opened to replace the dilapidated visitor centre once famously labelled 'the highest slum in Europe'. (p277)

6 GALLERIES OF MODERN LONDON, LONDON

Part of the fascinating Museum of London, the new £20-million Galleries of Modern London opened in 2010, encompassing everything from 1666 (the Great Fire) to the present day. (p76)

7 ROBERT BURNS BIRTHPLACE MUSEUM, ALLOWAY

Scotland's favourite poet is celebrated at the new Robert Burns Birthplace Museum, where displays include manuscripts and possessions. (p314)

8 MUSEUM OF LIVERPOOL, LIVERPOOL

Opened in 2011, Liverpool's new museum has themed galleries telling the stories of the city and its people, housed in a striking new building. (p223)

9 TURNER CONTEMPORARY, MARGATE

Launching in 2011, Margate's brand new state-of-the-art gallery stands right on the seafront, bathed in the sea-refracted light that the artist JMW Turner loved so much. (Rendezvous, Margate, Kent; www.turner contemporary.org)

Get Inspired

Books

○ **Oliver Twist** (1837) Tear-jerking social commentary from Charles Dickens.

○ **Sense and Sensibility** (1813) Jane Austen's quintessential tale of English manners.

○ **Waverley** (1814) Classic yarn of Scottish heroes by Sir Walter Scott.

○ **White Teeth** (2000) Zadie Smith's literary debut explores life in multicultural London.

○ **High Fidelity** (1995) British blokishness from Nick Hornby.

 Films

○ **Brief Encounter** (1945) David Lean's classic portrayal of typically British buttoned-up passion.

○ **Chariots of Fire** (1981) Oscar-winning story of Olympic endeavour.

○ **Trainspotting** (1996) Danny Boyle's break-through based on the heroin-laden novel.

○ **Billy Elliot** (2000) A boy's quest to learn ballet and escape post-industrial northern England.

○ **Shaun of the Dead** (2004) Zombie comedy: ballsy, bloody and thoroughly British.

♫ Music

○ **Sergeant Pepper's Lonely Hearts Club Band** (The Beatles) The Fab Four's finest moment.

○ **Exile on Main Street** (The Rolling Stones) Classic album from Britain's other iconic band.

○ **Village Green Preservation Society** (The Kinks) Poppy melodies and wry English observations.

○ **London Calling** (The Clash) Seminal punk with a point.

○ **Different Class** (Pulp) Brit-pop tales of English eccentricity.

✎ Websites

○ **BBC** (www.bbc.com) News and entertainment.

○ **British Council** (www.britishcouncil.org) Culture, arts and science.

○ **Traveline** (www.traveline.org) Invaluable public-transport planning.

○ **National Rail** (www.nationalrail.co.uk) Resource for train travel.

○ **Lonely Planet** (www.lonelyplanet.com) Destination information, traveller forums, hotels and more.

 ### Short on time?

This list will give you an instant insight into the country.

Read *Cider with Rosie* Cotswold childhood memories from Laurie Lee.

Watch *Withnail & I* Cult holiday disaster movie.

Listen *Definitely Maybe* Landmark album from Manchester bad boys Oasis.

Log-on *Visit Britain* (www .visitbritain.com) Britian's official tourism website; large and comprehensive.

New College, Oxford (p135)

Need to Know

Currency
British Pound (£)

Language
English – plus Welsh (Wales), Gaelic (Scotland)

ATMs
Widely available

Credit Cards
Visa and MasterCard widely used. Not always accepted at pubs and B&Bs.

Visas
Generally not required for citizens of Europe, Australia, NZ, USA and Canada on short stays

Mobile Phones
Phones from most countries operate, with roaming charges. Local SIM cards OK in European and Australian phones.

Wi-Fi
In some hotels and cafes

Internet Access
At internet cafes and public libraries; free to £5 per hour

Driving
Drive on the left. Steering wheels are on the right side.

Tipping
Not obligatory, but generally 10% to 15% for good service in restaurants

When to Go

■ Warm to hot summers, mild winters

Fort William GO May or Sep

Aberdeen GO May-Sep

Edinburgh GO May-Sep

Brecon GO May-Sep

Norwich GO May-Sep

London GO Any time

Exeter GO Apr-Oct

High Season
(Jun–Aug)
○ Weather at its best. Accommodation rates are high, especially for August school holidays.

○ Roads are busy, especially in seaside areas, national parks and popular cities such as Oxford, Edinburgh, Bath and York.

Shoulder
(Easter–end May; mid-Sep–end Oct)
○ Crowds reduce. Prices drop.

○ Weather often good; sunny spells mix with sudden showers March to May, while balmy 'Indian summers' feature September to October.

Low Season
(Dec–Feb)
○ Wet and cold; snow in mountain areas, especially in the north.

○ Opening hours reduced October to Easter; some places shut down. Big-city sights (especially London's) operate all year.

Advance Planning

○ **Two months before** Arrange long-distance transport and car rental to secure the cheapest deals. Book accommodation in London and other popular areas in high season.

○ **One month before** Book accommodation in country areas. Reserve tables at high-profile restaurants.

○ **Two weeks before** Confirm opening times and prices for attractions.

○ **One week before** Check the weather forecast. Then ignore it.

Your Daily Budget

BUDGET LESS THAN £50
- Budget B&B: £40 per double
- Cheap meals in cafes and pubs: £5 to £9
- Long-distance coach: £10 to £30

MIDRANGE £50–£100
- Midrange hotel or B&B: £50 to £130 per double
- Main course in midrange restaurant: £9 to £18
- Long-distance train average fare: £15 to £50
- Car rental: from £30 per day

TOP END OVER £100
- Four-star hotel room: from £200
- Three-course meal in a good restaurant: around £40 per person

Exchange Rates

Australia	A$1	£0.62
Canada	C$1	£0.62
Europe	€1	£0.84
Japan	¥100	£0.74
New Zealand	NZ$1	£0.46
USA	US$1	£0.62

For current exchange rates see www.xe.com

What to Bring

- **Comfortable shoes** Vital for enjoying your visits to museums, castles and historic cities.
- **Rain jacket** For those days when it will inevitably rain.
- **Small day-pack** For carrying that rain jacket when the sun will just as inevitably shine.
- **A taste for beer that isn't icy cold** Then try British 'real ale'.
- **Listening skills** Hold back on your own opinions – it'll be appreciated by the locals. And be aware that Brits rarely speak loudly in public – it's advisable to adjust your volume to match.

Arriving in Britain

Air London Heathrow – Direct train to Paddington (central London) every 15 minutes. www.heathrowexpress.com

London Gatwick – Direct train to Victoria (central London) every 15 minutes. www.gatwickexpress.com

Train Eurostar trains from Paris and Brussels arrive at St Pancras International (central London).

Long-distance bus & coach Arrive at London Victoria Coach Station (central London).

Getting Around

- **Air** Various carriers shuttle between major cities; for all but the longest flights it's often quicker to take the train.
- **Bus** Long-distance buses link towns and cities; local services in the countryside can be patchy.
- **Train** Fast and comfortable; book well ahead and travel off-peak for the best deals.
- **Car** Gives you freedom and helps reach out-of-the-way places.

Accommodation

- **B&Bs** The traditional Bed & Breakfast offers comfort and value; the best places give most boutique hotels a run for their money.
- **Hotels** Britain has a fantastic range of hotels to suit all budgets. You'll pay a premium in London and popular tourist spots.
- **Inns** In country areas, a room at the inn can be an excellent choice.

Be Forewarned

- **Public holidays** Banks and most shops close on public holidays, although many sights stay open. Everything closes on Christmas Day.
- **School holidays** Things get busier and rates rise during school holidays around Easter, summer and Christmas.
- **Traffic jams** A fact of life in Britain, especially during morning and evening 'rush hours' in cities (where public transport is usually preferable) and around holiday areas in summer.

London & its Day Trips

Everyone comes to London with a preconception shaped by a multitude of books, movies, TV shows and songs. Whatever your own ideas, prepare to have them shattered by this endlessly fascinating, amorphous city.

Don't believe anyone who claims to know London; the only thing that's constant here is change. You can spend a lifetime exploring the streets and parks, the famous buildings and the many attractions in the surrounding area, but there's always something new to discover.

And while the British Empire may be long gone, the engines of global capital continue to be stoked here, all adding to London's vibrant persona. It also makes it the third-most expensive city on the planet. Yet with endless reserves of cool, London rises above the fray and remains one of the world's great cities.

View of the London Eye (p81) from the River Thames **51**

London & its Day Trips

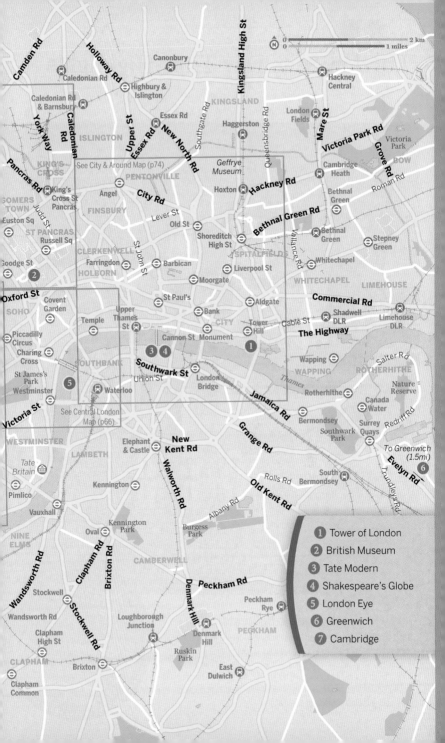

1 Tower of London
2 British Museum
3 Tate Modern
4 Shakespeare's Globe
5 London Eye
6 Greenwich
7 Cambridge

London & its Day Trips Highlights

1 Tower of London & Beefeaters

London's famous Tower (p71) has variously been a castle, palace and prison over almost 1000 years of history. Equally famous are the Yeoman Warders (or 'Beefeaters') who guard the tower. To qualify, all Beefeaters must have served at least 22 years in the armed forces and earned a Good Conduct Medal.

Need to Know

TOP TIP Book online to dodge queues **PHOTO OP** From atop the battlements **DID YOU KNOW?** The Yeomans' ceremonial outfits cost around £7000 **For further coverage, see p71**

Tower of London Don't Miss List

BY JOHN KEOHANE, CHIEF YEOMAN WARDER AT THE TOWER OF LONDON

1 A TOWER TOUR

To understand the Tower and its history, a guided tour with one of the Yeoman Warders is essential. Very few people appreciate that the Tower is actually our home as well; all the Warders live inside the outer walls. The Tower is rather like a miniature village – visitors are often rather surprised to see our washing hanging out beside the castle walls!

2 CROWN JEWELS

Visitors often think the Crown Jewels are the Queen's personal jewellery collection. They're not, of course; the Crown Jewels are actually the ceremonial regalia used during the Coronation. The highlights are the Sceptre and the Imperial State Crown, which contains the celebrated diamond known as the Star of Africa. People are often surprised to hear that the Crown Jewels aren't insured (as they could never be replaced).

3 WHITE TOWER

The White Tower is the original royal palace of the Tower of London, but it hasn't been used as a royal residence since 1603. It's the most iconic building here. Inside you can see exhibits from the Royal Armouries, including a suit of armour belonging to Henry VIII.

4 RAVENS

A Tower legend states that if its resident ravens ever left, the monarchy would topple – a royal decree states that we must keep a minimum of six ravens at any time. We currently have nine ravens, looked after by the Ravenmaster and his two assistants.

5 CEREMONY OF THE KEYS

We hold three daily ceremonies: the 9am Official Opening, the Ceremony of the Word (when the day's password is issued), and the 10pm Ceremony of the Keys, when the gates are locked after the castle has closed. Visitors are welcome to attend the last, but must apply directly to the Tower in writing.

British Museum

The British Museum (p84) is one of London's great wonders, with hundreds of galleries containing Egyptian, Etruscan, Greek, Roman, European and Middle Eastern artifacts. Among the must-sees are the Rosetta Stone, the controversial Parthenon Sculptures, and the Anglo-Saxon Sutton Hoo burial relics.

Need to Know

BEST TIME TO VISIT Weekdays are quieter than weekends **TIMING** Allow at least half a day **TOP TIP** Audioguides let you explore at your own pace **For further coverage, see p84**

THE AMERICAN SCENE

PRINTS FROM HOPPER TO POLLOCK

10 APRIL – 7 SEPTEMBER 2008

ADMISSION FREE
Prints and Drawings Gallery
Room 90

TERRA
AmericanAirlines

Cafés & shops

British Museum Don't Miss List

BY PAUL COLLINS, CURATOR IN THE MIDDLE EAST AT THE BRITISH MUSEUM

1 ENLIGHTENMENT GALLERY (ROOM 1)

This magnificent room contains an informative display that shows how collectors, antiquaries and travellers viewed and classified objects at the time the museum was founded (1753). It's an excellent introduction to the British Museum and its collections.

2 ASSYRIAN LION HUNT FROM NINEVEH (ROOM 10)

These are some of the greatest carvings from the ancient world. They originate from the city of Nineveh, in what is now modern-day Iraq. They've become especially important given the events of recent years in Iraq.

3 CLOCKS & WATCHES GALLERY (ROOMS 38 & 39)

These rooms contain a collection of mechanical devices for telling the time. It's quite a strange experience to be surrounded by the ticking, striking and chiming of hundreds of clocks!

4 EAST STAIRS

An impressive collection of casts of Persian, Mayan and Egyptian reliefs line the stairs. These were made in the 19th and early 20th centuries, and are historically important because the original objects left at the sites have been damaged or have disappeared.

5 NATIONAL PORTRAIT GALLERY

As well as visiting the British Museum, I'd encourage everyone to pay a visit to this wonderful art gallery (p70), which contains Britain's finest collection of historic portraits, from the early Tudors right through to the modern day; the rooftop cafe has the most wonderful view over Trafalgar Sq.

Far left: The Great Court; **Top:** British Museum exterior; **Bottom:** Ancient Egyptian sculpture

Tate Modern

This abandoned power station was once a real eyesore, but the inspired decision to transform it into a gallery (p79) in the late 1990s helped reinvigorate the nation's interest in modern art. Spread out over five floors, the permanent collection takes in everyone from Andy Warhol to Pablo Picasso, but it's the big-ticket exhibitions in the Turbine Hall that inevitably spark the most excitement. Best of all, it's completely free. Turbine Hall

Shakespeare's Globe

The original theatre where William Shakespeare premiered some of his plays burned down in 1613, but this modern-day reconstruction (p79) used traditional materials and building techniques to bring the Bard's open-air playhouse back to vivid life. It offers a fascinating insight into Shakespeare's theatrical world – you can take a guided tour or, better still, join the 'groundlings' for an afternoon performance.

London Eye

Alright, alright – it might be touristy, but this famous giant wheel (p81) is still a must-do. Jump into one of the space-age pods and enjoy a half-hour spin offering one of the finest views in all of London, stretching out to 25 miles on a good day. Book online and you won't even have to queue much.

Greenwich

Greenwich is a little way outside the centre, but it's worth making the time for a trip downriver – ideally by boat – to glorious Greenwich (p85). In days gone by, this elegant area was the centre of British maritime power, and relics of the nation's illustrious seafaring heritage linger on at the National Maritime Museum and the Old Royal Naval College. At the Royal Observatory the universal coordinate of Greenwich Mean Time was first established. Old Royal Naval College

Punting the Cambridge 'Backs'

The lovely university city of Cambridge (p116) is a day trip from London, and no visit is complete without taking a punt (a flat-bottomed boat) along the river by the picturesque 'Backs', the green lawns that run behind the city's finest colleges. Finish your cruise with a pint in one of the city's many historic pubs. You'll soon wonder how you could have studied anywhere else.

London & its Day Trips' Best...

City Views

o **London Eye** (p81) Ride the pods on the giant wheel, London's newest internationally recognised landmark

o **Greenwich** (p85) The Royal Observatory is an appropriate place from where to survey the cityscape

o **Westminster Cathedral** (p68) Climb the tower in this ancient church for views of Old London Town

o **Tower Bridge** (p76) Get another perspective on the River Thames

Things for Free

o **British Museum** (p84) London's flagship repository

o **National Gallery** (p70) Marvel at the masterpieces – gratis

o **Tate Modern** (p79) Thanks to Mr Tate, another great free gallery

o **Covent Garden** (p71) The perfect spot to wander, window-shop and watch street-art performers

o **Changing of the Guard** (p65) Classic daily London event outside Buckingham Palace

Acclaimed Restaurants

o **Great Queen Street** (p94) Cosy and informal, serving up the best of British

o **National Dining Rooms** (p94) Top-notch British food, fittingly located in the National Gallery, overlooking Trafalgar Sq

o **Gordon Ramsey** (p95) Whatever you think of the eponymous owner's TV persona, his restaurant is among the best

o **Veeraswamy** (p94) Britain's longest-running Indian restaurant, with excellent food and great service

Need to Know

Traditional Pubs

○ **Princess Louise** (p96)
Victorian classic, arguably London's most beautiful pub

○ **Lamb & Flag** (p96)
Everyone's favourite in Covent Garden; busy but worth a visit

○ **Ye Olde Watling** (p96)
Historic pub near St Paul's Cathedral dating from 1668

○ **Ye Olde Cheshire Cheese** (p96) An atmospheric icon of Fleet Street

ADVANCE PLANNING

○ **Two months before**
Reserve your hotel room and arrange theatre tickets

○ **Two weeks before**
Book a table at high-profile restaurants

○ **One week before**
Prebook online for top sights such as the London Eye, Madame Tussauds, St Paul's Cathedral and the Tower of London

RESOURCES

○ **Visit London**
(www.visitlondon.com) The official tourist website

○ **BBC London**
(www.bbc.co.uk/london) London-centric low-down from the BBC

○ **Evening Standard**
(www.thisislondon.co.uk) Latest news from the city's daily rag

○ **Urban Path**
(www.urbanpath.com) Online guide to 'nice things' – events, restaurants, hotels, spas and shops

GETTING AROUND

○ **Bus** Excellent network across the capital; good for sightseeing too, though the famous red double-deckers are not so common these days

○ **Underground train** London's 'tube' is the speediest way to get around town

○ **Waterbus** Useful and scenic way to get between riverside points

BE FOREWARNED

○ **Exhibitions** High-profile seasonal exhibitions at museums and galleries often charge extra and are sold out weeks ahead

○ **Restaurants** You'll need to book for the big-name establishments

○ **Public Transport** All-day Travelcards and Oyster cards (p104) offer the best value

○ **Rush hour** Morning peak-hours won't impact tourists much; during the evening rush, find a nice pub and wait until it's over

Left: Guard at Buckingham Palace (p65);
Above: Covent Garden Piazza (p71).

London Walking Tour

This walk takes you through the West End of London, and is an excellent introduction to some of the capital's major attractions and icons.

WALK FACTS

- **Start**
  Covent Garden
- **Finish**
  Trafalgar Sq
- **Distance**
  2.5 miles
- **Duration**
  Three hours

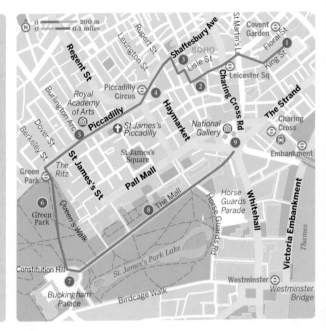

① Covent Garden Piazza

Yes it's touristy, but this wonderful square (designed by Inigo Jones), and former market hall, is a good place to start. Grab a coffee from one of the many open-air cafes to fuel you up for the walk, and sip it while watching the never-ending stream of buskers and street performers.

② Leicester Square

A walk down King St and over Charing Cross Rd brings you to Leicester Sq. Dominated by enormous nightclubs and cinemas, this is where movies premiere and stars make handprints in the pavement. It's a London landmark, but – to be blunt – not especially scenic.

③ Chinatown & Theatreland

Head north, across **Lisle St** – the heart of London's Chinatown – to reach **Shaftesbury Ave** – the heart of London's **theatreland** and home to some of the West End's most prestigious theatres.

④ Piccadilly Circus

Westwards down Shaftsbury Ave brings you to Piccadilly Circus, with the famous **Eros statue** at its centre. The Circus is always hectic and traffic-choked, with the buildings cloaked in massive flashing ads, but this is an icon of London, so it's worth making the stop.

5 Piccadilly

Running west from Piccadilly Circus is the elegant street of Piccadilly. It's lined with upmarket stores, including those on highly exclusive **Burlington Arcade**, thanks to the proximity of aristocratic neighbourhoods St James's and Mayfair.

6 Green Park

Walk past the **Ritz**, one of London's fanciest hotels, and turn left into Green Park for a chance to catch your breath, or rest your legs on one of the park benches under some stunning oak trees and olde-worlde street lamps.

7 Buckingham Palace

A stroll south through Green Park leads to one of London's best-known addresses: Buckingham Palace, the Queen's residence in London. If you made an early start, you might be here for the **changing of the guard** at 11.30am.

8 The Mall

With your back to Buckingham Palace you can march down The Mall, a grand avenue alongside **St James's Park**, where royal processions often take place and the Queen's limousine or carriage is escorted by her guards.

9 Trafalgar Square

The Mall leads you under **Admiralty Arch** and pops you out at Trafalgar Sq, with its fountains and statues, dominated by **Nelson's Column**. The square is also surrounded by grand buildings, including the **National Gallery** – where a seat on the steps outside the entrance is the perfect place to end your walk.

London in...

TWO DAYS

Start with our walking tour around the **West End**. In the afternoon, tick off more icons – **Westminster Abbey** and the **Houses of Parliament**, and the instantly recognisable tower of **Big Ben**. Cross Westminster Bridge to reach the **London Eye**, then spend the late afternoon at the **British Museum**. Day two starts at **St Paul's Cathedral**, followed by crossing the Millennium Bridge to the **Tate Modern**. From here stroll along the riverside walkways to reach **Tower Bridge**, then cross to visit the **Tower of London**.

FOUR DAYS

Day three could start with a morning of browsing – in the **Tate Gallery** or **National Gallery** if you're artistically inclined, or in the famous stores of **Regent St** or **Kensington** if you're more retail minded. Then spend the afternoon enjoying the splendours of **Greenwich**. Day four is for day trips: leave the capital behind for an excursion to **Windsor Castle**, **Cambridge** or **Canterbury Cathedral**.

The choir and apse of St Paul's Cathedral (p78)
NEIL SETCHFIELD / LONELY PLANET IMAGES ©

Discover London & its Day Trips

At a Glance

○ **Westminster** (p64) The hub of British political power.

○ **St James's** (p64) Playground of the rich, famous and royal.

○ **West End** (p69) London's hectic centre of shops and theatres.

○ **The City** (p71) Financial district.

○ **Chelsea, Kensington** (p80) **and Knightsbridge** (p100) The capital's poshest addresses.

○ **Greenwich** (p85) Where Britannia ruled the waves.

Big Ben, clock tower of the Houses of Parliament
PHOTOGRAPHER: DAVID TOMLINSON / LONELY PLANET IMAGES ©

LONDON

TELEPHONE CODE 020 / POP 7.51 MILLION / AREA 609 SQ MILES

Sights

Westminster & St James's

Purposefully positioned outside the old City (London's fiercely independent burghers preferred to keep the monarch and parliament at arm's length), Westminster has been the centre of the nation's political power for nearly a millennium. The area's many landmarks combine to form an awesome display of authority and gravitas.

Put on your best rah-rah voice to wander around St James's, an aristocratic enclave of palaces, famous hotels, historic shops and elegant buildings. There are some 150 historically noteworthy buildings within its 36 hectares.

HOUSES OF PARLIAMENT
Historic Building

(Map p66; www.parliament.uk; Parliament Sq SW1; ⊖ Westminster) Coming face to face with one of the world's most recognisable landmarks is always a surreal moment, but in the case of the Houses of Parliament it's a revelation.

The palace's most famous feature is its clock tower, aka **Big Ben** (Map p66). Ben is actually the 13-ton bell, named after Benjamin Hall, who was commissioner of works when the tower was completed in 1858.

At the business end, parliament is split into two houses. The green-hued **House of Commons** is the lower house, where the 650 elected Members of Parliament sit. Traditionally the home of hereditary bluebloods, the scarlet-decorated **House of Lords** now has peers appointed through various means.

Parliamentary recesses (ie holidays) last for three months over summer and a couple of weeks over Easter and Christmas. When parliament is in recess there are guided **tours** (☎ 0844 847 1672; www.ticketmaster.co.uk/housesofparliament; 75-min tours adult/child £14/6) of both chambers and other historic areas.

BUCKINGHAM PALACE   Palace

(Map p66; ☎ 020-7766 7300; www.royal collection.org.uk; Buckingham Palace Rd SW1; tours adult/child £17/9.75; ⏱ late Jul-Sep; ⊖ Victoria) With so many imposing buildings in the capital, the Queen's well-proportioned but relatively plain city pad is an anticlimax for some. When she's not off giving her one-handed wave in far-flung parts of the Commonwealth, Queen Elizabeth II divides her time between here, Windsor and Balmoral. If you've got the urge to drop in for a cup of tea, a handy way of telling whether she's home is to check whether the yellow, red and blue royal standard is flying.

Nineteen lavishly furnished State Rooms – hung with artworks by the likes of Rembrandt, van Dyck, Canaletto, Poussin and Vermeer – are open to visitors when HRH (Her Royal Highness) takes her holidays. The two-hour tour includes the **Throne Room**, with his-and-hers pink chairs initialled 'ER' and 'P'.

CHANGING OF THE GUARD

If you're a fan of bright uniforms, bearskin hats, straight lines, marching and shouting, join the throngs outside the palace at 11.30am (daily from May to July and on alternate days for the rest of the year, weather permitting), when the regiment of guards outside the palace changes over in one of the world's most famous displays of pageantry. It does have a certain freak show value but gets dull very quickly. If you're here in November, the procession leaving the palace for the State Opening of Parliament is much more impressive.

ROYAL MEWS

(Map p66; adult/child £7.50/4.80; ⏱ 11am-4pm) Indulge your Cinderella fantasies while inspecting the exquisite state coaches and immaculately groomed royal horses housed in the Royal Mews. Highlights include the 1910 royal wedding's Glass Coach and the 1762 Gold Coach, which has been used for every coronation since that of George IV. We're pretty sure that these aren't about to change back into pumpkins any time soon.

WESTMINSTER ABBEY   Church

(Map p66; ☎ 020-7654 4834; www.westminster -abbey.org; 20 Dean's Yard SW1; adult/child £15/6, tours £3; ⏱ 9.30am-4.30pm Mon, Tue, Thu & Fri, to 7pm Wed, to 2.30pm Sat; ⊖ Westminster) Not merely a beautiful place of worship, Westminster Abbey serves up the country's history cold on slabs of stone. For centuries the country's greatest have been interred here, including most of the monarchs from Henry III (died 1272) to George II (1760).

Every monarch since William the Conqueror has been crowned here, with the exception of a couple of unlucky Eds who were murdered (Edward V) or abdicated (Edward VIII) before the magic moment. Look out for the strangely ordinary-looking **Coronation Chair**.

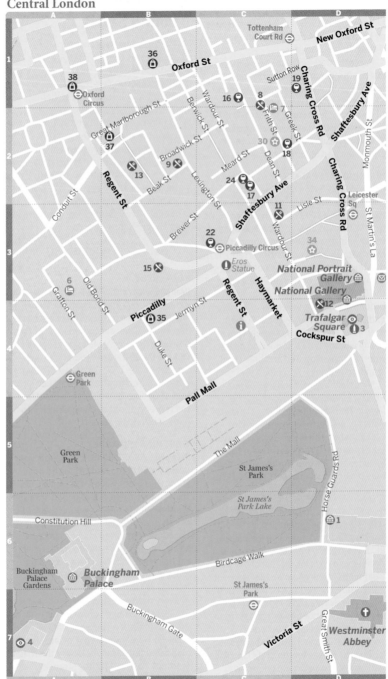

New Oxford St

Tottenham Court Rd

36

Oxford St

38 Oxford Circus

Sutton Row

19 Charing Cross Rd

Shaftesbury Ave

16   8

Great Marlborough St

Wardour St

Berwick St

Frith St   7

Greek St

Monmouth St

37

30

18

Broadwick St

Meard St

Dean St

Regent St

13

9

24

Charing Cross Rd

Beak St

Lexington St

17

Leicester Sq

St Martin's La

Conduit St

Brewer St

Shaftesbury Ave

11

Lisle St

34

22

Wardour St

Piccadilly Circus

National Portrait Gallery

15

Eros Statue

National Gallery

6

Gratton St

Old Bond St

Regent St

Haymarket

12

Piccadilly   35

Jermyn St

Trafalgar Square   3

Cockspur St

Duke St

Green Park

Pall Mall

Green Park

The Mall

St James's Park

St James's Park Lake

Horse Guards Rd

Constitution Hill

1

Buckingham Palace Gardens

Buckingham Palace

Birdcage Walk

St James's Park

Buckingham Gate

Victoria St

Great Smith St

Westminster Abbey

4

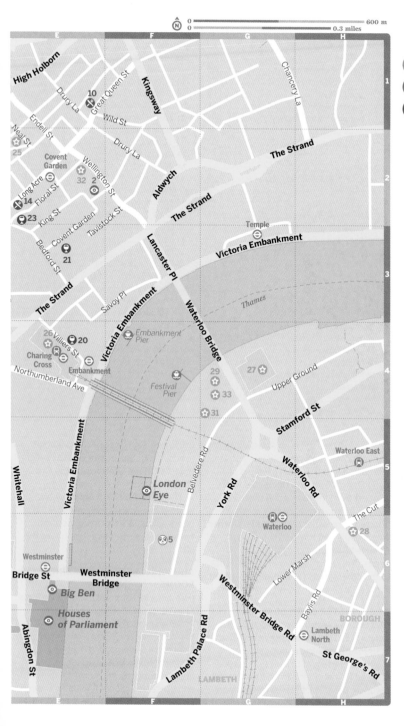

Central London

The building itself is an arresting sight. Though a mixture of architectural styles, it is considered the finest example of Early English Gothic in existence.

Apart from the royal graves, keep an eye out for the many famous commoners interred here, especially in **Poets' Corner**, where you'll find the resting places of Chaucer, Dickens, Hardy, Tennyson, Dr Johnson and Kipling as well as memorials to the other greats (Shakespeare, Austen, Brontë etc).

WESTMINSTER CATHEDRAL Cathedral
(Map p82; www.westminstercathedral.org.uk; Victoria St SW1; ⊙7am-7pm; ⊖Victoria) Begun in 1895, this neo-Byzantine cathedral is the headquarters of Britain's once sup-pressed Roman Catholic Church. It's still a work in progress, the vast interior part dazzling marble and mosaic and part bare brick; new sections are completed as funds allow. Look out for Eric Gill's highly regarded stone **Stations of the Cross** (1918).

The distinctive 83m red-brick and white-stone **tower** (adult/child £5/2.50) offers splendid views of London and, unlike St Paul's dome, you can take the lift.

CHURCHILL MUSEUM & CABINET WAR ROOMS Museum
(Map p66; www.iwm.org.uk/cabinet; Clive Steps, King Charles St SW1; adult/child £15/free; ⊙9.30am-6pm; ⊖Westminster) The Cabinet War Rooms were Prime Minister Winston Churchill's underground military HQ during WWII. Now a wonderfully evocative and atmospheric museum, the restored and preserved rooms (including Church-ill's bedroom) capture the drama of the

time. The interactive displays offer an intriguing exposé of the public and private faces of the man.

West End

Synonymous with big-budget musicals and frenzied flocks of shoppers, the West End is a strident mix of culture and consumerism. More a concept than a fixed geographical area, it nonetheless takes in Piccadilly Circus and Trafalgar Sq to the south, Regent St to the west, Oxford St to the north and Covent Garden and the Strand to the east.

Named after the elaborate collars (picadils) that were the sartorial staple of a 17th-century tailor who lived nearby, **Piccadilly** became the fashionable haunt of the well-heeled (and collared), and still boasts establishment icons such as the Ritz hotel and Fortnum & Mason department store. It meets Regent St, Shaftesbury Ave and Haymarket at neon-lit, turbo-charged **Piccadilly Circus**, home to the popular but unremarkable **Eros statue**. Ironically, the love god looks over an area that's long been linked to prostitution, both male and female, although it's less conspicuous these days.

Mayfair hogs all of the most expensive streets on the Monopoly board, including Park Lane and Bond St, which should give you an idea of what to expect: lots of pricey shops, Michelin-starred restaurants, society hotels and gentlemen's clubs. Elegant **Regent St** and frantic **Oxford St** are the city's main shopping strips.

At the heart of the West End lies **Soho**, a grid of narrow streets and squares hiding gay bars, strip clubs, cafes and advertising agencies. **Carnaby St** was the epicentre of the swinging London of the 1960s but is now largely given over to chain fashion stores. Lisle and Gerrard Sts form the heart of **Chinatown**, which is full of reasonably priced Asian restaurants and unfairly hip youngsters. Its neighbour, pedestrianised **Leicester Sq** (*les*-ter), heaves with tourists. Dominated by large cinemas, it sometimes hosts star-studded premieres.

TRAFALGAR SQUARE   Square
(Map p66; ⊖Charing Cross) Trafalgar Sq is the public heart of London, hosting rallies, marches and feverish New Year's festivities. Londoners congregate here

Fountain and Eros statue at Piccadilly Circus

69

to celebrate anything from football victories to the ousting of political leaders. Formerly ringed by gnarling traffic, the square's been tidied up and is now one of the world's grandest public places. At the heart of it, Nelson surveys his fleet from the 43.5m-high **Nelson's Column**, erected in 1843 to commemorate his 1805 victory over Napoleon off Spain's Cape Trafalgar. At the edges of the square are four plinths, three of which have permanent statues, while the **fourth plinth** is given over to temporary modern installations.

FREE **NATIONAL GALLERY** Gallery
(Map p66; www.nationalgallery.org.uk; Trafalgar Sq WC2; ☺10am-6pm Sat-Thu, to 9pm Fri; ⊖Charing Cross) Gazing grandly over Trafalgar Sq through its Corinthian columns, the National Gallery is the nation's most important repository of art. Four million visitors come annually to admire its 2300-plus Western European paintings, spanning the years 1250 to 1900.

Highlights include Turner's *The Fighting Temeraire* (voted Britain's greatest

painting), Botticelli's *Venus and Mars* and van Gogh's *Sunflowers*. The medieval religious paintings in the Sainsbury Wing are fascinating, but for a short, sharp blast of brilliance, you can't beat the truckloads of Monets, Manets, Cézannes and Renoirs in rooms 43 to 46.

FREE **NATIONAL PORTRAIT GALLERY**
Gallery
(Map p66; www.npg.org.uk; St Martin's Pl WC2; ☺10am-6pm Sat-Wed, to 9pm Thu & Fri; ⊖Charing Cross) The fascinating National Portrait Gallery is like stepping into a picture book of English history or, if you're feeling trashy, an *OK* magazine spread on history's celebrities ('what's *she* wearing?').

Founded in 1856, the permanent collection (around 11,000 works) starts with the Tudors on the 2nd floor and descends to contemporary figures (from pop stars to scientists). An audiovisual guide (£3) will lead you through the gallery's most famous pictures.

COVENT GARDEN Square
(Map p66; ⊖Covent Garden) A
hallowed name for opera fans due
to the presence of the esteemed Royal
Opera House (p99), Covent Garden is
one of London's biggest tourist traps,
where chain restaurants, souvenir shops,
balconied bars and street entertainers
vie for the passersby's pound.

The City

For most of its history, the City of London
was London. It's only in the last 250
years that the City has gone from being
the very essence of London and it's main
population centre to just its central business district. But what a business district
it is – despite the hammering its bankers
have taken in recent years, the 'square
mile' remains at the very heart of world
capitalism.

Currently fewer than 10,000 people
actually live here, although some
300,000 descend on it each weekday,
when they generate almost three-
quarters of Britain's entire GDP before
squeezing back onto the tube. On
Sundays it becomes a virtual ghost town;
it's a good time to poke around but come
with a full stomach – most shops and
eateries are closed.

TOWER OF LONDON Castle
**(Map p74; ☎0844-482 7777; www.hrp.org.uk;
Tower Hill EC3; adult/child £17/9.50, audioguides
£4/3; ⏱9am-5.30pm Tue-Sat, from 10am Sun
& Mon Mar-Oct, until 4.30pm Nov-Feb; ⊖Tower
Hill).** If you pay only one admission fee
while you're in London, make it the Tower.

In the 1070s, William the Conqueror
started work on the White Tower to
replace the castle he'd previously had
built here. By 1285, two walls with
towers and a moat were built around
it and the defences have barely been
altered since. A former royal residence,
treasury, mint and arsenal, it became
most famous as a prison when Henry VIII

Tower of London

Tackling the Tower

Although it's usually less busy in the late afternoon, don't leave your assault on the Tower until too late in the day. You could easily spend hours here and not see it all. Start by getting your bearings with the hour-long Yeoman Warder (Beefeater) tours; they're included in the cost of admission, entertaining and the only way to access the Chapel Royal of St Peter ad Vincula ❶ which is where they finish up.

When you leave the chapel, the Tower Green scaffold site ❷ is directly in front. The building immediately to your left is Waterloo Barracks , where the Crown Jewels ❸ are housed. These are the absolute highlight of a Tower visit, so keep an eye on the entrance and pick a time to visit when it looks relatively quiet. Once inside, take things at your own pace. Slow-moving travelators shunt you past the dozen or so crowns that are the treasury's centrepiece, but feel free to double-back for a second or even third pass – particularly if you ended up on the rear travela-tor the first time around. Allow plenty of time for the White Tower ❹, the core of the whole complex, starting with the exhibition of royal armour. As you continue onto the 2nd floor, keep an eye out for St John's Chapel ❺. The famous ravens ❻ can be seen in the courtyard around the White Tower. Head next through the towers that formed the Medieval Palace ❼, then take the East Wall Walk ❽ to get a feel for the castle's mighty battlements. Spend the rest of your time poking around the many, many other fascinating nooks and crannies of the Tower complex.

BEAT THE QUEUES

Buy your fast-track ticket in advance online or at the City of London Information Centre in St Paul's Churchyard.

Palacepalooza An annual Historic Royal Palaces membership allows you to jump the queues and visit the Tower (and four other London palaces) as often as you like.

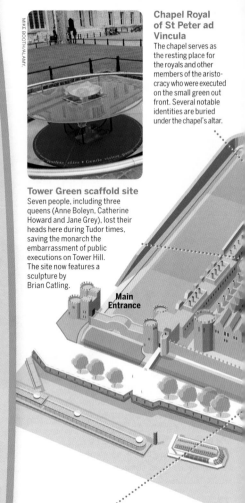

MIKE BOOTH/ALAMY

Chapel Royal of St Peter ad Vincula
The chapel serves as the resting place for the royals and other members of the aristocracy who were executed on the small green out front. Several notable identities are buried under the chapel's altar.

Tower Green scaffold site
Seven people, including three queens (Anne Boleyn, Catherine Howard and Jane Grey), lost their heads here during Tudor times, saving the monarch the embarrassment of public executions on Tower Hill. The site now features a sculpture by Brian Catling.

Main Entrance

White Tower
Much of the White Tower is taken up with this exhibition of 500 years of royal armour. Look for the virtually cuboid suit made to match Henry VIII's bloated body, complete with an oversized armoured pouch to protect his, ahem, crown jewels.

PAWEL LIBERA IMAGES/ALAMY

St John's Chapel

Kept as plain and unadorned as it would have been in Norman times, the White Tower's 2nd-floor chapel is the oldest surviving church in London, dating from 1080.

Crown Jewels

When they're not being worn for affairs of state, Her Majesty's bling is kept here. Among the 23,578 gems, look out for the 530-carat Cullinan diamond at the top of the Royal Sceptre, the largest part of what was (until 1985) the largest diamond ever found.·

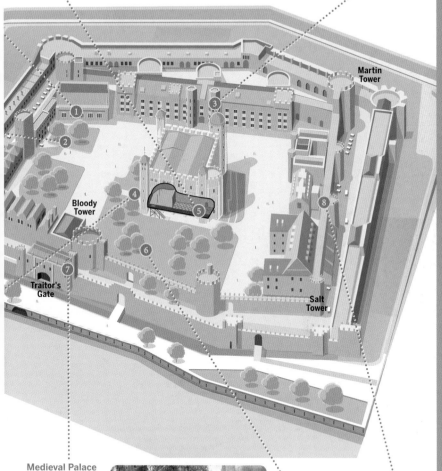

Martin Tower

Bloody Tower

Traitor's Gate

Salt Tower

Medieval Palace

This part of the Tower complex was commenced around 1220 and was home to England's medieval monarchs. Look for the recreations of the bedchamber of Edward I (1272–1307) in St Thomas's Tower and the throne room on the upper floor of the Wakefield Tower.

Ravens

This stretch of green is where the Tower's famous ravens are kept, fed on raw meat and blood-soaked bird biscuits. According to legend, if the birds were to leave the Tower, the kingdom would fall.

East Wall Walk

Follow the inner ramparts, starting from the 13th-century Salt Tower, passing through the Broad Arrow and Constable Towers, and ending at the Martin Tower, where the Crown Jewels were once stored.

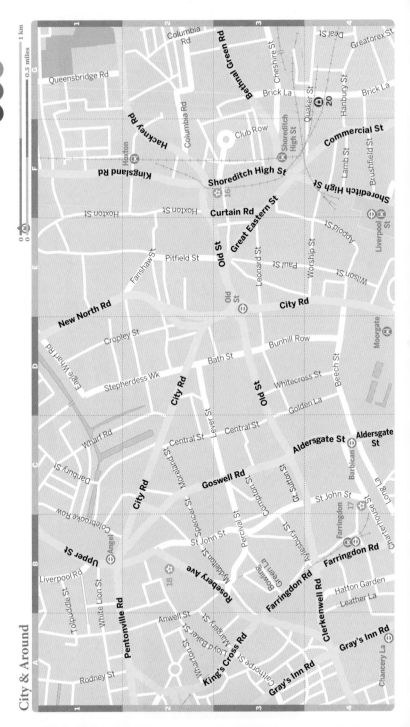

City & Around

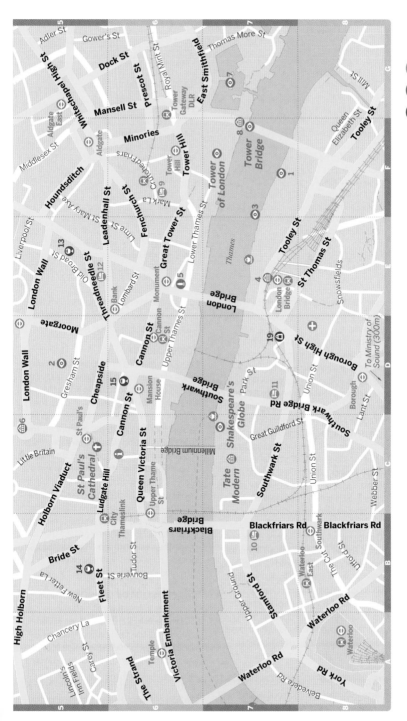

75

City & Around

moved to Whitehall Palace in 1529 and started dishing out his preferred brand of punishment.

The most striking building is the central **White Tower**, with its solid Romanesque architecture and four turrets. Today it houses a collection from the Royal Armouries. On the 2nd floor is **St John's Chapel**, dating from 1080 and therefore the oldest church in London. To the north is **Waterloo Barracks**, which now contains the spectacular **Crown Jewels**. On the far side of the White Tower is the **Bloody Tower**, where the 12-year-old Edward V and his little brother were held 'for their own safety' and later murdered, probably by their uncle, the future Richard III.

On the small green in front of the **Chapel Royal of St Peter ad Vincula** stood Henry VIII's **scaffold**, where seven people, including Anne Boleyn and her cousin Catherine Howard (Henry's second and fifth wives) were beheaded.

Look out for the latest in the Tower's long line of famous ravens, which legend says could cause the White Tower to collapse should they leave. Their wings are clipped in case they get any ideas.

To get your bearings, take the hugely entertaining free guided tour with any of the Tudor-garbed Beefeaters. Hour-long tours leave every 30 minutes from the bridge near the main entrance; the last tour's an hour before closing.

TOWER BRIDGE Landmark

London was still a thriving port in 1894 when elegant Tower Bridge was built. Designed to be raised to allow ships to pass, electricity has now taken over from the original steam engines. A lift leads up from the northern tower to the overpriced **Tower Bridge Exhibition** (Map p74; www.towerbridge. org.uk; adult/child £7/3; ⏰10am-5.30pm Apr-Sep, 9.30am-5pm Oct-Mar; ⊖Tower Hill), where the story of its building is recounted within the upper walkway. The same ticket gets you into the engine rooms below the southern tower. Below the bridge on the City side is Dead Man's Hole, where corpses that had made their way into the Thames (through suicide, murder or accident) were regularly retrieved.

FREE **MUSEUM OF LONDON** Museum (Map p74; www.museumoflondon.org.uk; 150 London Wall EC2; ⏰10am-6pm; ⊖Barbican) Visiting the fascinating Museum of London early in your stay helps to make sense of the layers of history that make up this place. The Roman section, in particular, illustrates how the modern is grafted onto the ancient; several of the city's main thoroughfares were once Roman roads, for instance.

The museum's £20 million Galleries of Modern London opened in 2010, encompassing everything from 1666 (the Great Fire) to the present day. While the Lord Mayor's ceremonial coach is the centrepiece, an effort has been made to create an immersive experience: you can enter reconstructions of an 18th-century debtors' prison, a Georgian pleasure garden and a Victorian street.

FREE **GUILDHALL** Historic Building
(Map p74; ☏020-7606 3030; www.guild hall.cityoflondon.gov.uk; Gresham St EC2; ⊙10am-4pm unless in use; ⊖Bank) In the middle of the 'square mile', the Guildhall has been the seat of the City's local government for eight centuries. The present building dates from the early 15th century.

Visitors can see the **Great Hall**, where the city's mayor is sworn in and where important fellows like the Tsar of Russia and the Prince Regent celebrated beating Napoleon. It's an impressive space decorated with the shields and banners of London's 12 principal livery companies, carved galleries (the west of which is

Maps

No Londoner would be without a pocket-size *London Mini A-Z*, which lists nearly 30,000 streets and still doesn't cover the capital in its entirety. If you're going to be in London for more than a few weeks, it's worth getting one.

protected by disturbing statues of giants Gog and Magog) and a beautiful oak-panelled roof. There's also a lovely bronze statue of Churchill sitting in a comfy chair.

MONUMENT Memorial
(Map p74; www.themonument.info; Monument St; adult/child £3/1; ⊙9.30am-5.30pm; ⊖Monument) Designed by Wren to commemorate the Great Fire, the Monument is 60.6m high, the exact distance from its base to the bakery on Pudding Lane where the blaze began. Climb the 311 tight spiral steps (not advised for claustrophobes) for an eye-watering view from beneath the symbolic vase of gold-leaf flames.

The Millenium Bridge across the River Thames (p85)

DOUG MCKINLAY / LONELY PLANET IMAGES ©

PHILIP GAME / LONELY PLANET IMAGES ©

Don't Miss St Paul's Cathedral

Dominating the City with a dome second in size only to St Peter's in Rome, St Paul's Cathedral was designed by Sir Christopher Wren after the Great Fire and built between 1675 and 1710.

The dome is renowned for somehow dodging the bombs during the Blitz and became an icon of the resilience shown in the capital during WWII. Outside the cathedral, to the north, is a **monument to the people of London**, a simple and elegant memorial to the 32,000 Londoners who weren't so lucky.

Inside, some 30m above the main paved area, is the first of three domes (actually a dome inside a cone inside a dome) supported by eight huge columns. The walkway round its base is called the **Whispering Gallery**, because if you talk close to the wall, your words will carry to the opposite side 32m away. It can be reached by a staircase on the western side of the southern transept (9.30am to 3.30pm only). There are 528 lung-busting steps to the **Golden Gallery** at the very top, and an unforgettable view of London.

Audio tours lasting 45 minutes are available for £4. Guided tours (adult/child £3/1) leave the tour desk at 10.45am, 11.15am, 1.30pm and 2pm (90 minutes). Evensong takes place at 5pm (3.15pm on Sunday).

THINGS YOU NEED TO KNOW

Map p74; www.stpauls.co.uk; adult/child £12.50/4.50; ⊗ 8.30am-4pm Mon-Sat; ⊖ St Paul's

---

ST KATHARINE DOCKS　　Harbour
(Map p74; ⊖ Tower Hill) A centre of trade and commerce for 1000 years, St Katharine Docks is now a buzzing waterside area of pleasure boats, shops and eateries. It was badly damaged during the war, but

survivors include the popular **Dickens Inn**, with its original 18th-century timber framework, and **Ivory House** (built 1854) which used to store ivory, perfume and other precious goods.

South Bank

Londoners once crossed the river to the area controlled by the licentious Bishops of Southwark for all kinds of raunchy diversions frowned upon in the City. It's a much more seemly area now, but the theatre and entertainment tradition remains.

FREE **TATE MODERN** Gallery
(Map p74; www.tate.org.uk; Queen's Walk SE1; ☺10am-6pm Sun-Thu, to 10pm Fri & Sat; ⊖Southwark) It's hard to miss this surprisingly elegant former power station on the side of the river, which is fortunate as the tremendous Tate Modern really shouldn't be missed. Focussing on modern art in all its wacky and wonderful permutations, it's been extraordinarily successful in bringing challenging work to the masses, becoming one of London's most popular attractions.

Outstanding temporary exhibitions (on the 4th floor; prices vary) continue to spark excitement, as does the periodically changing large-scale installation in the vast Turbine Hall. The permanent collection is organised into four themed sections, which change periodically but include works by the likes of Mark Rothko, Pablo Picasso, Francis Bacon, Roy Lichtenstein, Andy Warhol and Tracey Emin.

SHAKESPEARE'S GLOBE
Historic Theatre
(Map p74; ☏020-7401 9919; www.shakespeares-globe.org; 21 New Globe Walk SE1; adult/child £11/7; ☺10am-5pm; ⊖London Bridge) Originally built in 1599, the Globe burnt down in 1613 and was immediately rebuilt. The Puritans, who regarded theatres as dreadful dens of iniquity, eventually closed it in 1642. Its present incarnation was the vision of American actor and director Sam Wanamaker, who sadly died before the opening night in 1997.

Admission includes a guided tour of the open-roofed theatre, faithfully reconstructed from oak beams, handmade bricks, lime plaster and thatch. There's also an extensive

Tate-a-Tate

To get between London's Tate galleries in style, the **Tate Boat** (www.thamesclippers.com) will whisk you from one to the other, stopping en route at the London Eye. Services run from 10.10am to 5.28pm daily at 40-minute intervals. A River Roamer hop-on/hop-off ticket (purchased on board) costs £12; single tickets are £5.

exhibition about Shakespeare and his times.

From April to October plays are performed, and while Shakespeare and his contemporaries dominate, modern plays are also staged (see the website for upcoming performances). As in Elizabethan times, 'groundlings' can watch proceedings for a modest price (£5; seats are £15 to £35). There's no protection from the elements and you'll have to stand, but it's a memorable experience.

FREE **IMPERIAL WAR MUSEUM** Museum
(www.iwm.org.uk; Lambeth Rd SE1; ☺10am-6pm; ⊖Lambeth North) You don't have to be a lad to appreciate the Imperial War Museum and its spectacular atrium with spitfires hanging from the ceiling, rockets, field guns, missiles, submarines, tanks, torpedoes and other military hardware. The museum is on Lambeth Rd, a couple of minutes' walk southeast of Lambeth North tube station; turn right off St George's Rd.

CITY HALL
Landmark
(Map p74; www.london.gov.uk; Queen's Walk SE1; ☺8.30am-6pm Mon-Fri; ⊖London Bridge) The Norman Foster–designed, wonky-egg-shaped City Hall is an architectural feast and home to the mayor's office, the London Assembly and the Greater London Assembly (GLA). Visitors can see the mayor's meeting chamber and attend debates.

HMS BELFAST
Ship

(Map p74; http://hmsbelfast.iwm.org.uk; Queen's Walk SE1; adult/child £13/free; 10am-5pm; London Bridge) Launched in 1938, HMS *Belfast* took part in the D-day landings and saw action in Korea. Explore the nine decks and see the engine room, gun decks, galley, chapel, punishment cells, canteen and dental surgery.

SEA LIFE
Aquarium

(Map p66; 0871 663 1678; www.sealife.co.uk/london; County Hall SE1; adult/child £18/13; 10am-6pm; Waterloo) One of the largest aquariums in Europe, Sea Life has all sorts of aquatic creatures organised into different zones (coral cave, rainforest, River Thames), culminating with the shark walkway.

Pimlico

Handy to the big sights but lacking a strong sense of neighbourhood, the streets get prettier the further you stray from Victoria station.

FREE TATE BRITAIN
Gallery

(Map p52; www.tate.org.uk; Millbank SW1; 10am-5.40pm; Pimlico) Britannia rules the walls of Tate Britain. Reaching from 1500 to the present, it's crammed with local heavyweights like Blake, Hogarth, Gainsborough, Whistler, Spencer and, especially, Turner, whose work dominates the **Clore Gallery**. His 'interrupted visions' – unfinished canvasses of moody skies – wouldn't look out of place in the contemporary section, alongside the work of David Hockney, Francis Bacon, Tracey Emin, Angela Bulloch and Damien Hirst.

There are free hour-long guided tours, taking in different sections of the gallery, held daily at midday and 3pm (as well as 11am and 2pm on weekdays).

Chelsea & Kensington

This area is known as the royal borough. Residents of Chelsea and Kensington are certainly paid royally, earning the highest incomes in the UK (shops and restaurants will presume you do too). Kensington High St has a lively mix of chains and boutiques.

FREE VICTORIA & ALBERT MUSEUM
Museum

(V&A; Map p82; www.vam.ac.uk; Cromwell Rd SW7; 10am-5.45pm Sat-Thu, to 10pm Fri; South Kensington) A vast, rambling and wonderful museum of decorative art and design, the V&A is part of Prince Albert's legacy to Londoners in the wake of the Great Exhibition. It's a bit like the nation's attic, comprising four million objects collected from Britain and around the globe. Spread over nearly 150 galleries, it houses the world's greatest collection of decorative arts, including ancient Chinese ceramics, modernist architectural drawings, Korean bronzes, Japanese swords, cartoons by Raphael, spellbinding Asian

Workers at Borough Market (p100)

ORIEN HARVEY / LONELY PLANET IMAGES ©

Don't Miss **London Eye**

Originally designed as a temporary structure to celebrate the millennium, the Eye is now a permanent addition to the cityscape, joining Big Ben as one of London's most distinctive landmarks.

This 135m-tall, slow-moving Ferris-wheel-like attraction is the largest of its kind in the world. Passengers ride in an enclosed egg-shaped pod; the wheel takes 30 minutes to rotate completely and offers 25-mile views on a clear day.

Book your ticket online to speed up your wait (you also get a 20% discount), or you can pay an additional £10 to jump the queue. Joint tickets for the London Eye and Madame Tussauds (adult/child £43/31) are available, as is a 40-minute, sightseeing **River Cruise** (adult/child £12/6) with a multilingual commentary.

THINGS YOU NEED TO KNOW

Map p66; ☎0871 781 3000; www.londoneye.com; adult/child £18/9.50; ⏰10am-8pm; ⊖Waterloo

---

statues and Islamic carpets, Rodin sculptures, actual-size reproductions of famous European architecture and sculpture (including Michelangelo's *David*), Elizabethan gowns, ancient jewellery, an all-wooden Frank Lloyd Wright study and a pair of Doc Martens. Yes, you'll need to plan.

 NATURAL HISTORY MUSEUM
Museum
(Map p82; www.nhm.ac.uk; Cromwell Rd SW7; admission free; ⏰10am-5.50pm; ⊖South

Kensington) A sure-fire hit with kids of all ages, the Natural History Museum is jam-packed with interesting stuff, starting with the giant dinosaur skeleton that greets you in the main hall. In the dinosaur section, the fleshless fossils are brought to robotic life with a very realistic 4m-high animatronic Tyrannosaurus Rex alongside his smaller, but no less sinister-looking, cousins.

The other galleries are equally impressive. An escalator slithers up and

Hyde Park & Kensington

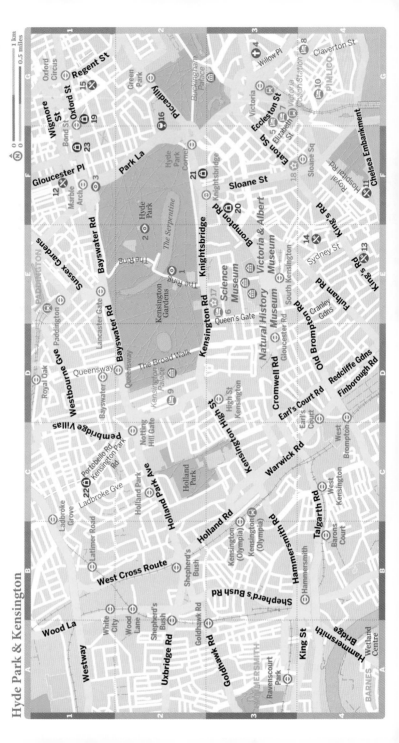

into a hollowed-out globe where two exhibits – The Power Within and Restless Surface – explain how wind, water, ice, gravity and life itself impact on the earth. For parents unsure of how to broach the facts of life, a quick whiz around the Human Biology section should do the trick.

The **Darwin Centre** houses a team of biologists and a staggering 20-million-plus species of animal and plant specimens. Take a lift to the top of the Cocoon, a seven-storey egg-shaped structure encased within a glass pavilion, and make your way down through the floors of interactive displays. Glass windows allow you to watch the scientists at work.

FREE **SCIENCE MUSEUM** Museum
(Map p82; www.sciencemuseum.org.uk; Exhibition Rd SW7; ⏰10am-6pm; ⊖South Kensington) With seven floors of interactive and educational exhibits, the Science Museum covers everything from the Industrial Revolution to the exploration of space. There is something for all ages, from vintage cars, trains and aeroplanes to labour-saving devices for the home, a wind tunnel and flight simulator. Kids love the interactive sections.

HYDE PARK Park
(Map p82; ⏰5.30am- midnight; ⊖Marble Arch, Hyde Park Corner or Queensway) At 145 hectares, Hyde Park is central London's largest open space. Henry VIII expropriated it from the Church in 1536, when it became a hunting ground and later a venue for duels, executions and horse racing. The 1851 Great Exhibition was held here, and during WWII the park became an enormous potato field. These days, it serves as an occasional concert venue and a full-time green space for fun and frolics. There's boating on the **Serpentine** for the energetic, while **Speaker's Corner** is for oratorical acrobats. Nearby **Marble Arch** was designed by John Nash in 1828 as the entrance to Buckingham Palace. It was moved here in 1851.

A soothing structure, the **Diana, Princess of Wales Memorial Fountain** is a circular stream that cascades gently and reassembles in a pool at the bottom; paddling is encouraged. It was unveiled in mid-2004, instigating an inevitable debate over matters of taste and gravitas.

Marylebone

Hip Marylebone isn't as exclusive as Mayfair, its southern neighbour, but it does have one of London's nicest high streets and the very famous, if somewhat

Hyde Park & Kensington

disappointing, Baker St. Apart from being immortalised in a hit song by Gerry Rafferty, Baker St is strongly associated with Sherlock Holmes (there's a museum and gift shop at his fictional address, 221B).

LONDON ZOO   Zoo

(Map p85; www.londonzoo.co.uk; Outer Circle, Regent's Park NW1; adult/child £18/14; ⏰10am-5.30pm Mar-Oct, to 4pm Nov-Feb; 🚇Camden Town) A huge amount of money has been spent to bring London Zoo, established in 1828, into the modern world. It now has a swanky £5.3 million gorilla enclosure and is involved in gorilla conservation in Gabon. Feeding times, reptile handling and the petting zoo are guaranteed winners with the kids.

MADAME TUSSAUDS   Waxworks

(Map p85; ☎0870 400 3000; www.madame-tussauds.co.uk; Marylebone Rd NW1; adult/child £26/22; ⏰9.30am-5.30pm; 🚇Baker St) With so much fabulous free stuff to do in London, it's a wonder that people still join lengthy queues to visit pricey Madame Tussauds, but in a celebrity-obsessed, camera-happy world, the opportunity to pose beside Posh and Becks is not short on appeal. The life-size wax figures are remarkably lifelike and are as close to the real thing as most of us will get.

Tickets are cheaper when ordered online; combined tickets with London Eye and London Dungeon are also available (adult/child £65/48).

Bloomsbury

With the University of London and British Museum within its genteel environs, it's little wonder that Bloomsbury has attracted a lot of very clever, bookish people over the years. Between the world wars, these pleasant streets were colonised by a group of artists and intellectuals known collectively as the Bloomsbury Group, which included novelists Virginia Woolf and EM Forster and the economist John Maynard Keynes.

FREE BRITISH MUSEUM   Museum

(Map p85; ☎020-7323 8000; www.british museum.org; Great Russell St WC1; ⏰10am-5.30pm Sat-Wed, to 8.30pm Thu & Fri; 🚇Russell

Sq) The country's largest museum and one of the oldest and finest in the world, this famous museum boasts vast Egyptian, Etruscan, Greek, Roman, European and Middle Eastern galleries, among many others.

Begun in 1753 with a 'cabinet of curiosities' bequeathed by Sir Hans Sloane to the nation on his death, the collection mushroomed over the ensuing years partly through the plundering of the empire. The grand **Enlightenment Gallery** was the first section of the redesigned museum to be built (in 1823).

Among the must-sees are the **Rosetta Stone**, the key to deciphering Egyptian hieroglyphics, discovered in 1799; the controversial **Parthenon Sculptures**, stripped from the walls of the Parthenon in Athens by Lord Elgin (the British ambassador to the Ottoman Empire), and which Greece wants returned; the stunning **Oxus Treasure** of 7th- to 4th-century-BC Persian gold; and the Anglo-Saxon **Sutton Hoo** burial relics.

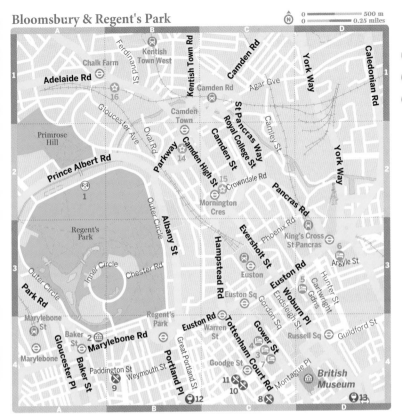

The **Great Court** was restored and augmented by Norman Foster in the year 2000 and now has a spectacular glass-and-steel roof, making it one of the most impressive architectural spaces in the capital. In the centre is the **Reading Room**, with its stunning blue-and-gold domed ceiling. This room is where Karl Marx wrote the *Manifesto of the Communist Party*.

You'll need multiple visits to savour even the highlights here; happily there are 15 half-hour free 'eye opener' tours between 11am and 3.45pm daily, focussing on different parts of the collection. Other tours include the 90-minute highlights tour at 10.30am, 1pm and 3pm daily (adult/child £8/5), and audioguides are available (£4.50).

Greenwich

Simultaneously the first and last place on earth, Greenwich (*gren*-itch) straddles the hemispheres as well as the ages. More than any of the villages swamped by London, Greenwich has retained its own sense of identity, based on splendid architecture and strong connections with the sea and science. All the great architects of the Enlightenment made their mark here, leaving an extraordinary cluster of buildings that have earned 'Maritime Greenwich' its place on Unesco's World Heritage list.

Greenwich is easily reached on the DLR or via train from London Bridge. **Thames River Services** (☎020-7930 4097; www.thamesriverservices.co.uk) has boats departing from Westminster Pier (single/return £9.50/12.50, one hour, every

The River Thames

A Floating Tour

London's history has always been determined by the Thames. The city was founded as a Roman port nearly 2000 years ago and over the centuries since then many of the capital's landmarks have lined the river's banks. A boat trip is a great way to experience the attractions.

There are piers dotted along both banks at regular intervals where you can hop-on/hop-off the regular services to visit places of interest.

The best place to board is Westminster Pier, from where boats head downstream, taking you from the City of Westminster, the seat of government, to the original City of London, now the financial district and dominated by a growing band of skyscrapers. Across the river, the once shabby and neglected South Bank now bristles with as many top attractions as its northern counterpart.

In our illustration we've concentrated on the top highlights you'll enjoy at a fish's-eye view as

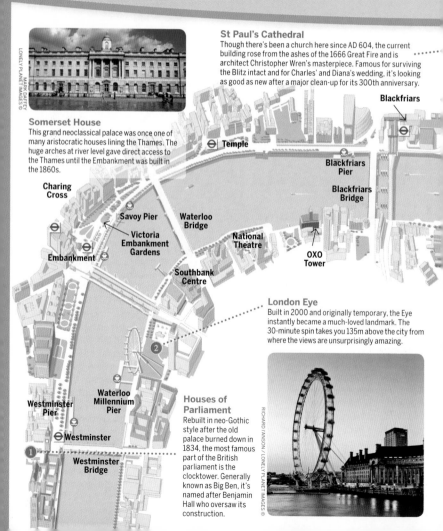

St Paul's Cathedral

Though there's been a church here since AD 604, the current building rose from the ashes of the 1666 Great Fire and is architect Christopher Wren's masterpiece. Famous for surviving the Blitz intact and for Charles' and Diana's wedding, it's looking as good as new after a major clean-up for its 300th anniversary.

Blackfriars

Somerset House

This grand neoclassical palace was once one of many aristocratic houses lining the Thames. The huge arches at river level gave direct access to the Thames until the Embankment was built in the 1860s.

Temple

Blackfriars Pier

Blackfriars Bridge

Charing Cross

Savoy Pier

Waterloo Bridge

Victoria Embankment Gardens

National Theatre

Embankment

OXO Tower

Southbank Centre

London Eye

Built in 2000 and originally temporary, the Eye instantly became a much-loved landmark. The 30-minute spin takes you 135m above the city from where the views are unsurprisingly amazing.

Waterloo Millennium Pier

Westminster Pier

Houses of Parliament

Rebuilt in neo-Gothic style after the old palace burned down in 1834, the most famous part of the British parliament is the clocktower. Generally known as Big Ben, it's named after Benjamin Hall who oversaw its construction.

Westminster

Westminster Bridge

you sail along. These are, from west to east, the Houses of Parliament **1**, the London Eye **2**, Somerset House **3**, St Paul's Cathedral **4**, Tate Modern **5**, Shakespeare's Globe **6**, the Tower of London **7** and Tower Bridge **8**.

Apart from covering this central section of the river, boats can also be taken upstream as far as Kew Gardens and Hampton Court Palace, and downstream to Greenwich and the Thames Barrier.

BOAT HOPPING

Thames Clippers hop-on/hop-off services are aimed at commuters but are equally useful for visitors, operating every 15 minutes on a loop from piers at Embankment, Waterloo, Blackfriars, Bankside, London Bridge and the Tower. Other services also go from Westminster. Oyster cardholders get a discount off the boat ticket price.

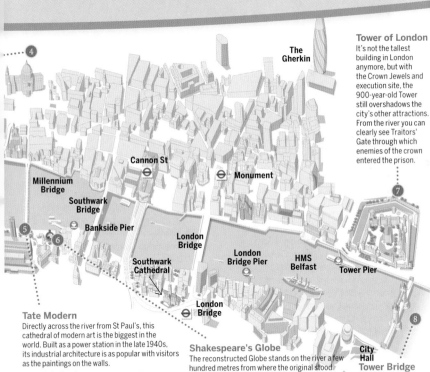

The Gherkin

Tower of London
It's not the tallest building in London anymore, but with the Crown Jewels and execution site, the 900-year-old Tower still overshadows the city's other attractions. From the river you can clearly see Traitors' Gate through which enemies of the crown entered the prison.

Cannon St

Monument

Millennium Bridge

Southwark Bridge

Bankside Pier

London Bridge

London Bridge Pier

HMS Belfast

Tower Pier

Southwark Cathedral

London Bridge

Tate Modern
Directly across the river from St Paul's, this cathedral of modern art is the biggest in the world. Built as a power station in the late 1940s, its industrial architecture is as popular with visitors as the paintings on the walls.

Shakespeare's Globe
The reconstructed Globe stands on the river a few hundred metres from where the original stood (and burnt down in 1613 during a performance). The life's work of American actor Sam Wanamaker, the theatre runs a hugely popular season from April to October each year.

City Hall

Tower Bridge
It might look as old as its namesake neighbour but one of the world's most iconic bridges was only completed in 1894. Not to be confused with London Bridge upstream, this one's famous raising bascules allowed tall ships to dock at the old wharves to the west and are still lifted up to 1000 times a year.

DOUG MCKINLAY / LONELY PLANET IMAGES ©

DOUG MCKINLAY / LONELY PLANET IMAGES ©

40 minutes), or alternatively take the cheaper Thames Clippers ferry.

FREE OLD ROYAL NAVAL COLLEGE
Historic Buildings

(www.oldroyalnavalcollege.org; 2 Cutty Sark Gardens SE10; ☽10am-5pm; DLR Cutty Sark) Designed by Wren, the Old Royal Naval College is a magnificent example of monumental classical architecture. Parts are now used by the University of Greenwich and Trinity College of Music, but you can visit the **chapel** and the extraordinary **Painted Hall**, which took artist Sir James Thornhill 19 years of hard graft to complete.

The complex was built on the site of the 15th-century Palace of Placentia, the birthplace of Henry VIII and Elizabeth I. This Tudor connection, along with Greenwich's industrial and maritime history, is explored in the **Discover Greenwich** centre. The tourist office is based here, along with a cafe and microbrewery. Tours of the complex leave at 2pm daily, taking in areas not otherwise open to the public (£5, 90

minutes). You can also buy 'walkcards' (50p) for themed self-guided tours of Greenwich: *Highlights* (40 minutes), *Royal* (80 minutes), *Viewpoints*, and *Architecture* (both 90 minutes).

Greenwich Guided Walks (☏0757-577 2298; www.greenwichtours.co.uk; adult/child £6/5; ☽12.15pm & 2.15pm) leave from the tourist office.

FREE NATIONAL MARITIME MUSEUM
Museum

(☏020-8858 4422; www.nmm.ac.uk; Romney Rd SE10; ☽10am-5pm; DLR Cutty Sark) Directly behind the old college, the National Maritime Museum completes Greenwich's trump hand of historic buildings. The museum itself houses a large collection of paraphernalia recounting Britain's seafaring history.

At the centre of the site, the elegant Palladian **Queen's House** has been restored to something like Inigo Jones' intention when he designed it in 1616 for the wife of Charles I. It's a refined setting for a gallery focusing on illustrious seafarers and historic Greenwich.

Left: View of 'the gherkin' (architect Norman Foster) from the Vertigo 42 bar (p97); **Below:** A double-decker bus passes nearby Big Ben (p64)
PHOTOGRAPHERS: (LEFT) DOUG MCKINLAY; (BELOW) DENNIS JOHNSON / LONELY PLANET IMAGES ©

Behind Queen's House, idyllic **Greenwich Park** climbs up the hill, affording great views of London. It's capped by the **Royal Observatory (same hours as rest of museum, until 7pm May-Aug)**, which Charles II had built in 1675 to help solve the riddle of longitude. Success was confirmed in 1884 when Greenwich was designated as the prime meridian of the world, and Greenwich Mean Time (GMT) became the universal measurement of standard time.

 Tours

One of the best ways to orientate yourself when you first arrive in London is with a 24-hour hop-on/hop-off pass for the double-decker bus tours. The buses loop around interconnecting routes throughout the day, providing a commentary as they go, and the price includes a river cruise and three walking tours. You'll save a couple of pounds by booking online.

Original London Sightseeing Tour
Bus tours
(020-8877 1722; www.theoriginaltour.com; adult/child £25/12)

Big Bus Company
Bus tours
(020-7233 9533; www.bigbustours.com; adult/child £26/10)

London Walks
Walking tours
(020-7624 3978; www.walks.com) Harry Potter tours, ghost walks and the ever popular Jack the Ripper tours.

London Mystery Walks
Walking tours
(07957 388280; www.tourguides.org.uk)

Black Taxi Tours of London
Taxi tours
(020-7935 9363; www.blacktaxitours.co.uk; 8am-6pm £100, 6pm-midnight £110, plus £5 on weekends) A two-hour spin past the major sights with a chatty cabbie as your guide.

London for Children

London has plenty of sights that parents and kids can enjoy together, and many of them are free, including the Natural History Museum, Science Museum and all of the city's parks, many of which have excellent playgrounds. Pricier but popular attractions include London Dungeon (for older children), London Zoo, Madame Tussauds, Tower of London, Sea Life and the London Eye. However, don't expect a warm welcome in swanky restaurants or pubs.

All top-range hotels offer in-house babysitting services. Prices vary enormously from hotel to hotel, so ask the concierge about hourly rates.

Sleeping

Take a deep breath and sit down before reading this section because no matter what your budget, London is a horribly pricey city to sleep in – one of the most expensive in the world, in fact. For this book we've defined the price categories for London differently than for the other chapters. Double rooms ranging between £80 and £180 per night are considered midrange; cheaper or more expensive options fall into the budget or the top-end categories, respectively.

Public transport is good, so you don't need to be sleeping at Buckingham Palace to be at the heart of things. However, if you're planning some late nights and don't fancy enduring the night buses (a consummate London experience, but one you'll want only once) it'll make sense not to wander too far from the action.

It's now becoming the norm for budget and midrange places to offer free wireless internet. The expensive places will offer it, too, but often charge. If your hotel charges for breakfast, check the prices; anything over £8 just isn't worth it when there are so many eateries to explore.

West End

This is the heart of the action, so naturally accommodation comes at a price, and a hefty one at that.

HAZLITT'S   Hotel £££
(Map p66; ☏020-7434 1771; www.hazlittshotel.com; 6 Frith St W1; s £206, d/ste from £259/646; @ ⓦ; ⊖Tottenham Court Rd) Staying in this charming Georgian house (1718) is a trip back into a time when four-poster beds and claw-foot baths were the norm for gentlefolk.

BROWN'S HOTEL   Hotel £££
(Map p66; ☏020-7493 6020; www.brownshotel.com; 30 Albemarle St W1; d £340-645, ste £885-3200; @ ⓦ; ⊖Green Park) Rudyard Kipling penned many of his works here, Kate Moss has frequented the spa and both Queen Victoria and Winston Churchill dropped in for tea. There's a lovely old-world feel to Browns, but without the snootiness of other Mayfair hotels.

The City

Bristling with bankers during the week, you can often pick up a considerable bargain in the City on weekends.

THREADNEEDLES   Hotel ££
(Map p74; ☏020-7657 8080; www.theetoncollection.com; 5 Threadneedle St EC2; r weekend/weekday from £175/345; @ ⓦ; ⊖Bank) The incredible stained-glass dome in the lobby points to Threedneedles' former status as a bank HQ. Today it's still popular with suits, but the atmosphere is chic rather than stuffy.

APEX CITY OF LONDON   Hotel ££
(Map p74; ☏020-7702 2020; www.apexhotels.co.uk; 1 Seething Lane EC3; r from £100; ⓦ; ⊖Tower Hill) Business-focused but close

enough to the Tower to hear the heads roll, the Apex offers particularly enticing weekend rates, a gym, huge TVs, free wi-fi and a rubber ducky in every room.

South Bank

Immediately south of the river is a good spot if you want to immerse yourself in workaday London and still be central.

MAD HATTER HOTEL Hotel ££

(Map p74; ☎ 020-7401 9222; www.fullershotels. com; 3-7 Stamford St SE1; r £155; ⊖ Southwark) There's nothing particularly mad (or even unusual) about it, but this is a good hotel with decent-sized rooms and unassuming decor hiding behind a lovely Victorian frontage. Prices fall considerably on weekends.

SOUTHWARK ROSE HOTEL Hotel ££

(Map p74; ☎ 020-7015 1480; www.southwark rosehotel.co.uk; 47 Southwark Bridge Rd SE1; r/ ste from £85/115; @ 🛜; ⊖ Borough) Though it's somewhat pricey during the week, this business hotel drops its rates considerably to attract the weekender visitors.

Pimlico

LUNA SIMONE HOTEL B&B ££

(Map p82; ☎ 020-7834 5897; www.lunasimone hotel.com; 47-49 Belgrave Rd SW1; s £70-75, d £95-120; @ 🛜; ⊖ Pimlico) The blue-and-yellow rooms aren't huge, but they're clean and calming; the ones at the back are quieter. Belgrave Rd follows on from Eccleston Bridge, directly behind Victoria Station.

WINDERMERE HOTEL
  B&B ££

(Map p82; ☎ 020-7834 5163; www.windermere -hotel.co.uk; 142-144 Warwick Way SW1; s £105-155, d £129-165; @ 🛜; ⊖ Victoria) Chintzy but comfortable early-Victorian town house. The cheapest rooms share bathrooms.

Belgravia

LIME TREE HOTEL B&B ££

(Map p82; ☎ 020-7730 8191; www.limetreehotel. co.uk; 135-137 Ebury St SW1; s £95, d £135-160; @ 🛜; ⊖ Victoria) A smartly renovated Georgian town house hotel with a beautiful back garden to catch the late afternoon rays.

B&B Belgravia B&B ££

(Map p82; ☎ 020-7259 8570; www.bb-belgravia. com; 64-66 Ebury St SW1; s/d £99/120; @ 🛜; ⊖ Victoria) This small hotel's unassuming facade belies a contemporary interior, although a new coat of paint wouldn't go astray.

Chelsea & Kensington

Classy Chelsea and Kensington offer easy access to the museums and fashion retailers. It's all a bit sweetie-darling, along with the prices.

GORE Hotel ££

(Map p82; ☎ 020-7584 6601; www.gorehotel. com; 190 Queen's Gate SW7; r from £135; @ 🛜; ⊖ Gloucester Rd) Located a short stroll from the Royal Albert Hall, the Gore serves

Morning in Regent's Park

Gay & Lesbian London

The West End, particularly Soho, remains the visible centre of gay and lesbian London, with numerous venues clustered around Old Compton St and its surrounds. However, Soho doesn't hold a monopoly on gay life. One of the nice things about the city is that there are local gay bars in many neighbourhoods.

Generally, London's a safe place for lesbians and gays. It's rare to encounter any problem with sharing rooms or holding hands in the inner city, although it would pay to keep your wits about you at night and be conscious of your surroundings.

The easiest way to find out what's going on is to pick up the free press from a venue *(Pink Paper, Boyz, QX)*. The gay section of *Time Out* is useful, as are www.gaydarnation.com (for men) and www.gingerbeer.co.uk (for women).

Some venues to get you started:

Candy Bar (Map p66; www.candybarsoho.co.uk; 4 Carlisle St W1; ⊖ Tottenham Court Rd) Long-running lesbian hang-out.

Friendly Society (Map p66; 79 Wardour St W1; ⊖ Piccadilly Circus) Soho's quirkiest gay bar, this Bohemian basement is bedecked in kid's-room wallpaper and Barbie dolls.

G-A-Y (Map p66; www.g-a-y.co.uk) Bar (30 Old Compton St W1; ⊖ Leicester Sq); Late (5 Goslett Yard WC2; ☺ 11pm-3am; ⊖ Tottenham Court Rd); Club @ Heaven (The Arches, Villiers St WC2; ☺ 11pm-4am Thu-Sat; ⊖ Charing Cross) Too camp to be restricted to one venue, G-A-Y now operates a pink-lit bar on the strip, a late-night bar a few streets away and club nights at one of gaydom's most internationally famous venues, Heaven. Cover charges vary; entry is usually cheaper with a flyer from G-A-Y Bar.

Village (Map p66; www.village-soho.co.uk; 81 Wardour St W1; ⊖ Piccadilly Circus) Glitzy gay bar with excellent, lengthy happy hours.

up British grandiosity (antiques, carved four-poster beds, a secret bathroom in the Tudor room) with a large slice of camp.

VICARAGE PRIVATE HOTEL B&B ££
(Map p82; ☎ 020-7229 4030; www.london vicaragehotel.com; 10 Vicarage Gate W8; s/d £95/125, without bathroom £56/95; @ 🛜; ⊖ High St Kensington) You can see Kensington Palace from the doorstep of this grand Victorian town house, which opens on to a cul-de-sac. The cheaper rooms (without bathrooms) are on floors three and four, so you may get a view as well as a workout.

Bloomsbury & St Pancras

Only one step removed from the West End and crammed with Georgian town-house conversions, these neighbourhoods are much more affordable.

ARRAN HOUSE HOTEL B&B ££
(Map p85; ☎ 020-7636 2186; www.arran hotel-london.com; 77-79 Gower St WC1; s/d/ tr/q £70/110/128/132, without bathroom £60/80/105/111; @ 🛜; ⊖ Goodge St) Period features such as cornicing and fireplaces, a pretty pergola-decked back garden and a comfy lounge with PCs and TV lift this hotel from the average to the attractive. Squashed en suites or shared bathrooms are the trade-off for these reasonable rates.

AROSFA HOTEL B&B ££
(Map p85; ☎ 020-7636 2115; www.arosfalondon. com; 83 Gower St WC1; s £60-65, d/tr/q £90/102/110; @ 🛜; ⊖ Goodge St) While the decor of the immaculately presented rooms is unremarkable, Arosfa's guest lounge has been blinged up with chande-

liers, clear plastic chairs and a free-internet terminal.

JESMOND DENE
B&B £

(Map p85; ☎020-7837 4654; www.jesmonddene hotel.co.uk; 27 Argyle St; s/d incl breakfast from £60/65; P @ 🛜; ⊖Kings Cross) A surprisingly pleasant option for a place so close to busy Kings Cross station, this modest hotel has clean but small rooms, some of which share bathrooms.

RIDGEMOUNT HOTEL
B&B £

(Map p85; ☎020-7636 1141; www.ridgemount hotel.co.uk; 65-67 Gower St WC1; s/d/tr/q £55/78/96/108, without bathroom £43/60/81/96; @ 🛜; ⊖Goodge St) There's a comfortable, welcoming feel at this old-fashioned, slightly chintzy place that's been in the same family for 40 years.

JENKINS HOTEL
B&B ££

(Map p85; ☎020-7387 2067; www.jenkinshotel. demon.co.uk; 45 Cartwright Gardens WC1; s/d from £52/95; ⊖Russell Sq) This modest hotel has featured in the TV series of Agatha Christie's *Poirot*. Rooms are small but the hotel has charm.

Airports

YOTEL
Capsule Hotel ££

(☎020-7100 1100; www.yotel.com; s/d £69/85, or per 4hr £29/45 then per additional hr £8; @ 🛜) Gatwick (South Terminal); Heathrow (Terminal 4) The best news for early-morning flyers since coffee-vending machines, Yotel's smart 'cabins' offer pint-sized luxury: comfy beds, soft lights, internet-connected TVs, monsoon showers and fluffy towels. Swinging cats isn't recommended, but when is it ever?

Eating

In this section, we steer you towards restaurants and cafes distinguished by their location, value for money, unique features, original settings and, of course, good food. Vegetarians needn't worry; London has a host of dedicated meat-free joints, while most others offer at least a token dish.

West End

Mayfair, Soho and Covent Garden are the gastronomic heart of London, with stacks of restaurants and cuisines to choose

A London double-decker bus

Want More?

For in-depth information, reviews and recommendations at your fingertips, head to the Apple App Store to purchase Lonely Planet's *London City Guide* iPhone app.

Alternatively, head to Lonely Planet (www.lonelyplanet.com/england/london) for planning advice, author recommendations, traveller reviews and insider tips.

from at budgets to suit both booze hounds and theatre-goers.

GREAT QUEEN STREET   British ££

(Map p66; ☎020-7242 0622; 32 Great Queen St WC2; mains £9-19; ⏰lunch daily, dinner Mon-Sat; ⊖Holborn) There's no tiara on this Great Queen, her claret-coloured walls and mismatched wooden chairs suggesting cosiness and informality. But the food's still the best of British, including lamb that melts in the mouth and Arbroath smokie (a whole smoked fish with creamy sauce).

VEERASWAMY   Indian ££

(Map p66; ☎020-7734 1401; www.veeraswamy.com; 99 Regent St W1; mains £15-30, pre- & post-theatre 2-/3-course £18/21; ⊖Piccadilly Circus) Since 1926 Veeraswamy has occupied this prime 1st-floor location, with windows looking over Regent St – making it Britain's longest-running Indian restaurant. The excellent food, engaging service and exotic, elegant decor make for a memorable eating experience. The entrance is on Swallow St.

WILD HONEY   Modern European ££

(Map p82; ☎020-7758 9160; www.wildhoney restaurant.co.uk; 12 St George St W1; mains £15-24; ⊖Oxford Circus) If you fancy a relatively affordable meal within the oak-panelled ambience of a top Mayfair restaurant, Wild Honey offers excellent lunch and pre-theatre set menus (respectively, £19 and £22 for three courses).

ARBUTUS   Modern European ££

(Map p66; ☎020-7734 4545; www.arbutus restaurant.co.uk; 63-64 Frith St W1; mains £14-20; ⊖Tottenham Court Rd) Focusing on seasonal produce, inventive dishes and value for money, Anthony Demetre's Michelin-starred restaurant just keeps getting better.

SACRED   Cafe £

(Map p66; www.sacredcafe.co.uk; mains £4-6); Ganton St (13 Ganton St W1; ⏰7.30am-8pm Mon-Fri, 10am-7pm Sat & Sun; ⊖Oxford Circus); Covent Garden (Stanfords, 12-14 Long Acre; ⏰9am-7.30pm Mon-Fri, 10am-8pm Sat, noon-6pm Sun) The spiritual paraphernalia and blatant Kiwiana don't seem to deter the smart Carnaby St set from lounging around this eclectic cafe. That's down to the excellent coffee and appealing counter food.

NATIONAL DINING ROOMS British £££

(Map p66; ☎020-7747 2525; www.thenational diningrooms.co.uk; Sainsbury Wing, National Gallery WC2; 2-/3-course meals £23/26; ⏰10am-5pm Sat-Thu, 10am-8.30pm Fri; ⊖Charing Cross) It's fitting that this acclaimed restaurant should celebrate British food, being in the National Gallery and overlooking Trafalgar Sq. For a much cheaper option with the same views, ambience, quality produce and excellent service, try a salad, pie or tart at the adjoining bakery.

FERNANDEZ & WELLS

Delicatessen Cafe £

(Map p66; www.fernandezandwells.com; 73 Beak St W1; mains £4-5; ⊖Piccadilly Circus) With its sister deli around the corner, there's no shortage of delicious charcuterie and cheese to fill the fresh baguettes on the counter of this teensy cafe. The coffee's superb.

HK DINER   Chinese £

(Map p66; 22 Wardour St W1; mains £6-13; ⏰11am-4am; ⊖Piccadilly Circus) If you've a hankering for soft-shell crab or barbecue pork in the wee hours of the morning, this Hong Kong–style cafe (delicious food, no-nonsense decor) is the place to come.

Chelsea & Kensington

These highbrow neighbourhoods harbour some of London's very best (and priciest) restaurants.

TOM'S KITCHEN
French ££

(Map p82; ☎ 020-7349 0202; www.tomskitchen. co.uk; 27 Cale St SW3; breakfast £4-15, mains £15-30; ⊙breakfast Mon-Fri, lunch & dinner daily; ⊖South Kensington) A much more informal and considerably cheaper option than Tom Aikens' eponymous restaurant, just around the corner, the firebrand chef's kitchen maintains the magic throughout the day. The breakfasts are excellent.

MADE IN ITALY
Italian £

(Map p82; ☎ 020-7352 1880; www.madeinitaly group.co.uk; 249 King's Rd SW3; pizzas £5-11, mains £8-17; ⊙lunch Sat & Sun, dinner daily; ⊖Sloane Sq) Pizza is served by the tasty quarter-metre at this traditional trattoria. Sit on the Chelsea roof terrace and dream of Napoli.

GORDON RAMSAY
French £££

(Map p82; ☎ 020-7352 4441; www.gordon ramsay.com; 68 Royal Hospital Rd SW3; 3-course lunch/dinner £45/90; ⊖Sloane Sq) Like or loathe the ubiquitous Scot, his eponymous restaurant is one of Britain's finest – one of only four in the country with three Michelin stars. Book ahead and dress up: jeans and T-shirts are forbidden – if you've seen the chef on the telly, you know not to argue.

Marylebone

You won't go too far wrong planting yourself on a table anywhere along Marylebone's charming High Street.

LA FROMAGERIE
Cafe, Deli £

(Map p85; www.lafromagerie. co.uk; 2-6 Moxon St W1; mains £6-13; ⊖Baker St)

This deli-cafe has bowls of delectable salads, antipasto, peppers and beans scattered about the long communal table. Huge slabs of bread invite you to tuck in, and all the while the heavenly waft from the cheese room beckons.

LOCANDA LOCATELLI
Italian ££

(Map p82; ☎ 020-7935 9088; www.locanda locatelli.com; 8 Seymour St W1; mains £11-30; ⊖Marble Arch) Known for its sublime pasta dishes, this dark but quietly glamorous restaurant in an otherwise unremarkable hotel is one of London's hottest tables.

Fitzrovia

Tucked away behind busy Tottenham Court Rd, Fitzrovia's Charlotte and Goodge Sts form one of central London's most vibrant eating precincts.

HAKKASAN
Chinese ££

(Map p85; ☎ 020-7927 7000; www.hakkasan. com; 8 Hanway Pl W1; mains £11-58; ⊖Totten-ham Court Rd) Hidden down a lane like all fashionable haunts need to be, the first Chinese restaurant to get a Michelin star

Food stall at Broadway Market (p100)
PHOTOGRAPHER: ORIEN HARVEY / LONELY PLANET IMAGES ©

Chain Eateries

Among the endless Caffe Neros, Pizza Expresses and All-Bar-Ones are some chain-restaurant gems, or, at least, great fallback options.

Some of the best you'll come across around the city:

GBK (www.gbk.co.uk) Gourmet Burger Kitchens dishing up creative burger constructions, including lots of vegetarian options.

Konditor & Cook (www.konditor andcook.com) London's best bakery chain, serving excellent cakes, pastries, bread and coffee.

Leon (www.leonrestaurants.co.uk) Bistro focussing on fresh, seasonal food (salads, wraps and the like).

Ping Pong (www.pingpongdimsum.com) Stylish Chinese dumpling joints.

S&M Cafe (www.sandmcafe.co.uk) The sausages and mash served in these retro diners won't give your wallet a spanking.

Wagamama (www.wagamama.com) Japanese noodles taking over the world from their London base.

Zizzi (www.zizzi.co.uk) Wood-fired pizza.

combines celebrity status, a dimly lit basement dining room, persuasive cocktails and sophisticated food.

SALT YARD   Spanish, Italian ££
(Map p85; 020-7637 0657; www.saltyard.co.uk; 54 Goodge St W1; tapas £4-8; Goodge St) Named after the place where cold meats are cured, this softly lit joint serves delicious Spanish and Italian tapas.

LANTANA   Cafe £
(Map p85; www.lantanacafe.co.uk; 13 Charlotte Pl W1; mains £4-10; breakfast & lunch Mon-Sat; Goodge St) Excellent coffee and substantial, inventive brunches induce queues on Saturday mornings outside this Australian-style cafe.

Drinking

As long as there's been a city, Londoners have loved to drink – and, as history shows, often immoderately. The pub is the focus of social life and there's always one near at hand. When the sun shines, drinkers spill out into the streets, parks and squares as well.

West End

GORDON'S WINE BAR   Bar
(Map p66; www.gordonswinebar.com; 47 Villiers St WC2; Embankment) What's not to love about this cavernous wine cellar that's lit by candles and practically unchanged over the last 120 years?

PRINCESS LOUISE   Pub
(Map p85; 208 High Holborn WC1; Holborn) This late 19th-century Victorian boozer is arguably London's most beautiful pub.

LAMB & FLAG   Pub
(Map p66; 33 Rose St WC2; Covent Garden) Everyone's Covent Garden 'find', this historic pub is often jammed.

GALVIN AT WINDOWS   Hotel Bar
(Map p82; www.galvinatwindows.com; The Hilton, 22 Park Lane W1; Hyde Park Corner) Drinks are pricey, but the view's magnificent from this 28th-floor eyrie.

JEWEL   Cocktail Bar
(Map p66; www.jewelbar.com); Piccadilly Circus (4-6 Glasshouse Street W1; Piccadilly Circus); Covent Garden (29-30 Maiden Lane WC2; Covent Garden) Chandeliers, banquettes, cocktails and, in Piccadilly, sunset views.

The City

YE OLDE WATLING   Pub
(Map p74; 29 Watling St; Mansion House) Atmospheric 1668 pub with a good selection of wine and tap beer.

YE OLDE CHESHIRE CHEESE   Pub
(Map p74; Wine Office Ct, 145 Fleet St EC4; Holborn) Touristy but always atmospheric and enjoyable for a pub meal.

VERTIGO 42
Champagne Bar

(Map p74; 020-7877 7842; www.vertigo42.
co.uk; Tower 42, Old Broad St, EC2; Liverpool
St) Book a two-hour slot in this 42nd-floor
bar with vertiginous views across London.

Marylebone
ARTESIAN
Hotel Bar

(Map p85; www.artesian-bar.co.uk; Langham
Hotel, 1C Portland Pl W1; Oxford Circus) For
a dose of colonial glamour with a touch
of the Orient, the sumptuous bar at the
Langham hits the mark.

 Entertainment

From West End luvvies to East End
geezers, Londoners have always loved a
spectacle. With bear-baiting and public
executions no longer an option, they've
learnt to make do with having one of the
world's best theatre, nightclub and live-
music scenes to divert them.

For a comprehensive list of what to do
on any given night, check out *Time Out*.
The listings in the free tube papers are
also handy.

Theatre

London is a world capital for theatre
and there's a lot more than mammoth
musicals to tempt you into the West End.
As far as the blockbuster musicals go, you
can be fairly confident that *Les Miserables*
and *Phantom of the Opera* will still be
chugging along, as well as Phantom's se-
quel *Love Never Dies*, plus *Legally Blonde*,
Sister Act and *The Wizard of Oz*.

On performance days, you can buy half-
price tickets for West End productions
(cash only) from the official agency **tkts**
(Map p66; www.tkts.co.uk; 10am-7pm Mon-Sat,
noon-4pm Sun; Leicester Sq), on the south
side of Leicester Sq. The booth is the one
with the clock tower; beware of touts
selling dodgy tickets.

The term 'West End' – as with
Broadway – generally refers to the big-
money productions like musicals, but
also includes other heavyweights. Some
recommended options:

Royal Court Theatre
Theatre

(Map p82; 020-7565 5000; www.
royalcourttheatre.com; Sloane Sq SW1; Sloane
Sq) The patron of new British writing.

Princess Louise pub

National Theatre
Theatre

(Map p66; ☎020-7452 3000; www.nationaltheatre.org.uk; South Bank SE1; ⊖Waterloo) Cheaper tickets for both classics and new plays from some of the world's best companies.

Old Vic
Theatre

(Map p66; ☎0844 871 7628; www.oldvictheatre.com; The Cut SE1; ⊖Waterloo) Kevin Spacey continues his run as artistic director (and occasional performer).

Donmar Warehouse
Theatre

(Map p66; ☎0844 871 7624; www.donmarwarehouse.com; 41 Earlham St WC2; ⊖Covent Garden) A not-for-profit company that has forged itself a West End reputation.

Nightclubs

Clubland's no longer confined to the West End, with megaclubs scattered throughout the city wherever there's a venue big enough, cheap enough or quirky enough to hold them. Admission prices vary widely; it's often cheaper to arrive early or prebook tickets.

FABRIC
Superclub

(Map p74; www.fabriclondon.com; 77A Charterhouse St EC1; admission £8-18; ⊗10pm-6am Fri, 11pm-8am Sat; 11pm-6am Sun; ⊖Farringdon) Consistently rated by DJs as one of the world's greatest, Fabric's three dance floors occupy a converted meat cold-store opposite the Smithfield meat market.

MINISTRY OF SOUND
Superclub

(www.ministryofsound.com; 103 Gaunt St SE1; admission £13-22; ⊗11pm-6.30am Fri & Sat; ⊖Elephant & Castle) Where the global brand started, it's London's most famous club and still packs in a diverse crew with big local and international names.

CARGO
Nightclub

(Map p74; www.cargo-london.com; 83 Rivington St EC2; admission free-£16; ⊖Old St) A popular club with a courtyard where you can simultaneously enjoy big sounds and the great outdoors. Hosts live bands and gay bingo too.

Rock, Pop & Jazz

You'll find interesting young bands gigging around venues all over the city. Big-

Royal Albert Hall

CHRISTER FREDRIKSSON / LONELY PLANET IMAGES ©

name gigs sell out quickly, so check www.seetickets.com before you travel.

KOKO
Club

(Map p85; www.koko.uk.com; 1A Camden High St NW1; Mornington Cres) Occupying the grand Camden Palace theatre, Koko hosts live bands most nights and the regular Club NME (£5) on Friday.

JAZZ CAFE
Club

(Map p85; www.jazzcafe.co.uk; 5 Parkway NW1; Camden Town) Jazz is just one part of the picture at this intimate club that stages a full roster of rock, pop, hip hop and dance, including famous names.

RONNIE SCOTT'S
Club

(Map p66; 020-7439 0747; www.ronniescotts.co.uk; 47 Frith St W1; Leicester Sq) London's legendary jazz club has been pulling in the hep cats since 1959.

ROUNDHOUSE
Concert hall

(Map p85; 0844 482 8008; www.roundhouse.org.uk; Chalk Farm Rd NW1; Chalk Farm) Iconic concert venue since the 1960s, hosting the likes of the Rolling Stones, Led Zeppelin and The Clash.

Classical Music

With four world-class symphony orchestras, two opera companies, various smaller ensembles, brilliant venues, reasonable prices and high standards of performance, London is a classical capital. Keep an eye out for the free (or nearly so) lunchtime concerts held in many of the city's churches.

ROYAL ALBERT HALL
Concert Hall

(Map p82; 020-7589 8212; www.royalalberthall.com; Kensington Gore SW7; South Kensington) A beautiful circular Victorian arena that hosts classical concerts and contemporary artists, but is best known as the venue for the annual classical music festival, the Proms.

SOUTHBANK CENTRE
Concert Halls

(Map p66; 0844 875 0073; www.southbankcentre.co.uk; Belvedere Rd; Waterloo) Home to the London Philharmonic Orchestra (www.lpo.co.uk), Sinfonietta (www.londonsinfonietta.org.uk) and the Philharmonia Orchestra (www.philharmonia.co.uk), among others, this centre hosts classical, opera, jazz and choral music in three premier venues: the **Royal Festival Hall**, the smaller **Queen Elizabeth Hall** and the **Purcell Room**. Look out for free recitals in the foyer.

Opera & Dance

ROYAL OPERA HOUSE
Opera, Ballet

(Map p66; 020-7304 4000; www.roh.org.uk; Bow St WC2; tickets £5-195; Covent Garden) Covent Garden is synonymous with opera thanks to this world-famous venue, which is also the home of the Royal Ballet, Britain's premier classical ballet company.

SADLER'S WELLS
Dance

(Map p74; 0844 412 4300; www.sadlers-wells.com; Rosebery Ave EC1; tickets £10-49; Angel) A glittering modern venue that was, in fact, first established in the 17th century, Sadler's Wells has been given much credit for bringing modern dance to the mainstream.

Shopping

From world-famous department stores to quirky backstreet retail revelations, London is a mecca for shoppers with an eye for style and a card to exercise. If you're looking for something distinctly British, eschew the Union Jack–emblazoned kitsch of the tourist thoroughfares and fill your bags with London fashion, music, books and antiques.

London's famous department stores are a tourist attraction in themselves, even if you don't intend to make a personal contribution to the orgy of consumption.

West End

Oxford St is the place for High St fashion, while Regent St cranks it up a notch. Carnaby St is no longer the hip hub that it was in the 1960s, but the lanes around it still have some interesting boutiques.

Roll out the Barrow

London has more than 350 markets selling everything from antiques and curios to flowers and fish.

Borough Market (Map p74; www.boroughmarket.org.uk; 8 Southwark St SE1; ⊙11am-5pm Thu, noon-6pm Fri, 8am-5pm Sat; ⊖London Bridge) A farmers market sometimes called London's Larder, it has been here in some form since the 13th century.

Portobello Road Market (Map p82; www.portobellomarket.org; Portobello Rd W10; ⊙8am-6.30pm Mon-Sat, closes 1pm Thu; ⊖Ladbroke Grove) One of London's most famous (and crowded) street markets, including clothes and antiques.

Broadway Market (www.broadwaymarket.co.uk; Broadway Mkt E8; ⊙9am-5pm Sat; ⊖Bethnal Green) Graze from the organic food stalls, choose a cooked meal and then sample one of the 200 beers on offer at the neighbouring Dove Freehouse. From the tube, head up Cambridge Heath Rd until you cross the canal. Turn left, following the canal and you'll see the market to the right after a few short blocks.

Brick Lane Market (Map p74; www.visitbricklane.org; Brick Lane E1; ⊙8am-2pm Sun; ⊖Liverpool St) An East End pearler, a sprawling bazaar featuring everything from fruit and veggies to paintings and bric-a-brac.

Bond St has designers galore, Savile Row is famous for bespoke tailoring and Jermyn St is the place for Sir to buy his smart clobber (particularly shirts). For musical instruments, visit Denmark St (off Charing Cross Rd).

SELFRIDGES — Department Store
(Map p82; www.selfridges.com; 400 Oxford St W1; ⊖Bond St) The funkiest and most vital of London's one-stop shops, where fashion runs the gamut from street to formal. The food hall is unparalleled, and the cosmetics hall the largest in Europe.

FORTNUM & MASON — Department Store
(Map p66; www.fortnumandmason.com; 181 Piccadilly W1; ⊖Piccadilly Circus) The byword for quality and service from a bygone era, steeped in 300 years of tradition.

LIBERTY — Department Store
(Map p66; www.liberty.co.uk; Great Marlborough St W1; ⊖Oxford Circus) An irresistible blend of contemporary styles and indulgent pampering in a mock-Tudor fantasyland of carved dark wood.

TOPSHOP OXFORD CIRCUS — Clothes
(Map p66; www.topshop.com; 216 Oxford St W1; ⊖Oxford Circus) Billed as the 'world's largest fashion store', the Topshop branch on Oxford Circus is a constant frenzy of shoppers searching for the latest look at reasonable prices.

GRAYS — Antiques
(Map p82; www.graysantiques.com; 58 Davies St W1; ⊖Bond St) Top-hatted doormen welcome you to this wonderful building full of specialist stallholders.

HMV — Music
(Map p66; www.hmv.com; 150 Oxford St W1; ⊖Oxford Circus) Giant store selling music, DVDs and magazines.

Knightsbridge

Knightsbridge draws the hordes with quintessentially English department stores.

Harrods — Department Store
(Map p82; www.harrods.com; 87 Brompton Rd SW1; ⊖Knightsbridge) A pricy but fascinating theme park for fans of Britannia.

Harvey Nichols Department Store
(Map p82; www.harveynichols.com; 109-125
Knightsbridge SW1; ⊖Knightsbridge) London's
temple of high fashion, jewellery and perfume.

ℹ Information

Dangers & Annoyances

Considering its size and disparities in wealth,
London is generally safe. That said, keep your
wits about you and don't flash your cash
unnecessarily. When travelling by tube, choose
a carriage with other people in it and avoid
deserted suburban stations. Following reports of
robberies and sexual attacks, shun unlicenced or
unbooked minicabs.

Watch out for pickpockets on crowded tubes,
night buses and streets. When using ATMs, guard
your PIN details carefully. Don't use one that looks
like it's been tampered with as there have been
incidents of card cloning.

Tourist Information

For a list of all tourist offices in London and around
Britain, see www.visitmap.info/tic.

Britain & London Visitor Centre (Map p66;
www.visitbritain.com; 1 Regent St SW1;
⊗9am-6.30pm Mon-Fri, 10am-4pm Sat & Sun;
⊖Piccadilly Circus) Accommodation, theatre
and transport tickets; *bureau de change*;
international phones; and internet. Longer
hours in summer.

City of London Information Centre (Map
p74; ☏020-7332 1456; www.visitthecity.co.uk;
⊗9.30am-5.30pm Mon-Sat, 10am-4pm Sun;
St Paul's Churchyard EC4; ⊖St Paul's) Tourist
information, fast-track tickets to City attractions
and guided walks (adult/child £6/4).

Websites

Londonist (www.londonist.com)

Time Out (www.timeout.com/london)

ℹ Getting There & Away

London is the major gateway to England, so
further transport information can be found in the
main Transport chapter.
AIR For information on flying to/from London,
see p403.
BUS Most long-distance coaches leave London
from **Victoria Coach Station** (Map p82; ☏020-
7824 0000; 164 Buckingham Palace Rd SW1;
⊖Victoria).
TRAIN London's main-line terminals are all linked
by the tube and each serve different destinations.

Selfridges department store

DOUG MCKINLAY / LONELY PLANET IMAGES ©

If you can't find your destination below, see the journey planner at www.nationalrail.co.uk.

Charing Cross (Map p66) Canterbury

Euston (Map p85) Manchester, Liverpool, Carlisle, Glasgow

King's Cross (Map p85) Cambridge, York, Scotland

Liverpool St (Map p74) Stansted airport, Cambridge

London Bridge (Map p74) Gatwick airport, Brighton

Marylebone (Map p85) Birmingham

Paddington (Map p82) Heathrow airport, Oxford, Bath, Plymouth, Cardiff

St Pancras (Map p85) Gatwick and Luton airports, Brighton, Sheffield, Leicester, Leeds, Paris

Victoria (Map p82) Gatwick airport, Brighton, Canterbury

Waterloo (Map p66) Windsor, Winchester, Plymouth

ⓘ Getting Around

To/From the Airports

GATWICK There are **National Rail** (www.nationalrail.co.uk) services from Gatwick's South Terminal to Victoria (from £12, 37 minutes), running every 15 minutes during the day and hourly through the night. Other trains head to St Pancras (from £12, 66 minutes). Fares are cheaper the earlier you book. If you're racing to make a flight, the **Gatwick Express** (☎0845 850 1530; www.gatwickexpress.com) departs Victoria every 15 minutes from 5am to 11.45pm (one-way/return £16/26, 30 minutes, first/last train 3.30am/12.32am).

Prices start from £2, depending on when you book, for the **EasyBus** (www.easybus.co.uk) minibus service between Gatwick and Earls Court (£10, allow 1¼ hours, every 30 minutes from 4.25am to 1am). You'll be charged extra if you have more than one carry-on and one check-in bag.

Gatwick's taxi partner, **Checker Cars** (www.checkercars.com), has a counter in each terminal. Fares are quoted in advance (about £95 for the 65-minute ride to Central London).

Left: The Houses of Parliament (p64) and a passing bus;
Below: Canary Wharf Underground station

HEATHROW The transport connections to Heathrow are excellent, and the journey to and from the city is painless. The cheapest option is the Underground. The Piccadilly line is accessible from every terminal (£4.50, one hour to central London, departing from Heathrow every five minutes from around 5am to 11.30pm). If it's your first time in London, it's a good chance to practice using the tube as it's at the beginning of the line and therefore not too crowded when you get on. If there are vast queues at the ticket office, use the automatic machines instead; some accept credit cards as well as cash.

You might save some time on the considerably more expensive **Heathrow Express** (☎ 0845 600 1515; www.heathrowexpress.co.uk), an ultramodern train to Paddington station (one-way/return £16.50/32, 15 minutes, every 15 minutes 5.12am to 11.42pm). You can purchase tickets on board (£5 extra), from self-service machines (cash and credit cards accepted) at both stations, or online.

There are taxi ranks for black cabs outside every terminal; a fare to the centre of London will cost between £50 and £70.

LONDON CITY The Docklands Light Railway connects London City Airport to the tube network, taking 22 minutes to reach Bank station (£4). A black taxi costs about £25 to central London.

LUTON There are regular **National Rail (www. nationalrail.co.uk)** services from St Pancras (£9.50, 29 to 39 minutes) to Luton Airport Parkway station, where a shuttle bus (£1) will get you to the airport within 10 minutes. EasyBus (p102) minibuses head from Victoria and Baker St to Luton (from £2, walk-on £10, allow 1½ hours, every 30 minutes). A taxi costs around £65.

STANSTED The **Stansted Express** (☎ 0845 850 0150; www.stanstedexpress.com) connects with Liverpool St station (one way/return £18/27, 46 minutes, every 15 minutes 6am to 12.30am).

EasyBus (p102) also has services between Stansted and Baker St (from £2, £10 walk-on, 1¼ hours, every 20 minutes). The **Airbus A6** (☎ 0870 580 8080; www.nationalexpress.com) links with Victoria Coach Station (£11, allow 1¾ hours, at least every 30 minutes).

A black cab to/from central London costs about £100.

London's Oyster Diet

To get the most out of London, you need to be able to jump on and off public transport like a local, not scramble to buy a ticket at hefty rates each time. You can do this with an **Oyster card**, a reusable smartcard on which you can load credit to be deducted as you go. The card itself is £3, which is fully refundable when you leave. Fares are deducted at a much lower rate than if you were buying a one-off paper ticket, and in any single day your fares will be capped at the equivalent of the day-pass rate (Zones 1–2 peak/off-peak £8/6.60) for the zones you've travelled in. All you need to do is touch your card to the yellow sensors on the station turnstiles or at the front of the bus. You can also purchase a weekly pass (£27.60) for unlimited travel within that period.

The alternative to Oyster is a **Travelcard**, which comes in daily and weekly varieties and is good for unlimited travel in the purchased period. They cost the same as the Oyster equivalent, but the Travelcard is not reusable (and there's no £3 charge to buy the card itself).

Bike

The central city is flat and relatively compact and the traffic moves slowly – all of which make it surprisingly good for cyclists. Recently TFL (www.tfl.gov.uk) launched the **Barclays Cycle Hire** scheme, with 6000 cycles available to hire from self-service docking stations within Zone 1 (£1/6/15/35/50 for up to one/two/three/six/24 hours, plus £1 access fee).

Car

London was recently rated western Europe's second-most congested city (congratulations Brussels). Don't even think about driving within it: traffic is heavy, roadwork continuous, parking is either impossible or expensive, and wheel-clampers keep busy. If you drive into central London from 7am to 6pm on a weekday, you'll need to pay an £8 per day congestion charge (visit www.tfl.gov.uk for payment options) or face a hefty fine. If you're hiring a car to continue your trip, take the tube to Heathrow and pick it up from there.

Public Transport

Although locals love to complain about it, London's public transport is excellent, with tubes, trains, buses and boats conspiring to get you anywhere you need to go. London is divided into concentric transport zones, although almost all of the places covered in this book are in Zones 1

and 2. TFL (www.tfl.gov.uk) is the glue that binds the network together. Its website has a handy journey planner and information on all services, including cabs.

LONDON UNDERGROUND 'The tube', as it's universally known, extends its subterranean tentacles throughout London and into the surrounding counties, with services running every few minutes from roughly 5.30am to 12.30am (from 7am to 11.30pm Sunday).

It's easy to use. Tickets, Travelcards and Oyster card top-ups can be purchased from counters and machines at the entrance to each station using either cash or credit card. They're then inserted into the slot on the turnstiles (or you touch your Oyster card on the yellow reader), and the barrier opens. Once you're through you can jump on and off different lines as often as you need to get to your destination.

Also included in the tube network are the driverless Docklands Light Railway (DLR), and some suburban train lines (branded as 'Overground' and included on tube maps).

The tube map itself is an acclaimed graphic design work, using coloured lines to show how the 14 different routes intersect. However, it's not remotely to scale. The distances between stations become greater the further from central London you travel, while Leicester Sq and Covent Garden stations are only 250m apart.

BUS Travelling round London by double-decker bus is an enjoyable way to get a feel for the city, but it's usually slower than the tube. Heritage 'Routemaster' buses with conductors operate on route 9 (from Aldwych to Royal Albert Hall) and 15 (between Trafalgar Sq and Tower Hill); these are the only buses without wheelchair access.

Buses run regularly during the day, while less frequent night buses (prefixed with the letter 'N') wheel into action when the tube stops. Single-journey bus tickets (valid for two hours) cost £2 (£1.20 on Oyster, capped at £3.90 per day); a weekly pass is £17. Children ride for free. At stops with yellow signs, you have to buy your ticket from the automatic machine (or use an Oyster) *before* boarding. Buses stop on request, so clearly signal the driver with an outstretched arm.

TRAIN As well as the specific 'Overground' lines that form part of the Underground network, London has a vast network of other suburban train services (particularly south of the river, where tube lines are in short supply) that are an important part of the public transport picture. As well as conventional one-off tickets, Travelcards and Oyster cards are valid on suburban trains within London.

BOAT The myriad boats that ply the Thames are a great way to travel, avoiding traffic jams while affording great views. Passengers with daily, weekly or monthly Travelcards (including on Oyster) get a third off all fares.

Thames Clippers (www.thamesclippers. com) runs regular commuter services between Embankment, Waterloo, Blackfriars, Bankside, London Bridge, Tower, Canary Wharf, Greenwich, North Greenwich and Woolwich piers (adult/child £5.30/2.65) from 7am to midnight (from 9.30am weekends).

Taxi

London's famous black cabs are available for hire when the yellow light above the windscreen is lit. To get an all-London licence, cabbies must do 'The Knowledge', which tests them on up to 25,000 streets within a 6-mile radius of Charing Cross and all points of interest from hotels to churches. Fares are metered, with flag fall of £2.20 and the additional rate dependent on time of day, distance travelled and taxi speed. A one-mile trip will cost between £4.60 and £8.60.

Licenced minicabs operate via agencies (most busy areas have a walk-in office with drivers waiting). They're a cheaper alternative to black cabs and quote trip fares in advance. The cars are recognisable by the ⊖ symbol displayed in the window. To find a local minicab firm, visit www.tfl.gov.uk.

Leeds Castle (p115)

HOLGER LEUE / LONELY PLANET IMAGES ©

DAY TRIPS FROM LONDON

Windsor & Eton

POP 30,568

Dominated by the massive bulk and heavy influence of Windsor Castle, these twin towns have a rather surreal atmosphere, with the morning pomp and ceremony of the changing of the guards in Windsor and the sight of school boys dressed in formal tailcoats wandering the streets of Eton.

 Sights

WINDSOR CASTLE
Castle

(www.royalcollection.org.uk; adult/child £16/9.50; ⏱9.45am-5.15pm) The largest and oldest occupied fortress in the world, Windsor Castle is a majestic vision of battlements and towers used for state occasions and as the Queen's weekend retreat.

William the Conqueror first established a royal residence in Windsor in 1070 when he built a motte and bailey here, the only naturally defendable spot in the Thames valley. Since then successive monarchs have rebuilt, remodelled and refurbished the castle complex to create the massive and sumptuous palace that stands here today.

The castle largely escaped the bombings of WWII, but in 1992 a devastating fire tore through the building, destroying or damaging more than 100 rooms. By chance, the most important treasures were in storage at the time, and with skilled craftsmanship and painstaking restoration, the rooms were returned to their former glory.

Join a free guided tour (every half hour) or take a multilingual audio tour of the lavish state rooms and beautiful chapels. The State Apartments and St George's Chapel are closed at times during the year; check the website for details.

Windsor Castle is one of England's most popular attractions. Come early and be prepared to queue.

QUEEN MARY'S DOLLS' HOUSE
Your first sight will be an incredible dolls' house, designed by Sir Edwin Lutyens for Queen Mary in 1924. The attention to detail is spellbinding – there's running

Changing of the guard ceremony at Windsor Castle

Windsor & Eton

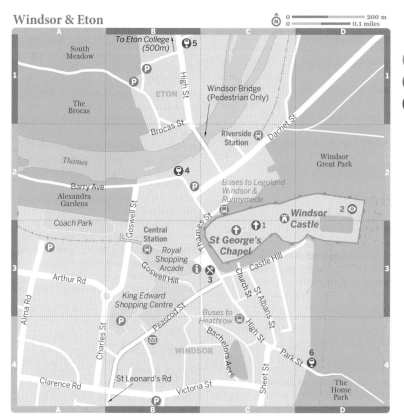

water, electricity and lighting and vintage wine in the cellar!

STATE APARTMENTS
After the dolls' house, a **gallery** with drawings by Leonardo da Vinci and a **China Museum**, you'll enter the stunning State Apartments, which are home to some exquisite paintings and architecture and are still used by the Queen.

The **Grand Staircase** sets the tone for the rooms, all of which are elaborate, opulent and suitably regal. Highlights include **St George's Hall,** which incurred the most damage during the fire of 1992. The dining chairs here, dwarfed by the scale of the room, are standard size. On the ceiling, the shields of the Knights of the Garter (originally from George IV's time here) were recreated after the fire.

Windsor & Eton

The **King's Dressing Room** has some of the most important Renaissance paintings in the royal collection. Charles II kipped in here instead of in the **King's**

107

Bedchamber – maybe George IV's magnificent bed (now on display) would have tempted him.

ST GEORGE'S CHAPEL
This elegant chapel, commissioned for the Order of the Garter by Edward IV in 1475, is one of Britain's finest examples of Perpendicular Gothic architecture.

The chapel – along with Westminster Abbey – serves as a **royal mausoleum**, and its tombs read like a history of the British monarchy.

ALBERT MEMORIAL CHAPEL
Originally built in 1240 and dedicated to Edward the Confessor, this small chapel was the place of worship for the Order of the Garter until St George's Chapel snatched that honour. After the death of Prince Albert at Windsor Castle in 1861, Queen Victoria ordered its elaborate redecoration as a tribute to her husband.

CHANGING OF THE GUARD
A fabulous spectacle of pomp, with loud commands, whispered conversations, triumphant tunes from a military band and plenty of shuffling and stamping of feet, the **changing of the guard (11am Mon-Sat Apr-Jul, alternate days Aug-Mar)** draws the crowds to the castle gates each day.

ETON COLLEGE   Boys' School
Cross the bridge over the Thames to Eton and you'll enter another world, one where old-school values and traditions seem to ooze from the very walls. The streets here are surprisingly hushed as you make your way down to the most enduring and illustrious symbol of England's class system, **Eton College** (www.etoncollege.com; adult/child £6.20/5.20; ☉ guided tours 2pm & 3.15pm daily during school holidays, Wed, Fri, Sat & Sun during term time).

Those who have studied here include 18 prime ministers, countless princes, kings and maharajahs, famous explorers, authors, and economists – among them the Duke of Wellington, Princes William and Harry, George Orwell, Ian Fleming, Aldous Huxley, Sir Ranulph Fiennes and John Maynard Keynes.

Eton is the largest and most famous public (meaning very private) school in England. It was founded by Henry VI in 1440 with a view towards educating 70 highly qualified boys awarded a scholarship from a fund endowed by the king. The boys still wear formal tailcoats, waistcoats and white collars to lessons, the school language is full of in-house jargon, and fencing, shooting, polo and beagling are on the list of school sporting activities.

Luckily for the rest of us, the college is open to visitors taking the guided tour, which gives a fascinating insight into how this most elite of schools functions. Tours take in the **chapel** (which you can see from Windsor Castle), the **cloisters**, the **Museum of Eton Life**, the **lower school** and the **school yard**. As you wander round, you may recognise some of the buildings, as the college is often used as a film set.

 Tours

Tourist Office   Walking tours
(☎ 01753-743900; www.windsor.gov.uk; adult/child £6/3; ☉ 11.30am Sat & Sun) Themed guided walks of the city.

 Eating & Drinking

TOWER   Classic British ££
(☎ 01753-863426; High St, Windsor; mains £9-16) Giant windows with views over the castle give this place an immediate allure, as do the grand chandeliers and high ceilings. The menu is brasserie style with a choice of classic British cuisine, featuring grills, fish and steaks simply and perfectly done. It's also a good spot to sample the finest of English institutions: afternoon tea.

TWO BREWERS   Traditional Pub
(34 Park St, Windsor) This 17th-century inn perched on the edge of Windsor Great Park is close to the castle's tradesmen's entrance and supposedly frequented by staff from the castle. It's a quaint and

cosy place, with dim lighting, obituaries to castle footmen and royal photographs with irreverent captions on the wall.

HENRY VI   Pub

(37 High St, Eton) Another old pub, but this time the low ceilings and subtle lighting are mixed with leather sofas and modern design. There's a nice garden for alfresco dining and live music at weekends.

. . . .

ⓘ Information

Royal Windsor Information Centre (www.windsor.gov.uk; Old Booking Hall, Windsor Royal Shopping Arcade; ⏲9.30am-5pm Mon-Sat, 10am-4pm Sun)

. . . .

ⓘ Getting There & Away

BUS Bus 702 connects Windsor with **London Victoria** coach station (£8.50, one hour, hourly), and bus 77 connects Windsor with **Heathrow** airport (one hour, hourly).

TRAIN Trains from Windsor Central station on Thames St go to **London Paddington** (30 to 45 minutes). Trains from Windsor Riverside station go to **London Waterloo** (one hour). Services run half-hourly from both stations and tickets cost £8.

Canterbury

POP 43,432

Canterbury tops the charts when it comes to English cathedral cities and is one of southern England's top attractions. The World Heritage–listed cathedral that dominates its centre is considered by many to be one of Europe's finest, and the town's narrow medieval alleyways, riverside gardens and ancient city walls are a joy to explore. But Canterbury isn't just a showpiece to times past; it's a spirited place with an energetic student population and a wide choice of contemporary bars, restaurants and arts.

Canterbury Pass

The **Canterbury Attractions Passport** (adult/child £19/15.25) gives entry to the cathedral, St Augustine's Abbey, the Canterbury Tales and any one of the city's museums. It's available from the tourist office.

◉ Sights

CANTERBURY CATHEDRAL   Cathedral

(www.canterbury-cathedral.org; adult/concession £8/7; ⏲9am-5pm Mon-Sat, 12.30pm-2.30pm Sun) The Church of England could not have a more imposing mother church than this extraordinary early Gothic cathedral, the centrepiece of the city's World Heritage Site and repository of more than 1400 years of Christian history.

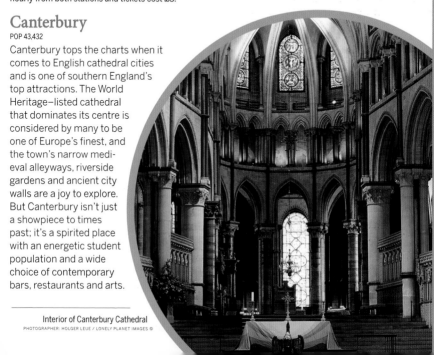

Interior of Canterbury Cathedral
PHOTOGRAPHER: HOLGER LEUE / LONELY PLANET IMAGES ©

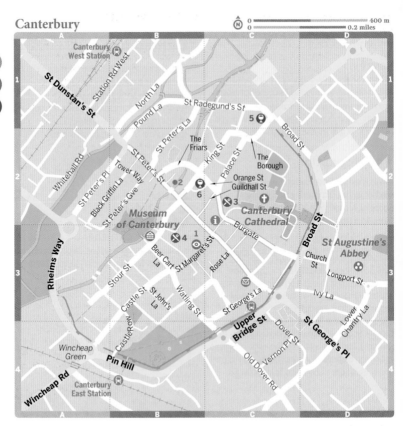

It's an overwhelming edifice filled with enthralling stories, striking architecture and a very real and enduring sense of spirituality, although visitors can't help but pick up on the ominous undertones of violence and bloodshed that whisper from its walls.

This ancient structure is packed with monuments commemorating the nation's battles. Also here is the grave and tunic of one of the nation's most famous warmongers, Edward the Black Prince (1330–76). The spot in the northwest transept where Archbishop Thomas Becket met his grisly end has been drawing pilgrims for centuries and is marked by a candle and modern altar.

The doorway to the crypt is beside the altar. This cavernous space is the cathedral's highlight, an entrancing 11th-century survivor from the cathedral's last devastating fire in 1174, which destroyed the rest of the building. Look for original carvings among the forest of pillars.

The wealth of detail in the cathedral is immense and unrelenting, so it's well worth joining a one-hour **tour** (adult/child £5/3; 10.30am, noon & 2.30pm Mon-Fri, 10.30am, noon & 1.30pm Sat Easter-Oct), or you can take a 40-minute self-guided **audiotour** (adult/concessions £3.50/2.50).

MUSEUM OF CANTERBURY Museum
(www.canterbury-museums.co.uk; Stour St; adult/child £3.60/2.30; 11am-4pm Mon-Sat year-round, also 1.30-4pm Sun Jun-Sep) A fine 14th-century building, once the Poor Priests' Hospital, now houses the city's absorbing museum which has a jumble of exhibits from pre-Roman times to the assassination of Becket, Joseph Conrad to locally born celebs.

ST AUGUSTINE'S ABBEY Abbey Ruins
(EH; adult/child £4.50/2.30; 10am-6pm Jul & Aug, to 5pm Apr-Jun) An integral but often overlooked part of the Canterbury World Heritage Site, St Augustine's Abbey was founded in AD 597, marking the rebirth of Christianity in southern England. Later requisitioned as a royal palace, it was to fall into disrepair and now only stumpy foundations remain.

CANTERBURY TALES Chaucer Attraction
(www.canterburytales.org.uk; St Margaret's St; adult/child £7.75/5.75; 10am-5pm Mar-Oct) A three dimensional interpretation of Chaucer's classic tales through jerky animatronics and audioguides, the ambitious Canterbury Tales is certainly entertaining but could never do full justice to Chaucer's tales. It's a lively and fun introduction for the young or uninitiated, however.

 Tours

Canterbury Historic River Tours River Tours
(07790-534744; www.canterburyrivertours. co.uk; adult/child £7.50/5; 10am-5pm Mar-Oct) Knowledgeable guides double up as energetic oarsmen on these fascinating minicruises that leave from behind The Old Weaver's House on St Peter's St.

Canterbury Walks Walking Tours
(01227-459779; www.canterbury-walks.co.uk; adult/under 12yr/senior & student £6/5.50/4.25; 11am daily Feb-Oct, also 2pm Jul-Sep) Chaperoned walking tours leave from the tourist office.

Keep Your Enemies Close...

Not one to shy away from nepotism, in 1162 King Henry II appointed his good mate Thomas Becket to the highest clerical office in the land, figuring it would be easier to force the increasingly vocal religious lobby to toe the line if he was pally with the archbishop. Unfortunately for Henry, he had underestimated how seriously Thomas would take the job, and the archbishop soon began disagreeing with almost everything the king said or did. By 1170 Henry had become exasperated with his former favourite and, after a few months of sulking, 'suggested' to four of his knights that Thomas was too much to bear. The dirty deed was done on December 29. Becket's martyrdom – and canonisation in double-quick time (1173) – catapulted Canterbury Cathedral to the top of the premier league of northern European pilgrimage sites. Mindful of the growing criticism at his role in Becket's murder, Henry arrived here in 1174 for a dramatic *mea culpa,* and after allowing himself to be whipped and scolded was granted absolution.

Eating & Drinking

DEESON'S   British ££

(☎ 01227-767854; 25-27 Sun St; mains £4.50-16; ◷ lunch & dinner) Kentish fruit and veg, local award-winning wines, beers and ciders, fish from Kent's coastal waters and the odd ingredient from the proprietor's very own allotment, all served in a straightforward, contemporary setting a Kentish apple's throw from the Cathedral gates. What more do you want?

VEG BOX CAFE   Vegetarian Cafe £

(1 Jewry Lane; soups £4.95, specials £6.95; ◷ 9am-5pm Mon-Sat) Perched above Canterbury's top veggie food store, this welcoming, laid-back spot uses only the freshest, locally sourced organic ingredients in its dishes; served at stocky timber tables under red paper lanterns.

PARROT   Pub

(1-9 Church Lane) Built in 1370 on Roman foundations, Canterbury's oldest boozer has a snug, beam-rich pub downstairs and a much-lauded dining room upstairs under yet more aging oak.

THOMAS BECKETT   Pub

(21 Best Lane) A classic English pub with a garden's worth of hops hanging from its timber frame, several quality ales to sample and a traditional decor of copper pots, comfy seating and a fireplace to cosy up to on winter nights. It also serves decent pub grub.

 Information

Tourist office (☎ 01227-378100; www. canterbury.co.uk; 12 Sun St; ◷ 9.30am-5pm Mon-Sat, 9.30am-4.30pm Sun) Situated opposite the Cathedral gate.

 Getting There & Away

Train

Canterbury connections:

London St Pancras High-speed service; £27.80, one hour, hourly

London Victoria/Charing Cross £23.40, one hour 40 minutes, two to three hourly

Brighton & Hove
POP 247,817

Raves on the beach, Graham Greene novels, Mods and Rockers in bank holiday fisticuffs, hens and stags on naughty weekends, classic car runs from London, the UK's biggest gay scene and the Channel's best clubbing – this city by the sea evokes many images among the British, but one thing is for certain: with its Bohemian, cosmopolitan, hedonistic vibe, Brighton is where England's seaside experience goes from cold to cool.

Brighton rocks all year round, but really comes to life during the summer months, when tourists, language students and revellers from London, keen to explore the city's legendary nightlife, summer festivals and multitude of trendy restaurants, slick boutique hotels and shops, pour into the city.

 Sights

ROYAL PAVILION   Royal Residence

(www.royalpavilion.org.uk; adult/child £9.50/5.40; ◷ 9.30am-5.45pm Apr-Sep, 10am-5.15pm Oct-Mar) The city's must-see attraction is the Royal Pavilion, the glittering party-pad and palace of Prince George, later Prince Regent then King George IV. It's one of the most decadent buildings in England and an apt symbol of Brighton's reputation for hedonism. The Indian-style domes and Moorish minarets outside are only a prelude to the palace's lavish oriental-themed interior, where no colour is deemed too strong, dragons swoop and snarl from gilt-smothered ceilings, gem-encrusted snakes slither down pillars, and crystal chandeliers seem ordered by the tonne. While gawping is the main activity, you can pick up an audiotour (included in the admission price) to learn more about the palace.

Brighton & Hove

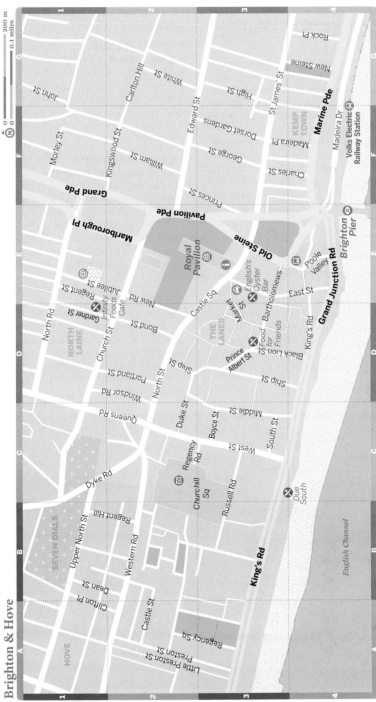

English Channel

0 200 m
0 0.1 miles

HOVE

SEVEN DIALS

NORTH LAINE

THE LANES

Royal Pavilion

KEMP TOWN

Marine Pde

Brighton Pier

Volks Electric Railway Station

Little Preston St
Preston St
Regency Sq
Castle St
Dean St
Clifton Pl
Upper North St
Regent Hill
Western Rd
Dyke Rd
Regent St
John St
Morley St
Kingswood St
William St
Carlton Hill
White St
Edward St
George St
Charles St
High St
St James's St
Madeira Pl
Madeira Dr
Rock Pl
New Steine
Dorset Gardens
Princes St
Grand Pde
Pavilion Pde
Marlborough Pl
Old Steine
Jubilee St
New Rd
Gardner St
Church St
Bond St
North Rd
North St
Portland St
Ship St
Windsor Rd
Queens Rd
Duke St
Boyce St
West St
Middle St
South St
Castle Sq
Market St
Bartholomews
East St
King's Rd
Grand Junction Rd
Poole Valley
Prince Albert St
Black Lion St
Ship St
Russell Rd
Churchill Sq
Regency Rd
King's Rd

Infinity Foods Cafe
English's Oyster Bar
Food for Friends
Due South

BRIGHTON PIER   Pier

(www.brightonpier.co.uk) This grand old centenarian pier, full of glorious gaudiness, is the place to come to experience the tackier side of Brighton. There are plenty of stomach-churning fairground rides and dingy amusement arcades to keep you amused, and candy floss and Brighton rock to chomp on while you're doing so.

Look west and you'll see the sad remains of the **West Pier** (www.westpier.co.uk), a skeletal iron hulk that attracts flocks of birds at sunset. It's a sad end for a Victorian marvel upon which the likes of Charlie Chaplin and Stan Laurel once performed.

Eating

INFINITY FOODS CAFE   Vegetarian   £

(50 Gardner St; mains £3-7; ☉10.30am-5pm Mon-Sat, noon-4pm Sun) The sister establishment of Infinity Foods wholefoods shop, a health-food cooperative and Brighton institution, serves a wide variety of vegetarian and organic food, with many vegan and wheat- or gluten-free options including tofu burgers, mezze plates and falafel.

FOOD FOR FRIENDS   Restaurant   ££

(www.foodforfriends.com; 17-18 Prince Albert St; mains £9-13; ☉lunch & dinner) This airy, glass-sided restaurant attracts the attention of passers-by as much as it does the loyalty of its customers with an ever-inventive choice of vegetarian and vegan food.

ENGLISH'S OYSTER BAR   Seafood   ££

(www.englishs.co.uk; 29-31 East St; mains £11-25; ☉lunch & dinner) A 60-year institution, this Brightonian seafood paradise dishes up everything from oysters to lobster to Dover sole. It's converted from fishermen's cottages, with echoes of the elegant Edwardian era inside and buzzing alfresco dining on the pedestrian square outside.

DUE SOUTH   Local Cuisine   ££

(www.duesouth.co.uk; 139 Kings Rd Arches; mains £12-18; ☉lunch & dinner Mon-Sat, lunch Sun) Sheltered under a cavernous Victorian arch on the seafront, with a curvaceous front window and small bamboo-screened terrace on the promenade,

Brighton Pier

Detour:
Leeds Castle

This immense moated pile is for many the world's most romantic **castle** (www. leeds-castle.com; adult/child £17.50/10; ⊙10am-6pm Apr-Sep), and it's certainly one of the most visited in Britain. While it looks formidable enough from the outside – a hefty structure balancing on two islands amid a large lake and sprawling estate – it's actually known as something of a 'ladies castle'. This stems from the fact that in its more than 1000 years of history, it has been home to a who's who of medieval queens, most famously Henry VIII's first wife, Catherine of Aragon.

The castle was transformed from fortress to lavish palace over the centuries, and its last owner, the high-society hostess Lady Baillie, used it as a princely family home and party pad to entertain the likes of Errol Flynn, Douglas Fairbanks and JFK.

The castle's vast estate offers enough attractions of its own to justify a day-trip: peaceful walks, a duckery, aviary and falconry demonstrations. You'll also find possibly the world's sole **dog collar museum**, plenty of kids' attractions and a **hedge maze**, overseen by a grassy bank where fellow travellers can shout encouragement or misdirections.

Leeds Castle is just east of Maidstone. Trains run from London Victoria to Bearsted (£17.10, one hour) where you catch a special shuttle coach to the castle (£5 return).

this refined yet relaxed and convivial restaurant specialises in dishes cooked with the best environmentally sustainable and seasonal Sussex produce.

 Shopping

A busy maze of narrow lanes and tiny alleyways that was once a fishing village, the **Lanes** is Brighton's most popular shopping district. Its every twist and turn is jam-packed with jewellers and gift shops, coffee shops and boutiques selling everything from antique firearms to hard-to-find vinyls. There's another, less-claustrophobic shopping district in **North Laine**, a series of streets north of the Lanes, including Bond, Gardner, Kensington and Sydney Sts, that are full of retro-cool boutiques and Bohemian cafes.

ⓘ Information

Brighton City Guide (www.brighton.co.uk)

Tourist office (✆0300-300 0088; www. visitbrighton.com; Royal Pavilion Shop, Royal Pavilion; ⊙10am-5.30pm)

ⓘ Getting There & Away

BUS **London Victoria** National Express, £11.80, two hours, hourly

Train

TRAIN All London-bound services pass through Gatwick Airport.

London St Pancras £16.90, 1¼ hours, half hourly

London Victoria £13.90, 50-70 minutes, half hourly

Cambridge

POP 108,863

Drowning in exquisite architecture, steeped in history and tradition and renowned for its quirky rituals, Cambridge is a university town extraordinaire. The tightly packed core of ancient colleges, the picturesque 'Backs' (college gardens) leading on to the river, and the leafy green meadows that seem to surround the city give it a far more tranquil appeal than its historic rival Oxford.

◉ Sights

Cambridge University

Cambridge University comprises 31 colleges, though not all are open to the public. Most colleges close to visitors for the Easter term and all are closed for exams from mid-May to mid-June. Opening hours vary from day to day, so contact the colleges or the tourist office for information as hours given below are only a rough guide.

TRINITY COLLEGE   College
(www.trin.cam.ac.uk; Trinity St; adult/child £1/50p; ⊙9am-4pm) The largest of Cambridge's colleges, Trinity, is entered through an impressive Tudor gateway first created in 1546. As you walk through, have a look at the statue of the college's founder, Henry VIII, that adorns it. His left hand holds a golden orb, while his right grips not the original sceptre but a table leg, put there by student pranksters and never replaced.

As you enter the **Great Court**, scholastic humour gives way to wonderment, for it is the largest of its kind in the world. To the right of the entrance is a small tree, planted in the 1950s and reputed to be a descendant of the apple tree made famous by Trinity alumnus Sir Isaac

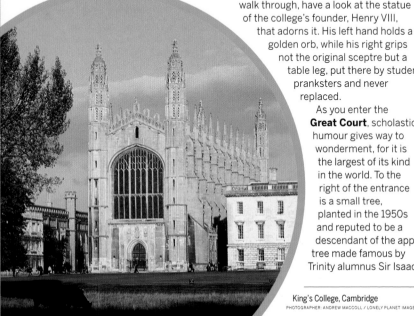

King's College, Cambridge
PHOTOGRAPHER: ANDREW MACCOLL / LONELY PLANET IMAGES ©

Cambridge

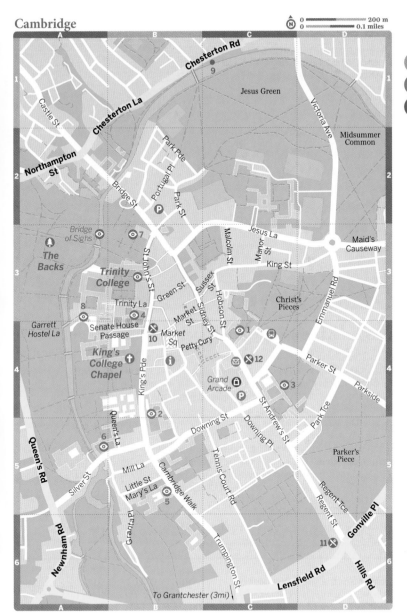

Newton. Other alumni include Tennyson, Francis Bacon, Lord Byron, HRH Prince Charles and at least nine prime ministers, British and international, and a jaw-dropping 32 Nobel Prize winners.

CORPUS CHRISTI COLLEGE College (www.corpus.cam.ac.uk; King's Pde; admission £2) Entry to this illustrious college is via the so-called New Court, which dates back a mere 200 years. To your right is the door to the Parker Library,

JON DAVISON / LONELY PLANET IMAGES ©

Don't Miss **King's College Chapel**

In a city crammed with show-stopping architecture, this is the show-stealer. It's one of the most extraordinary examples of Gothic architecture in England, and was begun in 1446 as an act of piety by Henry VI and finished by Henry VIII around 1516.

While you can enjoy stunning front and back views of the chapel from King's Pde and the river, the real drama is within. Mouths drop open upon first glimpse of the inspirational **fan-vaulted ceiling**, its intricate tracery soaring upwards before exploding into a series of stone fireworks.

The chapel is also remarkably light, its sides flanked by lofty **stained-glass windows** that retain their original glass – rare survivors of the excesses of the Civil War in this region. It's said that these windows were ordered to be spared by Cromwell himself, who knew of their beauty from his own studies in Cambridge.

THINGS YOU NEED TO KNOW

www.kings.cam.ac.uk/chapel; King's Pde; adult/child under 12 £5/free; ⊙9.30am-4.30pm Mon-Sat, 10am-5pm Sun

which holds the finest collection of Anglo-Saxon manuscripts in the world. Meanwhile, a monastic atmosphere still oozes from the inner Old Court, which retains its medieval form. Look out for the fascinating sundial and plaque to playwright and past student Christopher Marlowe (1564–93), author of *Dr Faustus* and *Tamburlaine*.

TRINITY HALL COLLEGE   College
(www.trinhall.cam.ac.uk; Trinity Lane; admission by donation) Henry James once wrote of the delightfully diminutive Trinity Hall, 'If I were called upon to mention the prettiest corner of the world, I should draw a thoughtful sigh and point the way to the gardens of Trinity Hall.'

Wedged cosily among the great and the famous, but unconnected to better-known Trinity College, Trinity Hall was founded in 1350 as a refuge for lawyers and clerics escaping the ravages of the Black Death, thus earning it the nickname, the 'Lawyers' College'.

GONVILLE & CAIUS COLLEGE   College
(www.cai.cam.ac.uk; Trinity St; admission free) Known locally as Caius (pronounced 'keys'), Gonville and Caius was founded twice, first by a priest called Gonville, in 1348, and then again in 1557 by Dr Caius (his given name was Keys – it was common for academics to use the Latin form of their names), a brilliant physician who supposedly spoilt his legacy by insisting the college admit no 'deaf, dumb, deformed, lame, chronic invalids, or Welshmen'! Fortunately for the college, his policy didn't last long, and the wheelchair-using megastar of astrophysics, Stephen Hawking, is now a fellow here.

CHRIST'S COLLEGE   College
(www.christs.cam.ac.uk; St Andrew's St; admission free 9.30am-noon, Darwin room £2.50; ⊙9.30am-noon, Darwin room 10am-noon & 2-4pm) Over 500 years old and a grand old institution, Christ's is worth visiting if only for its gleaming Great Gate emblazoned with heraldic carving of spotted Beaufort yale (antelope-like creatures), Tudor roses and portcullis. A stout oak door leads into First Court, which has an unusual circular lawn, magnolias and wisteria creepers. Pressing on through the Second Court there is a gate to the Fellows' Garden, which contains a mulberry tree under which 17th-century poet John Milton reputedly wrote *Lycidas*. Charles Darwin also studied here, and his room (admission £2; ⊙10am-noon & 2-4pm) has been restored as it would have been when he lived in it.

Other Sights

THE BACKS   Parklands
Behind the grandiose facades, stately courts and manicured lawns of the city's central colleges lies a series of gardens and parklands butting up against the river. Collectively known as the Backs, these tranquil green spaces and shimmering waters offer unparalleled views of the colleges and are often the most enduring image of Cambridge

St John's College, Cambridge (p120)

If You Like...
Cambridge Colleges

If you love the architecture and academic ambience of big-hitters such as Trinity and Caius, you may like to explore some of Cambridge's other colleges:

1 PETERHOUSE
(www.pet.cam.ac.uk; Trumpington St; admission free) The oldest and smallest college in Cambridge, Peterhouse is a charming place founded in 1284. Just to the north is **Little St Mary's Church**, which has a memorial to Peterhouse student Godfrey Washington, great-uncle of George. His family coat of arms was the stars and stripes, the inspiration for the US flag.

2 QUEENS' COLLEGE
(www.queens.cam.ac.uk; Silver St; adult/child £2.50/free; ⏱10am-4.30pm) The gorgeous 15th-century Queens' College sits elegantly astride the river and has two enchanting medieval courtyards: Old Court and Cloister Court.

3 ST JOHN'S COLLEGE
(www.joh.cam.ac.uk; St John's St; adult/child £3.20/free; ⏱10am-5.30pm) After King's College, St John's is one of the city's most photogenic colleges, and is also the second-biggest after Trinity. Founded in 1511, it sprawls along both banks of the river, joined by the Bridge of Sighs, a masterpiece of stone tracery.

4 EMMANUEL COLLEGE
(www.emma.cam.ac.uk; St Andrew's St) The 16th-century Emmanuel College is famous for its exquisite chapel, which was designed by Sir Christopher Wren. Here, too, is a plaque commemorating John Harvard (BA 1632), a scholar here who later settled in New England in the US, and left his money to found his namesake university in the Massachusetts town of Cambridge.

for visitors. The picture-postcard snapshots of college life, graceful bridges and weeping willows can be seen from the pathways that cross the Backs, from the comfort of a chauffeur-driven punt or from the lovely pedestrian bridges that criss-cross the river.

The fanciful **Bridge of Sighs** (built in 1831) at St John's is best observed from the stylish bridge designed by Wren just to the south. The oldest crossing is at **Clare College**, built in 1639 and ornamented with decorative balls. Its architect was paid a grand total of 15p for his design and, feeling aggrieved at such a measly fee, it's said he cut a chunk out of one of the balls adorning the balustrade so the bridge would never be complete. Most curious of all is the flimsy-looking wooden construction joining the two halves of Queen's College known as the **Mathematical Bridge**, first built in 1749. Despite what unscrupulous guides may tell you, it wasn't the handiwork of Sir Isaac Newton (he died in 1727), originally built without nails, or taken apart by students who then couldn't figure how to put it back together.

Tours

City Sightseeing　　　　Bus Tour
(www.city-sightseeing.com; adult/child £13/7; ⏱every 20min 10am-4.40pm) Hop-on/hop-off bus tours.

Riverboat Georgina　　　Boating
(☎01223-307694; www.georgina.co.uk) One-/two-hour cruises (£6/12) with the option of including lunch or a cream tea.

Tourist Office　　　Walking tour
(☎01223-457574; www.visitcambridge.org) Conducts two-hour city tours (adult/child £12.50/6, 11am and 1pm Monday to Saturday, 1pm Sunday) and 1½-hour city tours (adult/child £11/6, noon Monday to Friday, noon and 2pm Saturday). Book in advance.

The Cambridge vs Oxford boat race (p42)

SIMON GREENWOOD / LONELY PLANET IMAGES ©

 Eating

MICHAELHOUSE Modern British £
(www.michaelhousecafe.co.uk; Trinity St; mains
£7-9; ⊙8am-5pm Mon-Sat) Sip fair-trade
coffee and nibble focaccias among soaring medieval arches or else take a pew
within reach of the altar at this stylishly
converted church, which still has a working chancel.

ORIGIN8 Deli Cafe £
(www.origin8delicafes.com; 62 St Andrew's
St; mains £4-6.50; ⊙8am-6pm Mon-Sat, 11am-
5.30pm Sun) Bright and airy, this cafe, deli
and butchers shop prides itself on its
local organic ingredients. It's a great place
to stop for hearty soups, hog roast baps,
home-cooked sausage rolls, fresh salads
and luscious cakes.

OAK BISTRO Modern British ££
(☎01223-323361; www.theoakbistro.co.uk; 6
Lensfield Rd; mains £11-17, set 2-/3-course lunch
£12/15; ⊙closed Sun) This little place on

a busy corner is a great local favourite
and serves up simple, classic dishes with
modern flair. The atmosphere is relaxed
and welcoming, the decor minimalist and
the food perfectly cooked. There's even a
hidden walled garden for alfresco dining.
It's a popular spot so book ahead.

ⓘ Information

Tourist office (☎0871 266 8006; www.
visitcambridge.org; Old Library, Wheeler St;
⊙10am-5.30pm Mon-Fri, to 5pm Sat, 11am-3pm
Sun) Pick up a guide to the Cambridge colleges
(£4.99) in the gift shop or a leaflet (£1) outlining
two city walks. You can also download audio
tours from the website.

ⓘ Getting There & Away

TRAIN Trains run at least every 30 minutes to/
from **London's King's Cross** and **Liverpool St**
stations (£19, 45 minutes to 1¼ hours).

Oxford & Central England

Oxford sits proudly at the very heart of England. And just beyond this historic city's doorstep rise the tranquil, rolling hills of the Cotswolds. Dripping with charm and riddled with implausibly pretty villages, this part of the country is as close to the olde-worlde English idyll as you'll get, a haven of rose-clad cottages, graceful stone churches, cream teas and antique shops.

On the northern rim of this bucolic region are the major landmarks of Warwick Castle and Stratford-upon-Avon. And further north again the gentle landscape gives way to countryside with a slightly harder edge, with the rugged moors of the Peak District and Ironbridge Gorge, birthplace of the Industrial Revolution.

Central England also boasts two of the nation's finest stately homes – Blenheim Place and Chatsworth House. Add to these attractions simple access from London, and it's easy to see why the region is a magnet for visitors.

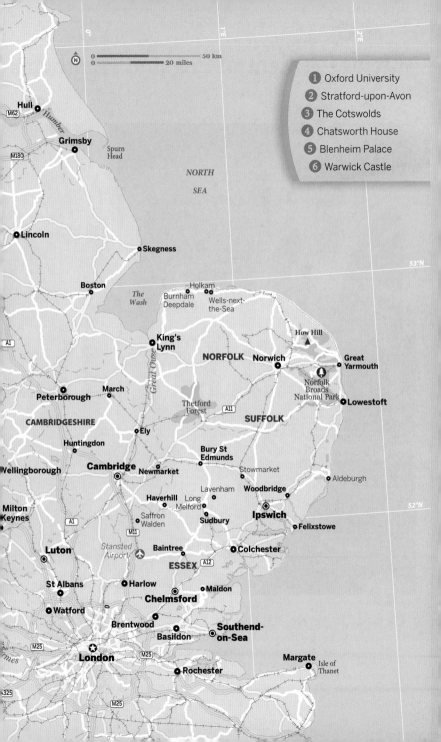

N

0   50 km
0   20 miles

Hull
M62
Humber
Grimsby
Spurn
Head

M180

NORTH

SEA

Lincoln

Skegness

53°N

Boston

The
Wash
Holkam
Burnham
Deepdale
Wells-next-
the-Sea

How Hill
A1
King's
Lynn
NORFOLK
Norwich
Great
Yarmouth

Peterborough
March
Great Ouse
Norfolk
Broads
National Park
Lowestoft

CAMBRIDGESHIRE
Thetford
Forest
A11
SUFFOLK

Ely

Huntingdon

Wellingborough
Cambridge
Newmarket
Bury St
Edmunds
Stowmarket
Aldeburgh

Lavenham
Woodbridge
Haverhill
Long
Melford
Milton
Keynes
A1
Saffron
Walden
Sudbury
Ipswich

M11
Felixstowe

Luton
Stansted
Airport
Baintree
Colchester

ESSEX
A12

St Albans
Harlow
Maldon

Chelmsford

Watford
Brentwood
Southend-
on-Sea
Basildon

Thames
M25
London
M25
Margate
Isle of
Thanet

A325
Rochester

M25

Oxford University's Colleges

Don't expect a neat campus here. Oxford University consists of 39 separate colleges scattered around the city, rubbing shoulders with other historic buildings and sometimes more prosaic modern streets. Each college is a historic and architectural gem in its own right.
Christ Church Cathedral (p139)

Need to Know

TOP TIP Check college opening hours; some colleges close for exams **BEST TIME TO VISIT** May or September **BEST PHOTO OP** Radcliffe Camera **For further coverage, see p134**

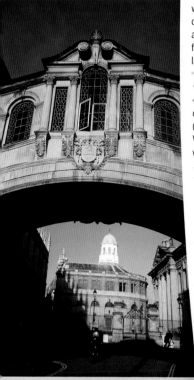

Oxford University Don't Miss List

PETER BERRY, WALKING-TOUR GUIDE,
BLACKWELL BOOKSHOP

1 CHRIST CHURCH

I've been showing visitors around for over 15 years, and many people say how much they enjoy the vibrant atmosphere. **Christ Church** (along with **Magdalen College**) is the most popular sight (pictured top left), partly thanks to its links with Lewis Carroll. These spots can be crowded, but going with a guide helps you jump the queues and make the most of your time here.

2 EXETER COLLEGE

To escape the crowds (a little), I recommend seeing slightly less-well-known places such as **Exeter College**, which has the most beautiful chapel of all the Oxford colleges, containing an exquisite tapestry by Pre-Raphaelite artists William Morris and Edward Burne-Jones. Another favourite is **New College**, also with a beautiful chapel and a large section of the ancient City Walls.

3 BRIDGE OF SIGHS

Hertford College has academic buildings on each side of New College Lane joined by the ornate **Bridge of Sighs** (pictured bottom left), named after the famous bridge in Venice (although as that bridge led to a prison it had small windows – ours are much larger). Alumni here include authors Jonathan Swift and Evelyn Waugh.

4 BODLEIAN LIBRARY

The 17th-century **Bodleian Library** is one of the oldest libraries in the world. Priceless items stored here include the original manuscripts of Tolkien's *The Hobbit*. On the other side of Broad St is the 20th-century part of the library; not many people know an underground conveyor belt carries books between the two.

5 UNIVERSITY CHURCH OF ST MARY THE VIRGIN

Originally just for the university, the services are now open to 'town and gown' (locals and students). Climb the tower's 127 steps – there's no lift in this medieval building – for spectacular views of the 'dreaming spires' of Oxford and out to the **Cotswold Hills** beyond.

Shakespeare at Stratford-upon-Avon

What could be more English than taking in a Shakespeare play in the birthplace of the nation's best-known playwright? After visiting William's birthplace and his grave – and all the houses he's connected with in between – make sure you leave time to see the Royal Shakespeare Company in action. Swan Theatre, Stratford-upon-Avon (p148)

Idle Exploration in the Cotswolds

The wonderful thing about the Cotswolds (p141) is that no matter where you go, you'll still end up in an impossibly pretty village of rose-clad cottages and honey-coloured stone. There'll be a quaint village green, a pub with sloping floors, and a view of the lush hills. It's surprisingly easy to leave the crowds behind and find your own slice of olde-worlde England. Cottage, the Cotswolds

Chatsworth House

In the heart of the Peak District National Park, the great stately home of Chatsworth House (p158) is known as the 'Palace of the Peak'. Inside, the lavish apartments and mural-painted staterooms are packed with paintings and priceless items of period furniture. The house sits in vast ornamental gardens and is surrounded by 25 sq miles of grounds, some landscaped by Lancelot 'Capability' Brown.

Blenheim Palace

The land and funds to build Blenheim Palace (p144) were granted to John Churchill, Duke of Marlborough, by a grateful Queen Anne after his decisive victory over the French in 1704. The Duke spared no expense on its design – it's universally acknowledged as a masterpiece of the baroque style. He didn't hold back on the furnishing either: statues, tapestries, ostentatious furniture and giant oil paintings are all still in place for us to admire today. Gardens at Blenheim Palace

Warwick Castle

Founded in 1068 by William the Conqueror, immensely popular Warwick Castle (p149) is ruined enough to be romantic, but still well preserved enough to be impressive. With sumptuous interiors, landscaped gardens, waxwork-populated private apartments, towering ramparts, armoury displays, medieval jousting and a theme-park dungeon there's plenty to keep the family busy for a whole day. Sword-fight display, Warwick Castle

Oxford & Central England's Best...

Historic Churches

○ **Christ Church Cathedral, Oxford** (p139) England's smallest cathedral in one of Oxford University's grandest colleges

○ **Holy Trinity Church, Stratford-upon-Avon** (p146) William Shakespeare's final resting place with famous epitaph

○ **St James, Chipping Campden** (p142) Classic 'wool church' in the heart of the Cotswolds

○ **Coventry Cathedral** (p154) Modernist masterpiece, attached to medieval remains and a WWII memorial

Castles & Stately Homes

○ **Warwick Castle** (p149) The region's finest medieval fortress, with attractions for all the family

○ **Peveril Castle** (p157) Ancient evocative ruin overlooking (and giving name to) Castleton

○ **Chatsworth House** (p158) One of England's grandest homes in the heart of the Derbyshire Peak District

○ **Blenheim Palace** (p144) Ultimate example of baroque architecture, with impressive gardens and grounds to match

Nature Spots

○ **Peak District** (p154) England's oldest national park, with wild moors and tranquil valleys, as well as gorges and lakes – but no peaks

○ **The Cotswolds** (p141) Bucolic region of rolling hills and picturesque villages – quintessential England

○ **Sherwood Forest** (p157) Famous as the home of Robin Hood and his Merry Men, this national nature reserve is now a popular day-trip spot

Need to Know

Country Towns

○ **Stratford-upon-Avon** (p145) A delightful Midlands market town and birthplace of the Bard

○ **Bakewell** (p159) Deep in the Peak District, famous for its eponymous pudding

○ **Buxton** (p154) Former spa town, still with trappings of Regency elegance

○ **Stow-on-the-Wold** (p143) A Cotswolds classic, famous for its large market square, surrounded by antique shops

○ **Chipping Campden** (p141) Of all the pretty Cotswolds towns, this is the gem

ADVANCE PLANNING

○ **Two months before** Book hotels in popular spots; reserve seats at Royal Shakespeare Theatre in Stratford-upon-Avon

○ **One month before** Arrange car hire and tickets for longer train journeys

○ **Two weeks before** Check opening times and ticket availability for key sights, especially Oxford colleges, Chatsworth House, Blenheim Palace, Warwick Castle and the main Shakespeare sights around Stratford-upon-Avon

RESOURCES

Major tourist information websites for the key cities and areas in this region:

○ **Oxford** (www.visitoxford.org)

○ **The Cotswolds** (www.visitcotswolds.co.uk)

○ **Heart of England** (www.visitheartofengland.com)

○ **East Midlands** (www.enjoyenglandseastmidlands.com)

○ **Peak District** (www.visitpeakdistrict.com)

○ **Warwick, Stratford, Coventry** (www.shakespeare-country.co.uk)

GETTING AROUND

○ **Bus** Long-distance buses between main centres are good; local buses infrequent in some rural areas

○ **Train** Connections between the major towns are fast and frequent

○ **Car** Easiest way of getting around the region, but cities and main motorways can get heavy with traffic. Popular spots have Park & Ride systems: park your car on the outskirts, take a shuttle bus into the centre.

BE FOREWARNED

○ **Oxford** Many colleges are closed for the Easter term and summer exams. Check www.ox.ac.uk/colleges for full details of opening days and hours.

○ **Major Sights** Popular areas including Stratford-upon-Avon, Warwick, Oxford and the Peak District get busy in summer

○ **Royal Shakespeare Company** Tickets for major productions are often sold out months in advance

◄: Viewpoint, Peak District National Park (p154); Above: Pavilion Gardens, Buxton (p155).

Oxford & Central England Itineraries

Follow the three-day itinerary to explore the best of the Cotswolds. The five-day trip leads further north, through the Midlands and into the Peak District. Combine them for a longer tour of the whole region.

IRISH SEA

NORTH SEA

7 CASTLETON
8 BUXTON
6 CHATSWORTH HOUSE
5 IRONBRIDGE GORGE
COVENTRY 4
3 WARWICK CASTLE
STRATFORD-UPON-AVON 2
STOW-ON-THE-WOLD 3 — 2 CHIPPING CAMPDEN
BLENHEIM PALACE 4
1 OXFORD

3 DAYS
OXFORD TO OXFORD
A Cotswolds Loop

Start your tour in the graceful city of **(1) Oxford**. It's easy to spend a day here, sauntering round the elegant colleges and other university buildings. Top sights include Christ Church, as well as architectural landmarks such as the Sheldonian Theatre and Bodleian Library.

On your second day, head west into the rural landscape of the Cotswolds. This is an area famous for pretty towns and villages, but finest of them all is **(2) Chipping Campden**, with its graceful curving main street flanked by a wonderful array of stone cottages, quaint shops and historic inns. There's also a good

selection of places to stay. Take a look at St James Church and the historic Market Hall, then enjoy an afternoon stroll in the surrounding countryside. Alternatively, visit **(3) Stow-on-the-Wold**, another classic Cotswolds town, its large market square featuring several antique shops.

Day three, and it's time to head back towards Oxford, stopping on the way at **(4) Blenheim Palace**, one of the region's (and the whole country's) greatest stately homes. Finish your tour with a good dinner at one of Oxford's excellent eateries.

OXFORD TO BUXTON
A Midlands Meander

5 DAYS

Start your tour in **(1) Oxford**, then head north to world-famous **(2) Stratford-upon-Avon**, birthplace of William Shakespeare. It's then a short hop to **(3) Warwick Castle**, for historical insights and family fun, possibly diverting to **(4) Coventry** for a moment of reflection at the famous cathedral. While fans of medieval monuments are never far from a highlight, if you're interested in more recent eras don't miss **(5) Ironbridge Gorge**, the crucible of the Industrial Revolution, now a World Heritage Site with several fascinating museums.

Then it's back to classic British history, and one of the country's finest stately homes, **(6) Chatsworth House**. Leave time to admire the stunning interiors and stroll in the ornamental gardens, famous for fountains and cascades, as well as exhibitions of contemporary sculpture. If time allows, take a longer stroll in the wilder landscape of the surrounding Peak District near **(7) Castleton**.

This tour ends in **(8) Buxton**, a picturesque sprawl of Georgian terraces, Victorian amusements and pretty parks.

Punting in Oxford (p134)

Discover Oxford & Central England

OXFORD

POP 134,248

The genteel city of Oxford is a privileged place, renowned as one of the world's most famous university towns – it's soaked in history, dripping with august buildings and yet incredibly insular. The 39 colleges that make up the University jealously guard their elegant honey-coloured buildings, and inside their grounds, a reverent hush and studious calm descends.

Oxford is highly aware of its international standing and yet is remarkably restrained for a city driven by its student population. It's a conservative, bookish kind of place where academic achievement and intellectual ideals are the common currency. The University buildings wrap around narrow cobbled lanes, gowned cyclists blaze along the streets and the vast library collections run along shelves deep below the city streets.

 Sights

MAGDALEN COLLEGE

College

(www.magd.ox.ac.uk; High St; adult/child £4.50/3.50; ☺1-6pm) Set amid 40 hectares of lawns, woodlands, river walks and deer park, Magdalen (*mawd*-len) is one of the wealthiest and most beautiful of Oxford's colleges. An elegant Victorian gateway leads into a medieval chapel, with its glorious 15th-century tower, and on to the remarkable cloisters, some of the finest in Oxford. The strange gargoyles and carved figures here are said to have inspired CS Lewis' stone statues

Boats on the River Avon, Stratford-upon-Avon (p145)
PHOTOGRAPHER: GLENN BEANLAND / LONELY PLANET IMAGES ©

Visiting the University

Much of the centre of Oxford is taken up by graceful university buildings and elegant colleges, each one individual in its appearance and academic specialities. However, not all are open to the public. For those that are, visiting hours change with the term and exam schedule. Check www.ox.ac.uk/colleges for full details of visiting hours and admission.

in *The Chronicles of Narnia*. Behind the cloisters, the lovely **Addison's Walk** leads through the grounds and along the banks of the River Cherwell for just under a mile.

SHELDONIAN THEATRE
Ceremonial Hall

(www.sheldon.ox.ac.uk; Broad St; adult/child £2.50/1.50; ⏱10am-12.30pm & 2-4.30pm Mon-Sat) The monumental Sheldonian Theatre was the first major work of Christopher Wren, at that time a university professor of astronomy. The Sheldonian is now used for college ceremonies and public concerts, but you can climb to the cupola for good views of the surrounding buildings.

BODLEIAN LIBRARY
Library

(www.bodley.ox.ac.uk; Broad St; ⏱9am-5pm Mon-Fri, 9am-4.30pm Sat, 11am-5pm Sun) Oxford's Bodleian Library is one of the oldest public libraries in the world, and one of England's three copyright libraries. It holds more than 7 million items on 118 miles of shelving and has seating space for up to 2500 readers.

RADCLIFFE CAMERA
Library

(Radcliffe Sq) The spectacular circular library, the reading room for the Bodleian Library, was built between 1737 and 1749 in grand Palladian style, and boasts Britain's third-largest dome. The only way to see the library is to join an **extended tour** (£13), which also explores the warren of underground tunnels leading to the library's vast book stacks.

FREE ASHMOLEAN MUSEUM
Museum

(www.ashmolean.org; Beaumont St; ⏱10am-6pm Tue-Sun) Britain's oldest pub-lic museum, the Ashmolean reopened in late 2009 after a massive £61 million redevelopment and is now being lauded as the finest university museum in the world. The makeover has made the once intimidating building and stuffy collection a real joy to browse, with a giant atrium, glass walls revealing galleries on different levels, and a beautiful rooftop restaurant.

NEW COLLEGE
College

(www.new.ox.ac.uk; Holywell St; admission £2; ⏱11am-5pm) This 14th-century college was the first in Oxford to accept undergraduates and is a fine example of the glorious Perpendicular style. The chapel here is full of treasures including superb stained glass, much of it original, and Sir Jacob Epstein's disturbing statue of Lazarus.

MERTON COLLEGE
College

(www.merton.ox.ac.uk; Merton St; admission £2; ⏱2-5pm Mon-Fri, 10am-5pm Sat & Sun) Founded in 1264, Merton was the first to adopt collegiate planning, bringing scholars and tutors together into a formal community. The charming 14th-century **Mob Quad** was the first of the college quads, while the **Old Library** is the oldest medieval library in use. It is said that Tolkien spent many hours here writing *The Lord of the Rings*.

OXFORD COVERED MARKET
Indoor Market

(www.oxford-covered-market.co.uk; ⏱9am-5.30pm) A haven of traditional butchers, fishmongers, cobblers and barbers, this is the place to go for Sicilian sausage,

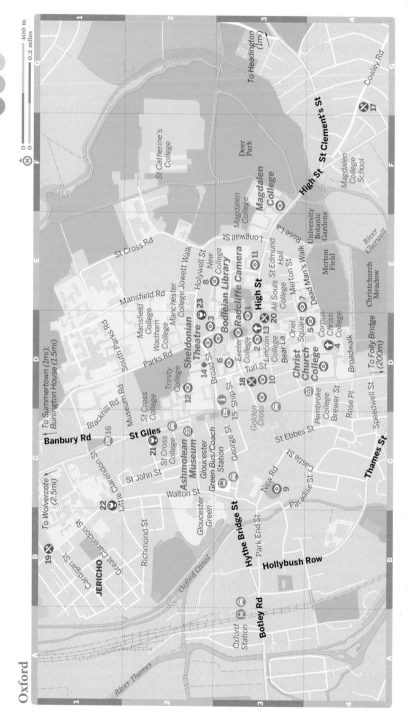

Oxford

Oxford

handmade chocolates, traditional pies, funky T-shirts and expensive brogues. It's a fascinating place to explore and, if you're in Oxford at Christmas, a must for its traditional displays of freshly hung deer, wild boar, ostrich and turkey.

 Tours

TOURIST OFFICE Walking Tours
(☏ 01865-252200; www.visitoxford.org; 15-16 Broad St; ⊗ 9.30am-5pm Mon-Sat, 10am-4pm Sun) Tours of Oxford city and colleges (adult/child £7/3.75) at 10.45am and 2pm year-round, and at 11am and 1pm in July and August, Inspector Morse tours (adult/child £7.50/4) at 1.30pm on Saturdays, family walking tours (adult/child £5.75/3.50) at 1.30pm on school holidays, and a bewildering array of themed tours (adult/child £7.50/4) – including an Alice [in Wonderland] tour, a Literary Tour, and a Harry Potter tour – that run on various dates throughout the year.

BLACKWELL Walking Tours
(☏ 01865-333606; oxford@blackwell.co.uk; 48-51 Broad St; adult/child £7/6.50; ⊗ mid-Apr–Oct) Oxford's most famous bookshop runs

1½-hour guided walking tours, including a literary tour at 2pm Tuesday and 11am Thursday, a tour devoted to 'Inklings' – an informal literary group whose membership included CS Lewis and JRR Tolkien – at 11.45am on Wednesday, plus a special tour every Friday on a topical theme. Book ahead.

BILL SPECTRE'S GHOST TRAIL
Walking Tours
(☏ 07941 041811; www.ghosttrail.org; adult/child £6/3; ⊗ 6.30pm Fri & Sat) For a highly entertaining and informative look at Oxford's dark underbelly, join Victorian undertaker Bill Spectre on a tour of Oxford's most haunted sites. The tour lasts one hour 45 minutes and departs from Oxford Castle Unlocked.

CITY SIGHTSEEING Bus Tours
(www.citysightseeingoxford.com; adult/child £12.50/6; ⊗ 9.30am-6pm Apr-Oct) Hop-on/hop-off bus tours depart every 10 to 15 minutes from the bus and train stations or any of the 20 dedicated stops around town.

Sleeping

OLD PARSONAGE HOTEL — Hotel £££

(☎01865-310210; www.oldparsonage-hotel.
co.uk; 1 Banbury Rd; r from £138; P @) Wonderfully quirky and instantly memorable, the Old Parsonage is a small boutique hotel with just the right blend of old-world character, period charm and modern luxury. The 17th-century building oozes style, with a contemporary-art collection, artfully mismatched furniture and chic bedrooms with handmade beds and marble bathrooms.

ETHOS HOTEL — Hotel ££

(☎01865-245800; www.ethoshotels.co.uk; 59 Western Rd; d from £80; @ 🔊) Hidden away off Abingdon Rd, this funky new hotel has bright, spacious rooms with bold, patterned wallpaper, enormous beds and marble bathrooms. You'll also get a minikitchen with a microwave, a breakfast basket and free wi-fi – all just 10 minutes' walk from the city centre. Some rooms open directly to the street, but with online deals for as little as £68, it's incredible value. To get here, cross Folly Bridge to Abingdon Rd and take the first right onto Western Rd.

BUTTERY HOTEL — Hotel ££

(☎01865-811950; www.thebutteryhotel.co.uk; 11-12 Broad St; s/d from £55/95; @) Right in the heart of the city with views over the college grounds, the Buttery is Oxford's most central hotel. It's a modest enough place, but considering its location, it's a great deal, with spacious if innocuous modern rooms, decent bathrooms and the pick of the city's attractions on your doorstep.

BURLINGTON HOUSE — B&B ££

(☎01865-513513; www.burlington-house.
co.uk; 374 Banbury Rd, Summertown; s/d from £65/85; P @ 🔊) Simple, elegant rooms decked out in restrained, classical style are available at this Victorian merchant house. The rooms are big, bright and uncluttered, with plenty of period character and immaculately kept bathrooms. The Burlington isn't central, but it has good public transport to town and is well worth the trip.

Eating

TROUT — Modern British ££

(☎01865-510930; www.thetroutoxford.co.uk; 195 Godstow Rd, Wolvercote; mains £8-16) Possibly the prettiest location in Oxford, 2½ miles north of the city centre, this charming olde-worlde pub has been a favourite haunt of town and gown for many years. Immortalised by Inspector Morse, it's generally crammed with happy diners enjoying the riverside garden and the extensive menu, though you can also just come for a quiet pint outside meal times. Book ahead.

VAULTS — Cafe £

(www.vaultsandgarden.com; Church of St Mary the Virgin; mains £3.50-5; ⊗10am-5pm) Set in a vaulted 14th-century Congregation House, this place serves a wholesome line of soups, salads, pastas and paellas with plenty of choice for vegetarians. It's one of the most beautiful lunch venues in Oxford, with a lovely garden overlooking Radcliffe Sq. Come early for lunch as it's a local favourite.

DOOR 74 — Modern British ££

(☎01865-203374; www.door74.co.uk; 74 Cowley Rd; mains £8-13; ⊗closed Mon & Sun dinner) This cosy little place woos its fans with a rich mix of British and Mediterranean flavours and friendly service. The menu is limited and the tables tightly packed, but the food is consistently good and combines classic ingredients with a modern twist. Book ahead as seating is limited.

JERICHO CAFÉ — Mediterranean ££

(www.thejerichocafe.co.uk; 112 Walton St; mains £7-12) Chill out and relax with the paper over a coffee and a slab of cake, or go for some of the wholesome lunch and dinner specials, which encompass everything from sausages and mash to Lebanese lamb *kibbeh*. There are plenty of hearty salads and lots of options for vegetarians.

BARBARA VAN ZANTEN / LONELY PLANET IMAGES ©

Don't Miss **Christ Church College**

The largest and grandest of all of Oxford's colleges, Christ Church is also its most popular.

The main entrance is below imposing **Tom Tower**, the upper part of which was designed by former student Sir Christopher Wren. Great Tom, the 7-ton tower bell, still chimes 101 times each evening at 9.05pm (Oxford is five minutes west of Greenwich), to sound the curfew imposed on the original 101 students.

Mere visitors, however, are not allowed to enter the college this way and must go further down St Aldate's to the side entrance. Immediately on entering is the 15th-century cloister, a relic of the ancient Priory of St Frideswide, whose shrine was once a focus of pilgrimage. From here, you go up to the **Great Hall**, the college's magnificent dining room, with its hammerbeam roof and imposing portraits of past scholars.

Coming down the grand staircase, you'll enter **Tom Quad**, Oxford's largest quadrangle, and from here, **Christ Church Cathedral**, the smallest cathedral in the country. Inside, brawny Norman columns are topped by elegant vaulting, and beautiful stained-glass windows adorn the walls.

THINGS YOU NEED TO KNOW

www.chch.ox.ac.uk; St Aldate's; adult/child £6/4.50; ⏰9am-5pm Mon-Sat, 2-5pm Sun

---

QUOD   Modern British **££**
(www.quod.co.uk; 92 High St; mains £12-15)
Bright, buzzing and decked out with modern art and beautiful people, this joint dishes up modern brasserie-style food to the masses. It's always bustling and at worst, will tempt you to chill by the bar with a cocktail while you wait.

The two-course set lunch (£9.95) is great value.

GEORGINA'S   Cafe **£**
(Ave 3, Oxford Covered Market; mains £3-6; ⏰8.30am-5pm Mon-Sat, 10am-4pm Sun) Hidden up a scruffy staircase in the covered market and plastered with old cinema

139

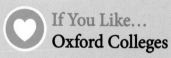

If You Like...
Oxford Colleges

Christ Church College and Magdalen College are the big draws, but Oxford has many more great colleges making up the university:

1 ALL SOULS COLLEGE
(www.all-souls.ox.ac.uk; High St; admission free; ⊙2-4pm Mon-Fri) One of the wealthiest of Oxford's colleges and primarily an academic research institution, dating from 1438. Unlike other older colleges, the front quad is largely unchanged in five centuries. It also contains a beautiful 17th-century sundial designed by Christopher Wren.

2 BRASENOSE COLLEGE
(www.bnc.ox.ac.uk; Radcliffe Sq; admission £1; ⊙noon-4pm) Small and select, this elegant 16th-century place is truly charming. Look out for the doorknocker above the high table in the dining hall – and ask about its fascinating history.

3 EXETER COLLEGE
(www.exeter.ox.ac.uk; Turl St; admission free; ⊙2-5pm) Known for its elaborate 17th-century dining hall and ornate Victorian Gothic chapel housing *The Adoration of the Magi,* a William Morris tapestry.

4 TRINITY COLLEGE
(www.trinity.ox.ac.uk; Broad St; adult/child £1.50/75p; ⊙10am-noon & 2-4pm Sun-Fri, 2-4pm Sat) Worth a visit for the exquisite carvings in its chapel and for Wren's beautiful Garden Quad.

5 ST EDMUND HALL
(www.seh.ox.ac.uk; Queen's Lane; admission free; ⊙noon-4pm Mon-Fri term time only) Sole survivor of the original halls, with a chapel decorated by William Morris and Edward Burne-Jones.

6 CORPUS CHRISTI COLLEGE
(www.ccc.ox.ac.uk; Merton St; admission free; ⊙1.30-4.30pm) A diminutive college but strikingly beautiful, Corpus Christi has a pelican sundial in the middle of the front quad.

posters, this is a funky little cafe serving a bumper crop of bulging salads, hearty soups and such goodies as goat-cheese quesadillas and scrumptious cakes.

 Drinking

TURF TAVERN Traditional Pub
(4 Bath Pl) Hidden away down a narrow alleyway, this tiny medieval pub is one of the town's best-loved and bills itself as 'an education in intoxication'. Home to real ales and student antics, it's always packed with a mix of students, professionals and the lucky tourists who manage to find it.

EAGLE & CHILD Traditional Pub
(49 St Giles) Affectionately known as the 'Bird & Baby', this atmospheric place dates from 1650 and is a hotchpotch of nooks and crannies. It was once the favourite haunt of Tolkien, CS Lewis and their literary friends and still attracts a mellow crowd.

RAOUL'S Cocktail Bar
(www.raoulsbar.co.uk; 32 Walton St; ⊙4pm-midnight) This trendy retro-look bar is one of Jericho's finest and is always busy.

Information

Tourist Information
Tourist office (☎01865-252200; www.visitoxford.org; 15-16 Broad St; ⊙9.30am-5pm Mon-Sat, 10am-4pm Sun)

Websites
Oxford City (www.oxfordcity.co.uk) Accommodation and restaurant listings as well as entertainment, activities and shopping.

Oxford Online (www.visitoxford.org) Oxford's official tourism website.

ℹ️ Getting There & Away

Bus

Services to **London** (£16 return) run up to every 15 minutes, day and night, and take about 90 minutes.

Airline (www.oxfordbus.co.uk) Runs to **Heathrow** (£20, 90 minutes) half-hourly from 4am to 10pm and at midnight and 2am, and **Gatwick** (£26, two hours) hourly 5.15am to 8.15pm and every two hours from 10pm to 4am.

Car

Driving and parking in Oxford is a nightmare. Use the five Park & Ride car parks on major routes leading into town. Parking is free and buses (10 to 15 minutes, every 10 minutes) cost £2.50.

Train

There are half-hourly services to **London Paddington** (£19.90, one hour). Hourly services also run to **Bath** (£22.50, 1¼ hours), but require a change at Didcot Parkway.

Chipping Campden
POP 2206

An unspoiled gem in an area full of achingly pretty villages, Chipping Campden is a glorious reminder of life in the Cotswolds in medieval times. The graceful curving main street is flanked by a wonderful array of wayward stone cottages, fine terraced houses, ancient inns and historic homes, liberally sprinkled with chichi boutiques and upmarket shops. Despite its obvious allure, the town remains relatively unspoiled by tourist crowds and is a wonderful place to visit.

Pop into the helpful **tourist office** (📞01386-841206; www.chippingcampdenonline. org; High St; ⊙9.30am-5pm) to pick up a town trail guide (£1) for information on the most historic buildings and to get you off the main drag and down some of the gorgeous back streets. If you're visiting on a Tuesday between July and September, it's well worth joining a **guided tour** at 2.30pm (suggested donation £3) run by the Cotswold Wardens.

DISCOVER OXFORD & CENTRAL ENGLAND

THE COTSWOLDS

Glorious honey-coloured villages filled with beautiful old mansions, thatched cottages, atmospheric churches and rickety almshouses draw crowds of tourists to the Cotswolds. The booming medieval wool trade brought the area its wealth and left it with such a glut of beautiful buildings that its place in history is secured for evermore. If you've ever dreamed of falling asleep under English-rose wallpaper or lusted after a cream tea in the midafternoon, there's no finer place to fulfil your fantasies.

Stone building, the Cotswolds.

Sights

The most obvious sight is the wonderful 17th-century **Market Hall**, with multiple gables and an elaborate timber roof. Further on, at the western end of the High St, is the 15th-century **St James**, one of the Cotswolds' great wool churches. Built in the Perpendicular style, it has a magnificent tower and some graceful 17th-century monuments. Nearby on Church St is a remarkable row of **almshouses** dating from the 17th century, and the Jacobean lodges and gateways of the now-ruined Campden House.

Sleeping & Eating

COTSWOLD HOUSE HOTEL

Hotel £££

(01386-840330; www.cotswoldhouse.com; The Square; r £140-650; P @) If you're after a spot of luxury, look no further than this chic Regency town house turned boutique hotel. Bespoke furniture, massive beds, Frette linens, cashmere throws, private gardens and hot tubs are the norm here. You can indulge in some treatments at the hotel spa, dine in luxuriant style at Juliana's (three-course set dinner, £49.50) or take a more informal approach at Hick's Brasserie (mains £10 to £19), a slick operation with an ambitious menu.

CHANCE

B&B ££

(01386-849079; www.the-chance.co.uk; 1 Aston Rd; d £75; P) Two pretty rooms with floral bedspreads, fresh flowers and a cast-iron fireplace make this B&B a good choice. The owners are particularly helpful, and little extras such as bathrobes and hot-water bottles are waiting in the rooms.

EIGHT BELLS

Pub ££

(01386-840371; www.eightbellsinn.co.uk; Church St; mains £13-17) Dripping with olde-worlde character and charm, but also decidedly modern, this 14th-century inn

Left: Weavers' cottages, the Cotswolds; **Below:** Cotswold sheep

PHOTOGRAPHER: (LEFT) & (BELOW) BARBARA VAN ZANTEN / LONELY PLANET IMAGES ©

serves real ales and a fine selection of modern British and Continental dishes in rustic settings.

ⓘ Getting There & Around

Between them, buses 21 and 22 run almost hourly to **Stratford-upon-Avon**. Bus 21 also stops in Broadway. There are no Sunday services.

Stow-on-the-Wold

POP 2794

A popular stop on a tour of the Cotswolds, Stow is anchored by a large market square surrounded by handsome buildings and steep-walled alleyways, originally used to funnel the sheep into the fair. The town has long held a strategic place in Cotswold history, standing as it does on the Roman Fosse Way and at the junction of six roads.

Sleeping & Eating

MOLE END   B&B ££

(☎ 01451-870348; www.moleendstow.co.uk; Moreton Rd; s/d from £55/80; **P @**) This charming and immaculately kept B&B on the outskirts of town is a real gem. There are three stunning rooms with acres of space, huge beds and a whiff of refined French styling. There's a large garden with bucolic views, as well as great breakfasts and amiable hosts.

NUMBER 9   B&B ££

(☎ 01451-870333; www.number-nine.info; 9 Park St; s/d from £45/65; 🛜) Centrally located and wonderfully atmospheric, this beautiful B&B is all sloping floors and exposed beams. The three rooms are cosy but spacious and have brand-new bathrooms and subtle decor.

143

GLENN BEANLAND / LONELY PLANET IMAGES ©

Don't Miss Blenheim Palace

One of the country's greatest stately homes, Blenheim Palace is a monumental baroque fantasy designed by Sir John Vanbrugh and Nicholas Hawksmoor between 1705 and 1722. The land and funds to build the house were granted to John Churchill, Duke of Marlborough, by a grateful Queen Anne after his decisive victory at the 1704 Battle of Blenheim. Now a Unesco World Heritage Site, Blenheim (*blen*-num) is home to the 11th duke and duchess.

Inside, the house is stuffed with statues, tapestries, ostentatious furniture and giant oil paintings in elaborate gilt frames. Highlights include the **Great Hall**, a vast space topped by 20m-high ceilings adorned with images of the first duke in battle; the opulent **Saloon**, the grandest and most important public room; the three **state rooms**, with their plush decor and priceless china cabinets; and the magnificent **Long Library**, which is 55m in length.

From the library, you can access the **Churchill Exhibition**, which is dedicated to the life, work and writings of Sir Winston, who was born at Blenheim in 1874. For an insight into life below stairs, the **Untold Story** exhibition explores the family's history through the eyes of the household staff.

If the crowds in the house become too oppressive, retire to the lavish gardens and vast parklands, parts of which were landscaped by Lancelot 'Capability' Brown. To the front, an artificial lake sports a beautiful bridge by Vanbrugh, and a minitrain takes visitors to a maze, adventure playground and butterfly house. Glorious walks lead to an arboretum, cascade and temple.

Blenheim Palace is near the small town of Woodstock, eight miles northwest of Oxford. Stagecoach bus S3 runs every half-hour (hourly on Sunday) from George St in Oxford.

THINGS YOU NEED TO KNOW

www.blenheimpalace.com; adult/child £18/10, park & garden only £10.30/5; ⊙10.30am-5.30pm daily mid-Feb–Oct, Wed-Sun Nov–mid-Dec

OLD BUTCHERS

Modern European ££

(☎ 01451-831700; www.theoldbutchers.com; 7 Park St; mains £13-18) Simple, smart and sophisticated, this is Stow's top spot for dining, serving robust, local ingredients whipped up into sublime dishes.

Getting There & Away

Bus 855 links Stow with Moreton, Bourton, Northleach and Cirencester (eight daily Monday to Saturday). Bus 801 runs to Cheltenham, Moreton and Bourton (four daily Monday to Friday, nine on Saturday).

The nearest train stations are 4 miles away at Kingham and Moreton-in-Marsh.

THE MIDLANDS
Stratford-upon-Avon
POP 22,187

The author of some of the most quoted lines ever written in the English language, William Shakespeare was born in Stratford in 1564 and died here in 1616, and the five houses linked to his life form the centrepiece of a tourist attraction that verges on a cult of personality.

Experiences in this unmistakably Tudor town range from the touristy (medieval re-creations and bard-themed tearooms) to the humbling (Shakespeare's modest grave in Holy Trinity Church) and the sublime (taking in a play by the world-famous Royal Shakespeare Company). Nevertheless, if can leave without buying at least a Shakespeare novelty pencil, you'll have resisted one of the most keenly honed marketing machines in the nation.

Sights & Activities

THE SHAKESPEARE HOUSES Museums
Five of the most important buildings associated with Shakespeare contain museums that form the core of the visitor experience at Stratford, run by the **Shakespeare Birthplace Trust** (☎ 01789-204016; www.shakespeare.org.uk; adult/child all five properties £19/12, three in-town houses £12.50/8; ⏱9am-5pm Apr-Oct, see website for low-season hours). You can buy individual tickets, but it's more cost-effective to buy a combination ticket covering the three houses in town, or all five properties.

SHAKESPEARE'S BIRTHPLACE
(Henley St) Start your Shakespeare tour at the house where the world's most famous playwright supposedly spent his childhood days. In fact, the jury is still out on whether this really was Shakespeare's birthplace, but devotees of the Bard have been dropping in since at least the 19th century, leaving their signatures scratched onto the windows. Set behind a modern facade, the house contains restored Tudor rooms, live presentations from famous Shakespearean characters, and an engaging exhibition on Stratford's favourite son.

NASH'S HOUSE & NEW PLACE
(☎ 01789-292325; cnr Chapel St & Chapel Lane) When Shakespeare retired, he swapped the bright lights of London for a comfortable town house at New Pl, where he died of unknown causes in April 1616. The house was demolished in 1759, but an attractive Elizabethan **knot garden** occupies part of the grounds.

Displays in the adjacent **Nash's House**, where Shakespeare's granddaughter Elizabeth lived, describe the town's history, and there's a collection of 17th-century furniture and tapestries.

HALL'S CROFT
(☎ 01789-292107, Old Town) Shakespeare's daughter Susanna married respected doctor John Hall, and their fine Elizabethan town house is south of the centre on the way to Holy Trinity Church. Deviating from the main Shakespearean theme, the exhibition offers fascinating insights into medicine in the 16th century.

ANNE HATHAWAY'S COTTAGE
(☎ 01789-292100, Cottage La, Shottery) Before marrying Shakespeare, Anne Hathaway lived in Shottery, a mile west of the centre, in this pretty thatched farmhouse. As well as period furniture,

145

there's an orchard and arboretum, with examples of all the trees mentioned in Shakespeare's plays. A footpath (no bikes allowed) leads to Shottery from Evesham Pl.

MARY ARDEN'S FARM

(01789-293455; Station Rd, Wilmcote) If you fancy going back even further, you can visit the childhood home of Shakespeare's mum at Wilmcote, 3 miles west of Stratford. Aimed firmly at families, the farm has exhibits tracing country life over the centuries, with nature trails, falconry displays and a collection of rare-breed farm animals. You can get here on the City Sightseeing bus, or cycle via Anne Hathaway's Cottage, following the Stratford-upon-Avon Canal towpath.

FREE **HOLY TRINITY CHURCH** Church (01789-266316; www.stratford-upon-avon.org; Old Town; admission to church free, Shakespeare's grave adult/child £1.50/50p; 8.30am-6pm Mon-Sat, 12.30-5pm Sun Apr-Sep, reduced low season hrs) The final resting place of the bard is said to be the most visited parish church in England. Inside are handsome 16th- and 17th-century tombs (particularly in the Clopton Chapel), some fabulous carvings on the choir stalls and, of course, the grave of William Shakespeare, with its ominous epitaph: 'cvrst be he yt moves my bones'.

 Tours

Popular and informative two-hour **guided town walks** (01789-292478; adult/child £5/2; 11am Mon-Wed, 2pm Thu-Sun) depart from Waterside, opposite Sheep St, which is also the starting point for the spooky **Stratford Town Ghost Walk** (adult/child £6/3; 7.30pm Mon, Thu, Fri & Sat).

City Sightseeing Bus Tours (01789-412680; www.citysightseeing-stratford.com; adult/child £11.50/6; every 20min Apr-Sep, less frequently in low season) Open-top, hop-on/hop-off bus tours leave from the tourist office and go to each of the Shakespeare properties. Tickets are valid for 24 hours.

 **Sleeping**

SHAKESPEARE HOTEL Hotel £££ (01789-294997; www.mercure.com; Chapel St; s/d £135/150; **P** **@**) For the full Tudor inn experience, head to this atmospheric Mercure property in a timbered medieval charmer on the main street. As well as enjoying a perfect location, you get tasteful rooms – some with four-poster beds and wood panels – as well as a sense of history that's missing from the competition.

ARDEN HOTEL Hotel £££ (01789-298682; www.theardenhotelstratford.com; Waterside; r incl breakfast from £125; **P** **@**) Formerly the Thistle, this elegant property facing the Swan Theatre has been stylishly revamped, with a sleek brasserie and champagne bar, and rooms featuring designer fabrics and bathrooms full of polished stone.

WHITE SAILS B&B ££ 01789-264326; www.white-sails.co.uk; 85 Evesham Rd; r from £95; **P** **@**) Plush fabrics, framed prints, brass bedsteads and shabby-chic tables and lamps set the scene at this gorgeous, intimate guest house.

Ambleside Guest House B&B £ (01789-297239; www.amblesideguesthouse.co.uk; 41 Grove Rd; s/d from £25/50; **P** **@**) Lovely, nonfrilly B&B with spotless rooms, amiable hosts and big organic breakfasts.

Ashgrove Guest House B&B £ (01789-297278; www.shgrovehousestratford.co.uk; 37 Grove Rd; s/d from £25/50; **P**) Tidy, airy rooms decked out in varying degrees of burgundy. Look for the wooden bear sculpture outside.

Broadlands Guest House B&B £ (01789-299181; www.broadlandsguesthouse.co.uk; 23 Evesham Pl; s/d from £48/80; **P**) Prim and blue, with classic English B&B rooms and filling breakfasts.

Salamander Guest House B&B £ (01789-205728; www.salamanderguesthouse.co.uk; 40 Grove Rd; s/d incl breakfast from £20/40; **P** **@**) Comfortable and homely, with the added appeal of wi-fi.

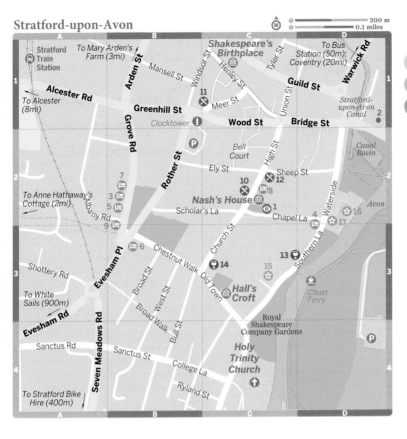

Stratford-upon-Avon

Stratford-upon-Avon

Woodstock Guest House B&B £

(☏ 01789-299881; www.woodstock-house.co.uk; 30 Grove Rd; s/d from £30/55; P) Agreeable flowery rooms, soft carpets, and a warm welcome, in a house with a tidy garden and gravel drive.

 Eating

EDWARD MOON'S

Modern British ££

(☏ 01789-267069; www.edwardmoon.com/moonsrestaurant; 9 Chapel St; mains £10-15) Named after a famous travelling chef, who cooked up the flavours of home for the British colonial service, this snug eatery serves delicious, hearty English dishes, many livened up with herbs and spices from the East.

VINTNER WINE BAR

Modern British ££

(☏ 01789-297259; www.the-vintner.co.uk; 5 Sheep St; mains £10-20; ☉ breakfast, lunch & dinner) Set in a town house from 1600, this quirky place is full of beams, exposed brickwork, and low ceilings on which to bang your head. Locals as well as out-of-towners come here for good food (mostly steaks, salads and roasts) and lively conversation.

Oscar's Cafe £

(13/14 Meer St; sandwiches & lunches £4-7; ☉ 11.30am-late) A casual cafe serving appetising breakfasts, lunches and afternoon teas; it turns into a bar after hours.

 **Drinking**

DIRTY DUCK Pub

(Waterside) Officially called the 'Black Swan', this enchanting riverside alehouse is a favourite thespian watering hole, and has a roll-call of former regulars that reads like an actors' Who's Who.

WINDMILL INN Pub

(Church St) Ale was flowing here at the same time as rhyming couplets flowed from Shakespeare's quill – this pub has been around a while. Despite its age it's still one of the liveliest places in town, and slightly removed from the tourist hubbub.

 Entertainment

ROYAL SHAKESPEARE COMPANY

Theatre

(RSC; ☏ 0844 800 1110; www.rsc.org.uk; tickets £8-38) Coming to Stratford without seeing a production of Shakespeare would be like going to Rome and not visiting the Vatican.

There are three grand stages in Stratford – **Royal Shakespeare Theatre** and **Swan Theatre** on Waterside and the **Courtyard Theatre** on Southern La. The first two properties were extensively redeveloped between 2007 and 2010 – contact the RSC for the latest news on performance times at the three venues. There are often special deals for under 25-year-olds, students and seniors and a few tickets are held back for sale on the day of the performance, but eager backpackers tend to snap these up fast. Wise theatregoers book well ahead.

ℹ Information

Tourist office (☏ 0870 160 7930; www.shakespeare-country.co.uk; Bridgefoot; ☉ call for opening times) Under refurbishment at the time of writing, but due to re-open on same site.

ℹ Getting There & Away

Chiltern Railways runs to **London Marylebone** (£49.50, 2¼ hours, four daily).

National Express coaches and other bus companies run from Stratford's Riverside bus station (behind the Stratford Leisure Centre on Bridgeway). Destinations served:

London Victoria National Express, £17.10, three to four hours, five daily

Oxford National Express £9.90, one hour, twice daily

Warwick Bus 16, 40 minutes, hourly

ⓘ Getting Around

A bicycle is handy for getting out to the outlying Shakespeare properties, and **Stratford Bike Hire** (☏07711-776340; www.stratfordbikehire.com; 7 Seven Meadows Rd; per half/full day from £7/13) will deliver to your accommodation.

Warwick

POP 25,434

Despite a devastating fire in 1694, Warwick remains a treasure-house of medieval architecture, dominated by the soaring turrets of Warwick Castle, which has been transformed into a major tourist attraction by the team behind Madame Tussauds. Unfortunately, the summer queues at the castle can resemble a medieval siege – you can escape the melee in the surrounding streets, which are jammed with interesting buildings and museums.

◎ Sights

WARWICK CASTLE   Castle

(☏0870 442 2000; www.warwick-castle.co.uk; castle adult/child £19.95/11.95, castle & dungeon adult/child £27.45/19.45; ⊙10am-6pm Apr-Sep, to 5pm Oct-Mar; Ⓟ) Founded in 1068 by William the Conqueror, the stunningly preserved Warwick Castle is the biggest show in town.

With waxwork-populated private apartments, sumptuous interiors, landscaped gardens, towering ramparts, displays of arms and armour, medieval jousting and a theme-park dungeon (complete with torture chamber and ham actors in grisly make-up), there's plenty to keep the family busy for a whole day. Tickets are discounted if you buy online.

Warwick

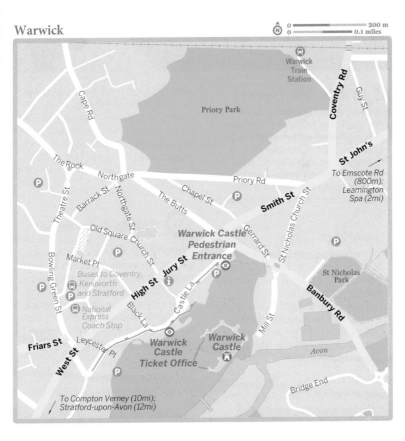

ℹ Getting There & Away

Stagecoach X17 runs to **Coventry** (1¼ hours, every 15 minutes Monday to Saturday). Stagecoach bus 16 goes to **Stratford-upon-Avon** (40 minutes, hourly) in one direction, and **Coventry** in the other. The main bus stops are on Market St.

Trains run to **Stratford-upon-Avon** (£5.20, 30 minutes, hourly) and **London** (£30, 1¾ hours, every 20 minutes), from the station northeast of the centre.

Ironbridge Gorge

Strolling or cycling through the woods, hills and villages of this peaceful river gorge, it's hard to believe such a sleepy enclave could really have been the birthplace of the Industrial Revolution. Nevertheless, it was here that Abraham Darby perfected the art of smelting iron-ore with coke in 1709, making it possible to mass-produce cast iron for the first time.

Abraham Darby's son, Abraham Darby II, invented a new forging process for producing single beams of iron, allowing Abraham Darby III to astound the world with the first-ever iron bridge, constructed in 1779. The bridge remains the focal point of this World Heritage Site, and a collection of very different museums tell the story of the Industrial Revolution in the very buildings where it took place.

◎ Sights & Activities

The Ironbridge museums are administered by the **Ironbridge Gorge Museum Trust** (☏ 01952-884391; www.ironbridge.org.uk), and all are open from 10am to 5pm from late March to early November, unless stated otherwise. You can buy tickets as you go, but the good-value **passport ticket** (adult/child £21.95/14.25) allows year-round entry to all of the sites.

MUSEUM OF THE GORGE   Museum
(The Wharfage; adult/child £3.60/2.35) Kick off your visit at the Museum of the Gorge, which offers an overview of the World

Left: Overlooking the grounds, Warwick Castle (p149);
Below: Tower, Warwick Castle
PHOTOGRAPHER: (LEFT) & (BELOW) MAX PAOLI & RUTH EASTHAM / LONELY PLANET IMAGES ©

Heritage Site using film, photos and 3-D models. Housed in a Gothic warehouse by the river, it's filled with entertaining, hands-on exhibits.

COALBROOKDALE MUSEUM OF IRON
Museum
(Wellington Rd; adult/child, £7.40/4.95) Set in the brooding buildings of Abraham Darby's original iron foundry, the Museum of Iron contains some excellent interactive exhibits. Combined tickets with Darby Houses also available.

DARBY HOUSES
Museums
(☎ 01952-433522; adult/child £4.60/3; ⊙ Apr-Oct) Just uphill from the Museum of Iron are these beautifully restored 18th-century homes, which housed generations of the Darby family in gracious but modest Quaker comfort.

IRON BRIDGE & TOLLHOUSE
Bridge
The flamboyant, arching **Iron Bridge** that gives the area its name was constructed to flaunt the new technology invented by the inventive Darby family. At the time of its construction in 1779, nobody could believe that anything so large could be built from cast iron without collapsing under its own weight. There's a small exhibition on the bridge's history at the former **tollhouse** (admission free).

BLISTS HILL VICTORIAN TOWN
Museum
(☎ 01952-433522; Legges Way, Madeley; adult/child £14.60/9.35) Set at the top of the Hay Inclined Plane (a cable lift that once transported coal barges uphill from the Shropshire Canal), Blists Hill is a lovingly restored Victorian village that has been repopulated with townsfolk in period costume, carrying out day-to-day activities like washing clothes, mending hobnail boots and working the village iron foundry.

Ironbridge Gorge

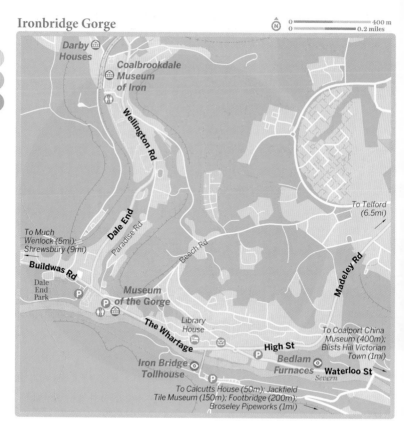

COALPORT CHINA MUSEUM Museum
(adult/child £7.40/4.95) Dominated by a pair of towering bottle kilns, the atmospheric old china works now contains an absorbing museum tracing the history of the industry, with demonstrations of traditional pottery techniques.

JACKFIELD TILE MUSEUM Museum
(Jackfield; adult/child £7.40/4.95) Gas-lit galleries re-create ornately tiled rooms from past centuries, from Victorian public conveniences to fairy-tale friezes from children's hospital wards. The museum is on the south bank of the Severn, near the footbridge to the Coalport China Museum.

BROSELEY PIPEWORKS Museum
(adult/child £4.55/3; ⏱1-5pm mid-May–Sep) This was once the biggest clay tobacco pipe-maker in the country, but the industry took a nose-dive following the introduction of pre-rolled cigarettes in the 1880s, and the factory has been preserved so it looks much as the last worker left it when the doors finally closed in 1957.

The pipeworks is a 1-mile walk south of the river, on a winding lane that passes the old workers' cottages (ask the tourist office for the *Jitties* leaflet).

ENGINUITY Museum
(Wellington Rd; adult/child £7.65/6.55) If the kids are getting tired of fusty historical museum displays, recharge their batteries at this levers-and-pulleys science

centre beside the Museum of Iron, where you can control robots, move a steam locomotive with your bare hands (and a little engineering know-how) and power up a vacuum cleaner with self-generated electricity.

 Sleeping

LIBRARY HOUSE　　　　　B&B ££
(☎01952-432299; www.libraryhouse.com; 11 Severn Bank; s/d from £60/70; P @ 🛜) Up an alley off the main street, this lovingly restored Georgian library building is hugged by vines, backed by a beautiful garden and decked out with stacks of vintage books, curios, prints and lithographs. There are three charming, individually decorated rooms, each named after a famous writer.

CALCUTTS HOUSE　　　　B&B ££
(☎01952-882631; www.calcuttshouse.co.uk; Calcutts Rd; s/d/tr from £45/53/90; P) This former ironmaster's pad, built in the 18th century, is tucked away on the south bank, a few paces from the Jackfield Tile Museum. Its traditionally decorated rooms have bags of character, and each is named after a famous former resident or guest at the house.

ℹ️ Information

Tourist office (☎01952-884391; www.visitironbridge.co.uk; The Wharfage; 🕙10am-5pm) Located at the Museum of the Gorge.

ℹ️ Getting There & Away

The nearest train station is six miles away at Telford, but you can continue on to Ironbridge on bus 96 (20 minutes, every two hours Monday to Saturday).

ℹ️ Getting Around

At weekends and on bank holidays from Easter to October, the Gorge Connect bus (free to Museum Passport holders) runs from Telford bus station to all of the museums on the north bank of the Severn. A Day Rover pass costs £2.50/1.50 per adult/child.

The flamboyant, arching Iron Bridge, Ironbridge Gorge (p151)

RDA / IMAGEBROKER

Detour:
Coventry

Over the centuries, Coventry has been a bustling hub for the production of cloth, clocks, bicycles, automobiles and munitions. It was this last industry that attracted the attention of the German Luftwaffe in WWII. The city was blitzed so badly that the Nazis coined a new verb, 'Coventrieren', meaning 'to flatten'. However, it's not all doom and gloom – a handful of medieval streets escaped the bombers, offering a taste of what the city must have been like in its heyday.

The evocative ruins of **St Michael's Cathedral** (Priory Row), built around 1300 but destroyed by Nazi incendiary bombs in the blitz of 14 November 1940, still stand as a permanent memorial to Coventry's darkest hour. You can climb the 180 steps of its **Gothic spire** for panoramic views (adult/child £2.50/1).

Symbolically adjoining the old cathedral's sandstone walls, the Sir Basil Spence–designed **Coventry Cathedral** (☏024-7652 1200; www.coventrycathedral. org.uk; Priory Row; adult/child under 7 £4.50/3.50; ⊙9.30am-4.30pm) is a modernist architectural masterpiece, with a futuristic organ, stained glass, a Jacob Epstein statue of the devil and St Michael, and ghostlike angels etched into its glass facade.

Bus X17 (every 20 minutes) goes to Warwick (1¼ hours). Trains go south to London Euston (£37.80; 1¼ hours, every 20 minutes) and Birmingham (30 minutes, every 10 minutes).

PEAK DISTRICT

Rolling across the southernmost hills of the Pennines, the Peak District is one of the most beautiful parts of the country. Ancient stone villages are folded into creases in the landscape and the hillsides are littered with famous stately homes and rocky outcrops that attract hordes of walkers, climbers and cavers.

No one knows for certain how the Peak District got its name – certainly not from the landscape, which has hills and valleys, gorges and lakes, moorland and gritstone escarpments, but no peaks. The most popular theory is that the region was named for the Pecsaetan, the Anglo-Saxon tribe who once populated this part of England.

Locals divide the Peak District into the Dark Peak – dominated by exposed moorland and gritstone 'edges' – and the White Peak, made up of the limestone dales to the south.

❶ Information

Peak District Tourist Board (www.visitpeakdistrict.com)
Peak District National Park Authority (☏01629-816200; www.peakdistrict.org)

Buxton
POP 24,112

Imagine Bath or Brighton, transported to the rolling hills of the Derbyshire dales. That's Buxton, a picturesque sprawl of Georgian terraces, Victorian amusements and pretty parks, set at the very heart of the Peak District National Park. The town built its fortunes on its natural warm-water springs, which attracted hordes of health tourists in Buxton's heyday. Today, visitors are drawn here by the flamboyant Regency architecture, the cute shops and cafes and the abundant natural wonders waiting in the surrounding countryside. Tuesday and Saturday are market days, bringing an extra dash of colour to the grey limestone market place.

Sights

VICTORIANA

At the foot of the Slopes, the historic centre of Buxton is a riot of Victorian pavilions, concert halls and glasshouse domes. The most famous building in town is the flamboyant, turreted **Opera House** (Water St), which hosts an impressive variety of stage shows, with a notable preference for Gilbert & Sullivan.

The Opera House shares an entrance with the equally flamboyant **Pavilion Gardens** (www.paviliongardens.co.uk; ⏱10am-4.30pm), where a series of domed pavilions sprawl across a pretty park like a seaside pier, dropped into the middle of the Derbyshire Dales. The main building contains a tropical greenhouse, a nostalgic cafe and the tourist office.

Uphill from the Pavilion Gardens is another glorious piece of Victoriana, the **Devonshire Hospital**, whose enormous dome contains part of the campus for the University of Derby. There is also – surprisingly – an opulent **spa** (☎01332-594408; www.devonshire-spa.co.uk) offering a full range of pampering treatments.

BUXTON SPA   Architecture

In Victorian times, spa activities were centred on the extravagant Buxton Baths complex, built in grand Regency style in 1854. The various bath buildings are fronted by a grand, curving facade, known as **the Crescent**, inspired by the Royal Crescent in Bath. Today it sits empty, awaiting a developer with enough money to restore the town spa. For a taste of what the baths looked like in their heyday, pop around the corner to **Cavendish Arcade**, whose walls retain their original eggshell-blue art-deco tiles.

Sleeping

OLD HALL HOTEL   Hotel £££

(☎01298-22841; www.oldhallhotelbuxton.co.uk; The Square; s/d incl breakfast from £65/100; @ 📶) There is a tale to go with every creak of the floorboards at this history-soaked establishment, supposedly the oldest hotel in England. Among other esteemed residents, Mary, Queen of Scots, stayed here from 1576 to 1578, albeit against her will. The rooms are still the grandest in town.

Farm cottage, the Peak District

155

ROSELEIGH HOTEL B&B ££

(📞 01298-24904; www.roseleighhotel.co.uk; 19 Broad Walk; s/d incl breakfast from £38/72; 🅿 @ 🛜) This gorgeous family-run B&B in a roomy old Victorian house has lovingly decorated rooms, many with fine views out over the Pavilion Gardens. The owners are a welcoming couple, both seasoned travellers, with plenty of interesting tales to tell.

Eating

COLUMBINE RESTAURANT

Modern British ££

(📞 01298-78752; 7 Hall Bank; mains £11-17; 🕑 dinner Mon-Sat, closed Tue Nov-Apr) On the lane leading down beside the Town Hall, this understated restaurant is top choice among Buxtonites in the know. The chef conjures up some imaginative dishes using mainly local produce and there's a sinful list of fattening puddings. Bookings recommended.

PAVILION CAFE Cafe £

(snacks £3-7; 🕑 9.30am-5pm Apr-Sep) Set in a renovated wing of the Pavilion, these peaceful tearooms conjure up images of jazz-fuelled tea-dances sometime between the wars.

Drinking & Entertainment

OLD SUN INN Pub

(33 High St) The cosiest of the High St pubs, with a warren of rooms full of original features and a lively crowd that spans the generations. The pub grub (mains £6 to £9.50), while predictable, is inexpensive and tasty.

OPERA HOUSE Opera

(www.buxtonoperahouse.org.uk; Water St) Buxton's gorgeously restored Victorian Opera House hosts a full program of drama, dance, concerts and comedy as well as some renowned festivals and events.

ℹ Information

Tourist office (www.visitpeakdistrict.com; Pavilion Gardens; 🕑 9.30am-5pm Oct-Mar, 10am-4pm Apr-Sep)

Archery practice, Sherwood Forest

Detour:
Sherwood Forest National Nature Reserve

If Robin Hood wanted to hide out in Sherwood Forest today, he'd have to disguise himself and the Merry Men as day trippers on mountain bikes. Covering 182 hectares of old-growth forest to the north of Nottingham, the park is a major destination for Nottingham city dwellers looking to fill their lungs with fresh air, but there are still some peaceful corners.

On the outskirts of the forest on the B6034, the **Sherwood Forest tourist office** (www.sherwoodforest.org.uk; Swinecote Rd; parking £3; ⏰10am-5pm) has visitor information, copious quantities of Robin Hood merchandise and the lame 'Robyn Hode's Sherwode', with wooden cut-outs, murals and mannequins telling the tale of the famous woodsman.

Numerous walking trails lead through the forest, passing such Sherwood Forest landmarks as the **Major Oak**, a broad-boughed oak tree that is certainly old enough to have sheltered Robin of Locksley, if he did indeed exist.

To reach the tourist office by car, drive north from Nottingham for about 10 miles on the A614. Or from Nottingham catch the Sherwood Arrow bus (30 minutes, four daily Monday to Saturday, two Sunday services).

ⓘ Getting There & Away

Northern Rail has trains to and from **Manchester** (£9.20, one hour, hourly). Buses stop on both sides of the road at Market Pl. The hourly Transpeak runs to **Nottingham** (2½ hours), via **Bakewell** (one hour).

Castleton
POP 1200

Guarding the entrance to the forbidding gorge known as Winnats Pass, Castleton is blessed with more than its fair share of visitor attractions. The streets are lined with leaning stone houses, walking trails criss-cross the surrounding hills, a wonderfully atmospheric castle crowns the ridge above town, and the bedrock under Castleton is riddled with caves which were once mined for Blue John Stone, a vivid violet form of flourspar.

Sights

PEVERIL CASTLE   Castle
(EH; adult/child £4.20/2.10; ⏰10am-5pm Apr-Oct, 10am-4pm Nov-Mar) Topping the ridge to the south of Castleton, this evoca-tive castle has been so ravaged by the centuries that it almost looks like a crag itself. Constructed by William Peveril, son of William the Conqueror, the castle was used as a hunting lodge by Henry II, King John and Henry III, and the crumbling ruins offer swoon-inducing views over the Hope Valley.

CASTLETON CAVES   Caves
The limestone caves around town have been mined for lead, silver and the semi-precious John Blue Stone for centuries and four are open to the public on guided tours.

PEAK CAVERN
(☏01433-620285; www.devilsarse.com; adult/child £7.75/5.75; ⏰10am-5pm, tours hourly till 4pm) A short walk from the castle tourist office is the largest natural cave entrance in England, known locally as the Devil's Arse. Should you choose to enter Bee-lzebub's rocky crevasse, you'll see some dramatic limestone formations, lit with fibreoptic cables.

157

ANDERS BLOMQVIST / LONELY PLANET IMAGES ©

Don't Miss **Chatsworth House**

It's easy to get stately home fatigue with all the grand manors dotted around, but sumptuous **Chatsworth House** is really something else. Known as the 'Palace of the Peak', this vast edifice has been occupied by the earls and dukes of Devonshire for centuries. The manor was founded in 1552 by the formidable Bess of Hardwick and her second husband, William Cavendish, who earned grace and favour by helping Henry VIII dissolve the English monasteries. Bess was onto her fourth husband, George Talbot, Earl of Shrewsbury, by the time Mary, Queen of Scots was imprisoned at Chatsworth on the orders of Elizabeth I in 1569.

While the core of the house dates from the 16th-century, Chatsworth was altered and enlarged repeatedly over the centuries, and the current building has a Georgian feel, dating back to the last overhaul in 1820. Inside, the lavish apartments and mural-painted staterooms are packed with paintings and priceless items of period furniture. Among the historic treasures, look out for the portraits of the current generation of Devonshires by Lucian Freud.

The house sits in 25 sq miles of grounds and ornamental gardens, some landscaped by Lancelot 'Capability' Brown. When the kids tire of playing hide-and-seek around the fountains, take them to the **farmyard adventure playground** with loads of ropes, swings and slides, and farmyard critters.

Chatsworth is 3 miles northeast of Bakewell.

THINGS YOU NEED TO KNOW

Chatsworth House (www.chatsworth.org; adult/child house & garden £10.50/6.25, garden only £7.50/4.50; ⊙11am-5.30pm); farmyard adventure playground (admission £5.25)

SPEEDWELL CAVERN

(01433-621888; www.speedwellcavern.co.uk; adult/child £8.25/6.25; ☺10am-5pm, tours hourly till 4pm) About half a mile west of Castleton at the mouth of Winnats Pass, this cave is reached via an eerie boat ride through flooded tunnels, emerging by a huge subterranean lake called the Bottomless Pit.

TREAK CLIFF CAVERN

(☏ 01433-620571; www.bluejohnstone.com; adult/child £7.95/4; ☺10am-5pm, last tour 4.20pm) A short walk across the fields from Speedwell Cavern, Treak Cliff is notable for its forest of stalactites and exposed seams of colourful Blue John Stone, which is still mined to supply the jewellery trade.

Eating & Drinking

Teashops abound in Castleton – probably the most popular purveyor of cream teas and light meals is **Three Roofs Cafe** (The Island; light meals £5-9; ☺10am-5pm), opposite the turn-off to the tourist office.

CASTLE INN   Pub £

(Castle St; mains £5-10) On the road up to the castle, unsurprisingly, with a cosy flagstone lounge bar, an open fire and a decent selection of hearty meals including good Sunday roasts.

ⓘ Getting There & Away

The nearest train station is at Hope, about 3 miles east of Castleton on the line between **Sheffield** and **Manchester**. On summer weekends, a bus runs between Hope station and Castleton to meet the trains, but it's an easy walk.

Bus 173 runs to Bakewell (50 minutes, three daily). From Monday to Saturday, bus 68 goes from **Castleton** to **Buxton** (one hour) in the morning, returning in the afternoon.

Bakewell
POP 3979

The second-largest town in the Peak District, Bakewell lacks the spa-town grandeur of Buxton, but it's still a pretty place to explore and a great base for exploring the White Peak. The town is ring-fenced by famous walking trails and stately homes, but it's probably best known for its famous pudding (of which the Bakewell Tart is just a poor imitation). Bakewell's streets are lined with cute teashops and bakeries, most with 'pudding' in the name.

Sights

Up on the hill above Rutland Sq, **All Saints Church** (☺9am-4.30pm) is packed with ancient features, including a 14th-century font, a pair of Norman arches, some fine heraldic tombs and a collection of crude stone gravestones and crosses dating back to the 12th century.

ⓘ Getting There & Away

Bakewell lies on the popular Transpeak bus route. Buses run hourly to **Buxton** (50 minutes). Five services a day continue to **Manchester** (1¾ hours).

Around Bakewell
Haddon Hall

Glorious **Haddon Hall** (www.haddonhall.co.uk; adult/child £8.95/4.95; ☺noon-5pm, last admission 4pm) looks exactly like a medieval manor house should look – all stone turrets, time-worn timbers and walled gardens. The house was founded in the 12th century, and then expanded and remodelled throughout the medieval period. The 'modernisation' stopped when the house was abandoned in the 18th century, saving Haddon Hall from the more florid excesses of the Victorian period. If the house looks familiar, it's because it was used as a location for the period blockbusters *Jane Eyre* (1996), *Elizabeth* (1998) and *Pride and Prejudice* (2005).

The house is 2 miles south of Bakewell on the A6. You can get here on the Transpeak bus from Bakewell to Matlock and Derby (hourly) or walk along the footpath through the fields, mostly on the east side of the river.

Bath & Southwest England

In England's southwest the past is ever present. This is the perfect region for close encounters with iconic stone circles and ancient Roman ruins, for admiring blockbuster stately homes and romantic castles, or marvelling at serene cathedrals and sumptuous Georgian cityscapes. Meanwhile, the landscape immerses you in the legends of King Arthur, the myths of Alfred the Great, and the literary worlds of Thomas Hardy, Jane Austen and Daphne du Maurier.

But the southwest also has an eye to the future. Here you can enjoy pioneering restaurants, stylish boutique hotels and cool surfer hang-outs. Then there are the pioneering eco-projects, wildlife-rich national parks, fossil-studded shores, and a coastline flecked with exquisite bays, towering rock formations and tranquil sweeps of sandy beach. All this gives you a bit of a dilemma – with the southwest it's not so much 'why go?', as 'what to do first?'.

Roman Baths complex, Bath (p186)

Bath & Southwest England

52°N

*St George's
Channel*

Strumble
Head ▲

Fishguard ● Preseli
Hills

Whitesands
Bay ▲ A40

Ramsey Ramsey
Newgale

A478

Cardigan ●

Carmarthen ●

A48

Black
Mountains ▲

*St Brides
Bay*

Grassholm
Island Skomer

Skokholm
Freshwater
West

● Haverfordwest
A4076

Pembroke ● Tenby ●

Stackpole
Head

Caldey

*Carmarthen
Bay*

Llanelli ●
A48

Swansea ◎

Gower
Peninsula ●

Mumbles ●

Port
Talbot ●

A485

A483

A40

Ilfracombe ●
Croyde ●

Lynton ● Porlock ●
Doone
Valley

Exmoor
National
Park ♦

Braunton ●

*Lundy
Island*

*Barnstaple
Bay*

Barnstaple ●

A396

Clovelly ●
A39

Bideford ●
A377

Tiverton ●

A386

DEVON

*Bude
Bay*

Bude ●

Okehampton ●

Exeter ◎

Boscastle ●
Tintagel ●

Brown
Willy
(420m) ▲
A30

CORNWALL

Launceston ●

*Range
Danger
Area*

Padstow ●

Wadebridge ●

Bodmin ●

Newquay Airport ✈

Newquay ●
Perranporth ●

St Agnes ●

③ *Eden
Project* ◎

St Austell ●

*Lanhydrock
House*

*Restormel
Castle*

Liskeard ●

Polperro ●
Polruan ●

Tavistock ●

*Dartmoor
National Park* ♦

A38

Torquay ●
Torbay

Totnes ●
Paignton ●

Dartmouth ●

Plymouth ◎
A379

*Whitsand
Bay*

⑥

Redruth ●
Camborne ●

Truro ●

Heligan

St Mawes ●

Kingsbridge ●

St Ives ●

Penzance ●
Hayle ●

Land's
End

St Michael's
Mount ⑤

*Mount's
Bay*

*Falmouth
Bay*

Falmouth ●

Minack
Theatre

The
Lizard ●

To Isles
of Scilly
(see inset)

*ATLANTIC

OCEAN*

51°N

50°N

To Isles
of Scilly
(see inset)

Isles of Scilly

St Martin's
*To Penzance
(38mi)*

Tresco
St Mary's

Hugh
Town

Peninnis
Head

0 —————— 10 km

5°W

4°W

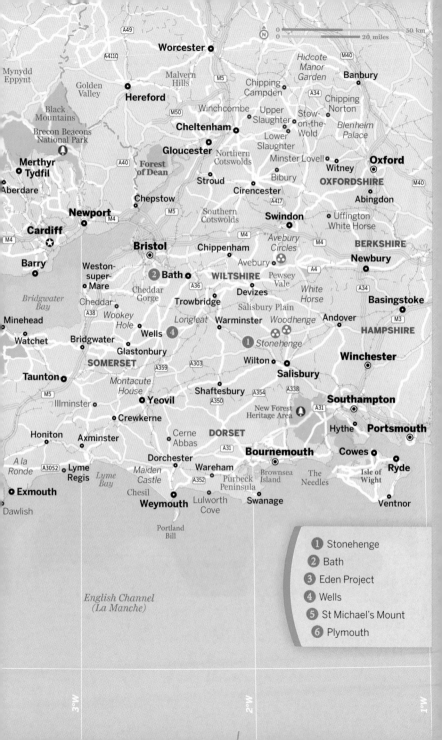

Bath & Southwest England Highlights

Stonehenge

1

The great stone circle of Stonehenge (p178) is Britain's most iconic archaeological site, a compelling ring of monolithic boulders that has been attracting a steady stream of pilgrims, poets and philosophers for the last 5000 years.

Need to Know
LOCATION Near Salisbury, 80 miles southwest of London **TOP TIP** Avoid crowds with an Access Visit **BEST PHOTO OP** Sunrise or sunset **For further coverage, see p178**

Stonehenge Don't Miss List

BY PAT SHELLEY, GUIDE, SALISBURY
& STONEHENGE GUIDED TOURS

1 THE MAIN CIRCLE
Stonehenge covers a fairly large area containing several features, but the focal point is, of course, the main circle of stones, including the distinctive **trilithons** – 'gateways' of two vertical stones with a lintel across the top. I've been running tours here for a few years – for me, nowhere sums up the magic and mystery of ancient Britain better than Stonehenge.

2 INSIDE THE CIRCLE
The main stones are fenced off, and you can't get very close. Many visitors simply turn up, wander around and snap a few photos through the fence. It's worth taking the audio tour or hiring a guide (I would say that, wouldn't I) to make it more than just 'a pile of stones'. Better yet, arrange a **special access tour**, which allows you to actually see inside the main circle.

3 THE SLAUGHTER STONE
Look out for the **Slaughter Stone**, once thought to be a Neolithic altar for human sacrifice. In reality it's a toppled monolith; over the centuries iron ore has mixed with rain in holes in the stone to give the appearance of blood.

4 THE CURSUS & THE AVENUE
I recommend this short walk to see the route to Stonehenge once used by the Neolithic people. Walk northeast along the bridleway from the car park to reach **the Cursus**, a long ditchlike earthwork that runs in an east–west line. Turn right to meet **the Avenue**, an ancient path leading back towards Stonehenge. Watching the giant stones looming up ahead is an unforgettable experience.

5 WOODHENGE & THE BARROWS
About 2 miles northeast of the stone circle, **Woodhenge** is an even older site where archaeologists are still discovering new evidence. There's not much to see, but it was featured on a TV show in the US called *Secrets of Stonehenge*, so many people want to visit. In the area surrounding Woodhenge and Stonehenge, the many hillocks or '**barrows**' are ancient burial mounds.

Bath's Royal Crescent

Often described as Britain's most beautiful city, it's no surprise that Bath has been designated a World Heritage Site. Much of the beauty is thanks to two pioneering 18th-century architects, the father and son team of John Wood Sr and John Wood Jr. Their work helped transform Bath from a sleepy spa town to a triumph of the Georgian Age, and the Royal Crescent (p182) is their masterpiece.

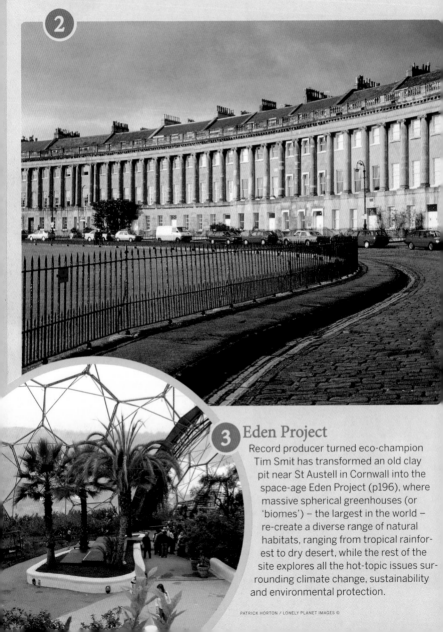

Eden Project

Record producer turned eco-champion Tim Smit has transformed an old clay pit near St Austell in Cornwall into the space-age Eden Project (p196), where massive spherical greenhouses (or 'biomes') – the largest in the world – re-create a diverse range of natural habitats, ranging from tropical rainforest to dry desert, while the rest of the site explores all the hot-topic issues surrounding climate change, sustainability and environmental protection.

Wells

4

The pretty little market town of Wells actually qualifies as England's smallest city, thanks to the magnificent medieval monument of Wells Cathedral (p188), which sits in the centre beside the grand Bishop's Palace – still the ecclesiastical seat of the Bishop of Bath and Wells. Ancient buildings and cobbled streets radiate out from the cathedral green to a marketplace that has been the bustling heart of Wells for some nine centuries.

5

St Michael's Mount

Looming up from the sea near the historic town of Penzance, the unmistakeable silhouette of St Michael's Mount (p197) is one of Cornwall's most iconic landmarks: a 12th-century abbey set on a craggy island connected to the mainland by a cobbled causeway covered at high tide. Highlights include the original armoury, the priory church and the abbey's sub-tropical gardens, which teeter dramatically above the waters. Causeway across to St Michael's Mount

6

Plymouth

In a region famous for picturesque gems, Plymouth stands out – but for an entirely different reason. There's no two ways about it, this place is a rough diamond. The gritty port is unappealing, but under the surface you'll find a rich nautical history: Sir Francis Drake famously spied the Spanish Armada from Plymouth Hoe (p191) in 1588, and the Pilgrim Fathers' *Mayflower* set sail for America from here in 1620. Smeaton's Tower (p192)

© TTL IMAGES / ALAMY

Bath & Southwest England's Best…

Cathedrals & Abbeys

○ **Salisbury Cathedral** (p177) Perhaps the grandest of all England's cathedrals

○ **Winchester Cathedral** (p174) Plain on the outside, but the interior is awe-inspiring

○ **Wells Cathedral** (p188) An oft-overlooked medieval gem

○ **Bath Abbey** (p181) The last great medieval church raised in England

○ **Glastonbury Abbey** (p189) Evocative ruins and burial place of mythical King Arthur

Iconic Landmarks

○ **St Michael's Mount** (p197) Cornwall's unique island-topped abbey, star of a thousand local postcards

○ **Glastonbury Tor** (p190) Focal point for numerous ancient and New Age myths, with stunning views

○ **The Eden Project** (p196) The world's largest greenhouses are as impressive as the tropical forests they contain

○ **Royal Crescent** (p182) The epitome of Georgian architecture in the beautiful city of Bath

Literary & Artistic Links

○ **St Ives** (p195) Home to the Tate Gallery's southwest outpost, and former home of sculptor Barbara Hepworth

○ **Jane Austen's Bath** (p181) Walk the streets of Bath, and you'll find little changed since Austen described them in books such as *Persuasion* and *Northanger Abbey*

○ **Agatha Christie's Greenway** (p191) The crime writer's summer hideaway

○ **King Arthur's Round Table** (p172) The stuff of legend, and a highlight of any visit to Winchester

Historic Sites

○ **Tintagel** (p194) Evocative clifftop castle ruins

○ **Mayflower Steps** (p192) The Pilgrim Fathers' 1620 departure point, in the Barbican

○ **Stonehenge** (p178) Britain's iconic prehistoric site

○ **Avebury** (p184) Southwest England's other great stone circle

Need to Know

ADVANCE PLANNING

○ **Two months before** Book hotels in popular spots; reserve a Special Access Visit at Stonehenge

○ **One month before** Arrange car hire and tickets for longer train journeys

○ **Two weeks before** Check opening times and ticket availability for key sights, such as the Roman Baths in Bath

RESOURCES

The key cities and areas in this region have useful information websites for travellers:

○ **Southwest England** (www.visitsouthwest.com)

○ **Bath** (www.visitbath.co.uk)

○ **Somerset** (www.visitsomerset.co.uk)

○ **Wiltshire** (www.visitwiltshire.co.uk)

○ **Hampshire** (www.visit-hampshire.co.uk)

○ **Devon** (www.visitdevon.co.uk)

○ **Cornwall** (www.visitcornwall.com)

GETTING AROUND

○ **Bus** Long-distance buses between main centres are good; local buses are infrequent in some rural areas

○ **Train** Connections between the major towns are fast and frequent

○ **Car** Easiest way of getting around the region, but cities and main motorways can get heavy with traffic. Popular spots such as Bath and Salisbury have Park & Ride systems: safely park your car on the outskirts, then take a shuttle bus into the centre.

BE FOREWARNED

○ **High season** The southwest counties (especially Devon and Cornwall) are prime holiday areas. British schools close for summer in July and August and thousands of families head for the beach.

○ **Bath** In summer, crowds are a fact of life in Bath; Spring and autumn are much less hectic

○ **Minor roads** Many of the southwest's minor roads are narrow, winding and tricky to navigate if you're more used to wide streets and open freeways

rt: Castle ruins, Tintagel (p194);
ove: St Michael's Mount (p197)

Bath & Southwest England Itineraries

Our suggested three-day loop from Bath takes in two spectacular medieval cathedral towns and the prehistoric icon of Stonehenge. The five-day trip saunters through the southwest, via the key highlights.

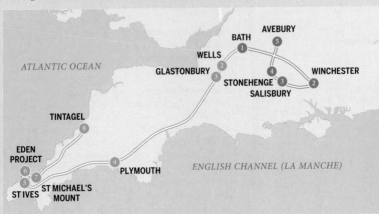

BATH TO BATH
History & Prehistory

3 DAYS

Start your tour in the beautiful city of **(1) Bath**. A day here should include a visit to the Roman Baths, which give the city its name – go early or late in the day to avoid the crowds. Other sights include Bath Abbey and the fabulous Georgian architecture around the centre, especially the Royal Crescent and the nearby Circus.

On your second day, head eastwards to **(2) Winchester**. The highlight here is undoubtedly the awe-inspiring Winchester Cathedral, but if time allows take in the Great Hall to see King Arthur's mythical Round Table.

Next stop is **(3) Salisbury**. There are very few structures that can top Winchester for grace and beauty, but one of them is Salisbury Cathedral – it's slender spire is an icon of the city and visible for miles around.

Just up the road is another iconic British sight, the prehistoric stone circle of **(4) Stonehenge**. If you're without a car, take a tour there from Salisbury. If you're driving, stop here on the way back to Bath. True fans of Ancient Britain might like to divert via the southwest's other great stone circle at **(5) Avebury** – even bigger than Stonehenge, and with a pub in the middle!

BATH TO ST IVES
A Southwest Saunter

5 DAYS

Start your tour with a couple of days in **(1) Bath**, admiring the elegant architecture and historic sites, then head south to the little city of **(2) Wells**, where the star of the show is the medieval gem of Wells Cathedral.

It's then a short hop to **(3) Glastonbury**, famous for its festival and home to mystical Glastonbury Tor, the site of King Arthur's grave and the court of the faery king, among other theories.

Head deeper southwest by crossing into Devon, famous for its lush farmland and cream teas. On the coast, the port town of **(4) Plymouth** isn't pretty, but the 1620 departure point of the Pilgrim Fathers,

marked today by the Mayflower Steps, is an evocative spot.

Final stop is the scenic holiday resort of **(5) St Ives**. Base yourself here for the last day or two of your tour, visiting the town's numerous galleries, lounging on the beach or maybe even surfing. Nearby are several more highlights, all making good day trips: the eco-spectacular **(6) Eden Project**, the iconic abbey and island of **(7) St Michael's Mount**, and the ruined castle of **(8) Tintagel**, for spectacular clifftop views and yet more King Arthur links.

Avebury Stone Circle (p184)

Discover Bath & Southwest England

HAMPSHIRE & WILTSHIRE

Winchester

POP 41,420

Calm, collegiate Winchester is a mellow must-see for all visitors. The past still echoes strongly around the flint-flecked walls of this ancient cathedral city. It was the capital of Saxon kings and a power base of bishops, and its statues and sights evoke two of England's mightiest myth-makers: Alfred the Great and King Arthur (he of the round table). Winchester's architecture is exquisite, from the handsome Elizabethan and Regency buildings in the narrow winding streets to the wondrous cathedral (p174) at its core.

 Sights

THE ROUND TABLE & GREAT HALL   Historic Artefact
(Castle Ave; suggested donation adult/child £1/50p; ⏰10am-5pm)
Winchester's other showpiece sight (after the cathedral) is the cavernous Great Hall, the only part of 11th-century Winchester Castle that Oliver Cromwell spared from destruction. Crowning the wall like a giant-sized dartboard of green and cream spokes is what centuries of mythology have dubbed King Arthur's Round Table. It's actually a 700-year-old copy, but is fascinating nonetheless. It's thought to have been constructed in the late 13th century and then painted in the reign of Henry VIII (King Arthur's image is unsurprisingly reminiscent of Henry's youthful face).

This hall was also the stage for several dramatic English courtroom dramas,

Harbour, St Ives (p195)
PHOTOGRAPHER: DOUG MCKINLAY / LONELY PLANET IMAGES ©

including the trial of Sir Walter Raleigh in 1603, who was sentenced to death but received a reprieve at the last minute.

FREE **WOLVESEY CASTLE** Castle
(EH; www.english-heritage.org.uk; ☉10am-5pm Apr-Sep) The fantastic, crumbling remains of early-12th-century Wolvesey Castle huddle in the protective embrace of the city's walls, despite the building having been largely demolished in the 1680s. It was completed by Henry de Blois, and it served as the Bishop of Winchester's residence throughout the medieval era. Queen Mary I and Philip II of Spain celebrated their wedding feast here in 1554. According to legend, its odd name comes from a Saxon king's demand for an annual payment of 300 wolves' heads. Access is via College St. Today the bishop lives in the (private) **Wolvesey Palace** next door.

 ## Tours

Guided Walks History
(adult/child £4/free; ☉11am & 2.30pm Mon-Sat Apr-Oct, 11am Sat Nov-Mar) Tourist office–run, 1½ hour, heritage-themed walks that include Jane Austen's Winchester, Ghost Walks and Canons and Courtesans.

 ## Sleeping

WYKEHAM ARMS Historic Inn ££
(☎01962-853834; www.fullershotels.com; 75 Kingsgate St; s/d/ste £70/119/150; **P**☎) At 250-odd years old, the Wykeham is bursting with history – it used to be a brothel and also put up Nelson for a night (some say the two events coincided). Creaking, winding stairs lead to the cosy, traditionally styled bedrooms above the pub, while sleeker rooms (over the converted post office, opposite) look out onto a pocked-sized courtyard garden.

5 CLIFTON TERRACE
Boutique B&B ££
(☎01962-890053; cliftonterrace@hotmail.co.uk; 5 Clifton Tce; s/d/f £60/70/110; **P**☎) Blending old and new, this tall Georgian town

house sees plush furnishings rub shoulders with antiques, and modern comforts coexist alongside claw-foot baths. The owners are utterly charming.

DOLPHIN HOUSE B&B ££
(☎01962-853284; www.dolphinhousestudios. co.uk; 3 Compton Rd; s/d £55/70; **P**☎) At this kind of B&B, plus your continental breakfast is delivered to a compact kitchen – perfect for lazy lie-ins. The terrace, complete with cast-iron tables and chairs, overlooks a gently sloping lawn.

 ## Eating

CHESIL RECTORY English ££
(☎01962-851555; www.chesilrectory.co.uk; 1 Chesil St; mains £16; ☉lunch & dinner Mon-Sat, lunch Sun) Duck through the hobbit-sized door, settle down amid the 15th-century beams and savour perfectly prepared modern British cuisine, cooked up by the former head chef at Fortnum & Mason.

BLACK RAT English ££
(☎01962-844465; www.theblackrat.co.uk; 88 Chesil St; mains £17-20; ☉dinner daily, lunch Sat & Sun) Worn wooden floorboards and warm red-brick walls give this relaxed restaurant a cosy feel.

WYKEHAM ARMS English ££
(☎01962-853834; www.fullershotels.com; 75 Kingsgate St; mains £10-17; ☉lunch & dinner Mon-Sat, lunch Sun; ☎) The food at this super-quirky pub is legendary – try the pan-fried salmon, or sausages flavoured with local bitter, then finish off with some seriously addictive sticky toffee pudding.

 ## Drinking

BLACK BOY Pub
(www.theblackboypub.com; 1 Wharf Hill; ☉noon-11pm, to midnight Fri & Sat) This adorable old boozer is filled with obsessive and sometimes freaky collections: from pocket watches to wax facial features; bear traps to sawn-in-half paperbacks. It's located just south of the Black Rat restaurant.

THOMAS WINZ / LONELY PLANET IMAGES ©

Don't Miss **Winchester Cathedral**

Almost 1000 years of history are crammed into Winchester's cathedral, which is not only the city's star attraction but one of southern England's most awe-inspiring buildings. The exterior, with a squat tower and a slightly sunken rear, isn't at first glance appealing, despite a fine Gothic facade. But the interior contains one of the longest **medieval naves** (164m) in Europe, and a fascinating jumble of features from all eras.

The cathedral sits beside foundations that mark the town's original 7th-century minster church. The cathedral was begun in 1070 and completed in 1093, and was subsequently entrusted with the bones of its patron saint, St Swithin (bishop of Winchester from 852 to 862). He is best known for the proverb that states that if it rains on St Swithin's Day (15 July) it will rain for a further 40 days and 40 nights.

Soggy ground and poor workmanship spelled disaster for the early church; the original tower collapsed in 1107 and major restructuring continued until the mid-15th century. Look out for the monument at the rear to diver William Walker, who saved the cathedral from collapse by delving repeatedly into its waterlogged underbelly from 1906 to 1912 to bolster rotting wooden foundations with vast quantities of concrete and brick.

The transepts are the most original parts of the cathedral, and the intricately carved **medieval choir stalls** are another must-see, sporting everything from mythical beasts to a mischievous green man.

Cathedral body tours last one hour. **Tower and roof tours** see you clambering up narrow stairwells, and being rewarded with fine views as far as the Isle of Wight.

THINGS YOU NEED TO KNOW

Cathedral (www.winchester-cathedral.org.uk; adult/child £6/free, combined admission & tower tour £9; ⊙9am-5pm Mon-Sat, 12.30-3pm Sun); cathedral body tours (free; ⊙hourly 10am-3pm Mon-Sat); tower and roof tours (£6; ⊙tours at 2.15pm Wed & Sat, plus 11.30am Sat)

Information

Tourist office (📞 01962-840500; www.visitwinchester.co.uk; High St; ⊙ 10am-5pm Mon-Sat plus 11am-4pm Sun May-Sep)

Getting There & Away

BUS Regular, direct National Express buses shuttle to **London Victoria** (£14.40, 1¾ hours). Stagecoach Explorer Tickets (adult/child £8/6) cover Winchester and Salisbury.

TRAIN Trains leave every 30 minutes for **London Waterloo** (£26, 1¼ hours).

Salisbury

POP 43,335

The gracious city of Salisbury is centred on a majestic cathedral that's topped by the tallest spire in England. It's been an important provincial city for more than a thousand years, and its streets form an architectural timeline ranging from medieval walls and half-timbered Tudor town houses to Georgian mansions and Victorian villas. Salisbury is also a lively, modern town, boasting plenty of bars, restaurants and terraced cafes, as well as a concentrated cluster of excellent museums.

Sights

CATHEDRAL CLOSE Significant Area

Salisbury's medieval cathedral close, a tranquil enclave surrounded by beautiful houses, has an other-worldly feel. Many of the buildings date from the same period as the cathedral, although the area was heavily restored during an 18th-century clean-up by James Wyatt.

The close is encircled by a sturdy outer wall, constructed in 1333; the stout gates leading into the complex are still locked every night. Just inside narrow High St Gate is the **College of Matrons**, founded in 1682 for widows and unmarried daughters of clergymen. South of the cathedral is the **Bishop's Palace**, now the private Cathedral School, parts of which date back to 1220.

Tours

Salisbury Guides   Heritage Tours

(www.salisburycityguides.co.uk; adult/child £4/2; ⊙ 11am Apr-Oct, 11am Sat & Sun Nov-Mar) Ninety-minute trips leave from the tourist office.

Salisbury Guided Tours   Guided Tours

(📞 0777 567 48 16; www.salisburyguidedtours.com; from £65 per group) Tours of Salisbury and the surrounding area.

Sleeping

ST ANNS HOUSE   Boutique B&B ££

(📞 01722-335657; www.stannshouse.co.uk; 32 St Ann St; s/d £60/110) For some perfectly priced indulgence head to this sumptuous town house which overflows with antiques, fine silk and linen direct from Istanbul. Gourmet breakfasts include beef and chilli sausages, smoked salmon and Parma ham.

ROKEBY GUEST HOUSE   B&B ££

(📞 01722-329800; www.rokebyguesthouse.co.uk; 3 Wain-a-long Rd; s/d from £50/60; P @ 🛜) Fancy furnishings, free-standing baths and bay windows make this B&B stand out from the crowd. The decking overlooking the lawn and the minigym help, too. Rokeby is a mile northeast of the cathedral.

WHITE HART   Hotel ££

(📞 01722-327476; www.mercure-uk.com; St John St; s from £90, d £122-142; P @) This 17th-century coaching inn is the place for a bit of pomp and pampering. Its white porticos face Cathedral Close, the service is appropriately attentive and rooms are suitably swish – the wood-rich four-poster bedrooms are positively opulent.

WEBSTERS   B&B ££

(📞 01722-339779; www.websters-bed-breakfast.com; 11 Hartington Rd; s £45-53, d £60-70; P @ 🛜) Websters' exterior charms include quaint blue shutters and arched windows. Inside it's all flowery wallpaper, patterned duvets, extra tea-tray treats and a genuinely warm welcome. Websters is a mile northwest of the cathedral.

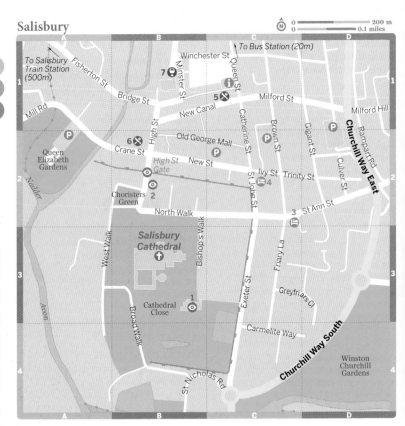

Salisbury

To Salisbury Train Station (500m)

To Salisbury Train Station

To Bus Station (20m)

Winchester St

Fisherton St

Bridge St

Mill Rd

Nadder

Queen Elizabeth Gardens

Crane St

High St

New Canal

Old George Mall

Minster St

Queen St

Catherine St

Milford St

Milford Hill

Brown St

Gigant St

Rampart Rd

Churchill Way East

Culver St

New St

High St Gate

Choristers Green

North Walk

Bishop's Walk

West Walk

Salisbury Cathedral

Cathedral Close

Broad Walk

Avon

St John St

Ivy St

Trinity St

St Ann St

Friary La

Greyfriars Cl

Exeter St

Carmelite Way

Churchill Way South

Winston Churchill Gardens

St Nicholas Rd

Salisbury

✗ Eating & Drinking

LEMON TREE English ££
(☎01722-333471; www.thelemontree.co.uk; 92 Crane St; mains £10; ⊗lunch & dinner Mon-Sat) The menu at this tiny eatery is packed with character – how about chicken laced with white wine, butternut squash with Provençal sauce, or crab claw and avocado salad?

BIRD & CARTER Deli £
(3 Fish Row, Market Sq; snacks from £4.50; ⊗8.30am-6pm Mon-Sat, 10am-4pm Sun) Nestling amid 15th-century beams, this deli-cafe blends olde-worlde charm with a tempting array of antipasti, charcuterie and local goodies.

GLENN BEANLAND / LONELY PLANET IMAGES ©

Don't Miss **Salisbury Cathedral**

England is endowed with countless stunning churches, but few can hold a candle to the grandeur and sheer spectacle of Salisbury Cathedral. Built between 1220 and 1258, the cathedral bears all the hallmarks of the early English Gothic style, with an elaborate exterior decorated with pointed arches and flying buttresses, and a sombre, austere interior designed to keep its congregation suitably pious.

Beyond the highly decorative **West Front**, a small passageway leads into the 70m-long nave, lined with handsome pillars of Purbeck stone. In the north aisle look out for a fascinating **medieval clock** dating from 1386, probably the oldest working timepiece in the world.

The **spire**, Salisbury's 123m crowning glory, was added in the mid-14th century, and is the tallest in Britain. It represented an enormous technical challenge for its medieval builders; it weighs around 6500 tons and required an elaborate system of cross-bracing, scissor arches and supporting buttresses to keep it upright. Look closely and you'll see that the additional weight has buckled the four central piers of the nave.

The cathedral **chapter house** is home to one of only four surviving original copies of the **Magna Carta**, the historic agreement made between King John and his barons in 1215 that acknowledged the fundamental principle that the monarch was not above the law. It's an evocative document; beautifully written and remarkably well-preserved.

For jaw-dropping views across the city and surrounding countryside, take a 90-minute **tower tour** up 332 vertigo-inducing steps to the base of the spire. Bookings are required.

THINGS YOU NEED TO KNOW

Cathedral (www.salisburycathedral.org.uk; requested donation adult/child £5/3; ⊙7.15am-6.15pm); chapter house (⊙10am-4.30pm Mon-Sat, 12.45-4.30pm Sun); tower tours (☏01722-555156; adult/child £8.50/6.50; ⊙1-4pm)

ONE English ££

(☎01722-411313; www.haunchofvenison.
uk.com; 1 Minster St; mains £9-13; ☺lunch &
dinner) Sloping floors, slanting beams
and fake pony-hide chairs surround
you in this chic eatery, located above
the Haunch of Venison pub. The menu
is equally eclectic, featuring mustard-
rubbed pork chops, duck mousse with
red onion marmalade and, yes: a haunch
of venison (with garlic mash).

HAUNCH OF VENISON Heritage Pub

(www.haunchofvenison.uk.com; 1 Minster St)
Featuring wood-panelled snugs, spiral
staircases and wonky ceilings, this 14th-
century drinking den is packed with
atmosphere – and ghosts.

ℹ Information

Tourist office (☎01722-334956; www.
visitwiltshire.co.uk/salisbury; Fish Row, Market
Sq; ☺9.30am-6pm Mon-Sat, 10am-4pm Sun Jun-
Sep, 9.30am-5pm Mon-Sat Oct-Apr)

ℹ Getting There & Away

BUS National Express operates coaches to
London via Heathrow (£16, three hours, three
daily), and **Bath** (£10, 1¼ hours, one daily).
TRAIN Trains run half-hourly from **London
Waterloo** (£32, 1½ hours) and hourly to **Exeter**
(£27, two hours) and further west. Another line
provides hourly connections to **Bath** (£8, one
hour).

Stonehenge

This compelling ring of monolithic **stones**
(EH; ☎01980-624715; www.english-heritage.org.
uk; adult/child £6.90/3.50; ☺9am-7pm Jun-Aug,
9.30am-6pm Mar-May & Sep-Oct, 9.30-4pm Oct-
Feb) has been attracting a steady stream
of pilgrims, poets and philosophers for
the last 5000 years and is Britain's most
iconic archaeological site.

Despite the constant flow of traffic
from the main road that runs beside the
monument, and the huge numbers of
intrigued visitors who traipse around the
perimeter on a daily basis, Stonehenge
still manages to be a mystical, ethereal

place – a haunting echo from Britain's forgotten past, and a reminder of the people who must have once walked the many ceremonial avenues across Salisbury Plain. Even more intriguingly, Stonehenge is still one of Britain's great archaeological mysteries. Despite the countless theories about what the site was originally used for – ranging from a sacrificial centre to a celestial timepiece – in truth, no one really knows for sure what drove prehistoric Britons to expend so much time and effort on its construction.

The Site

The first phase of construction at Stonehenge started around 3000 BC, when the outer circular bank and ditch were erected. A thousand years later, an inner circle of granite stones, known as bluestones, was added. It's thought that these mammoth 4-ton blocks were hauled from the Preseli Mountains in South Wales, some 250 miles away – an almost inexplicable feat for Stone Age builders equipped with only the simplest of tools. Although no one is entirely sure how the builders transported the stones so far, it's thought they probably used a system of ropes, sledges and rollers fashioned from tree trunks – Salisbury Plain was still covered by forest during Stonehenge's construction.

Around 1500 BC, Stonehenge's main stones were dragged to the site, erected in a circle and crowned by massive lintels to make the trilithons (two vertical stones topped by a horizontal one). The sarsen (sandstone) stones were cut from an extremely hard rock found on the Marlborough Downs, 20 miles from the site. It's estimated that dragging one of these 50-ton stones across the countryside would require about 600 people.

Also around this time, the bluestones from 500 years earlier were rearranged

179

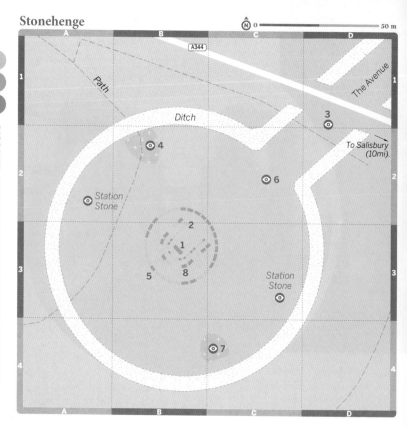

as an inner **bluestone horseshoe** with an **altar stone** at the centre. Outside this the **trilithon horseshoe** of five massive sets of stones was erected. Three of these are intact; the other two have just a single upright. Then came the major **sarsen circle** of 30 massive vertical stones, of which 17 uprights and six lintels remain.

Much further out, another circle was delineated by the 58 **Aubrey Holes**, named after John Aubrey, who discovered them in the 1600s. Just inside this circle are the **South and North Barrows**, each originally topped by a stone.

Prehistoric pilgrims would have entered the site via the **Avenue**, whose entrance to the circle is marked by the **Slaughter Stone** and the **Heel Stone**, located slightly further out on one side.

Stonehenge

◉ Sights

A marked pathway leads around the site, and although you can't walk freely in the circle itself, it's possible to see the stones fairly close up. An audioguide is included in the admission price, and can be obtained from the tourist office, which is 50m north of the main circle.

Tours

The **Stonehenge Tour** (☎01722-336855; www.thestonehengetour.info; return adult/child £11/5) leaves Salisbury's railway and bus stations half-hourly in June and August, and hourly between September and May. Tickets last all day. For guided tours, try **Salisbury Guided Tours** (☎0777 567 48 16; www.salisburyguidedtours.com; from £65 per group).

Getting There & Around

BUS No regular buses go to the site. For tours, see above.

TAXI Taxis charge £35 to go to the site from Salisbury, wait for an hour and come back.

BATH & SOMERSET
Bath
POP 90,144

Ask any visitor for their ideal image of an English city, and chances are they'll come up with something pretty close to Bath – an architectural icon, cultural trendsetter and fashionable haunt for the last 300 years.

This honey-stoned city is especially renowned for its architecture: along its stately streets you'll find a celebrated set of Roman bathhouses (p186), a grand medieval abbey and some of the finest Georgian terraces anywhere in England (in fact, Bath has so many listed buildings the entire place has been named a World Heritage Site by Unesco).

Throw in some fabulous restaurants, gorgeous hotels and top-class shopping (especially since the arrival of the new Southgate shopping centre), and you have a city that demands your undivided attention. Just don't expect to dodge the crowds.

Sights

BATH ABBEY   Church
(www.bathabbey.org; requested donation £2.50; ☺9am-6pm Mon-Sat Easter-Oct, to 4.30pm Nov-Easter, 1-2.30pm & 4.30-5.30pm Sun year-round) King Edgar was crowned in a church in Abbey Courtyard in 973 – though he had ruled since 959 – but the present Bath Abbey was built between 1499 and 1616, making it the last great medieval church raised in England. The nave's wonderful fan vaulting was erected in the 19th century.

Outside, the most striking feature is the west facade, where angels climb up and down stone ladders, commemorating a dream of the founder, Bishop Oliver King.

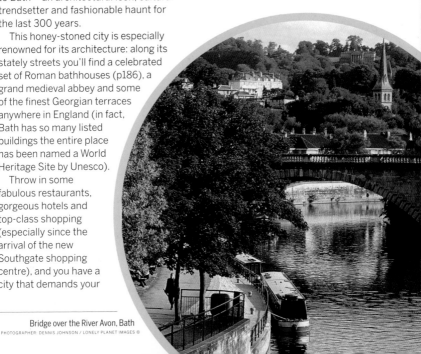

Bridge over the River Avon, Bath
PHOTOGRAPHER: DENNIS JOHNSON / LONELY PLANET IMAGES ©

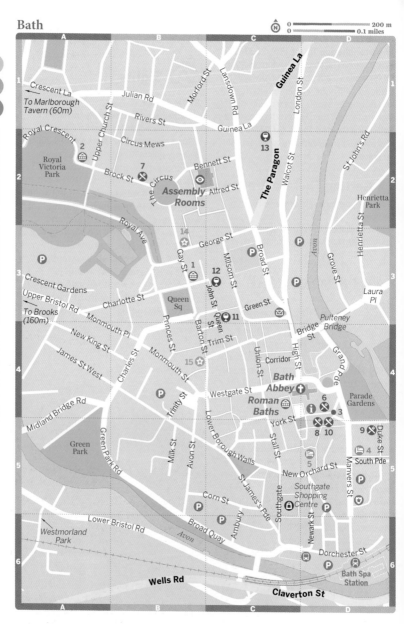

ROYAL CRESCENT & THE CIRCUS

Historic Area

Bath has so many listed buildings that the entire city has been named a World Heritage Site by Unesco. The city's crowning glory is the Royal Crescent, a semicircular terrace of majestic houses overlooking a private lawn and the green sweep of Royal Victoria Park. Designed by John Wood the Younger (1728–82) and built between 1767 and 1775, the houses would have

Bath

originally been rented for the season by wealthy socialites.

For a glimpse into the splendour and razzle-dazzle of Georgian life, head for **No 1 Royal Crescent** (www.bath-preservation-trust.org.uk; adult/child £6/2.50; ⊘10.30am-5pm Tue-Sun mid-Feb–mid-Oct, 10.30am-4pm mid-Oct–Dec), given to the city by the shipping magnate Major Bernard Cayzer, and since restored using only 18th-century materials. Among the rooms on display are the drawing room, several bedrooms and the huge kitchen, complete with massive hearth, roasting spit and mousetraps.

A walk east along Brock St from the Royal Crescent leads to the **Circus**, a ring of 30 symmetrical houses divided into three terraces. Plaques on the houses commemorate famous residents such as Thomas Gainsborough, Clive of India and David Livingstone.

FREE ASSEMBLY ROOMS Architecture
(Bennett St; ⊘10.30am-5pm Mar-Oct, 10.30am-4pm Nov-Feb) Opened in 1771, the city's glorious Assembly Rooms were where fashionable Bath socialites once gathered to waltz, play cards and listen to the latest chamber music. You're free to wander around the rooms, as long as they haven't been reserved for a special function. Highlights include the card room, tearoom and the truly splendid ballroom, all of which are lit by their original 18th-century chandeliers.

JANE AUSTEN CENTRE Museum
(www.janeausten.co.uk; 40 Gay St; adult/child £6.50/3.50; ⊘9.45am-5.30pm Apr-Sep, 11am-4.30pm Oct-Mar) Bath is known to many as a location in Jane Austen's novels. *Persuasion* and *Northanger Abbey* were both largely set in the city; the writer visited it many times and lived here from 1801 to 1806. The author's connections with the city are explored at the Jane Austen Centre, where displays also include period costume and contemporary prints of Bath.

 Tours

Bath City Sightseeing Bus Tour
(☎01225-330444; www.city-sightseeing.com; adult/child £10/6; ⊘9.30am-5pm Mar-May, Oct & Nov, to 6.30pm Jun-Sep) Hop-on/hop-off city tour on an open-topped bus. Buses stop every 20 minutes or so at various points around town.

Bizarre Bath Comedy Walk Walking Tour
(☎01225-335124; www.bizarrebath.co.uk; adult/student £8/5; ⊘8pm Mar-Oct) Daft city tour mixing street theatre and live performance. Leaves from outside the Huntsman Inn on North Parade Passage.

Jane Austen's Bath Walking Tour
(☎01225-443000; adult/child £5/4; ⊘11am Sat & Sun) Focuses on the Georgian city and Jane Austen sites. Tours leave from the Abbey Churchyard.

FREE Mayor's Guide Tours Walking Tour
(☎01225-477411; www.thecityofbath.co.uk; ⊘10.30am & 2pm Sun-Fri, 10.30am Sat) Excellent historical tours provided free by The

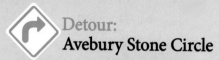

Detour:
Avebury Stone Circle

While the tour buses usually head straight for Stonehenge, prehistoric purists make for the massive stone circle at Avebury. Though it lacks the dramatic trilithons of its sister site across the plain, Avebury is arguably a much more rewarding place to visit. A large section of the village is actually inside the ring of stones; you get much closer to the action than you do at Stonehenge; and it's bigger, older and a great deal quieter. It may also have been a more important ceremonial site, judging by its massive scale and its location at the centre of a complex of barrows, burial chambers and processional avenues.

With a diameter of about 348m, Avebury is the largest stone circle in the world. It's also one of the oldest, dating from around 2500 to 2200 BC, between the first and second phase of construction at Stonehenge. The site originally consisted of an outer circle of 98 standing stones from 3m to 6m in length, many weighing up to 20 tonnes, carefully selected for their size and shape. The stones were surrounded by another circle delineated by a 5.5m-high earth bank and a 6m- to 9m-deep ditch. Inside were smaller stone circles to the north (27 stones) and south (29 stones).

The present-day site represents just a fraction of the circle's original size; many of the stones were buried, removed or broken up during the Middle Ages, when Britain's pagan past became something of an embarrassment to the church. In 1934, wealthy businessman and archaeologist Alexander Keiller supervised the re-erection of the buried stones, and planted markers to indicate those that had disappeared; he later bought the site for posterity using funds from his family's marmalade fortune.

Avebury is about 20 miles north of Stonehenge, just off the main road (A4) between London and Bath.

Mayors Corp of Honorary guides. Leave from outside the Pump Rooms. Extra tours at 7pm on Tuesday, Friday and Saturday May to September.

Sleeping

HALCYON
Hotel ££
(☏ 01225-444100; www.thehalcyon.com; 2/3 South Parade; d £99-125; 🛜) A shabby terrace of old hotels has been knocked through, polished up and totally rein-vented, and the Halcyon is now by far and away the best place in the city centre. It's style on a budget: the lobby is cool and monochrome; off-white rooms have splashes of colour, Philippe Starck bath fittings and White Company smellies; studio rooms even have kitchens. We like it a lot.

BROOKS
Bath ££
(☏ 01225-425543; www.brooksguesthouse.com; 1 & 1a Crescent Gardens; d £69-175; 🛜) On the west side of Bath, this is a plush option, with heritage fixtures blending attrac-tively with snazzy finishes. The owners have tried hard on the details: goosedown duvets, pocket-sprung mattresses, DAB radios and several breakfast spoils, including smoked salmon brioche and homemade muesli.

THREE ABBEY GREEN
B&B ££
(☏ 01225-428558; www.threeabbeygreen.com; 3 Abbey Green; d £85-135; 🛜) Considering the location, this place is a steal – tumble out of the front door and you'll find yourself practically on the abbey's doorstep. It's on a leafy square, and though the rooms lack sparkle, the suites have adjoining singles – ideal for travellers en famille.

APPLETREE GUEST HOUSE
B&B ££

(01225-337642; www.appletreeguesthouse.co.uk; 7 Pulteney Gardens; s £55-66, d £85-110, f £120-132;) It's absolutely tiny, but this welcoming B&B is worth recommending mainly for the sunny disposition of its husband-and-wife owners (Lynsay mainly sticks to the kitchen, while Les is a non-stop fizz of energy). Rooms are small and simple, but very cosy. Street parking is available free if you can find a space.

Eating

CIRCUS
Restaurant ££

(01225-318918; www.thecircuscafeandrestaurant.co.uk; 34 Brock St; lunch mains £5.50-9.70, dinner mains £11-13.90; lunch & dinner) Quite simply, our favourite place to eat in Bath. In a city that's often known for its snootiness, the Circus manages to be posh but not in the slightest pretentious. The attractive town house is steps from the Royal Crescent, and you can choose to eat on the ground floor or the intimate cellar dining room: either way, expect classic Modern British, beautifully presented, at bargain prices.

MARLBOROUGH TAVERN
Gastropub ££

(01225-423731; www.marlborough-tavern.com; 35 Marlborough Buildings; mains £10.95-15.95; lunch & dinner) Bath's best address for a gastrogrub, especially if you like your flavours rich and rustic.

DEMUTH'S
Restaurant ££

(01225-446059; 2 North Parade Passage; mains £9.75-14.25; lunch & dinner) For the last 20-something years this brilliant meat-free bistro has been turning out some of Bath's most creative and imaginative food – from a chive tart made with Devon Blue cheese to a simply divine apricot and fennel tagine.

ONEFISHTWOFISH
Restaurant ££

(01225-330236; 10a North Pde; mains £13-18; dinner Tue-Sun) Piscatarians would do well to plump for this super seafooderie, with cute little tables crammed in under a barrel-brick roof dotted with twinkly lights.

CAFÉ RETRO
Cafe £

(18 York St; mains £5-11; breakfast, lunch & dinner Tue-Sat, breakfast & lunch Mon) The paint-job's scruffy, the crockery's ancient and none of the furniture matches, but that's all part of the charm: this is a cafe

Section of the Avebury Stone Circle

ANDERS BLOMQVIST / LONELY PLANET IMAGES ©

STAEVEN VALLAK / LONELY PLANET IMAGES ©

Don't Miss **Roman Baths**

Ever since the Romans arrived in Bath, life in the city has revolved around the three natural springs that bubble up near the abbey. In typically ostentatious style, the Romans constructed a glorious complex of bathhouses above these thermal waters to take advantage of their natural temperature – a constant 46°C. The buildings were left to decay after the Romans departed and, apart from a few leprous souls who came looking for a cure in the Middle Ages, it wasn't until the end of the 17th century that Bath's restorative waters again became fashionable.

The 2000-year-old baths now form one of the best-preserved ancient Roman spas in the world. The site gets very, very busy in summer; you can usually dodge the worst crowds by visiting early on a midweek morning, or by avoiding July and August. Multilingual audioguides (including an optional one read by the bestselling author Bill Bryson) is included in the price.

The heart of the complex is the **Great Bath**. Head down to water level and along the raised walkway to see the Roman paving and lead base. A series of excavated passages and chambers beneath street level leads off in several directions and lets you inspect the remains of other smaller baths and hypocaust (heating) systems.

One of the most picturesque corners of the complex is the 12th-century **King's Bath**, built around the original sacred spring; 1.5 million litres of hot water still pour into the pool every day. You can see the ruins of the vast **Temple of Sulis-Minerva** under the **Pump Room**, and recent excavations of the **East Baths** give an insight into its 4th-century form.

THINGS YOU NEED TO KNOW

www.romanbaths.co.uk; Abbey Churchyard; adult/child £11.50/7.50, Jul & Aug £12.25/7.50; ⊙9am-8pm Jul & Aug, 9am-6pm Mar, Jun, Sep & Oct, 9.30am-5.30pm Jan, Feb, Nov & Dec, last admission one hour before closing from the old-school, and there's nowhere better for a hearty burger, a crumbly cake or a good old mug of tea.

Sally Lunn's Tearoom £
(4 North Parade Passage; lunch mains £5-6, dinner mains from £8; ⊘ lunch & dinner) Classic chintzy tearoom serving the trademark Sally Lunn's bun.

 Drinking

RAVEN Pub
(Queen St) Highly respected by real ale aficionados, this fine city drinking den commands a devoted following for its well-kept beer and trad atmosphere.

SALAMANDER Pub
(3 John St) The city's bespoke brewery, Bath Ales, owns this place, and you can sample all of their ales here.

STAR INN Pub
(www.star-inn-bath.co.uk; 23 The Vineyards off the Paragon; ☎) Not many pubs are registered relics, but the Star is – it still boasts many of its 19th-century bar fittings.

 **Entertainment**

MOLES Live Music
(www.moles.co.uk; 14 George St; ⊘ 9pm-2am Mon-Thu, to 4am Fri & Sat, 8pm-12.30am Sun) Bath's historic music club has hosted some big names down the years, and it's still the place to catch the hottest breaking acts.

THEATRE ROYAL Theatre
(www.theatreroyal.org.uk; Sawclose) Exclusive theatre featuring major drama, opera and ballet in the main auditorium, experimental productions in the Ustinov Studio, and young people's theatre at 'the egg'.

 **Shopping**

Bath's main shopping district is known as Southgate (www.southgate.com). It's one of the southwest's main meccas for high-street shoppers, with flagship stores for all the major retail names.

The more expensive designer stores and clothes shops are clustered around Milsom St, Milsom Place and Broad St. For quirky shops, vintage clothes and retro furniture, head for the bohemian boutiques dotted along Walcot St.

Bath's oldest shopping landmark is Pulteney Bridge, one of only a handful in the world to be lined by shops. It was built in 1773 and is now Grade-I listed.

ⓘ Information

Bath tourist office (enquiries ☎ 0906-711-2000, accommodation 0844-847-5256; www.visitbath.co.uk; Abbey Churchyard; ⊘ 9.30am-6pm Mon-Sat & 10am-4pm Sun Jun-Sep, 9.30am-5pm Mon-Sat & 10am-4pm Sun Oct-May)

ⓘ Getting There & Away

BUS Bath's **bus and coach station** (⊘ enquiries office 9am-5pm Mon-Sat) is on Dorchester St near the train station. National Express coaches run to **London** (£21.25, 3½ hours, 10 daily) via **Heathrow** (£17.50, 2¾ hours). Services to most other cities require a change at Bristol or Heathrow.

Local bus 173 runs to/from **Wells** (1 hour 10 minutes, hourly Monday to Saturday, seven on Sunday).

TRAIN There are several trains per hour from Bath Spa to **London Paddington** and **London Waterloo** (£22 to £39, 1½ hours, at least hourly), as well as **Cardiff Central** (£15.90, one hour, six to 10 daily).

Wells
POP 10,406

With Wells, small is beautiful. This tiny, picturesque metropolis is England's smallest city, and only qualifies for the 'city' title thanks to a magnificent medieval cathedral, which sits in the centre beside the grand Bishop's Palace. Wells has been the main seat of ecclesiastical power in this part of Britain since the 12th century, and is still the official residence of the Bishop of Bath and Wells. Medieval buildings and cobbled streets radiate out from the cathedral green to a marketplace that has been the bustling heart of Wells for some nine centuries (Wednesday and Saturday are market days).

 Sights

WELLS CATHEDRAL   Church
(www.wellscathedral.org.uk; Chain Gate, Cathedral Green; requested donation adult/child £5.50/2.50; ⊗7am-7pm Apr-Sep, 7am-dusk Oct-Mar) Set in a marvellous medieval close, the Cathedral Church of St Andrew was built in stages between 1180 and 1508. The building incorporates several Gothic styles, but its most famous asset is the wonderful **west front**, an immense sculpture gallery decorated with more than 300 figures, built in the 13th century and restored to its original splendour in 1986. The facade would once have been painted in vivid colours, but has long since reverted to its original sandy hue. Apart from the figure of Christ, installed in 1985 in the uppermost niche, all the figures are original.

Inside, the most striking feature is the pair of **scissor arches** that separate the nave from the choir, designed to counter the subsidence of the central tower. High up in the north transept you'll come across a wonderful **mechanical clock** dating from 1392 – the second-oldest surviving in England after the one at Salisbury Cathedral (p177). The clock shows the position of the planets and the phases of the moon.

Other highlights are the elegant **Lady Chapel** (1326) at the eastern end and the seven effigies of Anglo-Saxon bishops ringing the choir. The 15th-century **chained library** houses books and manuscripts dating back to 1472. It's only open at certain times during the year or by prior arrangement.

From the north transept follow the worn steps to the glorious **Chapter House** (1306), with its delicate ceiling ribs sprouting like a palm from a central column. Externally, look out for the **Chain Bridge** built from the northern side of the cathedral to Vicars' Close to enable clerics to reach the cathedral without getting their robes wet. The cloisters on the southern side surround a pretty courtyard.

Left: Street scene, Wells (p187); **Below:** Ruins of Glastonbury Abbey

PHOTOGRAPHER: (LEFT) GLENN BEANLAND; (BELOW) SHANNON NACE / LONELY PLANET IMAGES ©

Guided tours (⊘Mon-Sat) of the cathedral are free, and usually take place every hour. Regular concerts and cathedral choir recitals are held here throughout the year. You need to buy a permit (£3) from the cathedral shop to take pictures.

Glastonbury

POP 8429

If you suddenly feel the need to get your third eye cleansed or your chakras realigned, then there's really only one place in England that fits the bill: good old Glastonbury, a bohemian haven and centre for New Age culture since the days of the Summer of Love, and still a favourite hangout for hippies, mystics and counter-cultural types of all descriptions. The main street is more Haight Ashbury than Somerset hamlet, with a bewildering assortment of crystal sellers, veggie cafes, mystical bookshops and bong emporiums, but Glastonbury has been a spiritual centre since long before the weekend Buddhists and white witches arrived. It's

supposedly the birthplace of Christianity in England, and several of Britain's most important ley lines are said to converge on nearby Glastonbury Tor.

The town is also famous for the June **Glastonbury Festival** (www.glastonburyfestivals.co.uk), a massive extravaganza of music, dance, spirituality and general all-round weirdness

 Sights

GLASTONBURY ABBEY   Abbey
(www.glastonburyabbey.com; Magdalene St; adult/child £5.50/3.50; ⊘9.30am-6pm or dusk Sep-May, from 9am Jun-Aug) Legend has it that Joseph of Arimathea, great-uncle of Jesus, owned mines in this area and returned here with the Holy Grail (the chalice from the Last Supper) after the death of Christ. Joseph supposedly founded England's first church on the

189

site, now occupied by the ruined abbey, but the earliest proven Christian connection dates from the 7th century, when King Ine gave a charter to a monastery in Glastonbury. In 1184 the church was destroyed by fire; reconstruction began in the reign of Henry II.

In 1191, monks claimed to have had visions confirming hints in old manuscripts that the 6th-century warrior-king Arthur and his wife Guinevere were buried in the abbey grounds. Excavations uncovered a tomb containing a skeletal couple, who were reinterred in front of the high altar of the new church in 1278.

The remaining ruins at Glastonbury mainly date from the church that was built after the 1184 fire. It's still possible to make out some of the nave walls, the ruins of St Mary's chapel, and the remains of the crossing arches, which may have been scissor-shaped, like those in Wells Cathedral. The grounds also contain a small **museum**, cider **orchard** and **herb garden**, as well as the **Holy Thorn tree**, which supposedly sprung from Joseph's staff and mysteriously blooms twice a year, at Christmas and Easter.

GLASTONBURY TOR Landmark

The iconic hump of Glastonbury Tor looms up from the flat fields to the north-west of town.

This 160m-high grassy mound provides glorious views over the surrounding countryside, and is the focal point for a bewildering array of myths. According to some this is the home of a faery king, while an old Celtic legend identifies it as the stronghold of Gwyn ap Nudd (ruler of Annwyn, the Underworld). But the most famous legend identifies the tor as the mythic Isle of Avalon, where King Arthur was taken after being mortally wounded in battle by his nephew Mordred, and where Britain's 'once and future king' sleeps until his country calls again.

Whatever the truth of the legends, the tor has been a site of pilgrimage for many years, and was once topped by the medieval church of **St Michael**, although today only the tower remains.

It takes 45 minutes to walk up and down the tor. Parking is not permitted nearby, but the **Tor Bus** (adult/child £2.50/1.50) leaves from Dunstan's car park near the abbey. The bus runs every 30

Remains of the church of St Michael, Glastonbury Tor

GLENN BEANLAND / LONELY PLANET IMAGES ©

Detour:
Torquay & Agatha Christie

Torquay is the birthplace of the 'Queen of Crime', Agatha Christie (1890–1976), author of 75 novels and 33 plays, and creator of Hercule Poirot, the moustachioed, immodest Belgian detective, and Miss Marple, the surprisingly perceptive busy-body spinster. Born Agatha Miller, she grew up, courted and honeymooned in the resort town of Torquay and also worked as a hospital dispenser here during WWI, thus acquiring her famous knowledge of poisons.

The tourist office stocks the Agatha Christie Mile leaflet (free), which guides you round significant local sites, while **Torquay Museum** (529 Babbacombe Rd, Torquay; adult/child £4/2.50; ⊙10am-5pm Mon-Sat & 1.30-5pm Sun Jul-Sep) has a huge collection of photos, handwritten notes and display cases devoted to her famous detectives. The highlight though is **Greenway**, her summer home near Dartmouth. The **Greenway Ferry** (☎01803-844010; www.greenwayferry.co.uk) sails there from Princess Pier in Torquay, and from Dartmouth and Totnes. Boats sail only when the property is open; times vary and it's best to book.

minutes from 10am to 7.30pm from April to September, and from 10am to 3.30pm from October to March.

Eating & Drinking

RAINBOW'S END   Cafe £
(17a High St; mains £4-7; ⊙10am-4pm) A Glasto classic, this charming wholefood cafe cooks up generous portions of veggie chilli, fresh quiches and hearty soups, served up in a cheery dining room dotted with potted plants and mix-and-match furniture, plus a little patio out back.

WHO'D A THOUGHT IT INN   Pub ££
(17 Northload St; mains £8.25-16.95; ⊙lunch & dinner) In keeping with Glastonbury's outsider spirit, this town pub is brimming with wacky character, from the vintage signs and upside-down bike on the ceiling to the reclaimed red telephone box tucked in one corner.

ⓘ Information

Glastonbury Tourist Office (☎01458-832954; www.glastonburytic.co.uk; The Tribunal, 9 High St; ⊙10am-5pm Apr-Sep, to 4pm Oct-Mar) Stocks maps and accommodation lists, and sells leaflets describing local walks and the *Glastonbury Millennium Trail* (60p).

ⓘ Getting There & Away

Bus 376/377 travels to/from **Wells** (30 minutes, hourly Monday to Saturday, seven on Sundays).

DEVON & CORNWALL
Plymouth
POP 256,633

If parts of Devon are costume dramas or nature programs, Plymouth is a healthy dose of reality TV. Gritty, and certainly not always pretty, its centre has been subjected to buildings even the architects' mothers might question. But despite often being dismissed for its partying, poverty and urban problems, this is a city that's huge in spirit – and it comes with great assets.

Sights

PLYMOUTH HOE   Historic Headland
Francis Drake supposedly spied the Spanish fleet from this grassy strip overlooking Plymouth Sound; the fabled bowling green on which he finished his

191

Plymouth

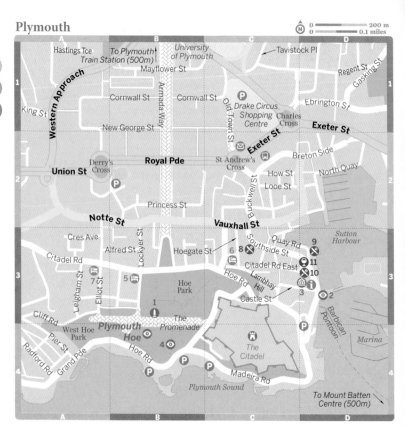

Plymouth

game was probably where his **statue** now stands.

Dominating the scene is the red-and-white-striped former lighthouse, **Smeaton's Tower** (The Hoe; adult/child £2/1; ⊙10am-noon & 1-4pm Tue-Sat Apr-Oct, 10am-noon & 1-3pm Tue-Sat Nov-Mar), which was built 14 miles off shore on the Eddystone Rocks in 1759, then moved to the Hoe in 1882. Climbing its 93 steps provides an illuminating insight into lighthouse keepers' lives and stunning views of the city, Dartmoor and the sea.

BARBICAN   Historic District
(www.plymouthbarbican.com) To get an idea of what old Plymouth was like, head for the Barbican, a district of cobbled streets and Tudor and Jacobean buildings, many now converted into galleries, craft shops and restaurants.

The Pilgrim Fathers' *Mayflower* set sail for America from the Barbican on 16 September 1620. The **Mayflower Steps** mark the point of departure – track down the passenger list displayed on the side of **Island House** nearby. Scores of other famous voyages are also marked by plaques at the steps, including one led by Captain James Cook, who set out from the Barbican in 1768 in search of a southern continent.

PLYMOUTH MAYFLOWER Museum
(3 The Barbican; adult/child £2/1; ⏱10am-4pm daily May-Oct, 10am-4pm Mon-Sat Nov-Apr) Runs through Plymouth's nautical heritage, providing the background to the Pilgrim Fathers' trip via interactive gizmos and multisensory displays.

 Sleeping

BOWLING GREEN Hotel ££
(📞01752-209090; www.bowling greenhotel. co.uk; 10 Osborne Pl; s/d/f £47/68/78; P 📶) Some of the airy cream-and-white rooms in this family-run hotel look out onto the modern incarnation of Drake's famous bowling green.

FOUR SEASONS B&B £
📞01752-223591; www.fourseasons guesthouse.co.uk; 207 Citadel Rd East; s £32-42, d £48-58, f £60) This place is crammed full of treats, from the big bowls of free sweets to the mounds of Devon bacon for breakfast.

JEWELL'S B&B £
(📞01752-254760; www. jewellsguesthouse.com; 220 Citadel Rd; s/d/f £28/50/65) Traces of the Victorian era linger in the high ceilings and ornate plasterwork of this friendly town house.

 Eating

BARBICAN KITCHEN British ££
(📞01752-604448; 60 Southside St; mains £11; ⏱lunch & dinner, closed Sun evening) In this bistro-style restaurant, the stone interior fizzes with bursts of shocking pink and lime. The food is attention grabbing too – try the calves' liver with horseradish mash or the honey, goat's cheese and apple crostini. Their Devon beefburger, with a slab of stilton, is divine.

CAP'N JASPERS Cafe £
(www.capn -jaspers.co.uk; Whitehouse Pier, Quay Rd; snacks £3-5; ⏱7.45am-11.45pm) Unique, quirky and slightly insane, this cabin-kiosk has been delighting bikers, tourists, locals and fishermen for decades with its motorised gadgets and teaspoons attached by chains.

Platters Seafood ££
(12 The Barbican; mains £16; hlunch & dinner) A down-to-earth eatery with fish so fresh

Traditional Cornish pasties

it's just stopped flapping – try the skate in butter or the locally caught sea bass.

DOLPHIN Pub

(14 The Barbican) This wonderfully unreconstructed Barbican boozer is all scuffed tables, padded bench seats and an authentic, no-nonsense atmosphere.

ℹ️ Information

Tourist office (☎ 01752-306330; www.visit plymouth.co.uk; Plymouth Mayflower, 3 The Barbican; ⏰ 9am-5pm Mon-Sat, 10am-4pm Sun Apr-Oct, 9am-5pm Mon-Fri, 10am-4pm Sat Nov-Mar)

ℹ️ Getting There & Away

BUS National Express services include **London** (£33, five to six hours, eight daily) and **Penzance** (£8, three hours, six daily).

TRAIN Services include those to **London** (£40, 3¼ hours, half-hourly), **Bristol** (£32, two hours, two or three per hour) and **Penzance** (£8, two hours, half-hourly).

Tintagel

POP 1822

The spectre of King Arthur looms large over the village of Tintagel and its spectacular clifftop **castle** (EH; ☎ 01840-770328; adult/child £5.20/2.60; ⏰ 10am-6pm Apr-Sep, 10am-5pm Oct, 10am-4pm Nov-Mar). Though the present-day ruins mostly date from the 13th century, archaeological digs have revealed the foundations of a much earlier fortress, fuelling speculation that the legendary king may indeed have been born at the castle, just as local fable claims. Part of the crumbling stronghold stands on a rock tower cut off from the mainland, accessed via a bridge and steep steps, and it's still possible to make out several sturdy walls and much of the castle's interior layout.

The village is awash with touristy shops and tearooms making the most of the King Arthur connection

Tintagel is on the north Devon coast, about 40 miles northwest of St Ives.

St Ives
POP 9870

Sitting on the fringes of a glittering arc-shaped bay, St Ives was once one of Cornwall's busiest pilchard-fishing harbours, but it's better known now as the centre of the county's arts scene. From the old harbour, cobbled alleyways and switchback lanes lead up into the jumble of buzzy galleries, cafes and brasseries that cater for thousands of summer visitors. It makes for an intriguing mix of boutique chic and traditional seaside, and while the high-season traffic can take the shine off things, St Ives is still an essential stop on any Cornish grand tour.

◎ Sights & Activities

TATE ST IVES   Gallery
(☎01736-796226; www.tate.org.uk/stives; Porthmeor Beach; adult/child £5.75/3.25; ◷10am-5pm Mar-Oct, 10am-4pm Tue-Sun Nov-Feb) The artwork almost takes second place to the surroundings at the stunning Tate St Ives, which hovers above Porthmeor Beach. Built in 1993, the gallery contains work by celebrated local artists, including Terry Frost, Patrick Heron and Barbara Hepworth, and hosts regular special exhibitions. On the top floor there's a stylish cafe-bar with some of the best sea views in St Ives. A joint ticket with the **Barbara Hepworth museum** can be purchased (adult/child £8.75/4.50).

BARBARA HEPWORTH MUSEUM & SCULPTURE GARDEN   Museum
(☎01736-796226; www.tate.org.uk/stives; Barnoon Hill; adult/child £5.75/3.25; ◷10am-5pm Mar-Oct, 10am-4pm Tue-Sun Nov-Feb) Barbara Hepworth (1903–75) was one of the leading abstract sculptors of the 20th century, and a key figure in the St Ives art scene; fittingly her former studio has been transformed into a moving archive and museum.

GLENN BEANLAND / LONELY PLANET IMAGES ©

Don't Miss **The Eden Project**

If any one thing is emblematic of Cornwall's regeneration, it's the Eden Project. Ten years ago the site was a dusty, exhausted clay pit, a symbol of the county's industrial decline. Now, thanks to the vision of ex-record producer turned environmental pioneer Tim Smit, it's home to two giant biomes, the largest greenhouses anywhere in the world.

Inside, a huge variety of plants recreate various habitats from dry savannah to tropical rainforest and wild jungle, elegantly illustrating the diversity of life on earth and our own dependence on its continued survival. It's informative, educational and enormous fun, but it does get very busy: booking in advance online will allow you to dodge the worst queues, and also bag a £1 discount.

The Eden Project is about 30 miles east of St Ives, near the town of St Austell, which is on the main train line between London and Penzance; you can catch buses from St Austell to the Eden Project. Last entry is 90 minutes before the site closes.

THINGS YOU NEED TO KNOW

☎ 01726-811911; www.edenproject.com; Bodelva; adult/child/family £16/6/39; ⏰ 10am-6pm Apr-Oct, 10am-4.30pm Nov-Mar

---

Sleeping

PRIMROSE VALLEY   Hotel £££
(☎ 01736-794939; www.primroseonline.co.uk; Porthminster Beach; d £105-155, ste £175-225; P ⁬ 🛜) A swash of style on the St Ives seafront. The rooms of the Edwardian house are all deliberately different: some chase a faintly maritime theme, with pale pine and soothing blues, while others plump for rich fabrics, cappuccino throws and exposed brick.

TRELISKA   B&B ££
(☎ 01736-797678; www.treliska.com; 3 Bedford Rd; d £60-80; 🛜) The smooth decor at this B&B is attractive – chrome taps, wooden

furniture, cool sinks – but what really sells it is the fantastic position, literally steps from St Ives' centre.

 ORGANIC PANDA B&B ££
(🕽01736-793890; www.organicpanda. co.uk; 1 Pednolver Tce; d £80-120; 🛜) Sleep with a clear conscience at this elegant B&B, run along all-organic lines. Spotty cushions, technicolour artwork and timber-salvage beds keep the funk factor high, and local artists showcase their works on the walls.

🍴 Eating

PORTHMINSTER BEACH CAFÉ
Bistro ££
(🕽01736-795352; www.porthminstercafe.co.uk; Porthminster Beach; lunch £10.50-16.50, dinner £10-22; 🕘9am-10pm) Fresh from scooping top prize in a recent survey to find Britain's top coastal cafe, the Porthminster boasts a sexy Riviera vibe, a suntrap patio and a seasonal menu ranging from Provençal fish soup to pan-fried scallops.

ALBA
Restaurant ££
(🕽01736-797222; Old Lifeboat House; mains £11-18; 🕘lunch & dinner) Split-level sophistication next to the lifeboat house, serving some of the best seafood this side of Padstow. In-the-know locals bag tables 5, 6 or 7 for their gorgeous harbour views.

LOFT
Restaurant ££
(🕽01736-794204; www.theloftrestaurantand terrace.co.uk; Norway Ln; dinner £10.95-19.95; 🕘lunch & dinner) Great new tip hidden away in a fisherman's net loft just behind the Sloop Craft Centre.

🍷 Drinking

HUB
Cafe
(www.hub-stives.co.uk; The Wharf) As its name suggests, the open-plan Hub is the heart of St Ives' (admittedly limited) nightlife. Think frothy lattes by day, cocktails and boutique beers after-dark, plus sliding

doors that open onto the harbour when the sun shines.

SLOOP INN
Pub
(The Wharf) A classic fishermen's boozer, complete with low ceilings, tankards behind the bar and a comprehensive selection of Cornish ales.

ℹ️ Information

Tourist office (🕽01736-796297; ivtic@penwith. gov.uk; Street-an-Pol; 🕘9am-5.30pm Mon-Fri, 9am-5pm Sat, 10am-4pm Sun) Inside Guildhall.

ℹ️ Getting There & Away

TRAIN St Ives is at the end of the branch line from **St Erth** (£3, 14 minutes, half-hourly), which is on the main line between London and Penzance. It's worth taking a ride on this line just for the gorgeous coastal views.

St Michael's Mount

Looming up from the waters of Mount's Bay is the unmistakeable silhouette of **St Michael's Mount** (NT; 🕽01736-710507; castle & gardens adult/child £8.75/4.25; 🕘10.30am-5.30pm Sun-Fri late-Mar–Oct), one of Cornwall's most iconic landmarks, set on a craggy island connected to the mainland by a cobbled causeway. There's been a monastery here since at least the 5th century, but the present abbey largely dates from the 12th century. After the Norman conquest, the Benedictine monks of Mont St Michel in Normandy raised a new chapel on the island in 1135, and the abbey later became the family seat of the aristocratic St Aubyns (who still reside here).

It's now under the stewardship of the National Trust. Highlights include the rococo drawing room, the original armoury, the 14th-century priory church and the abbey's subtropical gardens, which teeter dramatically above the sea. You can walk across the causeway at low tide, or catch a ferry at high tide in the summer from the little town of Marazion.

St Michael's Mount is near Penzance, about 8 miles south of St Ives.

York & Northern England

Northern England offers the perfect mix of lively cities and dramatic scenery. The region is dominated by giants such as Manchester and Liverpool, with their industrial foundations, musical heritage, cultural prowess and world-famous football teams. Meanwhile, much older cities like York and Chester tempt visitors with vast medieval cathedrals and cobbled streets of quirky 500-year-old buildings still circled by city walls.

Beyond the cities you'll find a totally different picture: the northern hills have a noticeably wilder edge than the manicured landscape 'down south'. Rolling moors and long slender valleys in the Yorkshire Dales give way to serious mountains in the Lake District, where vistas of lofty peaks, steep hillsides, and of course lakes, provide endless inspiration to hikers, poets and artists alike.

To top it off, in England's far north sits the Roman rampart of Hadrian's Wall, one of the country's most impressive relics from the classical age.

York Minster (p214)

Street in York (p212) and the towers of York Minster

York & Northern England

1. York
2. Grasmere
3. Hadrian's Wall
4. Yorkshire Dales
5. Castle Howard
6. Manchester
7. Liverpool

0° (Greenwich)

2°W
1°W

FIFE

A9 Kinross
Crail

Kirkcaldy

Falkirk
M9
Edinburgh

56°N

A68

A702 Moorfoot Hills

M74

Crookham
Bamburgh
Wooler
Alnwick

Hawick

NORTHUMBERLAND

A697 Rothbury

Moffat
Border Forest Park
Simonside Hills

A74(M)
Northumberland National Park
Morpeth

Dumfries
3 Hadrian's Wall
Newcastle-upon-Tyne

Brampton
Vindolanda Roman Fort & Museum
Housesteads Roman Fort & Museum
Hexham
Segedunum

Solway Firth
Carlisle
The Pennines
Sunderland

CUMBRIA
Seaham
Peterlee

Workington
Penrith
Durham
Hartlepool

Keswick
Kirkby Stephen
Stockton-on-Tees
Middlesbrough

Lake District National Park
A66
Whitby

A595
Keld
Darlington
Grosmont
Robin Hood's Bay

Windermere
2
Leyburn
North York Moors NP
Scarborough

Thirsk
Helmsley

Kendal
Yorkshire Dales National Park
Kilburn
Malton
Bridlington

Barrow-in-Furness
Ingleton
4
Cleveland Hills
Norton
Great Driffield

Barrow Island
Morecambe
Settle
A1
Castle Howard
5

Irish Sea
Lancaster
Skipton
Harrogate

54°N
Ilkley
1 **York**
54°N

M6
Keighley
YORKSHIRE

Blackpool
Haworth
Leeds
Beverley

Preston
Burnley
Selby
Hull

Liverpool Bay
Blackburn
Halifax
Goole

Southport
Bolton
Wakefield
Scunthorpe
M180

Wigan
Huddersfield
Doncaster
Grimsby

Liverpool
7
Manchester
6
Rotherham

Birkenhead
Warrington
Castleton
Sheffield
Gainsborough
A16

Liverpool Airport
Manchester Airport
Buxton
Chesterfield
Lincoln
Burgh le Marsh

Colwyn Bay
Rhyl
Chester
Peak District National Park
Sherwood Forest
Newark-on-Trent

Vale of Conwy
Clwydian Ranges
Dovedale
The Wash

Wrexham
Vale of Llangollen
Stoke-on-Trent
Nottingham
Grantham

Coed-y-Brenin Forest
Berwyn Mountains
A49
A38 Packington
Melton Mowbray

A458
Shrewsbury
Telford
Gailey
M1
A1

Llanidloes
Birmingham
M69
A10

Coventry

North Sea

Isle of Man

Point of Ayre
Bride

Dalby
Douglas

0
20 km

See Isle of Man Inset

York & Northern England Highlights

York

The ancient city of York (p212) is a medieval master-piece, with narrow streets and twisting alleyways en-circled by sturdy city walls, all crowned by the glorious architecture of the Minster. With even older Roman and Viking heritage too, it's not surprising that York is bidding for Unesco World Heritage status. Above: the Shambles (p213)

Need to Know

LOCATION 200 miles from London **BEST PHOTO OP** West face of the Minster, or on the city walls **TOP TIP** Walk slowly and look up to see building features **For more, see p212**

York Don't Miss List

MARK GRAHAM, GUIDE WITH THE ORIGINAL GHOST WALK OF YORK

1 YORK MINSTER

The Minster (p214) is the best-known sight in York, and rightly so. I highly recommend going to the top of the **Lantern Tower** for spectacular views over the medieval streets surrounding the Minster, with the modern city beyond and the North York Moors visible 30 miles away. It's a stiff climb up 275 steps, but well worth the effort.

2 BOOTHAM BAR

In York, a 'bar' is a medieval gateway (pictured bottom left) in the city walls (p213) and **Bootham Bar** is the oldest. To enjoy a great view of the city and a great sense of surrounding history, stop at the cafe in the square in front of **York Art Gallery**, opposite Bootham Bar. Beyond the city walls, you can see the massive towers of the Minster, while just to the right is the old **King's Manor** dating from the 15th century.

3 STROLLING THE STREETS

A great pleasure in York is just walking the old streets, admiring the architecture. My favourite strolls meander through the narrow 'gates' (streets) and 'snickleways' (alleys) from **Stonegate** – an old Roman road and one of the most beautiful streets in the city – to the best-known of York's medieval thoroughfares, the **Shambles** (p213).

4 DRINKING IN HISTORY

Many of York's old pubs have historic links and many are haunted too. My favourites include the **Blue Bell** (top left) on Fossgate and the **Olde Star** on Stonegate. The **King's Arms** is famous as the pub that floods in winter, but its riverside tables are a great meeting spot in the summer.

5 ST MARY'S ABBEY

A beautiful little bit of medieval York that's often overlooked is the ruin of **St Mary's Abbey** (p213), now sitting in the **Museum Gardens** near the Yorkshire Museum, on the western side of the city centre. The abbey dates from the 13th century and was mostly destroyed by Henry VIII in the Dissolution of the Monasteries in 1539.

Grasmere in the Lake District

The Lake District (p233) is one of the most beautiful areas in England, famously associated with William Wordsworth and the poets of the Romantic movement. In the heart of the district sits the pretty village of Grasmere – a centre of all things Wordsworth.

Need to Know

BEST TIME TO VISIT Avoid busy summer weekends **TRANSPORT** Local buses are a great way to travel in the area **LOCAL TREAT** Kendal Mint Cake **For more, see p236**

Grasmere Don't Miss List

BY SALLY ROBINSON OF THE WORDSWORTH TRUST

1 DOVE COTTAGE

The Romantic poets came to the Lake District for inspiration, and it's easy to see why. The whole region has a magical quality, and I love living here. In Grasmere I recommend a visit to **Dove Cottage** (pictured top left; p237), the first house in the Lake District occupied by William Wordsworth as an adult. He wrote some of his most famous poetry here and it's pretty much as he left it. The guided tours are really entertaining. Attached is the **Wordsworth Museum** with artefacts and manuscripts on display, and frequently changing exhibitions relating to the man himself and other Romantic poets.

2 ST OSWALD'S CHURCH

Many visitors come here to pay homage at Wordsworth's grave, but Grasmere's little **Church of St Oswald** (p237) is lovely on the inside, and worth a look.

3 RYDAL MOUNT

Just down the road from Grasmere, you can visit **Rydal Mount** (p239), the house where Wordsworth lived for 37 years with his wife, sister and children. Echoing the famous flowers of his best-known poem, Wordsworth planted a field of daffodils here in memory of his eldest daughter Dora, who died of tuberculosis.

4 WALKING

There are enough hills in the Lake District to fill a lifetime of walking, but my favourite is **Helm Crag**. Known locally as the 'Lion and the Lamb' after two distinctive rocks at the summit, it's a steep walk up from Grasmere but the views are worth it! For a flatter option, I love the walk round **Grasmere Lake**; my tip is to go clockwise for a great view of Helm Crag.

5 GRASMERE GINGERBREAD

Along with its Romantic connections, Grasmere is also famous for its gingerbread, made to a secret recipe in the village for almost 150 years. Buy some at **Sarah Nelson's Gingerbread Shop** (pictured bottom left; p237) to take on your walk. It's different to gingerbread you may've tasted elsewhere – sticky, crumbly and crunchy all at the same time. Delicious!

Hadrian's Wall Forts & Battlements

The awesome engineering project of Hadrian's Wall (p241) stretches for 117km across the north of England. The main feature is the wall itself, and you can walk beside it for a mile or more as it strides across the landscape. Along the wall, several of the original garrison forts are still standing, including wonderful examples at Vindolanda and Housesteads, offering a unique insight into the day-to-day world of Roman Britain. Vindolanda Roman fort (p244)

Yorkshire Dales Hiking & Biking

The green valleys, high hills and limestone escarpments and 'pavements' of the Yorkshire Dales (p217) have been a magnet for fans of the great outdoors for many years. With a network of track and trails, this is the place to go for a walk, or rent a mountain bike, and shake off city life for an hour or two – or even a day or two.

GLENN VAN DER KNIJFF / LONELY PLANET IMAGES ©

Castle Howard

The finest stately home in the north of England, and one of the best in the whole of Britain, the palatial edifice of Castle Howard (p213) was designed by the architect Sir John Vanbrugh for the third earl of Carlisle in the early 18th century, and it set the baroque benchmark for everyone else to follow. Surrounded by gardens and parkland, this is the quintessential English country estate.

Manchester

Like many of northern England's cities, Manchester (p226) has enjoyed a new lease of life in recent years. One of its most interesting new additions is the striking Imperial War Museum North, designed in typically imaginative style by the American architect Daniel Liebeskind. For many, the city's key attraction is a structure of a different kind: Old Trafford football stadium, home to Manchester United. Exchange Square

Liverpool

Forever famous as the birthplace of The Beatles, and still with a healthy Fab Four heritage industry, the city of Liverpool (p219) is only now rediscovering and celebrating its (sometimes glorious, sometimes harsh) maritime past, spearheaded by a major renaissance on the Victoria & Albert Waterfront, home to several fine museums, hotels and restaurants, and a clutch of classic old buildings. John Lennon statue, Cavern Quarter (p223)

York & Northern England's Best…

Cities

o **Manchester** (p226) England's second city and capital of the north, with world-class museums and galleries

o **Liverpool** (p219) Once down-at-heel, now revitalised, celebrating a rich musical heritage and maritime past

o **York** (p212) History served up in spades in this medieval epicentre, with Viking and Roman foundations

o **Chester** (p230) A fine collection of historic buildings, second only to York

Cathedrals & Abbeys

o **Liverpool Cathedral** (p221) 'If you want a cathedral, we've got one to spare' goes the song – and both are fabulous

o **York Minster** (p214) Vast and awe-inspiring, the zenith of medieval church construction

o **Chester Cathedral** (p231) Ancient abbey and church with a Victorian facelift in rose-pink sandstone

o **Fountains Abbey** (p219) Picturesque ruins and beautiful water gardens – a breathtaking picture of elegance and tranquillity

Architectural Highlights

o **Castle Howard** (p213) Opulent and spectacular stately home

o **Imperial War Museum North** (p227) Adventurous design, as thought-provoking as the exhibits

o **York City Walls** (p213) Medieval battlements circling the city, with great views

o **The Rows, Chester** (p231) Quirky two-tier shopping streets from Tudor times

o **The Three Graces, Liverpool** (p223) A trio of structures from the port's heyday

Nature Spots

o **Lake District** (p233) Of all England's national parks, this is simply the most beautiful

o **Yorkshire Dales** (p217) A perfect selection of hills, moors and valleys

o **Hadrian's Wall** (p241) Roman ruins are the main draw, but the surrounding landscape has a sparse grandeur

o **Museum Gardens, York** (p213) Miles away from wilder northern landscapes, but a perfect spot to rest between sightseeing

Need to Know

ADVANCE PLANNING

o **Two months before** Book hotels, especially in popular areas such as the Lake District, York and the Yorkshire Dales

o **One month before** Consider booking in advance for major sights such as Castle Howard, Hill Top and Jorvik. Book long-distance train tickets for the best deals.

o **One week before** Check the weather forecast if you plan to visit the Lake District or Yorkshire Dales, but remember conditions are always variable

RESOURCES

Major tourist information websites for the key cities and areas in this region:

o **Manchester** (www.visitmanchester.com)

o **Liverpool** (www.visitliverpool.com)

o **Northwest England** (www.visitnorthwest.com)

o **Lake District National Park** (www.lake-district.gov.uk)

o **Lake District** (www.golakes.co.uk)

o **Yorkshire** (www.visityorkshire.com)

o **Yorkshire Dales National Park** (www.yorkshiredales.org.uk)

o **Hadrian's Wall** (www.hadrians-wall.org)

GETTING AROUND

o **Bus** Good long-distance bus networks cover most of the north, but it's slower than train or car

o **Train** Lots of regular links between the big cities, plus several scenic branch-lines

o **Car** You'll regret taking a car into the big cities – use Park & Ride schemes or other public transport instead

BE FOREWARNED

o **Crowds** Be prepared for summer crowds and traffic jams, especially in the Yorkshire Dales and the Lake District

o **Weather** Statistically speaking, the north is colder and wetter than most of the rest of England – come prepared

o **Football** The beautiful game (also known as soccer) is practically a religion in Liverpool and Manchester; the cities can get rowdy on match days

t: Manchester's Museum of Science & Industry (p226); **Above:** Albert Dock, Liverpool (p222).

York & Northern England Itineraries

The three-day loop takes in the verdant Yorkshire Dales and the stately Castle Howard. The five-day trip mixes modern cities with countryside and rich history.

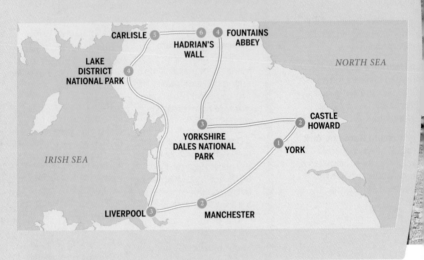

<table>
</table>

Map labels: CARLISLE, HADRIAN'S WALL, FOUNTAINS ABBEY, LAKE DISTRICT NATIONAL PARK, NORTH SEA, CASTLE HOWARD, YORK, YORKSHIRE DALES NATIONAL PARK, IRISH SEA, LIVERPOOL, MANCHESTER

3 DAYS

YORK TO YORK
History & Landscape

In the historic city of **(1) York**, start with a walk around the city walls, via the ancient 'bars' (gateways). Then head for York Minster, the finest medieval cathedral in northern England, and some say in all Europe. Other highlights include rickety-looking buildings in the cobbled lanes around the Shambles.

On day two, take a trip to **(2) Castle Howard**, a stately home of theatrical grandeur and architectural audacity a few miles outside York, recognisable from its starring role in the TV series and film of *Brideshead Revisited*. Return to York in time for a late afternoon river cruise, or have fun on an evening ghost tour.

On day three, head into the **(3) Yorkshire Dales National Park**, for picturesque hills and valleys and a classic rural landscape. Aim for the market town of Skipton, or go deeper into the park to Malham, where you can take a short walk to the geological formation of Malham Cove. If time allows, stop off at the classic ruins of **(4) Fountains Abbey** on the way back.

5 **DAYS**

YORK TO HADRIAN'S WALL
Big Cities & High Peaks

Start your tour with a couple of days in **(1) York**, admiring the elegant architecture and historic sites, then head southwest, across the Pennine Hills to **(2) Manchester**. Art and architecture fans will love the galleries, especially the imposing structure of the Imperial War Museum North. Fans of another kind will want to visit Old Trafford, home of Manchester United.

Then another great northern city: **(3) Liverpool**, famous as the birthplace of The Beatles. It's now rediscovering its maritime past, focused on the Victoria & Albert Waterfront, with fine museums, restaurants, and some classic old buildings.

After the cities, it's time for a breath of fresh air – a short journey northwards takes you to the **(4) Lake District**. This is where you find England's highest mountains and the region's most beautiful lakes, including Windermere and Grasmere.

Then it's back to the cities again, and the former border outpost of **(5) Carlisle**, with its historic castle and cathedral. It's also a good base for reaching **(6) Hadrian's Wall**, the country's most impressive remains from the Roman era.

A valley road, the Lake District (p233)
PHOTOGRAPHER: DAVID TOMLINSON / LONELY PLANET IMAGES ©

Discover York & Northern England

YORK

POP 181,100

Nowhere in northern England says 'medieval' quite like York, a city of extraordinary cultural and historical wealth that has lost little of its pre-industrial lustre. Its medieval spider's web of narrow streets is enclosed by a magnificent circuit of 13th-century walls. At the heart of the city lies the immense, awe-inspiring minster, one of the most beautiful Gothic cathedrals in the world. The city's long history and rich heritage is woven into virtually every brick and beam, and modern, tourist-orientated York – with its myriad museums, restaurants, cafes and traditional pubs – is a carefully maintained heir to that heritage.

Sights

JORVIK   Museum

(www.vikingjorvik.com; Coppergate; adult/child £8.95/6; ☉10am-5pm Apr-Oct, to 4pm Nov-Mar) Interactive multimedia exhibits aimed at 'bringing history to life' often achieve just the opposite, but the much-hyped Jorvik – the most visited attraction in town after the minster – manages to pull it off with admirable aplomb. It's a smells-and-all reconstruction of the Viking settlement that was unearthed here during excavations in the late 1970s, brought to you courtesy of a 'time-car' monorail that transports you through 9th-century Jorvik (the Viking name for York). You can cut time spent waiting in the queue by booking your tickets online and choosing the time you want to visit – it only costs £1 extra.

Foyer of the Lowry, Manchester (p228)
PHOTOGRAPHER: BEN BLACKALL / THE LOWRY

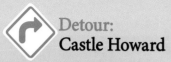

Detour:
Castle Howard

Stately homes may be two a penny in England, but you'll have to try pretty damn hard to find one as breathtakingly stately as **Castle Howard** (www.castlehoward.co.uk; adult/child house & grounds £12.50/7.50, grounds only £8.50/6; ☉house 11am-4.30pm, grounds 10am-6.30pm Mar-Oct & 1st 3 weeks of Dec), a work of theatrical grandeur and audacity set in the rolling Howardian Hills. This is one of the world's most beautiful buildings, instantly recognisable from its starring role in the 1980s TV series *Brideshead Revisited* and more recently in the 2008 film of the same name (both based on Evelyn Waugh's 1945 novel of nostalgia for the English aristocracy).

If you can, try to visit on a weekday, when it's easier to find the space to appreciate this hedonistic marriage of art, architecture, landscaping and natural beauty. As you wander about the peacock-haunted grounds, views open up over the hills, Vanbrugh's playful Temple of the Four Winds and Hawksmoor's stately mausoleum, but the great baroque house with its magnificent central cupola is an irresistible visual magnet. Inside, it is full of treasures – the breathtaking Great Hall with its soaring Corinthian pilasters, Pre-Raphaelite stained glass in the chapel, and corridors lined with classical antiquities.

Castle Howard is 15 miles northeast of York. There are several organised tours from York – check with the tourist office for up-to-date schedules.

FREE CITY WALLS City Walls

(☉8am-dusk) If the weather's good don't miss the chance to walk the city walls, it gives a whole new perspective on the city. The full circuit is 4.5 miles (allow 1½ to two hours); if you're pushed for time, the short stretch from Bootham Bar to Monk Bar is worth doing for the views of the minster.

Start and finish in the Museum Gardens or at **Bootham Bar** (on the site of a Roman gate), where a multimedia exhibit provides some historical context, and go clockwise. Highlights include **Monk Bar**, the best-preserved medieval gate, which still has a working portcullis, and **Walmgate Bar**, England's only city gate with an intact barbican (an extended gateway to ward off uninvited guests).

You can download a free guide to the wall walk at www.visityork.org/explore/walls.html.

YORKSHIRE MUSEUM Museum

(www.yorkshiremuseum.org.uk; Museum St; adult/child £7/free; ☉10am-5pm) Most of York's Roman archaeology is hidden beneath the medieval city, so the displays in the Yorkshire Museum are invaluable. There are excellent exhibits on Viking and medieval York too, including priceless artefacts such as the 8th-century Coppergate helmet; a 9th-century Anglian sword decorated with silver; and the 15th-century Middleham Jewel, an engraved gold pendant adorned with a giant sapphire.

In the peaceful **Museum Gardens** (☉dawn-dusk) are the ruins of **St Mary's Abbey** (founded 1089), dating from 1270–1294.

SHAMBLES Medieval Street

(www.yorkshambles.com) The narrow, cobbled lane known as the Shambles, lined with 15th-century Tudor buildings that overhang so much they seem to meet above your head, is the most visited street in Europe. It takes its name from the Saxon word *shamel*, meaning 'slaughterhouse' – in 1862 there were 26 butcher shops on this one street.

NEIL SETCHFIELD / LONELY PLANET IMAGES ©

Don't Miss **York Minster**

Not content with being Yorkshire's most important historic building, the awe-inspiring York Minster is also the largest medieval cathedral in all of Northern Europe. If this is the only cathedral you visit in England, you'll still walk away satisfied.

The first church on this spot was a wooden chapel built for the baptism of King Edwin of Northumbria on Easter Day 627; its location is marked in the crypt. It was replaced with a stone church that was built on the site of a Roman basilica, parts of which can be seen in the foundations. The first Norman minster was built in the 11th century; again, you can see surviving fragments in the foundations and crypt.

The present minster, built mainly between 1220 and 1480, manages to encompass all the major stages of Gothic architectural development. The transepts (1220–55) were built in Early English style; the octagonal chapter house (1260–90) and the nave (1291–1340) in the Decorated style; and the west towers, west front and central (or lantern) tower (1470–72) in Perpendicular style.

THINGS YOU NEED TO KNOW

www.yorkminster.org; adult/child £8/free; ⊗9am-5.30pm Mon-Sat, noon-3.45pm Sun

YORK CASTLE MUSEUM Museum (www.yorkcastlemuseum.org.uk; Tower St; adult/child £8/free; ⊗9.30am-5pm) This excellent museum contains displays of everyday life through the centuries, with reconstructed domestic interiors, a Victorian street, and a less-than-homely prison cell where you can try out a condemned man's bed – in this case the highwayman Dick Turpin's (he was imprisoned here before being hanged in 1739).

Tours

There's a bewildering range of tours on offer, from historic walking tours to a host of ever more competitive night-time ghost tours (York is reputed to be England's most haunted city). All tours listed here run daily, whatever the weather, no need to book just turn up.

Ghost Hunt of York _Walking Tours_
(www.ghosthunt.co.uk; adult/child £5/3; ⏰ tours 7.30pm) Award-winning tour laced with authentic ghost stories. Begins at the Shambles.

Yorkwalk _Walking Tours_
(www.yorkwalk.co.uk; adult/child £5.50/3.50; tours 10.30am & 2.15pm) A series of two-hour themed walks – Roman York, women in York, secret York and the inevitable graveyard and plague tour. Walks depart from Museum Gardens Gate on Museum St.

Original Ghost Walk of York
Walking Tours
(www.theoriginalghostwalkofyork.co.uk; adult/child £4.50/3; ⏰ tours 8pm) An evening of ghouls, ghosts, mystery and history courtesy of a well-established group departing from the King's Arms pub by Ouse Bridge.

York CitySightseeing _Bus Tours_
(www.city-sightseeing.com; day tickets adult/child £10/4; ⏰ 9am-5pm) Hop-on/hop-off route with 16 stops, calling at all the main sights. Buses leave from Exhibition Sq near York Minster.

Sleeping

ABBEYFIELDS _B&B_ ££
(☎ 01904-636471; www.abbeyfields.co.uk; 19 Bootham Tce; s/d from £49/78; 📶) Expect a warm welcome and thoughtfully arranged bedrooms here, with chairs and bedside lamps for comfortable reading.

ELLIOTTS B&B _B&B_ ££
(☎ 01904-623333; www.elliottshotel.co.uk; 2 Sycamore Pl; s/d from £55/80; P @ 📶) A beautifully converted 'gentleman's residence', Elliotts leans towards the boutique end of the guest house market

with stylish and elegant rooms, and hi-tech touches such as flatscreen TVs and free wi-fi.

HEDLEY HOUSE HOTEL _B&B_ ££
(☎ 01904-637404; www.hedleyhouse.com; 3 Bootham Tce; s/d/f from £50/80/90; P 📶 👪) Run by a couple with young children, this smart red-brick terrace-house hotel could hardly be more family-friendly – plus it has private parking at the back, and is barely five minutes' walk from the city centre through the Museum Gardens.

ARNOT HOUSE _B&B_ ££
(☎ 01904-641966; www.arnothouseyork.co.uk; 17 Grosvenor Tce; r £70-85; P) With three beautifully decorated rooms (provided you're a fan of Victorian floral patterns), including two with impressive four-poster beds, Arnot House sports an authentically old-fashioned look that appeals to a more mature clientele and there are no children allowed.

BRONTË HOUSE _B&B_ ££
(☎ 01904-621066; www.bronte-guesthouse.com; 22 Grosvenor Tce; s/d from £40/76; 📶) The Brontë offers five homely en-suite rooms, each decorated differently; our favourite is the double with a carved, 19th-century canopied bed, William Morris wallpaper and assorted bits and pieces from another era.

23 ST MARY'S _B&B_ ££
(☎ 01904-622738; www.23stmarys.co.uk; 23 St Mary's; s/d £55/90; P @) A smart and stately town house with nine chintzy, country-house-style rooms, some with hand-painted furniture to give them that rustic look, while other rooms are decorated with antiques, lace and polished mahogany.

DAIRY GUESTHOUSE _B&B_ ££
(☎ 01904-639367; www.dairyguesthouse.co.uk; 3 Scarcroft Rd; s/d from £55/75; 📶) A lovely Victorian home that has retained many of its original features, including pine doors, stained glass and cast-iron fireplaces. But the real treat is the flower- and plant-filled courtyard that leads to the cottage-style rooms.

Eating

GRAY'S COURT
Cafe ££

(www.grayscourtyork.com; Chapter House St; mains £6-7; ⏱breakfast & lunch) An unexpected find right in the very heart of York, this 16th-century house has more of a country atmosphere. Enjoy gourmet coffee and cake in the sunny garden, or indulge in a light lunch in the historic setting of the oak-panelled Jacobean gallery (extra points if you grab the alcove table above the main door).

ATE O'CLOCK
Bistro ££

(☎01904-644080; www.ateoclock.co.uk; 13a High Ousegate; mains £14-17; ⏱lunch & dinner Tue-Sat) A tempting menu of classic bistro dishes (fillet of beef with mushrooms, pork-and-chive sausage with mash and onion gravy) made with fresh Yorkshire produce has made this place hugely popular with locals – best book a table to avoid disappointment.

CAFÉ CONCERTO
Cafe/Bistro ££

(☎01904-610478; www.cafeconcerto.biz; 21 High Petergate; snacks £3-8, mains £10-17; ⏱8.30am-10pm) Walls papered with sheet music, chilled jazz on the stereo and battered, mismatched tables and chairs set the bohemian tone in this comforting coffee shop that serves breakfasts, bagels and cappuccinos big enough to float a boat in during the day, and a sophisticated bistro menu in the evening.

BETTY'S
Tearoom ££

(www.bettys.co.uk; St Helen's Sq; mains £6-11, afternoon tea £16; ⏱breakfast, lunch & dinner) Afternoon tea, old-school style, with

York

⊙ Top Sights

⊙ Sights

⊜ Sleeping

⊗ Eating

⊙ Drinking

white-aproned waitresses, linen table-cloths and a teapot collection ranged along the walls. House speciality is the Yorkshire Fat Rascal – a huge fruit scone smothered in melted butter – but the smoked haddock with poached egg and Hollandaise sauce is our favourite lunch dish.

Drinking

With only a couple of exceptions, the best drinking holes in town are the older, traditional pubs.

BLUE BELL   Pub

(53 Fossgate) This is what a real English pub looks like – a tiny, wood-panelled room with a smouldering fireplace, decor (and beer and smoke stains) dating from c 1798, a pile of ancient board games

in the corner, friendly and efficient bar staff, and Timothy Taylor and Black Sheep ales on tap.

YE OLDE STARRE   Pub

(40 Stonegate) Licenced since 1644, this is York's oldest pub – a warren of small rooms and a small beer garden, with a half-dozen real ales on tap.

Old White Swan   Pub

(80 Goodramgate) Popular and atmospheric old pub with small beer garden and a good range of guest real ales.

King's Arms   Pub

(King's Staith) York's best-known pub in fabulous riverside location, with tables spilling out onto the quayside – a perfect spot for a summer's evening, but be prepared to share it with a few hundred other people.

ℹ Information

York Visitor Centre (☏01904-550099; www.visityork.org; 1 Museum St; ⊙9am-6pm Mon-Sat, 10am-5pm Sun Apr-Sep, shorter hours Oct-Mar; @) Brand new visitor centre with tourist and transport info for all of Yorkshire, accommodation booking, ticket sales and internet access.

ℹ Getting There & Away

York is a major railway hub with frequent direct services to **London** (£80, two hours) and **Manchester** (£15, 1½ hours).

YORKSHIRE DALES NATIONAL PARK

The Yorkshire Dales – from the old Norse word dalr, meaning 'valleys' – is the central jewel in the necklace of three national parks strung across northern England, with the dramatic fells of the Lake District to the west and the brooding heaths of the North York Moors to the east.

From well-known names such as Wensleydale and Ribblesdale, to obscure and evocative Langstrothdale and Arkengarthdale, these glacial valleys are characterised by a distinctive landscape

Fountains Abbey ruins

VERONICA GARBUTT / LONELY PLANET IMAGES ©

of high heather moorland, stepped skylines and flat-topped hills rising above green valley floors patchworked with drystone dykes and dotted with picture-postcard towns and hamlets, where sheep and cattle still graze on village greens.

The Dales have been protected as a national park since the 1950s, assuring their status as a walker's and cyclist's paradise. But there's plenty for non-walkers as well, from exploring the legacy of literary vet James Herriot of *All Creatures Great and Small* fame, to sampling Wallace and Gromit's favourite teatime snack at the Wensleydale Creamery.

The *Visitor* newspaper, available from tourist offices, lists local events and walks guided by park rangers, as well as many places to stay and eat. The official park website at www.yorkshiredales.org.uk is also useful.

Skipton
POP 14,300

This busy market town on the southern edge of the Dales takes its name from the Anglo-Saxon *sceape ton* (sheep town) – no prizes for guessing how it made its money. Monday, Wednesday, Friday and Saturday are market days on High St, bringing crowds from all over and giving the town something of a festive atmosphere. The **tourist office** (☏01756-792809; www.skiptononline.co.uk; 35 Coach St; ⏱10am-5pm Mon-Fri, 9am-5pm Sat) is on the northern edge of the town centre.

◉ Sights & Activities

A pleasant stroll from the tourist office along the canal path leads to **Skipton Castle** (www.skiptoncastle.co.uk; High St; adult/child £6.20/3.70; ⏱10am-6pm Mon-Sat, noon-6pm Sun Mar-Sep, to 4pm Oct-Feb), one of the best-preserved medieval castles in England – a fascinating contrast to the ruins you'll see elsewhere.

From the castle, wander along Skipton's pride and joy – the broad and bustling High St, one of the most attractive shopping streets in Yorkshire. On the first Sunday of the month it hosts the Northern Dales farmers market.

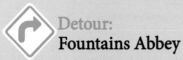

Detour:
Fountains Abbey

Nestled in the secluded valley of the River Skell lie two of Yorkshire's most beautiful attractions – an absolute must on any northern itinerary. The beautiful and strangely obsessive water gardens of the **Studley Royal** estate were built in the 19th century to enhance the picturesque ruins of 12th-century **Fountains Abbey** (NT; www.fountainsabbey.org.uk; adult/child £8.50/4.55; ☺10am-5pm Apr-Sep, to 4pm Oct-Mar). Together they present a breathtaking picture of pastoral elegance and tranquillity that have made them a Unesco World Heritage Site.

Fountains Abbey is about 25 miles northwest of York, near the town of Ripon.

 Eating

Bojangles Cafe, Bar £
(20 Newmarket St; mains £3-6) Best coffee in town. American-style breakfasts and burgers by day, tapas and cocktails in the evening.

Bizzie Lizzies Fish & Chips £
(36 Swadford St; mains £6-8; ☺11am-9pm, takeaway till 11.15pm) Award-winning, sit-down fish-and-chip restaurant overlooking the canal. There's also a takeaway counter (mains £3 to £5).

Narrow Boat Pub £
(38 Victoria St; mains £5-8) Traditionally styled pub with a great selection of local ales and foreign beers, friendly service and bar food.

Malham
POP 120

Stretching west from Grassington to Ingleton is the largest area of limestone country in England, which has created a distinctive landscape dotted with dry valleys, potholes, limestone pavements and gorges. Two of the most spectacular features in the area – Malham Cove and Gordale Scar – can be found near the pretty village of Malham.

 Sights & Activities

A half-mile walk north from Malham village leads to **Malham Cove**, a huge rock amphitheatre lined with 80m-high vertical cliffs. You can hike steeply up the left-hand end of the cove (on the Pennine Way footpath) to see the extensive limestone pavement above the cliffs.

A mile east of Malham along a narrow road (very limited parking) is spectacular **Gordale Scar**, a deep limestone canyon with scenic cascades and the remains of an Iron Age settlement.

The national park centre has a leaflet describing the **Malham Landscape Trail**, a 5-mile circular walk that takes in Malham Cove, Gordale Scar and the Janet's Foss waterfall.

NORTHWEST ENGLAND

Liverpool
POP 469,020

Beleaguered by a history of hard times and chronic misfortune, the city of Liverpool has seen its luck change dramatically in recent years. The city centre, which for decades was an unattractive mix of ugly retail outlets and depressing dereliction, is in the process of being transformed, largely on the back of a substantial program of urban regeneration.

Besides giving us a host of new buildings like the impressive, ultra-swish Liverpool ONE shopping district, the city's rebirth has breathed new life into its magnificent cultural heritage, established over 200 years ago when the city was a thriving trading port and one of the

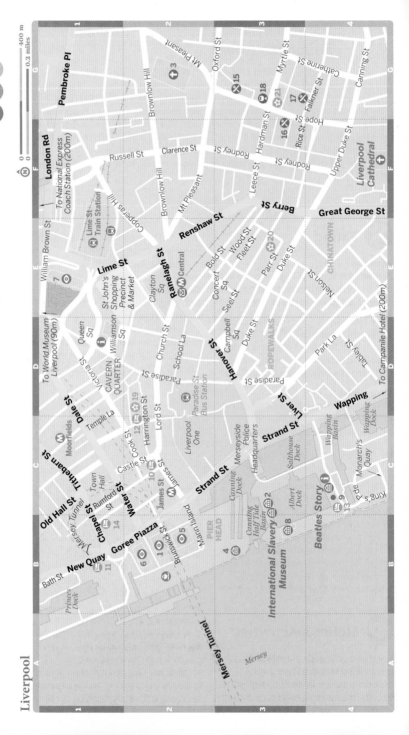

0   0.2 miles
0   400 m

Pembroke Pl

London Rd

To National Express
Coach Station (200m)

William Brown St

To World Museum
Liverpool (90m)

Russell St

Clarence St

Brownlow Hill

Mt Pleasant

Oxford St

Catherine St

Myrtle St

Falkner St

Canning St

Hope St

Hardman St

Rice St

Upper Duke St

Liverpool
Cathedral

Great George St

Rodney St

Leece St

Berry St

Renshaw St

Mt Pleasant

Brownlow Hill

Copperas Hill

Lime St Train Station

Lime St

St John's Shopping
Precinct & Market

Clayton St

Ranelagh St

Central

Bold St

Wood St

Fleet St

Concert
Sq

Seal St

Duke St

Parr St

Nelson St

CHINATOWN

ROPEWALKS

Campbell
Sq

Hanover St

Duke St

School La

Paradise St

Church St

Queen
Sq

Williamson
Sq

CAVERN
QUARTER

Victoria St

Temple La

Harrington St

Lord St

Dale St

Moorfields

Tithebarn St

Old Hall St

Chapel St

Town
Hall

Castle St

Rumford St

Water St

James St

Goree Piazza

New Quay

Bath St

Princes
Dock

Mersey Tunnel

Mann Island

Brunswick St

Liverpool
One

Paradise St
Bus Station

Merseyside
Police
Headquarters

Strand St

Liver St

Park La

Tabley St

To Campanile Hotel (200m)

Wapping

Strand St

Canning
Dock

Canning
Half Tide
Basin

PIER
HEAD

International Slavery
Museum

Albert
Dock

Salthouse
Dock

Wapping
Basin

Wapping
Dock

Beatles Story

Monarch's
Quay

King's

P de

Mersey

Mersey Tunnel

Liverpool

empire's most important cities. This legacy of power is best exemplified by the magnificent waterfront around Albert Dock, which has more listed buildings than any city in England except London and is now a Unesco World Heritage Site – proof that Liverpool doesn't want to celebrate its glorious past as much as create an exciting, contemporary equivalent of it.

 Sights

City Centre

FREE WORLD MUSEUM LIVERPOOL
Museum

(www.liverpoolmuseums.org.uk/wml; William Brown St; ⏰10am-5pm) Natural history, science and technology are the themes of this sprawling museum, whose exhibits range from birds of prey to space exploration. It also includes the country's only free planetarium.

FREE ST GEORGE'S HALL
Cultural Centre

(www.stgeorgesliverpool.co.uk; William Brown St; ⏰10am-5pm Tue-Sat, 1-5pm Sun) Arguably Liverpool's most impressive building is this magnificent example of neoclassical architecture that is as imposing today as it was when it was completed in 1854. Curiously, it was built as law courts and a concert hall – presumably a judge could pass sentence and then relax to a string quartet.

LIVERPOOL CATHEDRAL Cathedral
(www.liverpoolcathedral.org.uk; Hope St; ⏰8am-6pm) Liverpool's Anglican cathedral is a building of superlatives. Not only is it Britain's largest church; it's also the world's largest Anglican cathedral, and it's all thanks to Sir Giles Gilbert Scott, who made its construction his life's work.

The visitor centre features **The Great Space** (adult/child £5/3.50; ⏰9am-4pm Mon-Sat, noon-2.30pm Sun), a 10-minute, panoramic high-definition movie about the history of the cathedral. Your ticket also gives you access to the cathedral's 101m tower, from which there are terrific views of the city and beyond.

METROPOLITAN CATHEDRAL OF CHRIST THE KING Cathedral
(www.liverpoolmetrocathedral.org.uk; Mt Pleasant; ⏰8am-6pm Mon-Sat, 8am-5pm Sun Oct-Mar) Liverpool's Catholic cathedral is a mightily impressive modern building that looks like a soaring concrete tepee, hence its nickname – Paddy's Wigwam. The

central tower frames the world's largest stained-glass window, created by John Piper and Patrick Reyntiens.

Albert Dock

FREE INTERNATIONAL SLAVERY MUSEUM
Museum

(www.liverpoolmuseums.org.uk/ism; Albert Dock; ⊙10am-5pm) Museums are, by their very nature, like a still of the past, but the extraordinary International Slavery Museum resonates very much in the present. It reveals slavery's unimaginable horrors – including Liverpool's own role in the triangular slave trade – in a clear and uncompromising manner. It's heady, disturbing stuff, but as well as providing an insightful history lesson, we are reminded of our own obligations to humanity and justice throughout the museum, not least in the Legacies of Slavery exhibit, which explores the continuing fight for freedom and equality.

BEATLES STORY
Museum

(www.beatlesstory.com; Albert Dock; adult/child £12.95/6.50; ⊙9am-7pm, last admission 5pm) Liverpool's most popular museum doesn't illuminate any dark, juicy corners in the turbulent history of the world's most famous foursome – there's nary a mention of any internal discord, drugs or of Yoko Ono – but there's plenty of genuine memorabilia to keep a Beatles fan happy.

FREE TATE LIVERPOOL
Gallery

(www.tate.org.uk/liverpool; Albert Dock; special exhibitions adult/child from £5/4; ⊙10am-5.50pm) Touted as the home of modern art in the north, this gallery features a substantial checklist of 20th-century artists across its four floors, as well as touring exhibitions from the mother ship on London's Bankside.

FREE MERSEYSIDE MARITIME MUSEUM
Museum

(www.liverpoolmuseums.org.uk/maritime; Albert Dock; ⊙10am-5pm) The story of one of the world's great ports is the theme of this excellent museum and, believe us, it's a graphic and compelling page-turner. One of the many great exhibits is Emigration to a New World, which tells the story of nine million emigrants and their efforts to get to North America and Australia; the walk-through model of a typical ship shows just how tough conditions on board really were.

Liverpool Cathedral (p221)

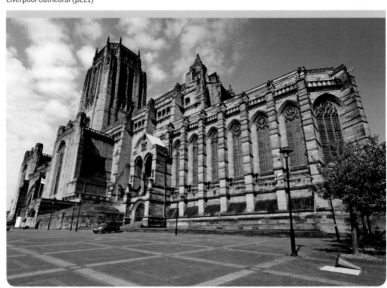

Doing The Beatles to Death

It doesn't matter that two of them are dead, that the much-visited Cavern Club is a reconstruction of the original club that was the scene of their earliest gigs, or that, if he were alive, John Lennon would have devoted much of his cynical energy to mocking the **'Cavern Quarter'** that has grown up around Mathew St. No, it doesn't matter at all, because the phenomenon lives on and a huge chunk of the city's visitors come to visit, see and touch anything – and we mean anything – even vaguely associated with The Beatles.

Which isn't to say that a wander around Mathew St isn't fun: from shucking oysters in the Rubber Soul Oyster Bar to buying a Ringo pillowcase in the From Me to You shop, virtually all of your Beatles needs can be taken care of.

True fans will undoubtedly want to visit the National Trust–owned **Mendips**, the home where John lived with his Aunt Mimi from 1945 to 1963 and **20 Forthlin Rd**, the plain terraced home where Paul grew up; you can only do so by prebooked **tour** (☎ 0151-427 7231; adult/child £16.80/3.15; ⏲ 10.30am & 11.20am Wed-Sun Easter-Oct) from outside the **National Conservation Centre** (www.liverpoolmuseums.org.uk/conservation; Whitechapel; ⏲ 10am-5pm).

If you'd rather do it yourself, the tourist offices stock the *Discover Lennon's Liverpool* guide and map, and *Robin Jones' Beatles Liverpool*.

North of Albert Dock

The area to the north of Albert Dock is known as **Pier Head**, after a stone pier built in the 1760s. This is still the departure point for ferries across the River Mersey, and was, for millions of migrants, their final contact with European soil.

Their story – and that of the city in general both past and present – is told in the eye-catching, giant-X-shaped **Museum of Liverpool** (www.liverpoolmuseums.org.uk/mol; Mann Island; admission free), built on an area known as Mann Island. The museum has only recently opened, with most of its galleries ready for visitors as of July 2011.

Prior to the arrival of the new museum, this part of the dock had been dominated by a trio of Edwardian buildings known as the 'Three Graces', dating from the days when Liverpool's star was still ascending. The southernmost, with the dome mimicking St Paul's Cathedral, is the **Port of Liverpool Building**, completed in 1907. Next to it is the **Cunard Building**, in the style of an Italian palazzo, once HQ to the Cunard Steamship Line. Finally, the **Royal Liver Building** (pronounced '*lie*-ver') was opened in 1911 as the head office of the Royal Liver Friendly Society. It's crowned by Liverpool's symbol, the famous 5.5m copper Liver Bird.

 Tours

BEATLES FAB FOUR TAXI TOUR

Musical Tours

(☎ 0151-601 2111; www.thebeatlesfabfour taxitour.co.uk; per tour £50) Get your own personalised 2½-hour tour of the city's moptop landmarks. Pick-ups arranged when booking.

YELLOW DUCKMARINE TOUR

Boat Tours

(☎ 0151-708 7799; www.theyellowduckmarine.co.uk; adult/child £11.95/9.95; ⏲ from 11am) Take to the dock waters in a WWII amphibious vehicle after a quickie tour of the city centre's main points of interest.

 Sleeping

City Centre

RACQUET CLUB Boutique Hotel ££
(☎ 0151-236 6676; www.racquetclub.org.uk;
Hargreaves Bldg, 5 Chapel St; r £110; ☎) Eight
individually styled rooms with influences
that range from French country house
to Japanese minimalist chic (often in the
same room) make this boutique hotel one
of the most elegant choices in town.

62 CASTLE ST Boutique Hotel ££
(☎ 0151-702 7898; www.62castlest.com; 62
Castle St; r from £79; P @ ☎) This elegant
property – voted one of Britain's top 100
lodgings in 2010 by the *Sunday Times* –
successfully blends the traditional Victorian features of the building with a sleek,
contemporary style.

HARD DAYS NIGHT HOTEL Hotel £££
(☎ 0151-236 1964; www.harddaysnighthotel.
com; Central Bldgs, North John St; r £110-160,
ste £750; @ ☎) You don't have to be a fan
to stay here, but it helps: unquestion-
ably luxurious, the 110 ultramodern,
fully equipped rooms are decorated with
specially commissioned drawings of the
band.

Around Albert Dock

CROWNE PLAZA LIVERPOOL Hotel ££
(☎ 0151-243 8000; www.cpliverpool.com; St
Nicholas Pl, Princes Dock, Pier Head; r from £79;
P @ ☎ ☎) The paragon of the modern
and luxurious business hotel, the Crowne
Plaza has a marvellous waterfront location and plenty of facilities including a
health club and swimming pool.

Campanile Hotel Hotel ££
(☎ 0151-709 8104; www.campanile-liverpool
-queens-dock.co.uk; Chaloner St, Queen's Dock; r
from £50; P ☎) Functional, motel-style rooms
in a purpose-built hotel. Great location and
perfect for families – children under 12 stay
for free.

Premier Inn Hotel ££
(☎ 0870 990 6432; www.premierinn.co.uk;
Albert Dock; r from £49; P ☎) Decent chain

hotel about two steps away from the Beatles Story museum.

🍴 Eating & Drinking

LONDON CARRIAGE WORKS
Modern British £££

(☏ 0151-705 2222; www.thelondoncarriage-works.co.uk; 40 Hope St; 2-/3-course meals £15/20, mains £14-33; ⏱ lunch & dinner) Liverpool's dining revolution is being led by Paul Askew's award-winning restaurant, which successfully blends ethnic influences from around the globe with staunch British favourites and serves up the result in a beautiful dining room – actually more of a bright glass box divided only by a series of sculpted glass shards. Reservations are recommended.

EVERYMAN BISTRO
Cafe £

(☏ 0151-708 9545; www.everyman.co.uk; 13 Hope St; mains £5-8; ⏱ noon-2am Mon-Fri, 11am-2am Sat, 7-10.30pm Sun) Out-of-work actors and other creative types on a budget make this great cafe-restaurant (beneath the Everyman Theatre) their second home – with good reason.

QUARTER
Bistro ££

(☏ 0151-707 1965; 7-11 Falkner St; mains £9-13; ⏱ lunch & dinner) A gorgeous little wine bar and bistro with outdoor seating for that elusive summer's day.

PHILHARMONIC
Traditional Pub

(36 Hope St; ⏱ 11am-11.30pm) This extraordinary bar, designed by the shipwrights who built the *Lusitania,* is one of the most beautiful bars in all of England. The interior is resplendent with etched and stained glass, wrought iron, mosaics and ceramic tiling – and if you think that's good, just wait until you see inside the marble men's toilets, the only heritage-listed lav in the country.

Entertainment

MASQUE Nightclub
(90 Seel St; ⏱11pm-3am Mon-Sat) This converted theatre is home to our favourite club in town.

CAVERN CLUB Live Music
(8-10 Mathew St) Reconstruction of the 'world's most famous club'; good selection of local bands.

ⓘ **Information**

Tourist Information

08 Place tourist office (☎0151-233 2008; Whitechapel; ⏱9am-8pm Mon-Sat, 11am-4pm Sun)

Albert Dock tourist office (☎0151-478 4599; ⏱10am-6pm) Two branches: Anchor Courtyard and Merseyside Maritime Museum.

Websites

Clubbing Liverpool (www.clubbingliverpool.co.uk) Everything you need to know about what goes on when the sun goes down.

Tourist office (www.visitliverpool.com)

ⓘ **Getting There & Away**

AIR Liverpool John Lennon Airport (☎0870-750 8484; www.liverpoolairport.com) Serves a variety of international destinations as well as destinations in the UK.

BUS National Express Coach Station (Norton St) Located 300m north of Lime St station. There are services to/from most major towns including **Manchester** (£6.30, 1¼ hours, hourly) and **London** (£25.60, five to six hours, six daily).

TRAIN Liverpool's main station is Lime St. It has hourly services to almost everywhere, including **Chester** (£4.35, 45 minutes), **London** (£65.20, 3¼ hours) and **Manchester** (£9.80, 45 minutes).

Manchester
POP 394,270

Manchester is the undisputed capital of the north. It's where capitalism was born, where communism and feminism were given theoretical legs, where the Industrial Revolution blossomed and where the first computer beeped into life. Today the city boasts world-class museums, heavyweight art galleries and a cultural heritage that spans the genres from the Hallé Orchestra to Oasis. Oh yes, and a rather famous football team.

 Sights

City Centre

FREE **MUSEUM OF SCIENCE & INDUSTRY** Museum
(MOSI; www.msim.org.uk; Liverpool Rd; charge for special exhibitions; ⏱10am-5pm) If there's anything you want to know

Exchange Square, Manchester
PHOTOGRAPHER: NEIL SETCHFIELD / LONELY PLANET IMAGES ©

NEIL SETCHFIELD / LONELY PLANET IMAGES ©

Don't Miss **Imperial War Museum North**

War museums generally appeal to those with a fascination for military hardware and battle strategy (toy soldiers optional), but Daniel Libeskind's visually stunning Imperial War Museum North, in Manchester, takes a radically different approach. War is hell, it tells us, but it's a hell we revisit with tragic regularity. Although the audiovisuals and displays are quite compelling, the extraordinary aluminium-clad building itself is a huge part of the attraction, and the exhibition spaces are genuinely breathtaking.

THINGS YOU NEED TO KNOW

www.iwm.org.uk/north; Trafford Wharf Rd; admission free; ⊙10am-5pm

about the Industrial (and post-Industrial) Revolution and Manchester's key role in it, you'll find the answers among the collection of steam engines and locomotives, factory machinery from the mills, and the excellent exhibition telling the story of Manchester from the sewers up.

FREE PEOPLE'S HISTORY MUSEUM
Museum

(www.phm.org.uk; Left Bank, Bridge St; 10am-5pm daily)
A major refurb of an Edwardian pumping station – including the construction of a striking new annexe – has resulted in the expansion of one of the city's best

museums, which is devoted to British social history and the labour movement. It's compelling stuff, and a marvellous example of a museum's relevance to our everyday lives.

NATIONAL FOOTBALL MUSEUM
Museum

(www.nationalfootballmuseum.com; Urbis, Cathedral Gardens, Corporation St) It's the world's most popular game and Manchester is home to the world's most popular team, so when this museum went looking for a new home, it made sense that it would find its way to the stunning glass triangle that is Urbis. Slated to open in 2011, the

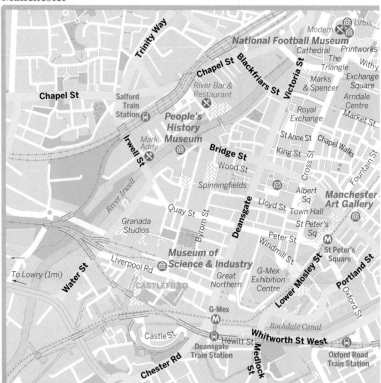

museum will be a major stop in the football fan's Manchester pilgrimage.

FREE MANCHESTER ART GALLERY
Gallery

(www.manchestergalleries.org; Mosley St; ⏱10am-5pm Tue-Sun) A superb collection of British art and a hefty number of European masters are on display at the city's top gallery. The newer gallery features a permanent collection of 20th-century British art starring Lucien Freud, Francis Bacon, Stanley Spencer, Henry Moore and David Hockney.

Salford Quays

It's a cinch to get here from the city centre via Metrolink (£2); for the Imperial War Museum North and the Lowry, look for the Harbour City stop; get off at Old Trafford for the eponymous stadium.

FREE LOWRY
Arts Centre

(www.thelowry.com; Pier 8, Salford Quays; ⏱11am-8pm Tue-Fri, 10am-8pm Sat, 11am-6pm Sun & Mon) Looking more like a shiny steel ship than an arts centre, the Lowry is the quays' most notable success. It attracts more than one million visitors a year to its myriad functions, which include everything from art exhibits and performances to bars, restaurants and, inevitably, shops.

The complex is home to more than 300 paintings and drawings by northern England's favourite artist, LS Lowry (1887–1976), who was born in nearby Stretford. He became famous for his humanistic depictions of industrial landscapes and northern towns, and gave his name to the complex.

 Eating

City Centre

MODERN Modern British ££

(0161-605 8282; Urbis, Cathedral Gardens, Corporation St; 2-/3-course lunch £12/15, dinner mains £11-21; ⊗lunch & dinner) Top fare on top of the world, or an excellent meal atop Manchester's most distinctive landmark, Urbis, is one of the city's most enjoyable dining experiences. The food – mostly Modern British cuisine – will not disappoint, but being able to sit at a table close to the floor-to-ceiling windows make this place worthwhile; book a table in advance.

LOVE SAVES THE DAY Cafe £
(0161-832 0777; Tib St; lunch £6-8; ⊗8am-7pm Mon-Wed, to 9pm Thu, to 8pm Fri, 10am-6pm Sat, 10am-4pm Sun) The Northern Quarter's most popular cafe is a New York–style deli, small supermarket and sit-down eatery in one large, airy room.

Salford Quays

RIVER BAR & RESTAURANT
Modern British £££
(0161-832 1000; www.theriverrestaurant. com; Lowry Hotel, 50 Dearman's Pl, Chapel Wharf; mains £18-39; ⊗lunch & dinner Mon-Sat) Head chef Oliver Thomas won the 'Taste of Manchester' award in 2010 for his outstanding British cuisine, which emphasises the use of local produce and traditional cooking methods.

MARK ADDY Modern British ££
(0161-832 4080; www.markaddy.co.uk; Stanley St; mains £8.90-12.50; ⊗lunch & dinner Wed-Fri, dinner Sat) A contender for best pub grub in town, the Mark Addy owes its culinary success to Robert Owen Brown, whose loving interpretations of standard British classics – pork hop with honey-roasted bramley, pan-fried Dab with cockles and spring onion et al (all locally sourced) – has them queuing at the door for a taste.

OLD TRAFFORD (MANCHESTER UNITED MUSEUM & TOUR) Stadium

(0870-442 1994; www.manutd.com; Sir Matt Busby Way; ⊗9.30am-5pm) Home of the world's most famous club, the Old Trafford stadium is both a theatre and a temple for its millions of fans worldwide, many of whom come in pilgrimage to the ground to pay tribute to the minor deities disguised as highly paid footballers that play there. We strongly recommend that you take the **tour** (adult/child £12.50/8.50; ⊗every 10min 9.40am-4.30pm except match days), which includes a seat in the stands, a stop in the changing rooms, a peek at the players' lounge (from which the manager is banned unless invited by the players) and a walk down the tunnel to the pitchside dugout, which is as close to ecstasy as many of the club's fans will ever get.

Bridge, Salford Quays, Manchester (p228)

NEIL SETCHFIELD / LONELY PLANET IMAGES ©

ℹ Information

Tourist office (www.visitmanchester.com; Piccadilly Plaza, Portland St; ⏱10am-5.15pm Mon-Sat, 10am-4.30pm Sun)

ℹ Getting There & Away

AIR Manchester Airport (☎0161-489 3000; www.manchesterairport.co.uk) South of the city, The largest airport outside London.

BUS National Express (www.nationalexpress. com) Serves most major cities almost hourly from Chorlton St coach station in the city centre. Destinations include **Liverpool** (£6.30, 1¼ hours, hourly) and **London** (£24.40, 3¾ hours, hourly).

TRAIN Manchester Piccadilly is the main station for trains to and from the rest of the country. Trains head to **Liverpool Lime St** (£9.80, 45 minutes, half-hourly) and **London Euston** (£131, three hours, seven daily). Off-peak fares are considerably cheaper.

ℹ Getting Around

TO/FROM THE AIRPORT The airport is 12 miles south of the city. A train to or from Victoria station costs £2, and a coach is £3. A taxi is nearly four times as much in light traffic.

BUS Centreline bus 4 provides a free service around the heart of Manchester every 10 minutes. Pick up a route map from the tourist office.

METROLINK There are frequent **Metrolink** (www.metrolink.co.uk) trams between Victoria and Piccadilly train stations as well as further afield to Salford Quays. Buy your tickets from the platform machine.

Chester

POP 80,130

Marvellous Chester is one of English history's greatest gifts to the contemporary visitor. Its red-sandstone wall, which today gift-wraps a tidy collection of Tudor and Victorian buildings, was built during Roman times.

It's hard to believe today, but throughout the Middle Ages Chester made its money as the most important port in the northwest. However, the River Dee silted up over time and Chester fell behind Liverpool in importance.

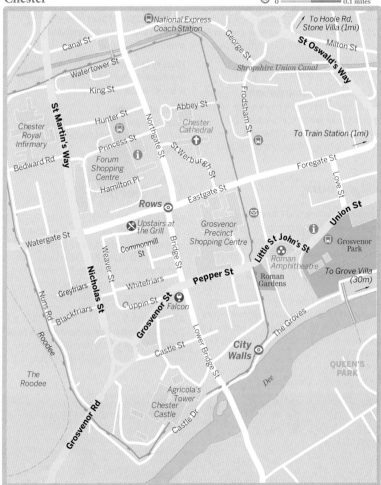

 Sights

THE ROWS Architecture

Chester's great draw is the Rows, a series of two-level galleried arcades along the four streets that fan out in each direction from the **central Cross**. The architecture is a handsome mix of Victorian and Tudor (original and mock) buildings that house a fantastic collection of individually owned shops. The origin of the Rows is a little unclear, but it is believed that as the Roman walls slowly crumbled, medieval traders built their shops against the resulting rubble banks, while later arrivals built theirs on top.

CHESTER CATHEDRAL Cathedral
(www.chestercathedral.com; Northgate St; adult/child £5/2.50; 9am-5pm Mon-Sat, 1-4pm Sun)
Originally a Benedictine abbey built on the remains of an earlier Saxon church dedicated to St Werburgh (the city's patron saint), it was shut down in 1540 as part of Henry VIII's dissolution frenzy but

reconsecrated as a cathedral the following year. Although the cathedral itself was given a substantial Victorian facelift, the 12th-century cloister and its surrounding buildings are essentially unaltered and retain much of the structure from the early monastic years.

 ROMAN AMPHITHEATRE Ruins
Just outside the city walls is what was once an arena that seated 7000 (making it the country's largest); now it's little more than steps buried in grass.

Tours

The tourist office and Chester Visitors' Centre offer a broad range of walking tours departing from both centres. Each tour lasts between 1½ and two hours.

CITY SIGHTSEEING CHESTER
Bus Tours
(01244-347452; www.city-sightseeing.com; adult/child £8.50/3; every 15-20min) Offers open-top bus tours of the city, picking up from the tourist office and Chester Visitors' Centre.

Section of the Rows, Chester (p231)

Chester Rows: The Inside Story
Walking Tours
(adult/child £5/4; 2pm) The fascinating history of Chester's most outstanding architectural feature.

History Hunter
Walking Tours
(adult/child £5/4; 10.30am) Two thousand years of Chester history.

Taste of Chester
Walking Tours
(adult/child £5/4; 2pm Thu & Sat May-Oct) Two thousand years of Chester history and samples of local produce.

Sleeping

GREEN BOUGH Boutique Hotel £££
(01244-326241; www.chestergreenbough hotel.co.uk; 60 Hoole Rd; r from £150; P @) The epitome of the boutique hotel, this exclusive, award-winning Victorian town house has individually styled rooms dressed in the best Italian fabrics.

STONE VILLA B&B ££
(01244-345014; www.stonevillachester.co.uk; 3 Stone Pl, Hoole Rd; s/d from £45/75) Twice winner of Chester's B&B of the Year in the

GLENN BEANLAND / LONELY PLANET IMAGES ©

City Walls

A good way to get a sense of Chester's unique character is to walk the 2-mile circuit along the walls that surround the historic centre. Originally built by the Romans around AD 70, the walls were altered substantially over the following centuries but have retained their current position since around 1200.

last 10 years, this beautiful villa has everything you need for a memorable stay.

BAWN LODGE   B&B   ££
(☎01244-324971; www.bawnlodge.co.uk; 10 Hoole Rd; r from £75; P🅿🛜) Spotless rooms with plenty of colour make this charming guest house a very pleasant option.

 Eating & Drinking

UPSTAIRS AT THE GRILL
Steakhouse   £££
(☎01244-344883; www.upstairsatthegrill.co.uk; 70 Watergate St; mains £15-25; ⊗dinner Mon-Sat, lunch & dinner Sun) A superb Manhattan-style steakhouse almost hidden on the 2nd floor, this is the place to devour every cut of meat from American-style porterhouse to a sauce-sodden chateaubriand.

OLD HARKER'S ARMS   Pub   ££
(www.harkersarms-chester.co.uk; 1 Russell St; mains £9-14; ⊗11am-late) An old-style boozer with a gourmet kitchen, this is the perfect place to tuck into Cumberland sausages or a Creole rice salad with sweet potatoes. To get here, follow Eastgate St east for 100m and take a left onto Russell St.

FALCON   Traditional Pub
(Lower Bridge St) This is an old-fashioned boozer with a lovely atmosphere; the surprisingly adventurous menu offers up dishes such as Jamaican peppered beef or spicy Italian sausage casserole. Great for both a pint and a bite (mains from £5.50).

ℹ Information

Chester Visitors' Centre (www.visitchester.com; Vicar's Lane; ⊗9.30am-5.30pm Mon-Sat & 10am-4pm Sun)

Tourist office (www.chester.gov.uk; Town Hall, Northgate St; ⊗9am-5.30pm Mon-Sat & 10am-4pm Sun)

ℹ Getting There & Away

BUS National Express (www.nationalexpress.com) Destinations include **Liverpool** (£7.20, one hour, four daily), **London** (£24.60, 5½ hours, three daily) and **Manchester** (£6.80, 1¼ hours, three daily).

TRAIN The train station is about a mile from the city centre. City-Rail Link buses (free) operate between the station and the centre. Trains travel to **Liverpool** (£4.35, 45 minutes, hourly), **London Euston** (£65.20, 2½ hours, hourly) and **Manchester** (£12.60, one hour, hourly).

THE LAKE DISTRICT

If you're a lover of the great outdoors, the Lake District is one corner of England where you'll want to linger. This sweeping panorama of slate-capped fells, craggy hilltops, misty mountain tarns and glittering lakes has been pulling in the crowds ever since the Romantics pitched up in the early 19th century, and it remains one of the country's most popular beauty spots.

Windermere & Bowness
POP 8432

Of all England's lakes, none carries quite the cachet of regal Windermere. Stretching for 10.5 silvery miles from Ambleside to Newby Bridge, it's one of the classic Lake District vistas, and has been a centre for Lakeland tourism since the first steam trains chugged into town in 1847 (much to the chagrin of the local gentry, including William Wordsworth).

The town itself is split between Windermere, 1.5 miles uphill from the lake, and bustling Bowness – officially 'Bowness-on-Windermere' – where a bevy of boat trips, ice-cream booths and frilly teashops jostle for space around the shoreline. It's busy, brash and a touch tatty in places, but the lake itself is still a stunner, especially viewed from one of Windermere's historic cruise boats.

The train and bus stations are in Windermere town. Most of the hotels and B&Bs are dotted around Lake Rd, which leads downhill to Bowness and the lakeshore.

Sights & Activities

WINDERMERE LAKE CRUISES

Lake Cruises

(☎ 015395-31188; www.windermere-lakecruises. co.uk) Top on the list of things to do in Windermere is to take a lake cruise. The first passenger ferry was launched back in 1845, and cruising on the lake is still a hugely popular pastime: some of the vessels are modern, but there are a couple of period beauties dating back to the 1930s.

Sleeping

WHEATLANDS LODGE

B&B ££

(☎ 015394-43789; www.wheatlandslodge -windermere.co.uk; Old College Lane; d £70-150; P 🛜) Set back from the hustle of Windermere town, this elegant detached residence looks venerably Victorian, but inside it reveals some contemporary surprises: lovely, large rooms each with their own keynote colour (maroon, coffee, pistachio), big bathrooms with a choice of walk-in shower or jacuzzi hot tub, and an extremely upmarket dining room serving one of the best breakfasts we had in Windermere.

APPLEGARTH HOTEL

Hotel £££

(☎ 015394-43206; www.lakesapplegarth. co.uk; College Rd; s £57-62, d £100-196; P) Traditional in style, undoubtedly, but then this is one of the loveliest Arts & Crafts houses in Windermere, built in the 19th century by industrial bigwig John Riggs.

ARCHWAY

B&B ££

(☎ 015394-45613; www.the-archway. com; 13 College Rd; d £50-55) There's nothing particularly fancy about the rooms at this stone-fronted B&B (although there are spanking fell views from the front rooms), but it's worth a mention for its breakfast: Manx kippers, smoked haddock and American-style pancakes are all on offer.

Waterfall at Ambleside, the Lake District (p233)

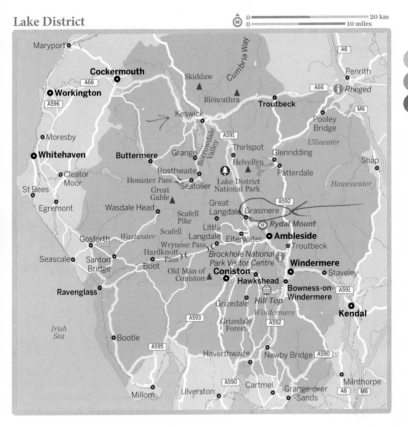

NUMBER 80 BED THEN BREAKFAST

B&B ££

(☎ 015394-43584; www.number80bed.co.uk; 80 Craig Walk; d £80-90; 🛜) Just four rooms, but each one has its own decorative tics: Room 1 feels traditional with a pine four-poster, but the other three are more modern.

 ## Eating & Drinking

JERICHO'S

Restaurant £££

(☎ 015394-42522; www.jerichos.co.uk; Waverly Hotel, College Rd; dinner mains £15-24; 🕒 dinner Tue-Sun) Now installed at the Waverley Hotel, the town's most upmarket restaurant is a favourite with the foodie guides, and head chef Chris Blaydes has acquired a deserved name as one of the Lake District's most talented chefs.

LUCY 4 AT THE PORTHOLE

Bistro ££

(3 Ash St; tapas £5-10; 🕒 lunch Sat & Sun, dinner daily) The homely old Porthole has been overhauled courtesy of Lucy Nicholson, of Lucy's of Ambleside fame. It boasts the same laid-back atmosphere, pick-and-mix tapas menu and wine-bar feel as the original Lucy 4, only this time steps from the Windermere shoreline.

ANGEL INN

Gastropub ££

(☎ 015394-44080; www.the-angelinn.com; Helm Rd; mains £11-16; 🕒 lunch & dinner) This area isn't just about cosy inns – it has its share of gastropubs too, like this one beside the Bowness shoreline. Stripped wood, banquette seats and leather sofas conjure an urban-chic ambiance, and the menu's solid gastropub stuff – mussels, beer-battered haddock and seared sea bass.

235

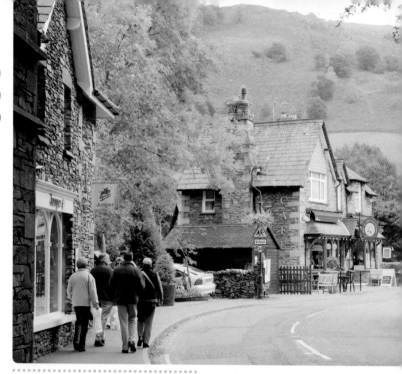

ℹ Information

Brockhole National Park Visitor Centre
(☏ 015394-46601; www.lake-district.gov.uk;
🕙 10am-5pm Easter-Oct) The Lake District's
flagship visitor centre is 3 miles north of
Windermere on the A591, with a teashop,
adventure playground and gardens.

Tourist office Bowness (☏ 015394-42895;
bownesstic@lake-district.gov.uk; Glebe Rd;
🕙 9.30am-5.30pm Easter-Oct, 10am-4pm Fri-Sun
Nov-Easter); Windermere (☏ 015394-46499;
windermeretic@southlakeland.gov.uk; Victoria St;
🕙 9am-5.30pm Mon-Sat, 9.30am-5.30pm Sun
Apr-Oct, shorter hrs in winter) The latter branch
is opposite NatWest Bank.

ℹ Getting There & Around

BUS There's one daily National Express coach
from **London** (£37, eight hours). Local buses:
555/556 Lakeslink Tracks the lake to
Brockhole Visitor Centre (seven minutes,
at least hourly), **Ambleside** (15 minutes) and
Grasmere (30 minutes), or Kendal in the
opposite direction.

599 Lakes Rider (three times hourly Monday
to Saturday, hourly on Sunday, reduced service
in winter) To **Bowness**, **Windermere**, **Rydal
Church** (for Rydal Mount), **Dove Cottage** and
Grasmere.

TRAIN Windermere is the only town inside the
national park accessible by train. It's reached on
the branch line from Oxenholme (on the main line
between Scotland and London).

Grasmere

POP 1460

Even without its Romantic connections,
gorgeous Grasmere would still be one
of the Lakes' biggest draws. It's one of
the prettiest of the Lakeland hamlets,
huddled at the base of a sweeping valley
dotted with woods, pastures and slate-
coloured hills, but most of the thousands
of trippers come in search of its famous
former residents: opium-eating Thomas de Quincey, unruly Coleridge and
grand old man William Wordsworth. With
such a rich literary heritage, Grasmere
unsurprisingly gets crammed; avoid high
summer if you can.

Left: Street in Grasmere; **Below:** Walker in the Lake District
PHOTOGRAPHER: (LEFT) © 1STOPIMAGES / ALAMY; (BELOW) RICHARD I'ANSON / LONELY PLANET IMAGES ©

◉ Sights

DOVE COTTAGE
Historic Home

(☎015394-35544; www.wordsworth.org.uk;
adult/child £7.50/4.50; ⏰9.30am-5.30pm,
last admission 4pm winter) Originally an inn
called The Dove and Olive, this tiny cottage just outside Grasmere is the most
famous former home of William Wordsworth. Covered with climbing roses, hon-
eysuckle and tiny latticed windows, the
cottage contains some fascinating artefacts – keep your eyes peeled for some
fine portraits of Wordsworth, a cabinet
containing his spectacles, shaving case
and razor, and a set of scales used by de
Quincey to weigh out his opium.

Next door is the **Wordsworth Museum
& Art Gallery**, which houses a collection
of letters, portraits and manuscripts
relating to the Romantic movement,
and regularly hosts events and poetry
readings.

SARAH NELSON'S GINGERBREAD SHOP
Confectionery Shop

(☎015394-35428; www.grasmeregingerbread.
co.uk; Church Stile; 12 pieces of gingerbread
£3.50; ⏰9.15am-5.30pm Mon-Sat, 12.30-5pm
Sun) Don't think about leaving Grasmere
without sampling Sarah Nelson's legendary gingerbread, produced to the same
secret recipe for the last 150 years and
still served by ladies in frilly pinnies and
starched bonnets.

ST OSWALD'S CHURCH
Church

The Wordsworth family regularly came
here to worship: inside you'll see a
memorial to the poet alongside his own
prayer book, and in the churchyard you'll
find the graves of William, Mary and
Dorothy; the Wordsworth children Dora,
Catherine and Thomas; and Samuel
Taylor Coleridge's son Hartley.

 Sleeping

MOSS GROVE ORGANIC
Hotel £££

(☎015394-35251; www.mossgrove.com; r £225-325; P 🛜) This Victorian villa has been lavishly redeveloped as Lakeland's loveliest eco-chic hotel, second to none in terms of green credentials: sheep-fleece insulation, natural-ink wallpapers, organic paints, reclaimed-timber beds. It's expensive, but definitely one to remember.

HOW FOOT LODGE
B&B ££

(☎015394-35366; www.howfoot.co.uk; Town End; d £70-78; P) Wordsworth fans will adore this stone cottage just a stroll from William's digs at Dove Cottage. The six rooms are light and contemporary, finished in fawns and beiges; ask for the one with the private sun lounge for that indulgent edge.

RAISE VIEW HOUSE
B&B ££

(☎015394-35215; www.raiseviewhouse.co.uk; White Bridge; s/d £90/110; P 🛜) For that all-essential fell view, you can't really top this excellent B&B. All the rooms have a different outlook (the ones from Helm Crag, Easedale and Stone Arthur are particularly

impressive), and the rest of the house is beautifully appointed: Farrow & Ball paints, Gilchrist & Soames bath-stuffs, and Wedgwood china on the breakfast table.

Eating

JUMBLE ROOM
Restaurant £££

(☎015394-35188; Langdale Rd; mains £13-24; ⏲lunch weekends, dinner Wed-Mon) Mixing quality Lakeland produce with Mediterranean influences (particularly from Spain and Italy), it attracts diners from far and wide, and the decor oozes oddball appeal, from the jumble-shop-chic furniture and polka-dot plates to the colourful cow pictures on the downstairs walls.

SARA'S BISTRO
Bistro ££

(Broadgate; mains £10-16; ⏲lunch & dinner) Hearty homespun cooking is Sarah's raison d'être – big portions of roast chicken, lamb shanks and apple crumble, served without the faintest hint of fuss.

❶ Getting There & Away

The hourly 555 runs from Windermere to **Grasmere** (15 minutes), via Ambleside, **Rydal**

Green hills of the Lake District National Park

DAVID ELSE / LONELY PLANET IMAGES ©

Detour:
Rydal Mount

While most people flock to Dove Cottage (p237) in search of William Wordsworth, those in the know head for Rydal Mount, the Wordsworth family home from 1813 until his death in 1850. Still owned by the poet's distant descendants, the house is a treasure trove of Wordsworth memorabilia. On the top floor is Wordsworth's attic study, containing his encyclopedia and a sword belonging to his younger brother John, killed in a shipwreck in 1805.

The house is 1.5 miles northwest of Ambleside, off the A591. Bus 555 (and bus 599 from April to October), between Grasmere, Ambleside, Windermere and Kendal, stops at the end of the drive.

Church and Dove Cottage. The open-top 599 (two or three per hour March to August) runs from Grasmere south via Ambleside, Troutbeck Bridge, Windermere and Bowness.

Hill Top

In the tiny village of Near Sawrey, 2 miles south of Hawkshead, this **farmhouse** (NT; ☎ 015394-36269; hilltop@nationaltrust.org.uk; adult/child £6.50/3.10; ⏱10am-4.30pm mid-May–Aug, 10.30am-4.30pm mid-Mar–mid-May & Sep-Oct, 11.30am-3.30pm mid-Feb–mid-Mar) is a must for Beatrix Potter buffs: it was the first house she lived in after moving to the Lake District, and it's also where she wrote and illustrated many of her famous tales.

Purchased in 1905 (largely on the proceeds of her first bestseller, *The Tale of Peter Rabbit*), Hill Top is crammed with decorative details that fans will recognise from the author's illustrations.

Thanks to its worldwide fame (helped along by the 2006 biopic *Miss Potter*), Hill Top is one of the Lakes' most popular spots. Entry is by timed ticket, and the queues can be seriously daunting during the summer holidays.

Carlisle

POP 69,500

Precariously perched on the tempestuous border between England and Scotland, in the area once ominously dubbed the 'Debatable Lands', Carlisle is a city with a notoriously stormy past. The battlements and keeps of the stout medieval castle still stand watch, built from the same rosy red sandstone as the city's cathedral and terraced houses, but Carlisle is a more peaceful place these days, with a buzzy student population that keeps this old city young at heart.

 Sights & Activities

CARLISLE CASTLE   Castle
(☎ 01228-591922; www.english-heritage.org.uk/daysout/properties/carlisle-castle; adult/child £4.50/2.30; ⏱9.30am-5pm Apr-Sep, 10am-4pm Oct-Mar) The castle has witnessed some dramatic events over the centuries: Mary, Queen of Scots was imprisoned here in 1568, and the castle was the site of a notorious eight-month siege during the English Civil War, when the Royalist garrison survived by eating rats, mice and the castle dogs before finally surrendering in 1645. Look out for the 'licking stones' in the dungeon, which Jacobite prisoners supposedly lapped for moisture.

CARLISLE CATHEDRAL   Church
(www.carlislecathedral.org.uk; 7 The Abbey; donation £2; ⏱7.30am-6.15pm Mon-Sat, to 5pm Sun) Built from the same rosy stone as many of the city's buildings, Carlisle's cathedral began life as a priory church in 1122, before later being raised to cathedral status when its first abbot, Athelwold, became the first Bishop of Carlisle. Among its notable features are the 15th-century choir stalls, the impressive barrel-vaulted roof and the

wonderful 14th-century East Window, one of the largest Gothic windows in England.

 Sleeping

HALLMARK HOTEL
Hotel ££

(01228-531951; carlisle.reception@hallmark hotels.co.uk; Court Sq; d from £75-95; P 🛜) Chain it may be, but the reborn Lakes Court Hotel is now a superior Carlisle sleep. It's certainly not 'boutique' (despite what the brochure says), but it's perfectly comfortable: rooms in golds and yellows (all with big beds, wi-fi and flatscreen tellies), posh function rooms, and a handy location steps from the station.

NUMBER THIRTY ONE
B&B ££

(01228-597080; www.number31.freeservers. com; 31 Howard Pl; s/d from £70/100; P) Stylish B&B a short walk from the centre. Only three rooms, but all have something different to recommend them, from a Zen-print headboard in the Red room to a half-tester in the Yellow room.

Cornerways
B&B ££

(01228-521733; www.cornerwaysguesthouse. co.uk; 107 Warwick Rd; s £30-35, d £55-65; P @ 🛜) This rambling red-brick is basic as they come, but offers some of the cheapest B&B rooms in the city.

Eating

HOLME BISTRO
Restaurant ££

(56-58 Denton St; mains £11-15; ⊗lunch & dinner Mon-Sat) A little stroll southwards from the train station brings you to this little-known local gem, where the British bistro food is streets ahead of the competition. There's nary a whiff of pretension here, either in the simply done dining room or the simply done food.

PRIOR'S KITCHEN RESTAURANT
Cafe £

(Carlisle Cathedral; lunch £4-6; ⊗9.45am-4pm Mon-Sat) Afternoon tea in this stone-vaulted cafe (formerly a monk's mess hall) has been a tradition in Carlisle for

Left: Chesters Roman Fort, Hadrian's Wall (p242); **Below:** Snow-dusted hills surrounding a lake, Lake District National Park (p233)

PHOTOGRAPHER: (LEFT) © JOHN DEVLIN / ALAMY; (BELOW) FEARGUS COONEY / LONELY PLANET IMAGES ©

as long as anyone cares to remember.

❶ Information

Tourist office (☎01228-625600; www.historic-carlisle.org.uk; Greenmarket; ⏰9.30am-5pm Mon-Sat, 10.30am-4pm Sun)

❶ Getting There & Away

BUS Carlisle is Cumbria's main transport hub. National Express coaches travel to **London** (£35, 7½ hours, three direct daily), **Glasgow** (£20.70, two hours, 14 daily) and **Manchester** (£28, 3¼ hours, eight daily).

TRAIN Carlisle is on the **London Euston** (£91, 3¼ to 4¼ hours) to **Glasgow** (£22, 1¼ to 1½ hours) line.

HADRIAN'S WALL

Hadrian's Wall, named in honour of the emperor who ordered it built, was one of Rome's greatest engineering projects, a spectacular 73-mile testament to ambition and the practical Roman mind. Even today, almost 2000 years after the first stone was laid, the sections that are still standing remain an awe-inspiring sight, proof that when the Romans wanted something done, they just knuckled down and did it.

It wasn't easy. When completed, the mammoth structure ran across the narrow neck of England, from the Solway Firth in the west almost to the mouth of the Tyne in the east. Every Roman mile (1.62 miles) there was a gateway guarded by a small milecastle and between each milecastle were two observation turrets.

A series of forts was developed as bases some distance south (and may predate the wall), and 16 lie astride it. The prime remaining forts on the wall are Cilurnum (Chesters), Vercovicium (Housesteads) and Banna (Birdoswald). The best forts behind the wall are Corstopitum at Corbridge, and Vindolanda, north of Bardon Mill.

Hadrian's Wall

Rome's Final Frontier

Of all Britain's Roman ruins, Emperor Hadrian's 2nd-century wall, cutting across northern England from the Irish Sea to the North Sea, is by far the most spectacular; Unesco awarded it world cultural heritage status in 1987.

We've picked out the highlights, one of which is the prime remaining Roman fort on the wall, Housesteads, which we've reconstructed here.

Housesteads' granaries
Nothing like the clever underground ventilation system, which kept vital supplies of grain dry in Northumberland's damp and drizzly climate, would be seen again in these parts for 1500 years.

Milecastle

North Gate

Birdoswald Roman Fort
Explore the longest intact stretch of the wall, scramble over the remains of a large fort then head indoors to wonder at a full-scale model of the wall at its zenith. Great fun for the kids.

Housesteads Roman Fort
See Illustration Right

Interval Tower

Birdoswald Roman Fort • Harrow Scar Milecastle • Greenhead • Irthing • Roman Army Museum • Housesteads Roman Fort & Museum • Once Brewed • Sewingshields • Hadrian's Wall • B6318 • Vindolanda Roman Fort & Museum • Bardon Mill • Chesters Roman Fort & Museum • Acomb • Chollerford • Low Brunton • Haydon Bridge • Hexham • Haltwhistle • South Tyne • A69 • Brampton

0 — 10 km / 0 — 5 miles

Chesters Roman Fort
Built to keep watch over a bridge spanning the River North Tyne, Britain's best-preserved Roman cavalry fort has a terrific bathhouse, essential if you have months of nippy northern winter ahead.

Hexham Abbey
This may be the finest non-Roman sight near Hadrian's Wall, but the 7th-century parts of this magnificent church were built with stone quarried by the Romans for use in their forts.

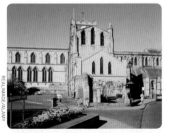

Housesteads' hospital
Operations performed at the hospital would have been surprisingly effective, even without anaesthetics; religious rituals and prayers to Aesculapius, the Roman god of healing, were possibly less helpful for a hernia or appendicitis.

GLYN THOMAS/ALAMY

Housesteads' latrines
Communal toilets were the norm in Roman times and Housesteads' are remarkably well preserved – fortunately no traces remain of the vinegar-soaked sponges that were used instead of toilet paper.

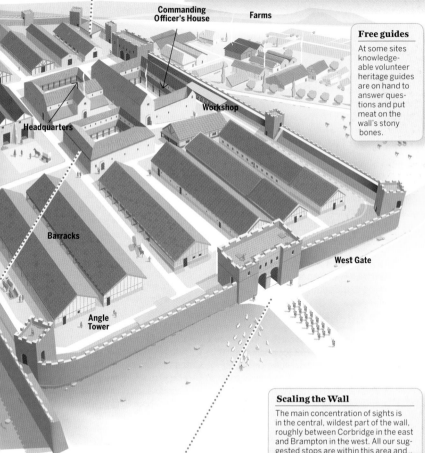

Commanding Officer's House

Farms

Workshop

Headquarters

Free guides
At some sites knowledgeable volunteer heritage guides are on hand to answer questions and put meat on the wall's stony bones.

Barracks

West Gate

Angle Tower

Housesteads' gatehouses
Unusually at Housesteads neither of the gates faces the enemy, as was the norm at a Roman fort – builders aligned them east-west. Ruts worn by cart wheels are still visible in the stone.

Scaling the Wall
The main concentration of sights is in the central, wildest part of the wall, roughly between Corbridge in the east and Brampton in the west. All our suggested stops are within this area and follow an east-west route. The easiest way to travel is by car, scooting along the B6318, but special bus AD122 will also get you there. Hiking along the designated Hadrian's Wall Path (84 miles) allows you to appreciate the achievement up close.

If You Like...
Roman History

If you like the excellent forts and museums at Housesteads and Vindolanda, check out the area around Haltwhistle, which boasts many more relics from the Roman era.

1 **ROMAN ARMY MUSEUM**
(www.vindolanda.com; adult/child £4.50/2.50, with Vindolanda £9/5; ◷10am-6pm) A few miles northwest of Haltwhistle, near the settlement of Greenhead, this kid-pleasing museum provides lots of colourful background detail on the Roman army, such as how the soldiers spent their R&R time in this lonely outpost of the empire.

2 **BIRDOSWALD ROMAN FORT**
(EH; adult/child £4.80/2.40; ◷10am-5.30pm Mar-Oct) The remains of this once-formidable fort on an escarpment overlooking the beautiful Irthing Gorge are on a minor road off the B6318, about 3 miles west of Greenhead.

Carlisle, in the west, and Newcastle, in the east, are obviously good starting points, but Brampton, Haltwhistle, Hexham and Corbridge all make good bases. The B6318 follows the course of the wall from the outskirts of Newcastle to Birdoswald. The main A69 road and the train line run parallel to the wall, 3 or 4 miles to the south.

ℹ Information

Northumberland National Park Visitor Centre
(☏01434-344396; ◷9.30am-5pm Apr-Oct) This centre is in the tiny settlement of Once Brewed just off the B6318. The official portal for the whole of Hadrian's Wall Country is www.hadrianswall.org.

ℹ Getting There & Around

BUS The AD 122 Hadrian's Wall bus (eight daily, April to October) is a hail-and-ride service that runs between Hexham and **Carlisle**, via all the important sights.

TRAIN The train line between Newcastle and **Carlisle** (Tyne Valley Line) has stations at Corbridge, Hexham, Haydon Bridge, Bardon Mill, **Haltwhistle** and Brampton. Trains run hourly but not all services stop at all stations.

Haltwhistle & Around
POP 3810

The market town of Haltwhistle makes a good base for exploring Hadrian's Wall. Access is straightforward, there's a good choice of places to stay and eat, and many major sights – including some of the best-preserved and most dramatic stretches of the wall itself – are nearby.

◉ Sights

**VINDOLANDA ROMAN FORT &
MUSEUM** _Roman Fort_
(www.vindolanda.com; adult/child £5.90/3.50, with Roman Army Museum £9/5; ◷10am-6pm Apr-Sep, to 5pm Feb-Mar & Oct) The extensive site of Vindolanda offers a fascinating glimpse into the daily life of a Roman garrison town. The time-capsule museum displays leather sandals, signature Roman toothbrush-flourish helmet decorations, and a new exhibition featuring numerous writing tablets recently returned from the British Library. These include a student's marked work ('sloppy'), and a parent's note with a present of socks and underpants (things haven't changed – in this climate you can never have too many).

The museum is just one part of this large, extensively excavated site, which includes impressive parts of the fort and town (excavations continue) and reconstructed turrets and temple.

Vindolanda is a mile south of the B6318, about 8 miles east of Haltwhistle.

🛏 Sleeping

ASHCROFT _B&B_ **££**
(☏01434-320213; www.ashcroftguesthouse.co.uk; Lanty's Lonnen, Haltwhistle; s/d from £48/78; 🛜) In the world of British B&Bs,

MANFRED GOTTSCHALK / LONELY PLANET IMAGES ©

Don't Miss **Housesteads Roman Fort & Museum**

The wall's most dramatic site – and the best-preserved Roman fort in the whole country – is at Housesteads. From here, high on a ridge and covering 2 hectares, you can survey the moors of Northumberland National Park, and the snaking wall, with a sense of awe at the landscape and the aura of the Roman lookouts.

The substantial foundations bring fort life alive. The remains include an impressive hospital, granaries with a carefully worked-out ventilation system and barrack blocks. Most memorable are the spectacularly situated communal flushable latrines, which summon up Romans at their most mundane. Information boards show what the individual buildings would have looked like in their heyday and there's a scale model of the entire fort in the small museum at the ticket office.

Housesteads is on the B6318, about 6 miles from Haltwhistle.

THINGS YOU NEED TO KNOW
EH; adult/child £4.80/2.40; ⏰10am-6pm Apr-Sep

things don't get better than this. Picture a large, elegant Edwardian vicarage surrounded by two acres of beautifully manicured, layered lawns and gardens from which there are stunning views.

CENTRE OF BRITAIN Hotel ££
(☎01434-322422; www.centre-of-britain.org. uk; Haltwhistle; s/d from £59/70) Just across from where locals claim the 'centre of Britain' to be, this Norwegian-owned

hotel (hence the slightly Scandinavian feel) incorporates a sturdy 15th-century *pele* tower, one of the oldest chunks of architecture in town.

ℹ️ Information

Tourist office (☎01434-322002; ⏰9.30am-1pm & 2-5.30pm Mon-Sat, 1-5pm Sun)
Haltwhistle's tourist office is in the train station, but may soon be moving to the library in Main St.

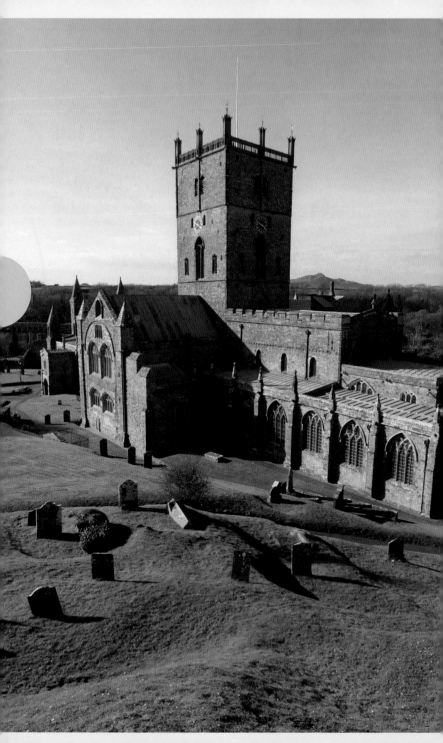

Snowdonia & Wales

Wales is a separate nation, with its own language and culture. And you can feel the difference as soon as you cross the border. Although this ancient Celtic country was under English rule from around 1300, the flame of independence never died, and in 1998 Wales finally regained control of its own destiny.

So after centuries of oppression and decades in the doldrums, Wales is now rediscovering itself with energy and determination. Cultural landmarks across the country have been restored; the capital city of Cardiff has decorated the once-abandoned waterfront with stunning new buildings; and even the summit of Snowdon, the highest peak in the land, has received a brand-new 21st-century visitor centre.

Whether you're marvelling at the medieval castles in the north, exploring pubs and shops in the south, or hiking airy clifftops in the west, you certainly won't regret spending some time in Wales.

St David's Cathedral (p265)

Hikers in Snowdonia National Park (p276)

Snowdonia & Wales

Legend:

1 Snowdon
2 Cardiff Bay
3 St Davids
4 Pembrokeshire Coast
5 Portmeirion
6 Caernarfon Castle

40 km
20 miles

ATLANTIC OCEAN

53°N
52°N
51°N

Blackpool
Southport
Carmel Head
Isle of Anglesey
Amlwch
Holyhead
ANGLESEY
Holy Island
Great Ormes
Llandudno
Birkenhead
Liverpool
Beaumaris
Conwy
Rhyl
Prestatyn
Ellesmere Port
Caernarfon
Bangor
Abergele
Holywell
Pen-y-Pass
Llanberis
Denbigh
Flint
Clynnog Fawr
Betws-y-Coed
Ruthin
Chester
Morfa Nefyn
Mt Snowdon (1085m)
Brymbo
Porthmadog
Blaenau Ffestiniog
Corwen
Wrexham
Abersoch
Pwllheli
Portmeirion
Llangollen
Chirk
Harlech
Snowdonia National Park
Oswestry
Knockin
Barmouth
Dolgellau
Centre for Alternative Technology
Shrewsbury
Welshpool
Machynlleth
Church Stretton
Aberystwyth
Llanidloes
Newtown
POWYS
Ludlow
Llanon
Rheidol
Llandrindod Wells
Leominster
New Quay
Tregaron
Cambrian Mountains
Pembrokeshire Coast National Park
Cardigan
Newport
Hay-on-Wye
Hereford
Fishguard
Llandovery
St Davids
Newgale
CARMARTHENSHIRE
Carmarthen
Brecon
Llanthony
Haverfordwest
Crickhowell
Freshwater West
Milford Haven
Amroth
Kidwelly
Ammanford
Brecon Beacons National Park
Abergavenny
Monmouth
Pembroke
Tenby
Llanelli
Pontarddulais
Merthyr Tydfil
Tredegar
Ebbw Vale
Raglan
Tintern Abbey
Manorbier
Clydach
Aberdare
Abersychan
Usk
Pembrokeshire Coast National Park
Swansea
Neath
Pontypool
Cwmbran
Chepstow
Swansea Airport
Port Talbot
Pontypridd
Castell Coch
Mumbles
Caerphilly
Cardiff International Airport
St Mellons
Chipping Sodbury
Porthcawl
Llandaff
Cardiff
Barry
Penarth
Clevedon
Bristol
Ilfracombe
Weston-super-Mare
Bath
Barnstaple
Exmoor National Park
Minehead
Burnham-on-Sea
Radstock
Bude
Tiverton
Taunton
Glastonbury
Wincanton

Snowdonia & Wales Highlights

① Snowdon

Dominating the map of North Wales is the spectacular mountainous landscape of Snowdonia (p276), much of it protected as a national park. The region gets its name from Snowdon, the highest peak in Wales and the most popular spot for visitors.

Need to Know

LOCATION 120 miles north of Cardiff, 200 miles northwest of London **WEATHER** Can be warm and sunny; can be wet and gloomy **For further coverage, see p276**

Snowdon Don't Miss List

SAM ROBERTS, SENIOR WARDEN
(RETIRED) OF SNOWDONIA NATIONAL
PARK

1 HIKE TO SNOWDON'S SUMMIT

I've lived in this area all my life, and as a Welshman I'm naturally proud of my homeland. My favourite hike up to Snowdon's summit (p277) is the **Rhyd-Ddu Path**; it's on the western side of the mountain which sees fewer visitors. Alternatively, take the Snowdon Sherpa bus to **Pen-y-Pass**, reach the summit from there and descend on the **Llanberis Path**.

2 LLANBERIS PATH

This is one of the most popular walking trails up the mountain, starting from **Llanberis** (p278). You can stroll up just for a short distance, or it's easy enough to go all the way to the summit. On your way back down the Llanberis Path, enjoy a drink and a warm welcome at my favourite cafe, **Penceunant Tearoom**.

3 SNOWDON RAILWAY

If you can't hike up to the summit, or haven't got time, you can take a ride on the unique **Snowdon Railway** (p277), built in the 19th century for Victorian tourists and still working today. Be aware that queues at the ticket office in Llanberis can be long on sunny days in the summer, so I recommend booking ahead if you can.

4 HAFOD ERYRI

Not only does a railway run up Snowdon, you can get a cup of tea at the top as well! **Hafod Eryri** (p277) was built in 2009 and is the highest cafe in Wales. It can be very busy, but to escape the crowds you need walk only a short distance back down the mountain. If you get a return ticket on the train, the half-hour allowed at the top is not really enough; I recommend train up, walk down.

5 PEN-Y-GWYRD HOTEL

To immerse yourself in Snowdon tradition and atmosphere, stay a night at this historic hotel (p279). It's been a base for hikers and mountaineers for more than a century.

Cardiff Bay

The Welsh capital city is buzzing with confidence, and nowhere is this more apparent than the revitalised waterfront of Cardiff Bay (p259). Once a derelict dock and down-at-heel neighbourhood called Tiger Bay, now it's home to a collection of fascinating structures including the historic Pierhead building, the new Wales Millennium Centre and the Senedd (the Assembly Building for Wales's devolved government) – not to mention several film locations for *Dr Who*. Wales Millennium Centre

St Davids

It's little more than a village but St Davids (p265) ranks as Britain's smallest city thanks to the presence of a magnificent 12th-century cathedral that marks the burial place of the nation's patron saint. It's been a place of pilgrimage for more than 1500 years, and today St Davids still attracts many visitors, as it makes a good base for exploring this beautiful corner of West Wales. St David's Cathedral

Pembrokeshire Coast

4

At the end of the peninsula that makes up the southwest part of Wales is the old county of Pembrokeshire (p264), edged on two sides by the sea, and some of the most beautiful stretches of coastline in Britain. It's protected as a national park, and provides excellent hiking, surfing and wildlife-watching opportunities – as well as bucket-and-spade beaches perfect for family holidays.

Puffin, Pembrokeshire

5

Portmeirion

Perhaps the wackiest attraction in Wales is the seaside fantasy-land of Portmeirion (p275), an Italianate village perched above the sea, created by the eccentric architect Sir Clough Williams-Ellis in the early 20th century. Brimming with follies, colonnades, pastel-coloured palaces and other architectural oddities, with nods to styles as varied as Moorish and Greek, it provided the perfect setting for the classic cult TV series *The Prisoner* in the 1960s.

6

Caernarfon Castle

One of an 'iron ring' of fortresses built by (English) King Edward I to control Wales in the late 13th century, Caernarfon Castle (p273) was a military stronghold, seat of government and royal palace. It's dramatic and unusual thanks to colour-banded masonry and polygonal towers, supposedly inspired by the ancient walls of Constantinople. Today, it's a Unesco World Heritage Site.

Snowdonia & Wales' Best…

Castles

○ **Cardiff Castle** (p258)
Roman foundations, Norman additions, Victorian frills – the capital's stronghold has a chequered past

○ **Chepstow Castle** (p263)
Classic fortress, guarding Wales's southeast border

○ **Conwy Castle** (p272) Part of the English 'iron ring' that controlled North Wales for centuries

○ **Caernarfon Castle** (p273)
Yet another 'magnificent badge of our subjection', as Welsh writer Thomas Pennant put it

Architecture

○ **Cardiff Bay** (p259)
Victorian Gothic splendour at the Pierhead and modernist style at the Millennium Centre

○ **Pontcysyllte Aqueduct, Llangollen** (p269) Slender pillars carry a canal high across the Dee Valley

○ **Portmeirion** (p275)
Bizarre fantasy-land of follies, colonnades and architectural oddities

○ **St David's Cathedral** (p265) Small maybe, but one of the loveliest cathedrals in Wales

Culture Spots

○ **Hay-on-Wye** (p267) Self-proclaimed secondhand bookshop capital of the world, and home of the Hay Literary Festival

○ **Llangollen** (p268) The International Musical Eisteddfod takes place here every July

○ **Wales Millennium Centre, Cardiff** (p262) The capital's stunning showpiece centre for music and the performing arts

○ **Tintern Abbey** (p263)
Evocative ruins in the Wye Valley, and the inspiration for poets and artists through the centuries

Need to Know

Natural Beauty

○ **Pembrokeshire** (p264)
In the far west of Wales, a beautiful rural area with a dramatic coastline

○ **Snowdonia** (p276) The largest national park in Wales, a wild landscape of glacier-scarred valleys and rugged jagged mountains, including Snowdon

○ **Wye Valley** (p263)
A snaking, steep-sided valley flanked by fields and woodland

ADVANCE PLANNING

○ **Six months before**
Make accommodation plans if you're interested in the Hay Literary Festival, the Eisteddfod or other major events

○ **Two months before**
Book long-distance train and bus tickets for the best deals

○ **Two weeks before**
Confirm opening times and prices for the major sights

RESOURCES

Major tourist information websites for the key cities and areas in this region:

○ **Wales**
(www.visitwales.co.uk)

○ **Cardiff**
(www.visitcardiff.com)

○ **Wye Valley**
(www.visitwyevalley.com)

○ **Snowdonia**
(www.visitsnowdonia.info)

○ **Snowdonia National Park** (www.eryri-npa.co.uk; www.pembrokeshirecoast. org.uk)

○ **Pembrokeshire** (www. visitpembrokeshire.com)

○ **South Wales**
(www.visitsouthwales.com)

GETTING AROUND

○ **Bus** Long-distance buses between main centres are good; local buses are infrequent in some rural areas

○ **Train** Wales has very useful rail arteries through the south and north of the country, plus the famously scenic Heart of Wales line through the centre

○ **Car** Gives you maximum freedom, but many roads are narrow and twisting; don't be trying to get anywhere in a hurry

BE FOREWARNED

○ **Festivals**
Accommodation is practically impossible to find during major events such as the Eisteddfod and the Hay Festival. If you're not coming for the festivals, you're better off avoiding these towns at these times.

○ **Welsh** In some parts of Wales (but not all) the first language is Welsh. Trying a few words can help break the ice, but remember not everyone's a Welsh speaker! Try: *sut mae* (pronounced 'sit mai') – hello; *bore da* ('boray da') – good morning; *diolch* ('dee-olkh') – thanks and *hwyl fawr* ('hueyl vowrr') – goodbye.

Left: Conwy Castle (p272);
Above: Pontcysyllte Aqueduct (p269)

Snowdonia & Wales Itineraries

Our three-day trip runs along the southern edge of Wales, while the five-day option heads up through the borders to the mountains and castles of the north. The routes intersect at Cardiff.

3 DAYS

CHEPSTOW TO ST DAVIDS
City Buzz & Coastal Peace

If you're coming into South Wales from England by road, you'll probably cross the River Severn on one of two gigantic suspension bridges. It's worth detouring to the ancient border town of **(1) Chepstow** to visit Chepstow Castle. If time allows, continue a few miles up the Wye Valley to see the evocative ruins of **(2) Tintern Abbey**.

Continue to **(3) Cardiff**, the lively Welsh capital. Top sights here include Cardiff Castle and, down at revitalised Cardiff Bay, the iconic Pierhead building (dubbed Cardiff's Big Ben) and Wales Millennium Centre. Rugby fans may want to visit the Millennium Stadium in the city centre. In the evening, you're spoilt for choice with bars and restaurants lining the waterfront.

Next, head to the far tip of Wales and the stunningly scenic area of **(4) Pembrokeshire** for a spot of surfing, clifftop hiking or just lounging on the beach. Base yourself in charming **(5) St Davids**, a rural outpost with an impressive medieval cathedral.

Top left: Cafe fare, Cardiff (p261); **Top right:** Harlech Castle (p273)

5
DAYS

CARDIFF TO CAERNARFON

Books, Mountains & Castles

Start your tour in **(1) Cardiff,** the capital of Wales. On day two head north to the whacky little border town of **(2) Hay-on-Wye**, famous for its more than 30 secondhand bookshops and a literary festival that Bill Clinton famously called 'the Woodstock of the mind'. Continue through the borders to reach **(3) Llangollen**, home to another famous festival – the International Eisteddfod – and also noted for a sinuous canal aqueduct, an engineering marvel in its day.

Then it's back into the heartland of Wales, and the mountainous landscape of **(4) Snowdonia National Park**. From **(5) Llanberis**, hikers can ascend Snowdon, the highest peak in Wales, while those with a more relaxed state of mind can ride the mountain railway to the top.

On the edge of the park sit four sturdy fortresses, together forming a World Heritage Site. Base yourself in **(6) Caernarfon** for the castle of the same name, then visit nearby Conwy Castle and Harlech Castle. If time allows, detour to **(7) Portmeirion** to sample architecture of a very different sort.

Discover
Snowdonia & Wales

At a Glance

- **Cardiff** (p258) The Welsh capital.

- **South Wales** (p263) Some post-industrial landscapes, interspersed with visual gems.

- **Pembrokeshire** (p264) Distinct identity and outpost ambience.

- **Mid-Wales** (p266) The Welsh heartland. Hay-on-Wye is a gateway to the area.

- **North Wales** (p268) Mountainous and moody.

- **Snowdonia National Park** (p276) The biggest park in Wales.

Millennium Stadium, Cardiff
PHOTOGRAPHER: NEIL SETCHFIELD / LONELY PLANET IMAGES ©

CARDIFF (CAERDYDD)

POP 324,800

The capital of Wales since only 1955, Cardiff has embraced its new role with vigour, emerging as one of Britain's leading urban centres in the 21st century. Caught between its ancient fort and its ultramodern waterfront, compact Cardiff seems to have surprised even itself with how interesting it's become.

◉ Sights

Central Cardiff

CARDIFF CASTLE   Castle

(www.cardiffcastle.com; Castle St; adult/child £8.95/6.35, incl guided tour £11.95/8.50; ⏱9am-6pm Mar-Oct, 9am-5pm Nov-Feb) The grafting of Victorian mock-Gothic extravagance onto Cardiff's most important historical relics makes Cardiff Castle the city's leading attraction. It's far from a traditional Welsh castle, more a collection of disparate castles scattered around a central green, encompassing practically the whole history of Cardiff. The most conventional castle-y bits are the 12th-century motte-and-bailey **Norman keep** at its centre and the 13th-century **Black Tower**, which forms the entrance gate.

In the 19th century it was discovered that the Normans had built their fortifications on top of the original 1st-century Roman fort. The high walls that surround the castle now are largely a Victorian reproduction of the 3rd-century 3m-thick Roman walls. Also from the 19th century are the towers and turrets on the west side, dominated by the colourful 40m **clock tower**.

FREE NATIONAL MUSEUM CARDIFF
Museum

(www.museumwales.ac.uk; Gorsedd Gardens Rd; ⏰10am-5pm Tue-Sun) Set around the green lawns and colourful flowerbeds of **Alexandra Gardens** is the Civic Centre, an early-20th-century complex of neo-baroque buildings in gleaming white Portland stone. They include the **City Hall**, police headquarters, law courts, crown offices, Cardiff University and this excellent museum, one of Britain's best, covering natural history, archaeology and art.

MILLENNIUM STADIUM
Stadium

(☎029-2082 2228; www.millenniumstadium.com; Westgate St; tours adult/child £6.50/4; ⏰10am-5pm Mon-Sat, 10am-4pm Sun) The spectacular Millennium Stadium squats like a stranded spaceship on the River Taff's east bank. Attendance at international rugby and football matches has increased dramatically since this 72,500-seat, three-tiered stadium with sliding roof was completed in time to host the 1999 Rugby World Cup. The famous **Cardiff Arms Park**, its predecessor, lies literally in its shadow.

Cardiff Bay

CARDIFF BAY WATERFRONT
Neighbourhood

Lined with important national institutions, Cardiff Bay is where the modern Welsh nation is put on display in an architect's playground of interesting buildings, large open spaces and public art.

FREE SENEDD (NATIONAL ASSEMBLY BUILDING)
Government Building

(☎0845 010 5500; www.assemblywales.org/sen-home; ⏰10.30am-4.30pm, extended during plenary sessions) Designed by Lord Richard Rogers (the architect

behind London's Lloyd's Building and Paris' Pompidou Centre), the Senedd is a striking structure of concrete, slate, glass and steel with an undulating canopy roof lined with red cedar. The lobby and surrounding area are littered with public artworks.

FREE PIERHEAD
Museum

(☎029-0845 010 5500; www.pierhead.org; ⏰10.30am-4.30pm Mon-Fri & most weekends) One of the area's few Victorian remnants, Pierhead is a red-brick French-Gothic Renaissance confection – nicknamed Wales' Big Ben.

Sleeping

Central Cardiff

PARK PLAZA
Hotel ££

(☎029-2011 1111; www.parkplazacardiff.com; Greyfriars Rd; r from £109; @ 🛜 ﹰ) Luxurious without being remotely stuffy, the Plaza has all the five-star facilities you'd expect from a business-orientated hotel.

Arcade cafes, Cardiff

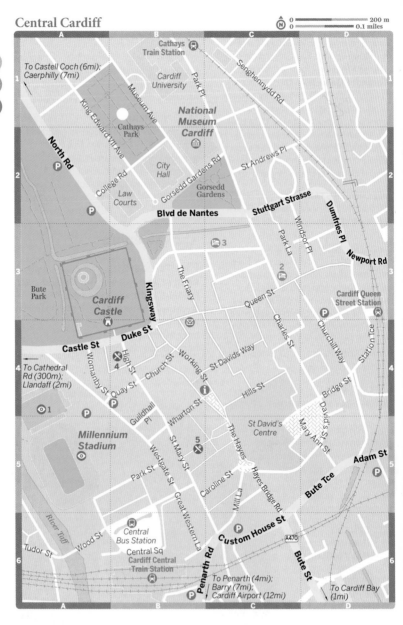

Central Cardiff

0   200 m
0   0.1 miles

DISCOVER SNOWDONIA & WALES CARDIFF (CAERDYDD)

PARC HOTEL   Hotel ££

(0871-376 9011; www.thistle.com/theparc
hotel; Park Pl; r from £99; @ ⊙) A smart contemporary hotel located right at the heart
of the main shopping area, with tasteful
rooms, good facilities and helpful staff.

Cardiff Bay

JOLYON'S BOUTIQUE HOTEL   Hotel ££

(029-2048 8775; www.jolyons.co.uk; 5 Bute
Cres; r £65-140; ⊙) A touch of Georgian
elegance in the heart of Cardiff Bay,

Central Cardiff

Jolyon's has six individually designed rooms combining antique furniture with contemporary colours and crisp cotton sheets.

ST DAVID'S HOTEL & SPA Hotel ££
(☎029-2045 4045; www.thestdavidshotel.com; Havannah St; r from £99; @ 🛜 ☒) A glittering, glassy tower topped with a sail-like flourish, St David's epitomises Cardiff Bay's transformation from wasteland to stylish place-to-be. Every room has a private balcony with a harbour view.

 Eating & Drinking

Central Cardiff

PLAN Cafe £
(28 Morgan Arcade; mains £5-8; ⊘9am-5pm; 🖋) Serving quite possibly Wales' best coffee, this satisfying cafe specialises in healthy, organic, locally sourced food, including vegan options.

GOAT MAJOR Pub £
(33 High St; mains £7-8; ⊘food noon-6pm Mon-Sat, noon-4pm Sun) A solidly traditional pub with armchairs, a fireplace and lip-smacking Brains Dark real ale on tap, the Goat Major's gastronomic contribution comes in the form of its selection of homemade pies.

Cardiff Bay
WOODS BAR & BRASSERIE
Modern European ££
(☎029-2049 2400; Stuart St; mains £11-18; ⊘closed Sun dinner) The historic Pilotage Building has been given a modern makeover – including zany wallpaper, exposed stone walls and a floor-to-ceiling glass extension – to accommodate Cardiff Bay's best restaurant. The cuisine is modern European, light and flavoursome, with an emphasis on using local ingredients.

CWTCH Bar
(5 Bute Cres) A cwtch is either a warm, safe place or a cuddle and this little bar, below Jolyon's hotel, is certainly the former and imparts a cosy feeling that's almost as good as the latter. Lethal two-for-one cocktail deals add to the merriment, as do occasional open-mic nights. Sink into a sofa and slip into Cwtch's warm embrace.

SALT Bar
(Mermaid Quay) A large, modern, nautical-themed bar with plenty of sofas and armchairs for lounging around and a 1st-floor open-air terrace with a view of the yachts out in the bay.

 Shopping

If you thought Cardiff's 21st-century makeover was all about political edifices, arts centres and sports stadia, think again. One of the most dramatic developments in the central city is the transformation of the Hayes shopping strip, with the giant, glitzy extension of the St David's shopping centre now eating up its entire eastern flank. Costing £675 million, it's one of the UK's largest. Balancing this ultramodern mall is a historic network of Victorian and Edwardian arcades spreading their dainty tentacles either side of St Mary St.

MEL / IMAGEBROKER

Don't Miss **Wales Millennium Centre**

The centrepiece and symbol of Cardiff Bay's regeneration, the Millennium Centre is an architectural masterpiece of stacked Welsh slate in shades of purple, green and grey topped with an overarching bronzed steel shell – designed by Capita Percy Thomas.

The roof above the main entrance is pierced by 2m-high, letter-shaped windows, spectacularly backlit at night, that spell out phrases from poet Gwyneth Lewis: '*Creu Gwir fel Gwydr o Ffwrnais Awen*' (Creating truth like glass from inspiration's furnace) and 'In these stones horizons sing'.

You can wander through the public areas at will, or take an official **guided tour** (adult/child £5.50/4.50; ⏰9am-5pm) that leads behind the giant letters, onto the main stage and into the dressing rooms, depending on what shows are on.

THINGS YOU NEED TO KNOW

☎029-2063 6464; www.wmc.org.uk; Bute Pl; admission free

ℹ Information

Cardiff Bay Visitor Centre (☎029-2087 7927; Harbour Dr; ⏰10am-6pm)

Cardiff tourist office (☎029-2087 3573; www.visitcardiff.com; Old Library, The Hayes; ⏰9.30am-5.30pm Mon-Sat, 10am-4pm Sun; @)

ℹ Getting There & Away

BUS The First (www.firstgroup.com) *Shuttle100* service heads regularly between Cardiff and Swansea (peak/off-peak £6.50/5 return, one hour). National Express (www.nationalexpress.com) coach destinations include **Swansea** (£7.30, one hour), **Brecon** (£4.10, 1¼ hours), **Monmouth** (£9.70, 1¼ hours), **Chepstow** (£5.20, one hour) and **London** (£22, 3¼ hours).

TRAIN Direct services from Cardiff include **London Paddington** (£43, 2¾ hours) and **Fishguard Harbour** (£20, 2¼ hours).

SOUTH WALES
Chepstow

Magnificent **Chepstow Castle** (Bridge St; adult/child £3.60/3.20; ⏰9am-5pm Apr-Oct, 9.30am-4pm Mon-Sat, 11am-4pm Sun Nov-Mar) perches atop a limestone cliff overhanging the river, guarding the main river crossing from England into South Wales. It is one of the oldest castles in Britain (building began in 1067) and the impressive Great Tower retains its original Norman architecture.

Lower Wye Valley

The A466 road follows the snaking, steep-sided valley of the River Wye from Chepstow to Monmouth, passing through the straggling village of Tintern. It's a beautiful drive, given a particularly mysterious quality when a twilight mist rises from the river and shrouds the illuminated ruins of **Tintern Abbey** (Cadw; www.cadw.wales.gov.uk; adult/child £3.60/3.20; ⏰9am-5pm Apr-Oct, 9.30am-4pm Mon-Sat & 11am-4pm Sun Nov-Mar; P). Founded in 1131 by the Cistercian order, this sprawling monastic complex and its riverside setting has served as inspiration for poets and artists through the centuries. The huge abbey church was built between 1269 and 1301, the stone shell of which remains surprisingly intact; the finest feature is the tracery that once contained the magnificent west windows.

Gower Peninsula (Y Gŵyr)

With its broad butterscotch beaches, pounding surf, precipitous clifftop walks and rugged, untamed uplands, the Gower Peninsula feels a million miles away from Swansea's urban bustle – yet it's just on the doorstep. The peninsula also has the best surfing in Wales outside Pembrokeshire.

Sights

Heading west along the south coast from the family-magnet beach of **Port Eynon**, the village of **Rhossili** looks north along the 3-mile sweep of **Rhossili Bay** at the western tip of the peninsula. From Rhossili village follow the 1-mile tidal causeway to rocky, wave-blasted **Worm's Head** (from Old English *wurm,* meaning dragon) but *only* for a two-hour period either side of low tide. At the heart of the peninsula is Cefn Bryn, a ruggedly beautiful expanse of moorland that rises to a height of 186m. On a suitably desolate ridge above the village of **Reynoldston** stands a mysterious neolithic burial chamber capped by the 25-tonne quartz boulder known as **Arthur's Stone** (Coeten Arthur).

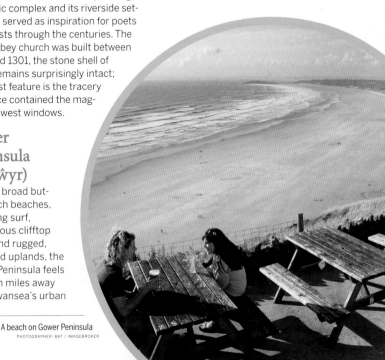

A beach on Gower Peninsula
PHOTOGRAPHER: BAT / IMAGEBROKER

Detour:
Castell Coch

Fanciful **Castell Coch** (Cadw; ☎029-2081 0101; Tongwynlais; adult/child £3.60/3.20; ⏱9am-5pm Apr-Oct, 9.30am-4pm Mon-Sat & 11am-4pm Sun Nov-Mar) was the summer retreat of the third marquess of Bute and, like Cardiff Castle, was designed by William Burges in gaudy Victorian Gothic style.

Lady Bute's huge, circular bedroom is pure fantasy – her bed, with crystal globes on the bedposts, sits in the middle beneath an extravagantly decorated and mirrored cupola, with 28 painted panels around the walls depicting monkeys (fashionable at the time, apparently; just plain weird now).

Lord Bute's bedroom is small and plain in comparison, but the octagonal drawing room is another hallucinogenic tour de force, the walls painted with scenes from Aesop's fables, the domed ceiling a flurry of birds and stars, and the fireplace topped with figures depicting the three ages of men and women.

From Cardiff, Stagecoach buses 26 and 132 (30 minutes) stop at Tongwynlais, a 10-minute walk to the castle. Bus 26A (four daily Monday to Friday) stops right at the castle gates.

Laugharne (Talacharn)
POP 2900

Sleepy little Laugharne (pronounced 'larn') sits above the tide-washed shores of the Taf Estuary, overlooked by a Norman castle. Dylan Thomas, one of Wales' greatest writers, spent the last four years of his life here, during which he produced some of his most inspired work, including *Under Milk Wood;* the town is one of the inspirations for the play's fictional village of Llareggub (spell it backwards and you'll get the gist).

 Sights

DYLAN THOMAS BOATHOUSE   Museum
(www.dylanthomasboathouse.com; Dylan's Walk; adult/child £3.50/1.75; ⏱10am-5.30pm May-Oct, 10.30am-3.30pm Nov-Apr) Dylan Thomas lived here from 1949 to 1953 with his wife Caitlin and their three children. It's a beautiful setting, looking out over the estuary with its 'heron-priested shore'. The parlour has been restored to its 1950s appearance, with the desk that once belonged to Thomas' schoolmaster father and recordings of the poet reading his own works.

Along the lane from the Boathouse is the old shed where Thomas did most of his writing. It looks as if he has just popped out, with screwed-up pieces of paper littered around.

Dylan and Caitlin Thomas are buried in a grave marked by a simple white, wooden cross in the grounds of **St Martin's Church**, on the northern edge of the town. **Dylan's Walk** is a scenic 2-mile loop that continues north along the shore beyond the Boathouse, then turns inland past a 17th-century farm and back via St Martin's Church.

PEMBROKESHIRE (SIR BENFRO)

The rugged Pembrokeshire coast is what you would imagine the world would look like if God was a geology teacher. There are knobbly hills of volcanic rock, long thin inlets scoured by glacial meltwaters, and stratified limestone pushed up vertically and eroded into natural arches, blowholes and sea stacks. Stretches of towering red and grey cliff give way to perfect sandy beaches, only to resume around the headland painted black.

It's a landscape of Norman castles, Iron Age hill forts, holy wells and Celtic saints – including the nation's patron, Dewi Sant (St David). Predating even the ancient Celts are the remnants of an older people, who left behind them dolmens and stone circles – the same people who may have transported their sacred bluestones all the way from the Preseli Hills to form the giant edifice at Stonehenge.

St Davids (Tyddewi)

POP 1800

Charismatic St Davids (yes, it has dropped the apostrophe from its name) is Britain's smallest city, its status ensured by the magnificent 12th-century cathedral that marks Wales' holiest site. The birth and burial site of the nation's patron saint, St Davids has been a pilgrimage destination for more than 1500 years. Today, St Davids attracts hordes of nonreligious pilgrims too, drawn by the town's laid-back vibe and the excellent hiking, surfing and wildlife-watching in the surrounding area.

 Sights

ST DAVID'S CATHEDRAL　Cathedral
(www.stdavidscathedral.org.uk; £4 donation invited; ⏰8.30am-5.30pm Mon-Sat, 12.45-5.30pm Sun) Hidden in a hollow and behind high walls, St David's Cathedral is intentionally unassuming. The valley site was chosen in the vain hope that the church would be overlooked by Viking raiders, but it was ransacked at least seven times. Yet once you pass through the gatehouse that separates it from the town and its stone walls come into view, you see it's as imposing as any of its contemporaries.

The atmosphere inside is one of great antiquity. As you enter the **nave**, the oldest surviving part of the cathedral, the first things you notice are the sloping floor and the outward lean of the massive, purplish-grey pillars linked by semicircular Norman Romanesque arches, a result of subsidence. Above is a richly carved 16th-century oak ceiling, adorned with pendants and bosses.

Castell Coch

© DAVID NEWHAM / ALAMY

 ## Sleeping & Eating

RAMSEY HOUSE B&B ££
(☎ 01437-720321; www.ramseyhouse.co.uk;
Lower Moor; r £100; P 🛜) The young owners
have fashioned a fresh-looking B&B from
their new house on the outskirts of town,
which is still only a short stroll west from
the centre.

ALANDALE B&B ££
(☎ 01437-720404; www.stdavids.co.uk/guest-
house/alandale.htm; 43 Nun St; s/d £36/80;
@ 🛜) A neat terraced house built in the
1880s for coastguard officers, Alandale
has a bright, cheerful atmosphere. Ask for
one of the rooms at the back, which are
quieter and have sweeping views.

CWTCH Modern Welsh £££
(☎ 01437-720491; www.cwtchrestaurant.co.uk;
22 High St; 3-course dinner £29; ⏰ dinner Wed-
Sun, daily summer) Stone walls and wooden
beams mark this out as a place with a
sense of occasion, as indeed does the

price, yet there's a snugness that lives up
to its name (*cwtch* means a cosy place or
a cuddle).

FARMER'S ARMS Pub
(14 Goat St) Even though St Davids is a bit
of a tourist trap, you'd be hard-pressed
finding a more authentic country pub.

MID-WALES
Brecon Beacons National Park

High mountain plateaux of grass and
heather, their northern rims scalloped
with glacier-scoured hollows, rise above
wooded, waterfall-splashed valleys and
green, rural landscapes. There are four
distinct regions within the park, neatly
bounded by main roads: the wild, lonely
Black Mountain in the west, with its high
moors and glacial lakes; Fforest Fawr,
which lies between the A4067 and A470,
whose rushing streams and spectacular
waterfalls form the headwaters of the

Rivers Tawe and Neath;
the Brecon Beacons proper, a
group of very distinctive, flat-topped
hills that includes **Pen-y-Fan** (886m), the
park's highest peak; and, from the A40
northeast to the English border, the rolling
heathland ridges of the Black Mountains –
don't confuse them with the Black Mountain (singular) in the west.

The handsome stone market town
of Brecon stands at the meeting of the
River Usk and the River Honddu. For
centuries the town thrived as a centre
of wool production and weaving; today
it's the main hub of the national park
and a natural base for exploring the
surrounding countryside.

Information

National Park Visitor Centre (☎01874-
623366; www.breconbeacons.org; Libanus;
⊙9.30am-5pm) The centre is off the A470 road
5 miles southwest of Brecon.

Tourist office (☎01874-622485; Market car park;
⊙9.30am-5.30pm Mon-Sat, 10am-4pm Sun)

Hay-on-Wye
(Y Gelli Gandryll)
POP 1500

Hay-on-Wye, a pretty little town on the
banks of the River Wye just inside the
Welsh border, has developed a reputation
disproportionate to its size. First came
the explosion in secondhand bookshops,
a charge led by the charismatic local
maverick Richard Booth. Later, a festival
was established. The 10-day Hay Festival
in late May has become Britain's leading
festival of literature and the arts – a kind
of bookworm's Glastonbury.

 Sleeping & Eating

START B&B ££
(☎01497-821391; www.the-start.net; Bridge
St; s/d £45/70; P 🖃) Peacefully set on
the fringes of town, this little place

267

boasts an unbeatable riverside setting, homely rooms in a renovated 18th-century house and a flagstone-floored breakfast room.

OLD BLACK LION Gastropub, B&B ££
(☎ 01497-820841; www.oldblacklion.co.uk; Lion St; s/d £53/90; P) As traditional and atmospheric as they come, this inn looks 17th-century but parts of it date from the 13th – expect low ceilings and uneven floors. The accumulated weight of centuries of hospitality is cheerfully carried by the current staff.

THREE TUNS Gastropub ££
(☎ 01497-821855; Broad St; mains £12-19; ☺ Wed-Sun) Rebuilt and expanded after a fire partially destroyed the 16th-century building, this smart gastropub has a large garden area for alfresco food and a fancier restaurant upstairs.

ⓘ Information

Tourist office (☎ 01497-820144; www.hay-on-wye.co.uk; Oxford Rd; ☺ 11am-4pm; @)

NORTH WALES
Llangollen
POP 3500

Llangollen (lan-goch-len), huddled in the fertile Vale of Llangollen around the banks of the tumbling River Dee, has long been a scenic gem of North Wales. It was traditionally seen as more of a day-trip destination, but its appeal has evolved rapidly in recent years with a slew of smart new places to eat, a burgeoning walking and outdoors scene, and a growing reputation for its arts festivals.

The **International Musical Eisteddfod** (see the boxed text, opposite) is staged at the Royal International Pavilion in early July. The **Llangollen Fringe Festival** (www.llangollenfringe. co.uk), a smaller version of the famous Edinburgh Fringe Festival, is staged at the Town Hall each July, and the recently launched **Llangollen Comedy Festival** (www.llancomedy.com) now comes to the Royal International Pavilion every June.

Llangollen

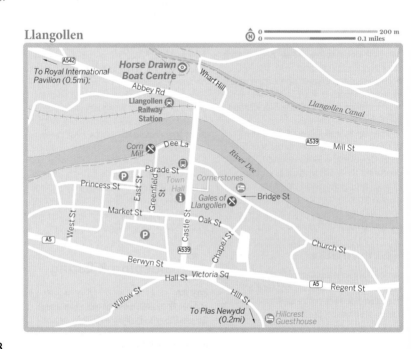

Essential Eisteddfod

The **National Eisteddfod** (www.eisteddfod.org.uk), pronounced 'ey-steth-vot', a celebration of Welsh culture, is Europe's largest festival of competitive music-making and poetry. Descended from ancient Bardic tournaments, it is conducted in Welsh, but the festival welcomes all entrants and visitors. Many people come in search of Welsh ancestry, while musical fringe events featuring local bands lend a slight Glastonbury-style atmosphere. It's generally held in early August, and the venue swings annually between North and South Wales.

Most famous of all is the **International Musical Eisteddfod** (www.llangollen2010.co.uk), established after WWII to promote international harmony. Held in early July, it attracts participants from more than 40 countries, transforming the town into a global village. In addition to daily folk music and dancing competitions, gala concerts feature international stars. It was nominated for the Nobel Peace Prize in 2004.

Sights & Activities

HORSE DRAWN BOAT CENTRE
Boat trip

(www.horsedrawnboats.co.uk; adult/child £5/2.50; ⊙11am-4.30pm Apr-Oct) The 45-minute, horse-drawn boat excursion from Llangollen Wharf cruises along the canal to Pontcysyllte Aqueduct and back.

PONTCYSYLLTE AQUEDUCT Landmark
(admission free) A few miles out of town, carrying a canal across a steep-sided valley, this is the tallest navigable aqueduct in the world and an engineering marvel. It's also a Unesco World Heritage Site. You can walk across the towpath beside the canal – but it's not a trip for anyone with vertigo.

LLANGOLLEN RAILWAY Heritage rail
(www.llangollen-railway.co.uk; adult/child return £11/5.50; ⊙return daily high season, special services low season) The 7.5-mile jaunt through the Dee Valley via Berwyn (near Horseshoe Falls) and Carrog on the former Ruabon to Barmouth line is a superb day out for families and heritage rail lovers alike.

Sleeping & Eating

CORNERSTONES GUESTHOUSE
B&B ££

(☎01978-861569; www.cornerstones-guesthouse.co.uk; 15 Bridge St; r £80-100; P @) This converted 16th-century house, all sloping floorboards and oak beams, has charm and history. The River Room is the cosiest of the five rooms, with the gentle lapping of the River Dee to send you off to sleep.

HILLCREST GUESTHOUSE B&B £
(☎01978-860208; www.hillcrest-guesthouse.com; Hill St; r from £50; 🐾) Pet friendly and charmingly traditional, it's a simple but homely place that attracts consistently good reports from visitors.

GALES OF LLANGOLLEN Wine bar ££
(☎01978-860089; www.galesofllangollen.co.uk; 18 Bridge St; mains £7.95-15.95; ⊙noon-2pm & 6-9.30pm Mon-Sat) Gales, a Llangollen institution, is consistently the best place in town to eat.

CORN MILL Gastropub ££
(Dee Lane; mains £8.75-16.50; ⊙noon-9pm) The water mill still turns at the heart of this converted mill – now an all-day bar and eatery – while the deck is the best spot in town for an alfresco lunch.

269

Llangollen tourist office (☏01978-860828; The Chapel, Castle St; ⏰9.30am-5.30pm high season, 9.30am-5pm low season)

Getting There & Away

The nearest mainline train station is at Ruabon, 6 miles east on Arriva Trains' Holyhead–Cardiff line.

Llandudno

POP 15,000

Llandudno is a master of reinvention. Developed as an upmarket Victorian holiday town, it still retains much of its 19th-century grandeur today, yet continues to find new fans with its booming boutique accommodation, upmarket dining, big-name retail outlets and Welsh art and performance. No wonder the American travel writer Bill Bryson was moved to describe Llandudno as his 'favourite seaside resort'.

Sights

GREAT ORME Headland

The dominating feature in the area is the Great Orme (207m), a spectacular 2-mile-long limestone headland jutting into the Irish Sea. Old-school tramway and cable-car rides go to the summit, providing breathtaking views of the Snowdonia range.

LLANDUDNO PIER Seaside

(⏰9am-6pm) The 1878-built Victorian pier is, at 670m, the longest pier in Wales and extends into the sea with amusements, candyfloss and slot machines. High art it isn't, but the kids will love it.

Sleeping

ESCAPE B&B Hotel **££**

(☏01492-877776; www.escapebandb.co.uk; 48 Church Walks; r £85-135; P ?) Escape, Llandudno's first boutique B&B, recently

Left: Bridge over the River Dee, Llangollen (p268);
Below: Hilltop view over Llangollen (p268)

PHOTOGRAPHERS: (LEFT) ANDERS BLOMQVIST; (BELOW) MICAH WRIGHT / LONELY PLANET IMAGES ©

upped the ante again, giving the rooms a major, design-led makeover to include a host of energy-saving and trendsetting features.

OSBORNE HOUSE — Hotel £££

(☎ 01492-860330; www.osbornehouse.com; 17 North Pde; ste £150-190; **P** **@**) All marble, antique furniture and fancy drapes, the lavish Osbourne House takes a more classical approach to aesthetics, but the results are no less impressive.

ABBEY LODGE — B&B ££

(☎ 01492-878042; 14 Abbey Rd; s/d £45/75; **P** **@**) The owners of Abbey Lodge keep this four-room property fresh and provide some homely touches, such as a small collection of local-interest books in each room.

Eating & Drinking

SEAHORSE — Seafood ££

(☎ 01492-875315; www.the-seahorse.co.uk; 7 Church Walks; set menu £21; ☺5pm-late Tue-Sat) It's a split-level affair with the more intimate cellar room better suited to informal dining and the street-level restaurant the domain of a good-value set menu (except weekends).

Cottage Loaf — Pub ££

(www.the-cottageloaf.co.uk; 1 Market St; mains £9-12) A cosy pub with real ales and satisfyingly hearty pub food.

ℹ Information

Llandudno tourist office (☎ 101492-577577; www.visitllandudno.org.uk; Mostyn St; ☺9am-5.30pm Mon-Sat & 9.30am-4.30pm Sun Apr-Oct, 9am-5pm Mon-Sat Nov-Mar)

Seafront at Llandudno (p270)

❶ Getting There & Away

BUS Arriva (www.arrivabus.co.uk) runs bus 5 to **Caernarfon** (1¾ hours, half-hourly Monday to Saturday, hourly Sunday) and bus 19/19A to **Llanrwst** (30 minutes, half-hourly Monday to Saturday, hourly Sunday). **National Express** (www.nationalexpress.com) runs to **London** (£32, 8½ hours).

TRAIN Arriva Trains (www.arrivatrainswales. co.uk) runs services to **Holyhead** (£11, 1½ hours) and nearby **Llandudno Junction** station (£2.10, 10 minutes) on the North Coast line. The latter station connects to direct services to **London Euston** (£70, three hours) with **Virgin Trains** (www.virgintrains.co.uk) on the West Coast Main Line. Arriva also runs services from **Llandudno Junction** station to **Betws-y-Coed** (£4.70, 30 minutes) on the Conwy Valley Line.

Conwy

POP 4000

Conwy Castle, the Unesco-designated cultural treasure, dominates the walled town of Conwy. Even today, it invests the approach to town with a sense of pomp and ceremony, while the three bridges spanning the river – namely Thomas Telford's 1826 (now-pedestrianised) suspension bridge, Robert Stephenson's 1848 steel railway bridge and the newer road-crossing bridge – add a sense of theatrical flourish.

⊙ Sights

CONWY CASTLE & TOWN WALL Castle
(Cadw; adult/child £4.60/4.10; ⊗9am-5pm high season, 9.30am-4pm Mon-Sat & 11am-4pm Sun low season) Probably the most stunning of all Edward I's Welsh fortresses, built between 1277 and 1307, Conwy Castle rises from a rocky outcrop with commanding views across the estuary and Snowdonia National Park. Exploring the castle's nooks and crannies makes for a superb, living-history visit but, best of all, head to the battlements for panoramic views and an overview of Conwy's majestic complexity. The 1200m-long **town wall** was built simultaneously with the castle, guarding Conwy's residents at night. You can walk part-way round the wall; the best views are to be had from Upper Gate.

Caernarfon

POP 9600

Wedged between the gleaming Menai Strait and the deep-purple mountains of Snowdonia, Caernarfon 's main claim to fame is its fantastical castle. Given the town's crucial historical importance, its proximity to the national park and its reputation as a centre of Welsh culture (it has the highest percentage of Welsh speakers of anywhere), parts of the town centre are surprisingly down-at-heel. Still, there's a lot of charm and a tangible sense of history in the streets around the castle. Within the cobbled lanes of the old walled town are some fine Georgian buildings, while the waterfront area has started on the inevitable march towards gentrification. The castle was built by Edward I as the last link in his 'iron ring' and it's now part of the *Castles and Town Walls of King Edward in Gwynedd* Unesco World Heritage Site.

Sights & Activities

CAERNARFON CASTLE

Castle, Museum

(Cadw; adult/child £4.95/4.60; ⊙9am-5pm Apr-Oct, 9.30am-4pm Mon-Sat & 11am-4pm Sun Nov-Mar) Majestic Caernarfon Castle was built between 1283 and 1330 as a military stronghold, a seat of government and a royal palace. Inspired by the dream of Macsen Wledig recounted in the *Mabinogion*, Caernarfon echoes the 5th-century walls of Constantinople, with colour-banded masonry and polygonal towers, instead of the traditional round towers and turrets.

Despite its fairytale aspect it is thoroughly fortified. It repelled Owain Glyndŵr's army in 1404 with a garrison of only 28 men, and resisted three sieges during the Civil War before surrendering to Cromwell's army in 1646.

A year after the construction of the building was begun, Edward I's second son was born here, becoming heir to the throne four months later when his elder

If You Like...
North Wales Castles

If you like the castles and defences of Caernarfon and Conwy (part of a World Heritage Site snappily titled *The Castles and Town Walls of King Edward in Gwynedd*), you may want to visit the other two members of the group:

1 HARLECH CASTLE

(Cadw; www.cadw.wales.gov.uk; adult/child £3.60/3.20; ⊙9am-5pm Apr-Oct, 9.30am-4pm Mon-Sat, 11am-4pm Sun Nov-Mar) Edward I finished this intimidating building in 1289, the southernmost of his 'iron ring' of fortresses designed to keep the Welsh firmly beneath his boot. Despite its might, the storybook fortress has been called the 'Castle of Lost Causes' because it has been lucklessly defended so many times. Owain Glyndŵr captured it after a long siege in 1404. He was in turn besieged here by the future Henry V. The grey sandstone castle's massive gatehouse and outer walls are still intact and give the illusion of impregnability even now. Four round towers guard the corners and you can climb onto the ramparts for views in all directions.

2 BEAUMARIS CASTLE

(Cadw; www.cadw.wales.gov.uk; adult/child £3.60/3.20; ⊙9.30am-6pm high season, 9.30am-4pm Mon-Sat, 11am-4pm Sun low season) The last of Edward I's great castles of North Wales, and the largest, Beaumaris sits on the Isle of Angelsey, just off the North Wales coast, reached via the bridge near Bangor. The four successive lines of fortifications and concentric 'walls within walls' make it the most technically perfect castle in Britain, and definitely a site with the wow factor.

brother died. To consolidate Edward's power he was made Prince of Wales in 1301, and his much-eroded statue is over the **King's Gate**.

Caernarfon Castle is a large, relatively intact structure. You can walk on and through the interconnected walls and towers gathered around the central green, most of which are well preserved but empty.

FREE SEGONTIUM ROMAN FORT
Ruins, Museum

(www.segontium.org.uk; Ffordd Cwstenin; ⏲12.30-4.30pm Tue-Sun) Just east of the centre, these excavated foundations represent the westernmost Roman legionary fort of the Roman Empire. Overlooking the Menai Strait, the fort dates back to AD 77, when the conquest of Wales was completed by capturing the Isle of Anglesey. It was designed to accommodate a force of up to 1000 infantrymen, and coins recovered from the site indicate that it was an active garrison until AD 394 – a reflection of its crucial strategic position.

 Sleeping & Eating

VICTORIA HOUSE
B&B ££

(☎01286-678263; www.thevictoriahouse.co.uk; 15 Church St; d £50-70; 🛜) Victoria House is an exceptional four-bedroom guest house with a homely feel, spacious modern rooms and some nice touches, such as an impressive selection of free toiletries and a DVD on the town's history in each room.

BLACK BOY INN
Pub, B&B ££

(☎01286-673604; www.black-boy-inn.com; Northgate St; s/d £65/95; P 🛜) Dating from 1522, the creaky but atmospheric rooms at this traditional inn have original wooden beams and panelling but a modern sensibility.

CAER MENAI
B&B ££

(☎01286-672612; www.caermenai.co.uk; 15 Church St; s/d from £40/60; @ 🛜) A former county school (1894), this elegant building is the biggest and brightest on the street.

❶ Information

Tourist office (☎01286-672232; Castle Ditch; ⏲9.30am-4.30pm Apr-Oct, 10am-3.30pm Mon-Sat Nov-Mar)

❶ Getting There & Away

BUS Buses include 87/88 to **Llanberis** (30 minutes). Snowdon Sherpa (www

.snowdoniagreenkey.co.uk)
bus S4 heads to **Beddgelert** (30
minutes) via the Snowdon Ranger (20
minutes) and Rhyd Ddu (24 minutes) trailheads.
A National Express coach stops here daily, en
route to **London** (£31, 10½ hours).
TRAIN Caernarfon is the northern terminus
of the Welsh Highland Railway tourist train,
which currently runs to just past **Beddgelert**
(£22 return, 1½ hours) and will connect to
Porthmadog in 2011.

Portmeirion

Set on its own tranquil peninsula
reaching into the estuary, **Portmeirion**
(www.portmeirion-village.com; adult/child
£8/4; ⏱9.30am-5.30pm) is an oddball,
gingerbread collection of buildings with
a heavy Italian influence, masterminded
by the Welsh architect Sir Clough
Williams-Ellis. Starting in 1926, Clough
collected bits and pieces from disintegrating stately mansions to create this
weird and wonderful seaside utopia
over the course of 50 years. When it was
deemed to be finished in 1976, Clough

had reached the ripe old age of 90 and
had designed and built many of the
structures himself.

It's really much more like an
amusement park or a stage set than
an actual village and, indeed, it formed
the ideally surreal set for the cult TV
series *The Prisoner*, which was filmed
here from 1966 to 1967; it still draws
fans of the show in droves, with *Prisoner*
conventions held annually in April.

Most of the kooky cottages or scaled-
down mansions scattered about the site
are available for holiday lets, while other
buildings contain cafes, restaurants
and gift shops. Portmeirion pottery
(the famously florid pottery designed
by Susan, Sir Clough's daughter) is
available, even though these days it's
made in Stoke-on-Trent (England).

Portmeirion is 2 miles east of
Porthmadog.

SNOWDONIA NATIONAL PARK

Snowdonia National Park (Parc Cenedlaethol Eryri) was founded in 1951 (making it Wales' first national park), primarily to keep the area from being loved to death. No Snowdonia experience is complete without coming face-to-face with Snowdon (1085m), one of Britain's most awe-inspiring mountains and the highest summit in Wales (it's actually the

Snowdonia

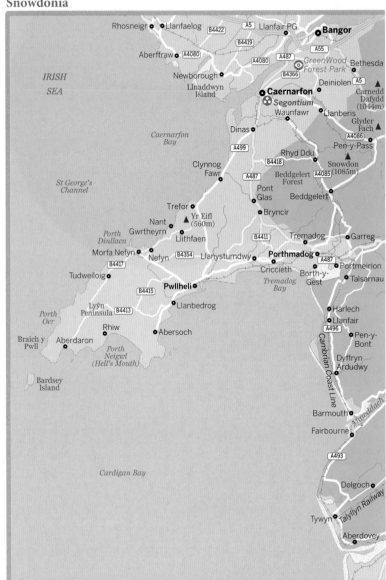

61st highest in Britain, with the other 60 all in Scotland). On a clear day the views stretch to Ireland and the Isle of Man over Snowdon's fine jagged ridges, which drop away in great swoops to sheltered *cwms* (valleys) and deep lakes.

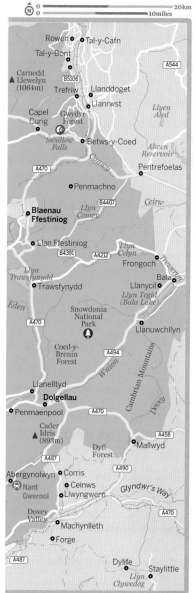

◉ Sights & Activities

SNOWDON
Walking

Six paths of varying length and difficulty lead to the summit of Snowdon. From Llanberis on the north side of the mountain, the **Llanberis Path** (10 miles, six hours return) is easiest to follow, running beside the railway line in places.

On the east side, two options start from Pen-y-Pass and require the least amount of ascent: the **Miner's Track** (7 miles, six hours) starts out gently but ends steeply; the **Pyg Track** (7 miles, six hours) is more interesting and meets the Miners Track where it steepens.

On the west side of the mountain are two minor routes: the relatively little-used **Rhyd Ddu Path** (8 miles, six hours) and the **Snowdon Ranger Path** (7 miles, five hours).

The most challenging route is the **Watkin Path** (8 miles, six hours) on the southerly approach from Nantgwynant.

SNOWDON MOUNTAIN RAILWAY
Railway

(☎0844 493 8120; www.snowdonrailway.co.uk; return adult/child £25/18; ⊙9am-5pm Mar-Oct) If you're not physically able to climb a mountain, short on time or just plain lazy, those industrious, railway-obsessed Victorians have gifted you an alternative. Opened in 1896, this is the UK's highest and only public rack-and-pinion railway. Vintage steam and modern diesel locomotives haul carriages from Llanberis up to Snowdon's very summit in an hour. Return trips involve a scant half-hour at the top before heading back down again. Single tickets can only be booked for the journey up (adult/child £18/15).

HAFOD ERYRI
Visitor Centre

Just below the cairn that marks Snowdon's summit, this striking piece of architecture opened in 2009 to replace the dilapidated 1930s visitor centre, which Prince Charles famously labelled 'the highest slum in Europe'. Clad in granite and curved to blend into the mountain, it's a wonderful building, housing a cafe, toilets and ambient interpretative

Be Prepared

In the alpine reaches of Snowdonia, the sudden appearance of low cloud and mist is common, even on days that start out clear and sunny. Never head into isolated reaches without food, drink, warm clothing and waterproofs, whatever the weather. Also be aware that even some walks described as easy may follow paths that go near very steep slopes and over loose scree.

The park authority publishes a free annual visitor newspaper, which includes information on getting around, park-organised walks and other activities. The Met Office keeps the weather conditions constantly updated on its website (www.metoffice.gov.uk/loutdoor/mountainsafety).

elements built into the structure itself. The centre (including the toilets) closes in the winter or if the weather's terrible; it's open whenever the train is running.

Llanberis

POP 1900

While not the most instantly attractive town in the area, Llanberis is a mecca for walkers and climbers, especially in July and August when accommodation is at a premium. It's actually positioned just outside the national park but functions as a hub, partly because the Snowdon Mountain Railway leaves from here. The town was originally built to house workers in the Dinorwic slate quarry; the massive waste tips are hard to miss as you approach from the east. While tourism is the cornerstone of Llanberis life these days, the town wears its industrial heritage on its sleeve.

🛏 Sleeping & Eating

GLYN AFON　　　　B&B　££
(☏ 01286-872528; www.glyn-afon.
co.uk; 72 High St; s/d £38/60; P)
The recently refurbished rooms have no frills but are warm and homely at this midrange guest house.

DOLAFON
B&B, Tearooms　££
(☏ 01286-870993; www.
dolafon.com; High St; s/d from £30/60; P) Set back from the road, this imposing 19th-century house offers a series of traditional rooms, most of them with en suites.

Narrow-gauge railway, Llanberis
PHOTOGRAPHER: GRANT DIXON / LONELY PLANET IMAGES ©

PEAK RESTAURANT — Welsh ££

(☎ 01286-872777; www.peakrestaurant.co.uk; 86 High St; mains £12-15; ⏱ dinner Wed-Sun) Charming owners and adventurer-sized portions underpin this restaurant's popularity and longevity.

PETE'S EATS — Cafe £

(☎ 01286-870117; www.petes-eats.co.uk; 40 High St; meals £4-6; @ 🛜) A busy, bright cafe where hikers and climbers swap tips over monster portions in a hostel-like environment.

ℹ️ Information

Tourist office (☎ 01286-870765; 41 High St; ⏱ 9.30am-4.30pm Apr-Oct, 9.30am-3pm Fri-Mon Nov-Mar)

ℹ️ Getting There & Away

Snowdon Sherpa bus S1 heads to **Pen-y-Pass** (15 minutes) while S2 continues on to **Betws-y-Coed** (33 minutes). Buses 87 and 88 head to **Caernarfon** (30 minutes).

Betws-y-Coed

POP 950

If you're looking for a base with an Alpine feel from which to explore Snowdonia National Park, the bustling little stone village of Betws-y-Coed (bet-us-ee-koyd) stands out as a natural option. The town has been Wales' most popular inland resort since Victorian days when a group of countryside painters founded an artistic community to record the diversity of the landscape. The arrival of the railway in 1868 cemented its popularity and today Betws-y-Coed is as busy with families and coach parties as it is with walkers.

Sleeping & Eating

TŶ GWYN HOTEL — Hotel, Restaurant ££

(☎ 01690-710383; www.tygwynhotel.co.uk; r £52-120; P 🛜) This ex-coaching inn has been welcoming guests since 1636, its venerable age borne out by misshapen rooms, low ceilings and exposed beams.

Detour:
Pen-y-Gwyrd

Eccentric but full of atmosphere, **Pen-y-Gwyrd** (☎ 01286-870211; www.pyg.co.uk; Nant Gwynant; r with/without bathroom £48/40) was used as a training base by the 1953 Everest team, and memorabilia from their stay includes their signatures on the dining-room ceiling. You'll find it below Pen-y-Pass, at the junction of the A498 and A4086.

MAES-Y-GARTH — B&B ££

(☎ 01690-710441; www.maes-y-garth.co.uk; Lon Muriau, off A470; r £66-70; P 🛜) Just across the river and a field from the township, this completely ordinary-looking newly built home has earned itself many fans.

BISTRO BETWS-Y-COED — Restaurant ££

(☎ 01690-710328; www.bistrobetws-y-coed.com; Holyhead Rd; lunch £6-9, dinner £12-17; ⏱ Wed-Sun, daily summer) This cottage-style eatery's statement of intent is 'modern and traditional Welsh'.

ℹ️ Information

National Park Information Centre (www.betws-y-coed.co.uk; Royal Oak Stables; ⏱ 9.30am-4.30pm) Sells books and maps.

ℹ️ Getting There & Away

BUS Snowdon Sherpa buses S2 and S6 stop outside the train station, with services to **Pen-y-Pass** (25 minutes) and **Llanberis** (33 minutes).

TRAIN Betws-y-Coed is on the **Conwy Valley Line** (www.conwyvalleyrailway.co.uk), with six daily services (three on Sundays) to **Llandudno** (£4.70, 52 minutes). Llandudno Junction is on the main line with connections to Manchester and the rest of the country.

Edinburgh & Central Scotland

Edinburgh is a city that just begs to be explored. From the narrow lanes and alleys that riddle the Old Town to the elegant streets and Georgian squares of the New Town, it's filled with icons and big-name attractions, topped of course by Edinburgh Castle. And every corner turned reveals unexpected vistas of the landscape beyond – green sunlit hills, a glimpse of rust-red crags, a blue flash of distant sea.

So leave the city behind and venture out to Central Scotland's other sights. The neighbouring city of Glasgow offers quirky museums and sublime art nouveau architecture. Stirling tempts with a castle to rival Edinburgh while Loch Lomond and the Trossachs serve up lake and mountain scenery.

For a final inducement there's St Andrews, the home of golf; Balmoral Castle, the holiday retreat of British monarchs since Victorian times; and glorious Speyside dotted with dozens of whisky distilleries.

An Edinburgh street viewed through kilt-clad legs

Statue outside Greyfriars Kirkyard, Edinburgh
WILL SALTER / LONELY PLANET IMAGES ©

Edinburgh & Central Scotland

1 Edinburgh Castle
2 Speyside
3 Rosslyn Chapel
4 Royal Yacht *Britannia*
5 Stirling Castle
6 Palace of Holyroodhouse
7 St Andrews

Edinburgh & Central Scotland Highlights

Edinburgh Castle

The brooding, black crags of Castle Rock are the very reason for Edinburgh's existence – it was the most easily defended hilltop on the invasion route from England. Crowning the crag with a profusion of battlements, Edinburgh Castle (p294) is now Scotland's most popular pay-to-enter tourist attraction. Military Tattoo performance, Edinburgh Castle

Need to Know
BEST TIME TO VISIT
Lunchtime (for the one o'clock gun) TOP TIP Buy tickets online SECRET SPOT The cemetery for officers' dogs For further coverage, see p294

Edinburgh Castle Don't Miss List

PETER YEOMAN, HISTORIC SCOTLAND'S HEAD OF CULTURAL RESOURCES

1 HONOURS OF SCOTLAND

The crown, sceptre and sword of state are glittering symbols of our nationhood. They were first used at the coronation of Mary, Queen of Scots in 1543 when she was only nine months old. The centuries-old regalia are displayed in the Royal Palace alongside the Stone of Destiny.

2 ST MARGARET'S CHAPEL

The oldest building in the castle is a wee gem, possibly part of a tower keep built in the early 1100s to commemorate Scotland's royal saint, who died in the castle in 1093. The chapel (pictured top left) is delightfully decorated inside with fine Romanesque architecture.

3 MONS MEG

Step outside the chapel and you are confronted by the great bombard Mons Meg, gifted to James II in 1457. This is a great vantage point for the firing of the one o' clock gun (fired daily except Sunday), causing many visitors to jump out of their skins! The views from here across the Georgian New Town to the Forth Estuary are truly magnificent.

4 DAVID'S TOWER

Deep beneath the Half Moon Battery lies David's Tower, built as a fancy residence for David II in 1371. Badly damaged in the siege of 1573, the tower became hidden in the foundations for the new battery, and was only rediscovered in 1912. The Honours of Scotland spent much of WWII here, hidden down a medieval loo!

5 CASTLE VAULTS

In 1720, 21 pirates captured in Argyll were thrown into the castle dungeons. They had all sailed with one of the most infamous pirate-captains of the Caribbean, 'Black Bart' Roberts. The following decades saw a busy time for this State Prison, stuffed full of prisoners from the wars with America and France. The reconstructed cells allow you to experience something of the squalor!

285

Speyside Whisky Trail

No trip to Scotland is complete without visiting a whisky distillery, and the Speyside region is the heartland of Scotch whisky, with no fewer than 50 distilleries. Dufftown (p324) lies at the middle of it all, within easy reach of seven distilleries, and sporting its own whisky museum. Interior of a whisky distillery

Need to Know

TOP TIP Book ahead for tours **BEST TIME TO VISIT** May or September, for the Speyside festivals **BEST PHOTO OP** Casks at Speyside Cooperage **For further coverage, see p324**

Speyside Don't Miss List

IAN LOGAN, BRAND AMBASSADOR, CHIVAS BROTHERS

1 THE GLENLIVET DISTILLERY

The home of the most iconic single malt whisky in the world, the Glenlivet offers a great mix of old and new, and a chance to see how modern technology has been adapted to work alongside traditional techniques. If you are a whisky connoisseur, join me on my weekly tour and discover behind the scenes secrets. It's at Ballindalloch, 10 miles west of Dufftown.

2 SPEYSIDE COOPERAGE

The Speyside Cooperage (bottom left; p324) gives you a chance to watch a craft that has changed little over the centuries – the quality of the cask is one of the biggest contributing factors to the flavour of a single malt. The team here supply barrels to distilleries all over the world and share with the distillers the passion of creating the finest whiskies in the world.

3 GORDON & MACPHAIL

The most famous whisky shop in the world, Gordon & MacPhail in the town of Elgin, is home to some of the oldest whiskies in the world including a 70-year-old Mortlach. The owners have played an important part in making single malt whisky what it is today, bottling these whiskies long before the distillers ever did.

4 CORGARFF CASTLE

The impressive and remote Corgarff Castle (pictured top left) was once home to the redcoats whose job it was to chase down illegal distillers in the early 19th century. The castle is near Cockbridge, 30 miles south of Dufftown on the road to Ballater.

5 GROUSE INN

Set deep in the heart of the old smuggling country, this remote pub at Cabrach, in the hills 10 miles south of Dufftown, has nearly 250 single malts on optic with many more on display around the bar, a collection that is home to several rare and unique bottlings.

Rosslyn Chapel

The success of Dan Brown's novel *The Da Vinci Code* and the subsequent Hollywood movie has seen a flood of visitors descend on this beautiful and enigmatic 15th-century chapel (p303). Wreathed in ornate and mysterious stone carvings, it's been the subject of Knights Templar and Holy Grail conspiracy theories for decades, and provides the setting for both book and movie dénouement.

Royal Yacht Britannia

The *Britannia* (p302) served as the royal family's floating home during their foreign travels. Decommissioned in 1997 the ship is now permanently moored in Leith, and offers an intriguing insight into the Queen's private tastes. Don't expect a sumptuous royal residence – it's more like a comfortable country house with old fashioned charm. The only double bed is in the honeymoon suite, once used by Bill and Hilary Clinton.

Stirling Castle

5

While Edinburgh Castle tops the visitor stakes, in terms of history and heritage its sister fortress at Stirling (p317) is arguably more rewarding. This sturdy bastion has played a pivotal role in many key events of Scottish history, and was once a residence of the Stuart monarchs. Highlights include the Great Hall, the largest medieval banqueting hall ever built in Scotland.

6

Palace of Holyroodhouse

This 16th-century tower house was extended in the 17th-century to create a royal palace (p299), now Her Majesty the Queen's official residence in Scotland. The building is more famous for its association with Mary, Queen of Scots, who spent six eventful years (1561–67) living here. As well as Mary's private bedchamber, the palace brims with fascinating antiques and artworks, and after your visit you can wander around delightful Holyrood Park.

7

St Andrews

Scotland is the home of golf, and playing at the Old Course at St Andrews (p322) – the world's oldest golf course – is on every golfer's wish list. But there's more to the town than golf. This was once Scotland's religious capital, and the remains of the castle and cathedral are well worth visiting. And don't miss the magnificent West Sands where scenes from the movie *Chariots of Fire* were filmed. A bridge on the Old Course

Edinburgh & Central Scotland's Best...

Churches & Cathedrals

o **St Giles Cathedral** (p295) A great grey bulk dominating Edinburgh's High St, with beautiful crown spire

o **Glasgow Cathedral** (p312) Shining example of Gothic architecture; the imposing interior sends a shiver down the spine

o **St Andrews Cathedral** (p322) Evocative ruins of one of Britain's most magnificent medieval buildings

o **Rosslyn Chapel** (p303) Beloved by conspiracy theorists thanks to *The Da Vinci Code*

Castles

o **Edinburgh Castle** (p294) Icon of the capital and home to the Stone of Destiny

o **Stirling Castle** (p317) Always in the shadow of Edinburgh, but can be a more rewarding visit

o **Culzean Castle** (p315) Gorgeous castle, with surrounding park giving fabulous views

o **Balmoral Castle** (p325) The royal family's holiday home in Scotland built for Queen Victoria in 1855

History & Culture Spots

o **Robert Burns Birthplace Museum** (p314) Brand new museum dedicated to Scotland's best-known poet

o **Palace of Holyroodhouse** (p299) The British monarch's official residence in Scotland, also a former home of Mary, Queen of Scots

o **Scott Monument** (p299) Lofty perch with stunning views of Edinburgh's Old Town skyline

o **Braemar Gathering** (p320) Most famous Highland games in the country

Natural Beauty

○ **Arthur's Seat, Holyrood Park, Edinburgh** (p297) Unexpected touch of the wilds and great viewpoint in the heart of the city

○ **Loch Lomond** (p315) Beautiful loch immortalised in song, easily reached from Edinburgh or Glasgow

○ **Speyside** (p324) Valley of the 'slivery Spey' and the heartland of Scotch whisky

○ **The Trossachs** (p321) Craggy hills and scenic lochs; often described as 'the Highlands in miniature'

Need to Know

ADVANCE PLANNING

○ **Six months before** Reserve a tee time for playing golf on St Andrews Old Course. Book accommodation if you plan to visit during festival time (August) or Hogmanay (New Year).

○ **One month before** Reserve accommodation for any other time of year

○ **One week before** Make bookings for Speyside distillery tours and Trossachs boat trips

RESOURCES

Major tourist information websites:

○ **Edinburgh Tourist Board** (www.edinburgh.org)

○ **Edinburgh Museums & Galleries** (www.edinburghmuseums.org.uk)

○ **Edinburgh Festivals** (www.edinburghfestivals.co.uk)

○ **Stirling and the Trossachs** (www.visitscottishheartlands.com)

○ **Glasgow** (www.seeglasgow.com)

○ **Speyside** (www.greaterspeyside.com; www.maltwhiskytrail.com)

○ **Loch Lomond & the Trossachs National Park** (www.lochlomond-trossachs.org)

○ **St Andrews** (www.visitfife.com)

GETTING AROUND

○ **Bus** Useful network of intercity buses; Edinburgh has a good city bus network

○ **Car** The most time-efficient way to get around this region. Parking in Edinburgh city centre is difficult – best to use public transport

○ **Train** OK for reaching major centres from Edinburgh or Glasgow, but less useful for day-to-day getting around – the train lines skirt the region to the east and west

BE FOREWARNED

○ **Golf** Check to see if the Open Championship is being staged in St Andrews before you go – if so, accommodation will be impossible to find, and the roads approaching town will be clogged with traffic

Left: Stained glass , Glasgow Cathedral (p312);
Above: Scott Monument, Edinburgh (p299).
PHOTOGRAPHERS: (LEFT) NEIL SETCHFIELD / LONELY PLANET IMAGES ©; (ABOVE) JONATHAN SMITH / LONELY PLANET IMAGES ©

Edinburgh & Central Scotland Itineraries

Do a three-day loop and explore the best of the capital and surrounds. The five-day trip leads further north, into the central Scottish heartland.

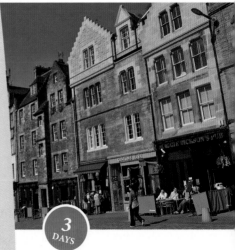

3 DAYS

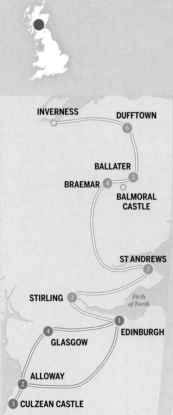

EDINBURGH TO EDINBURGH

Capital Classics

On your first day in **(1) Edinburgh**, orientate yourself with an open-top bus tour. Then enjoy the Georgian streets and squares of the New Town before going up the Scott Monument. Start exploring the Old Town with a visit to the Palace of Holyroodhouse, then work your way up the Royal Mile. Visit Edinburgh Castle later in the afternoon, when it's usually quieter.

On day two, head to **(2) Alloway** and the Robert Burns Birthplace Museum, then on to magnificent **(3) Culzean Castle**, one of the most impressive of Scotland's stately homes. If time allows, fans of cityscapes and architecture should detour to **(4) Glasgow**, where highlights include the art nouveau work of Charles Rennie Mackintosh.

Return to **(5) Edinburgh** for a closer look at the city via the underground chambers of Real Mary King's Close or Royal Museum of Scotland. In the afternoon, head out to Leith to visit the Royal Yacht Britannia. End with dinner at one of Leith's excellent restaurants, or head back to the city and scare yourself silly on a ghost tour.

Top left: Grassmarket bars and boutiques, Edinburgh (p294);
Top right: Ruins of St Andrews Castle (p322)

5 DAYS

EDINBURGH TO DUFFTOWN

Histories & Distilleries

Spend your first day or two in **(1) Edinburgh** then it's a short journey to **(2) Stirling** where visiting the castle and the nearby Wallace Monument will take the best part of the day, before you head east to **(3) St Andrews**. Allow a day to explore Scotland's old ecclesiastical capital, and perhaps enjoy a game of golf on one of several world-famous courses.

From here, cross the Tay Bridge and head north to the classic Highland village of **(4) Braemar**. After a look at Braemar Castle, a short drive east brings you to **Balmoral Castle**, the royal family's holiday home (they usually visit in August). Allow at least two hours for exploring this fascinating royal estate before continuing to the pretty village of **(5) Ballater** for an overnight stop.

Next day, another scenic drive awaits, on the famous A939 Cockbridge to Tomintoul road, over the northern flank of the tundra-like Cairngorm Mountains. Drop down into the Spey valley at the town of Grantown-on-Spey then follow the valley northeast to end in **(6) Dufftown**, the whisky capital. (If you're travelling further into Scotland, note that it's a 90-minute drive to **Inverness**, the start of our Highlands itinerary, p336.)

Discover Edinburgh & Central Scotland

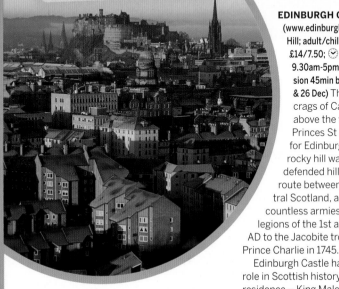

View of Edinburgh Castle and Old Town, Arthur's Seat (p298)
PHOTOGRAPHER: JONATHAN SMITH / LONELY PLANET IMAGES ©

EDINBURGH

 Sights

Old Town

Edinburgh's Old Town stretches along
a ridge to the east of the castle, and
tumbles down Victoria St to the broad
expanse of the Grassmarket. It's a jagged
and jumbled maze of masonry riddled
with closes (alleys) and wynds (narrow
lanes), stairs and vaults, and cleft along
its spine by the cobbled ravine of the
Royal Mile. This mile-long street earned
its regal nickname in the 16th century
when it was used by the king to travel
between the castle and the Palace of
Holyroodhouse.

EDINBURGH CASTLE   Castle
(www.edinburghcastle.gov.uk; Castle
Hill; adult/child incl audioguide
£14/7.50; ☉9.30am-6pm Apr-Sep,
9.30am-5pm Oct-Mar, last admission 45min before closing, closed 25
& 26 Dec) The brooding, black
crags of Castle Rock rising
above the western end of
Princes St are the very reason
for Edinburgh's existence. This
rocky hill was the most easily
defended hilltop on the invasion
route between England and central Scotland, a route followed by
countless armies from the Roman
legions of the 1st and 2nd centuries
AD to the Jacobite troops of Bonnie
Prince Charlie in 1745.

Edinburgh Castle has played a pivotal
role in Scottish history, both as a royal
residence – King Malcolm Canmore (r
1058–93) and Queen Margaret first made
their home here in the 11th century – and
as a military stronghold. The castle last

saw military action in 1745; from then until the 1920s it served as the British army's main base in Scotland. Today it is one of Scotland's most atmospheric, most popular – and most expensive – tourist attractions.

The **Entrance Gateway**, flanked by statues of Robert the Bruce and William Wallace, opens to a cobbled lane that leads up beneath the 16th-century **Portcullis Gate** to the cannon ranged along the Argyle and Mills Mount batteries. The battlements here have **great views** over New Town to the Firth of Forth.

At the far end of Mills Mount Battery is the famous **one o'clock gun**, where crowds gather to watch a gleaming WWII 25-pounder fire an ear-splitting time signal at exactly 1pm (every day except Sundays, Christmas Day and Good Friday).

The **Castle Vaults** beneath the Great Hall (entered from Crown Sq via the Prisons of War exhibit) were used variously as storerooms, bakeries and a prison. The vaults have been renovated to resemble 18th- and early-19th-century prisons, where graffiti carved by French and American prisoners can be seen on the ancient wooden doors.

On the eastern side of the square is the **Royal Palace**, built during the 15th and 16th centuries, where a series of historical tableaux leads to the highlight of the castle – a strongroom housing the **Honours of Scotland** (the Scottish crown jewels), the oldest surviving crown jewels in Europe. Locked away in a chest following the Act of Union in 1707, the crown (made in 1540 from the gold of Robert the Bruce's 14th-century coronet), sword and sceptre lay forgotten until they were unearthed at the instigation of the novelist Sir Walter Scott in 1818. Also on display here is the **Stone of Destiny**.

SCOTCH WHISKY EXPERIENCE
Whisky Exhibition

(www.scotchwhiskyexperience.co.uk; 354 Castle Hill; adult/child incl tour & tasting £11.50/5.95; ☺10am-6.30pm Jun-Aug, 10am-6pm Sep-May;

📶) A short distance downhill from the Castle Esplanade, a former school houses this multimedia centre explaining the making of whisky from barley to bottle in a series of exhibits, demonstrations and tours that combine sight, sound and smell, including the world's largest collection of malt whiskies; look out for Peat the distillery cat!

ST GILES CATHEDRAL Church

(www.stgilescathedral.org.uk; High St; £3 donation suggested; ☺9am-7pm Mon-Fri, 9am-5pm Sat, 1-5pm Sun May-Sep, 9am-5pm Mon-Sat, 1-5pm Sun Oct-Apr) Dominating High St is the great grey bulk of St Giles Cathedral. The present church dates largely from the 15th century – the beautiful **crown spire** was completed in 1495 – but much of it was restored in the 19th century. The interior lacks grandeur but is rich in history: St Giles was at the heart of the Scottish Reformation, and John Knox served as minister here from 1559 to 1572.

REAL MARY KING'S CLOSE
Historic Building

(☎0845 070 6255; www.realmarykingsclose. com; 2 Warriston's Close, Writers Ct, High St; adult/child £11/6; ☺10am-9pm Apr-Oct, to 11pm Aug, 10am-5pm Sun-Thu & 10am-9pm Fri & Sat Nov-Mar) Part of the Royal Exchange was built over the sealed-off remains of Mary King's Close, and the lower levels of this medieval Old Town alley have survived almost unchanged in the foundations of the City Chambers for 250 years. Now open to the public as the Real Mary King's Close, this spooky, subterranean labyrinth gives a fascinating insight into the daily life of 16th- and 17th-century Edinburgh.

SCOTTISH PARLIAMENT BUILDING
Landmark

(☎0131-348 5200; www.scottish.parliament. uk; admission free; ☺9am-6.30pm Tue-Thu, 10am-5.30pm Mon & Fri in session, 10am-6pm Mon-Fri in recess Apr-Oct, 10am-4pm in recess Nov-Mar; 📶) The Scottish parliament building built on the site of a former brewery close to the Palace of Holyroodhouse, was officially opened by HM the Queen in October 2005. The public areas of the parliament building – the

Edinburgh

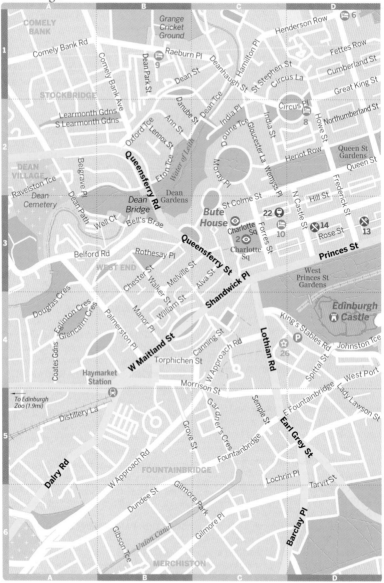

Main Hall, where there is an exhibition, a shop and cafe, and the **public gallery** in the Debating Chamber – are open to visitors (tickets needed for public gallery – see website for details). The **Main Hall**, inside the public entrance, has a

low, triple-arched ceiling of polished concrete, like a cave, or cellar, or castle vault. It is a dimly lit space, the starting point for a metaphorical journey from this relative darkness up to the **Debating Chamber** (sitting directly above the

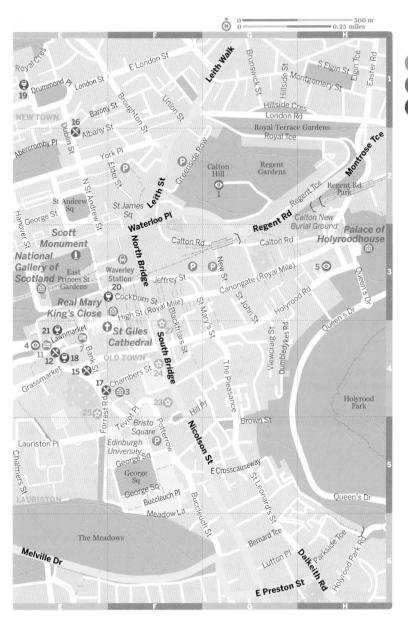

Main Hall), which is, in contrast, a palace of light – the light of democracy. This magnificent chamber is the centrepiece of the parliament, designed not to glorify but to humble the politicians who sit within it.

HOLYROOD PARK   Park

In Holyrood Park Edinburgh is blessed with a little bit of wilderness in the heart of the city. The former hunting ground of Scottish monarchs, the park covers 263 hectares of varied landscape, including

Edinburgh

crags, moorland and loch. The highest point is the 251m summit of **Arthur's Seat**, offering fantastic views.

South of the Royal Mile

NATIONAL MUSEUM OF SCOTLAND
Museum

(www.nms.ac.uk; Chambers St; admission free, fee for special exhibitions; ⊙10am-5pm) The golden stone and striking modern architecture of the museum building, opened in 1998, is one of the city's most distinctive landmarks. The five floors of the museum trace the history of Scotland from geological beginnings to the 1990s, with many imaginative and stimulating exhibits – audioguides are available in several languages. Highlights include the **Monymusk Reliquary**, a tiny silver casket dating from AD 750, which is said to have been carried into battle with Robert the Bruce at Bannockburn in 1314, and some of the **Lewis chessmen**, a set of charming 12th-century chess pieces made from walrus ivory. Don't forget to take the lift to the **roof terrace** for a fantastic view of the castle.

New Town

Edinburgh's New Town lies north of the Old Town, on a ridge running parallel to the Royal Mile and separated from it by the valley of Princes Street Gardens. Its regular grid of elegant, Georgian terraces is a complete contrast to the chaotic tangle of tenements and wynds that characterise the Old Town. Today Edinburgh's New Town remains the world's most complete and unspoilt example of Georgian architecture and town planning. Along with the Old Town, it was declared a Unesco World Heritage site in 1995.

PRINCES STREET

Princes St is one of the world's most spectacular shopping streets. Built up on the north side only, it catches the sun in summer and allows expansive views across Princes Street Gardens to the castle and the crowded skyline of the Old Town. **Princes Street Gardens** lie in a valley that was once occupied by the Nor' Loch, a boggy depression that was drained in the early 19th century.

WILL SALTER / LONELY PLANET IMAGES ©

Don't Miss **Palace of Holyroodhouse**

This palace is the royal family's official residence in Scotland, but is most famous as the 16th-century home of the ill-fated **Mary, Queen of Scots**. The palace is closed to the public when the royal family is visiting and during state functions (usually in mid-May, and mid-June to early July; check the website for exact dates).

The guided tour leads you through a series of impressive royal apartments, ending in the **Great Gallery**. The 89 portraits of Scottish kings were commissioned by Charles II and supposedly record his unbroken lineage from Scota, the Egyptian pharaoh's daughter who discovered the infant Moses in a reed basket on the banks of the Nile.

But the highlight of the tour is **Mary, Queen of Scots' Bed Chamber**, home to the unfortunate Mary from 1561 to 1567, and connected by a secret stairway to her husband's bedchamber.

THINGS YOU NEED TO KNOW

www.royalcollection.org.uk; Canongate; adult/child £10.25/6.20; ☺9.30am-6pm Apr-Oct, 9.30am-4.30pm Nov-Mar

---

SCOTT MONUMENT　　　Monument
(East Princes Street Gardens; admission £3; ☺10am-7pm Apr-Sep, 9am-4pm Mon-Sat, 10am-4pm Sun Oct-Mar) The eastern half of Princes Street Gardens is dominated by the massive Gothic spire of the Scott Monument, built by public subscription in memory of the novelist Sir Walter Scott after his death in 1832. The exterior is decorated with carvings of characters from his novels; inside you can see an exhibition on Scott's life, and climb the 287 steps to the top for a superb view of the city.

FREE **NATIONAL GALLERY OF SCOTLAND**　　　Art Gallery
(www.nationalgalleries.org; The Mound; fee for special exhibitions; ☺10am-5pm daily, to 7pm Thu; 🛜) Designed by William Playfair,

Royal Mile

A Grand Day Out

Planning your own procession along the Royal Mile involves some tough decisions – it would be impossible to see everything in a single day, so it's wise to decide in advance what you don't want to miss and shape your visit around that. Remember to leave time for lunch, for exploring some of the Mile's countless side

alleys and, during festival time, for enjoying the street theatre that is bound to be happening in High St.

The most pleasant way to reach the Castle Esplanade at the start of the Royal Mile is to hike up the zigzag path from the footbridge behind the Ross Bandstand in Princes Street Gardens (in springtime you'll be knee-deep in daffodils). Starting at Edinburgh Castle ① means that the rest of your walk is downhill. For a superb view up and down the length of the Mile, climb the Camera Obscura's Outlook Tower ② before visiting Gladstone's Land ③ and St Giles Cathedral ④. If history's your

Edinburgh Castle
If you're pushed for time, visit the Great Hall, the Honours of Scotland and the Prisons of War exhibit. Head for the Half Moon Battery for a photo looking down the length of the Royal Mile.

Royal Visits to the Royal Mile

1561: Mary, Queen of Scots arrives from France and holds an audience with John Knox.
1745: Bonnie Prince Charlie fails to capture Edinburgh Castle, and instead sets up court in Holyroodhouse.
2004: Queen Elizabeth II officially opens the Scottish Parliament building.

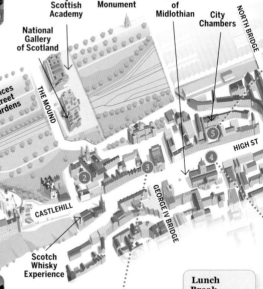

Royal Scottish Academy

Scott Monument

Heart of Midlothian

City Chambers

NORTH BRIDGE

National Gallery of Scotland

Princes Street Gardens

THE MOUND

HIGH ST

CASTLEHILL

GEORGE IV BRIDGE

Scotch Whisky Experience

Gladstone's Land
The 1st floor houses a faithful recreation of how a wealthy Edinburgh merchant lived in the 17th century. Check out the beautiful Painted Bedchamber, with its ornately decorated walls and wooden ceilings.

Lunch Break

Pie and a pint at **Royal Mile Tavern**; soup and a sandwich at **Always Sunday**; bistro nosh at **Café Marlayne**.

thing, you'll want to add Real Mary King's Close **5**, John Knox House **6** and the Museum of Edinburgh **7** to your must-see list.

At the foot of the mile, choose between modern and ancient seats of power – the Scottish Parliament **8** or the Palace of Holyroodhouse **9**. Round off the day with an evening ascent of Arthur's Seat or, slightly less strenuously, Calton Hill. Both make great sunset viewpoints.

TAKING YOUR TIME

Minimum time needed for each attraction:

Edinburgh Castle: two hours

Gladstone's Land: 45 minutes

St Giles Cathedral: 30 minutes

Real Mary King's Close: one hour (tour)

Scottish Parliament: one hour (tour)

Palace of Holyroodhouse: one hour

Real Mary King's Close
The guided tour is heavy on ghost stories, but a highlight is standing in an original 17th-century room with tufts of horsehair poking from the crumbling plaster, and breathing in the ancient scent of stone, dust and history.

Canongate Kirk

CANONGATE

ST MARY'S ST

SOUTH BRIDGE

Tron Kirk

Our Dynamic Earth

Scottish Parliament
Don't have time for the guided tour? Pick up a *Discover the Scottish Parliament Building* leaflet from reception and take a self-guided tour of the exterior, then hike up to Salisbury Crags for a great view of the complex.

Palace of Holyroodhouse
Find the secret staircase joining Mary, Queen of Scots' bedchamber with that of her husband, Lord Darnley, who restrained the queen while his henchmen stabbed to death her secretary (and possible lover), David Rizzio.

St Giles Cathedral
Look out for the Burne-Jones stained-glass window (1873) at the west end, showing the crossing of the River Jordan, and the bronze memorial to Robert Louis Stevenson in the Moray Aisle.

EUROPHOTOS/ALAMY

COLIN PALMER PHOTOGRAPHY/ALAMY

JEAN-CHRISTOPHE GODET/ALAMY

Don't Miss **Royal Yacht Britannia**

One of Scotland's biggest tourist attractions is the former Royal Yacht *Britannia*. She was the British royal family's floating home during their foreign travels from the time of her launch in 1953 until her decommissioning in 1997, and is now moored permanently in front of Ocean Terminal.

The tour, which you take at your own pace with an audioguide (available in 20 languages), gives an intriguing insight into the Queen's private tastes – *Britannia* was one of the few places where the royal family could enjoy true privacy. The entire ship is a monument to 1950's decor and technology, and the accommodation reveals Her Majesty's preference for simple, unfussy surroundings – the Queen's own bed is surprisingly tiny and plain.

THINGS YOU NEED TO KNOW

www.royalyachtbritannia.co.uk; Ocean Terminal, Leith; adult/child £10.50/6.75; ⊘9.30am-6pm Jul-Sep, 10am-5.30pm Apr-Jun & Oct, 10am-5pm Nov-Mar, last admission 1½hr before closing

---

this imposing classical building, with its Ionic porticoes, dates from the 1850s. The basement galleries dedicated to **Scottish art** include glowing portraits by Allan Ramsay and Sir Henry Raeburn, rural scenes by Sir David Wilkie and impressionistic landscapes by William MacTaggart. Look out for Raeburn's iconic *Reverend Robert Walker Skating on Duddingston Loch,* and Sir George Harvey's hugely entertaining *A Schule Skailin* (A

School Emptying) – a stern dominie (teacher) looks on as the boys stampede for the classroom door, one reaching for a spinning top confiscated earlier.

GEORGE STREET & CHARLOTTE SQUARE

Until the 1990s George St – the major axis of New Town – was the centre of Edinburgh's financial industry and Scotland's equivalent of Wall St. Today the big financial firms have moved to premises in the Exchange office district west of Lothian Rd, and George St's former banks and offices house upmarket shops, pubs and restaurants. At the western end of George St is **Charlotte Square**, the architectural jewel of New Town, designed by Robert Adam shortly before his death in 1791. The northern side of the square is Adam's masterpiece and one of the finest examples of Georgian architecture anywhere. **Bute House**, in the centre at No 6, is the official residence of Scotland's first minister.

CALTON HILL

Calton Hill (100m), rising dramatically above the eastern end of Princes St, is Edinburgh's acropolis, its summit scattered with grandiose memorials mostly dating from the first half of the 19th century. It's also one of the best viewpoints in Edinburgh, with a panorama that takes in the castle, Holyrood, the Firth of Forth, New Town and the full length of Princes St.

Leith

Two miles northeast of the city centre, Leith has been Edinburgh's seaport since the 14th century. Like many of Britain's dockland areas, it fell into decay in the decades following WWII but has been undergoing a revival since the late 1980s. Old warehouses have been turned into luxury flats, and a lush crop of trendy bars and restaurants has sprouted along the waterfront.

Around Edinburgh
ROSSLYN CHAPEL
Church

(Collegiate Church of St Matthew; www. rosslynchapel.com; Roslin; adult/child £7.50/free; 9.30am-6pm Mon-Sat, noon-4.45pm Sun Apr-Sep,

9.30am-5pm Mon-Sat, noon-4.45pm Sun Oct-Mar) The success of Dan Brown's novel *The Da Vinci Code* and the subsequent Hollywood film has seen a flood of visitors descend on Scotland's most beautiful and enigmatic church: Rosslyn Chapel. The chapel was built in the mid-15th century for William St Clair, third earl of Orkney, and the ornately carved interior – at odds with the architectural fashion of its time – is a monument to the mason's art, rich in symbolic imagery. As well as flowers, vines, angels and biblical figures, the carved stones include many examples of the pagan 'Green Man'; other figures are associated with Freemasonry and the Knights Templar. Intriguingly, there are also carvings of plants from the Americas that predate Columbus' voyage of discovery. The symbolism of these images has led some researchers to conclude that Rosslyn is some kind of secret Templar repository, and it has been claimed that hidden vaults beneath the chapel could conceal anything from the Holy Grail or the head of John the Baptist to the body of Christ himself. The chapel is owned

Outside the Scottish Parliament building (p295)

Rosslyn Chapel

Deciphering Rosslyn

Rosslyn Chapel is a small building, but the density of decoration inside can be overwhelming. It's well worth buying the official guidebook by the Earl of Rosslyn first; find a bench in the gardens and have a skim through before going into the chapel – the background information will make your visit all the more interesting. The book also offers a useful self-guided tour of the chapel, and explains the legend of the Master Mason and the Apprentice.

Entrance is through the north door ❶. Take a pew and sit for a while to allow your eyes to adjust to the dim interior; then look up at the ceiling vault, decorated with engraved roses, lilies and stars (can you spot the sun and the moon?). Walk left along the north aisle to reach the Lady Chapel, separated from the rest of the church by the Mason's Pillar ❷ and the Apprentice Pillar ❸. Here you'll find carvings of Lucifer ❹, the Fallen Angel, and the Green Man ❺. Nearby are carvings ❻ that appear to resemble Indian corn (maize). Finally, go to the western end and look up at the wall – in the left corner is the head of the Apprentice ❼; to the right is the (rather worn) head of the Master Mason ❽.

ROSSLYN CHAPEL & THE DA VINCI CODE

Dan Brown was referencing Rosslyn Chapel's alleged links to the Knights Templar and the Freemasons – unusual symbols found among the carvings, and the fact that a descendant of its founder, William St Clair, was a Grand Master Mason – when he chose it as the setting for his novel's denouement. Rosslyn is indeed a coded work, written in stone, but its meaning depends on your point of view. See *The Rosslyn Hoax?* by Robert LD Cooper (www.rosslynhoax .com) for an alternative interpretation of the chapel's symbolism.

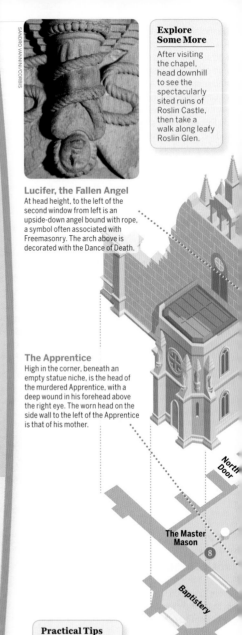

SANDRO VANNINI/CORBIS

Explore Some More

After visiting the chapel, head downhill to see the spectacularly sited ruins of Roslin Castle, then take a walk along leafy Roslin Glen.

Lucifer, the Fallen Angel
At head height, to the left of the second window from left is an upside-down angel bound with rope, a symbol often associated with Freemasonry. The arch above is decorated with the Dance of Death.

The Apprentice
High in the corner, beneath an empty statue niche, is the head of the murdered Apprentice, with a deep wound in his forehead above the right eye. The worn head on the side wall to the left of the Apprentice is that of his mother.

North Door

The Master Mason

❽

Baptistery

Practical Tips

Buy your tickets in advance through the chapel's website (except in August, when no bookings are taken). No photography is allowed inside the chapel.

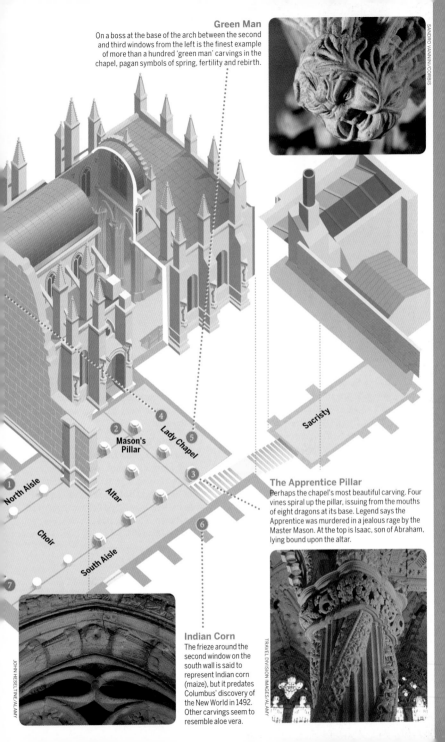

Green Man

On a boss at the base of the arch between the second and third windows from the left is the finest example of more than a hundred 'green man' carvings in the chapel, pagan symbols of spring, fertility and rebirth.

SANDRO VANNINI/CORBIS

Sacristy

Lady Chapel

Mason's Pillar

② ④ ⑤

North Aisle ①

Altar

③

Choir

South Aisle

⑥

⑦

The Apprentice Pillar

Perhaps the chapel's most beautiful carving. Four vines spiral up the pillar, issuing from the mouths of eight dragons at its base. Legend says the Apprentice was murdered in a jealous rage by the Master Mason. At the top is Isaac, son of Abraham, lying bound upon the altar.

TRAVEL DIVISION IMAGES/ALAMY

Indian Corn

The frieze around the second window on the south wall is said to represent Indian corn (maize), but it predates Columbus' discovery of the New World in 1492. Other carvings seem to resemble aloe vera.

JOHN HESELTINE/ALAMY

by the Episcopal Church of Scotland and services are still held here on Sunday mornings.

The chapel is on the eastern edge of the village of Roslin, 7 miles south of Edinburgh's centre. Lothian Bus 15 (not 15A) runs from the west end of Princes St in Edinburgh to Roslin (£1.20, 30 minutes, every 30 minutes).

 Tours

Bus Tours

Open-topped buses leave from Waverley Bridge outside the main train station and offer hop-on/hop-off tours of the main sights, taking in New Town, the Grassmarket and the Royal Mile. Tours run daily, year-round, except for 24 and 25 December.

City Sightseeing   Bus Tours
(www.edinburghtour.com; adult/child £12/5)
Lothian Buses' bright red open-top buses depart every 20 minutes from Waverley Bridge.

MacTours   Bus Tours
(www.edinburghtour.com; adult/child £12/5)
Offers similar tours to City Sightseeing, but in a vintage bus.

Majestic Tour   Bus Tours
(www.edinburghtour.com; adult/child £12/5)
Runs every 30 minutes (every 20 minutes in July and August) from Waverley Bridge to the Royal Yacht *Britannia* at Ocean Terminal via the New Town, Royal Botanic Garden and Newhaven, returning via Leith Walk, Holyrood and the Royal Mile.

Walking Tours

There are plenty of organised walks around Edinburgh, many of them related to ghosts, murders and witches.

Black Hart Storytellers   Ghost Tours
(www.blackhart.uk.com; adult/concession £9.50/7.50) Not suitable for young children. The 'City of the Dead' tour of Greyfriars Kirkyard is probably the scariest of Edinburgh's 'ghost' tours.

Left: Bustling pub, Edinburgh; **Below:** National Monument, Calton Hill (p303)

PHOTOGRAPHERS: (LEFT) IZZET KERIBAR / LONELY PLANET IMAGES ©; (BELOW) WILL SALTER / LONELY PLANET IMAGES ©

Edinburgh Literary Pub Tour

Literary Tours

(www.edinburghliterarypubtour.co.uk; adult/ student £10/8) An enlightening two-hour trawl through Edinburgh's literary history – and its associated howffs – in the entertaining company of Messrs Clart and McBrain.

 Sleeping

Old Town

HOTEL MISSONI   Boutique Hotel   £££

(☎0131-220 6666; www.hotelmissoni.com; 1 George IV Bridge; r £180; 🛜) The Italian fashion house has established a style icon in the heart of the medieval Old Town with this bold statement of a hotel – modernistic architecture, black and white decor with well-judged splashes of colour, impeccably mannered staff and – most importantly – very comfortable bedrooms and bathrooms with lots of nice little touches, from fresh milk in the minibar to plush bathrobes.

WITCHERY BY THE CASTLE

Boutique B&B   £££

(☎0131-225 5613; www.thewitchery.com; Castle Hill, Royal Mile; ste £295) Set in a 16th-century Old Town house in the shadow of Edinburgh Castle, the Witchery's seven lavish suites are extravagantly furnished with antiques, oak panelling, tapestries, open fires and roll-top baths, and supplied with flowers, chocolates and complimentary champagne.

New Town & Around

SIX MARY'S PLACE   B&B   ££

(☎0131-332 8965; www.sixmarysplace.co.uk; 6 Mary's Pl, Raeburn Pl; s/d/f from £50/94/150; @🛜) Six Mary's Place is an attractive Georgian town house with a designer mix of period features, contemporary furniture and modern colours. Breakfasts are vegetarian-only, served in an attractive

307

conservatory with a view of the garden, while the lounge, with its big, comfy sofas, offers free coffee and newspapers.

ONE ROYAL CIRCUS — B&B £££
(📞0131-625 6669; www.oneroyalcircus.com; 1 Royal Circus; r £180-260; 📶👪) Live the New Town dream at this incredibly chic Georgian mansion where genuine antiques and parquet floors sit comfortably alongside slate bathrooms and Philippe Starck furniture.

TIGERLILY — Boutique Hotel £££
(📞0131-225 5005; www.tigerlilyedinburgh. co.uk; 125 George St; r from £195; 📶) Georgian meets gorgeous at this glamorous, glittering boutique hotel (complete with its own nightclub) decked out in mirror mosaics, beaded curtains, swirling Timorous Beasties textiles and wall coverings, and atmospheric pink uplighting.

DENE GUEST HOUSE — B&B ££
(📞0131-556 2700; www.deneguesthouse.com; 7 Eyre Pl; per person £25-50; 👪) The Dene is a friendly and informal place, set in a charming Georgian town house, with a welcoming owner and spacious bedrooms. The inexpensive single rooms

Looking out from Calton Hill (p303)

make it ideal for solo travellers; children under 10 staying in their parents' room pay half price.

Eating

Old Town

OUTSIDER — Bistro ££
(📞0131-226 3131; 15 George IV Bridge; mains £8-13; 🕐noon-11pm) This Edinburgh stalwart is known for its rainforest interior (potted ferns in atmospheric dimness) and has a brilliant menu that jumps straight in with mains such as chorizo and chickpea casserole.

TOWER — Scottish £££
(📞0131-225 3003; www.tower-restaurant.com; Museum of Scotland, Chambers St; mains £15-25; 🕐noon-11pm) Chic and sleek, with a great view of the castle, Tower is set atop the Museum of Scotland building.

MAXIE'S BISTRO — Bistro ££
(5b Johnston Tce; mains £8-14; 🕐11am-11pm) Maxie's candle-lit bistro, with its cushion-lined nooks set amid stone walls and wooden beams is a pleasant enough

setting for a cosy dinner, but at summer lunchtimes people queue for the outdoor tables on the terrace overlooking Victoria St.

New Town

OLOROSO
Scottish £££

(☎0131-226 7614; www.oloroso.co.uk; 33 Castle St; mains £16-25; ⊙restaurant noon-2.30pm & 7-10.30pm, bar 11am-1am) Oloroso is one of Edinburgh's most stylish restaurants, perched on a glass-encased New Town rooftop with views across a Mary Poppins' chimney-scape to the Firth of Forth and Fife hills. Swathed in sophisticated cream linen and charcoal upholstery enlivened with splashes of deep yellow, the dining room serves top-notch Scottish produce with Asian and Mediterranean touches.

MUSSEL INN
Seafood ££

(www.mussel-inn.com; 61-65 Rose St; mains £10-22; ⊙noon-3pm & 5.30-10pm Mon-Thu, noon-10pm Fri-Sun) Owned by west-coast shellfish farmers, the Mussel Inn provides a direct outlet for fresh Scottish seafood. The busy restaurant, decorated with bright beechwood indoors, spills out onto the pavement in summer.

STAC POLLY
Scottish £££

(☎0131-556 2231; www.stacpolly.com; 29-33 Dublin St; mains £18-22; ⊙lunch Mon-Fri, dinner Mon-Sat) Named after a mountain in northwestern Scotland, Stac Polly's kitchen adds sophisticated twists to fresh Highland produce.

 **Drinking**

Old town

BOW BAR
Pub

(80 West Bow) One of the city's best traditional-style pubs (it's not as old as it looks) serving a range of excellent real ales and a vast selection of malt whiskies, the Bow Bar often has standing room only on Friday and Saturday evenings.

JOLLY JUDGE
Pub

(www.jollyjudge.co.uk; 7a James Crt; ☎) A snug little howff tucked away down a close, the Judge exudes a cosy 17th-century atmosphere (low, timber-beamed painted ceilings) and has the added attraction of a cheering open fire in cold weather.

ECCO VINO
Wine Bar

(www.eccovinoedinburgh.com; 19 Cockburn St) With outdoor tables on sunny afternoons, and cosy candle-lit intimacy in the evenings, this comfortably cramped Tuscanstyle wine bar offers a tempting range of Italian wines, though not all are available by the glass – best to share a bottle.

New Town

OXFORD BAR
Pub

(www.oxfordbar.com; 8 Young St) The Oxford is that rarest of things these days – a real pub for real people, with no 'theme', no music, no frills and no pretensions. 'The Ox' has been immortalised by Ian Rankin, author of the Inspector Rebus novels, who is a regular here, as is his fictional detective.

CUMBERLAND BAR
Pub

(www.cumberlandbar.co.uk; 1-3 Cumberland St) Immortalised as the stereotypical New Town pub in Alexander McCall-Smith's serialised novel *44 Scotland Street,* the Cumberland has an authentic, traditional wood-brass-and-mirrors look (despite being relatively new), and serves well-looked-after, cask-conditioned ales and a wide range of malt whiskies.

⭐ **Entertainment**

WHISTLE BINKIE'S
Rock/Blues

(www.whistlebinkies.com; 4-6 South Bridge) This crowded cellar-bar just off the Royal Mile has live music every night till 3am, from rock and blues to folk and jazz.

JAZZ BAR
Jazz

(www.thejazzbar.co.uk; 1a Chambers St; ☎) This atmospheric cellar bar, with its polished parquetry floors, bare stone walls, candle-lit tables and stylish steel-framed chairs is owned and operated by jazz musicians.

SANDY BELL'S   Folk
(25 Forrest Rd) This unassuming bar has been a stalwart of the traditional-music scene since the Corrs were in nappies. There's music almost every evening at 9pm, and also from 3pm Saturday and Sunday.

EDINBURGH FESTIVAL THEATRE
Ballet/Opera
(www.eft.co.uk; 13-29 Nicolson St; ☉box-office 10am-6pm Mon-Sat, to 8pm show nights, 4pm-showtime Sun) A beautifully restored art deco theatre with a modern frontage, the Festival is the city's main venue for opera, dance and ballet, but also stages musicals, concerts, drama and children's shows.

TRAVERSE THEATRE   Drama/Dance
(www.traverse.co.uk; 10 Cambridge St; ☉box-office 10am-6pm Mon-Sat, till 8pm on show nights) The Traverse is the main focus for new Scottish writing and stages an adventurous program of contemporary drama and dance.

 Shopping

Princes St is Edinburgh's principal shopping street, lined with all the big high-street stores, with many smaller shops along pedestrianised Rose St, and more expensive designer boutiques on George St. For more off-beat shopping – including fashion, music, crafts, gifts and jewellery – head for the cobbled lanes of Cockburn, Victoria and St Mary's Sts, all near the Royal Mile in the Old Town, William St in the western part of New Town, and the Stockbridge district, immediately north of the New Town.

 Information

Edinburgh Festival Guide (www.edinburgh festivals.co.uk) Everything you need to know about Edinburgh's many festivals.

Edinburgh & Scotland Information Centre (ESIC; ☎0845 225 5121; www.edinburgh.org; Princes Mall, 3 Princes St; ☉9am-9pm Mon-Sat, 10am-8pm Sun Jul & Aug, 9am-7pm Mon-Sat,

10am-7pm Sun May, Jun & Sep, 9am-5pm Mon-Wed, 9am-6pm Thu-Sun Oct-Apr)

The List (www.list.co.uk) Listings of restaurants, pubs, clubs and nightlife.

 Getting There & Away

Air
Edinburgh Airport (☎0131-333 1000; www.edinburghairport.com) Eight miles west of the city. Numerous flights to other parts of Scotland and the UK, Ireland and mainland Europe.

Bus
Scottish Citylink (☎0871 266 3333; www.citylink.co.uk) buses connect Edinburgh with all of Scotland's cities and major towns. The following are sample one-way fares departing from Edinburgh.

DESTINATION	FARE (£)	DURATION (HR)	FREQU-ENCY
Fort William	30	4-5	8 daily
Glasgow	6	1¼	every 15min
Inverness	26	4	hourly
Portree	46	7	1 daily
Stirling	7	1	hourly

Train
The main terminus in Edinburgh is **Waverley train station** located in the heart of the city. You can buy tickets, make reservations and get travel information at the **Edinburgh Rail Travel Centre** (☉4.45am-12.30am Mon-Sat, 7am-12.30am Sun) in Waverley station. First ScotRail operates a regular shuttle service between Edinburgh and **Glasgow** (£11, 50 minutes, every 15 minutes), and frequent daily services to all Scottish cities including **Inverness** (£55, 3¼ hours).

GLASGOW
Forever overshadowed by neighbouring Edinburgh, the city of Glasgow is a fascinatingly vital place. Fine restaurants, cafes and bars await to tickle your taste buds, and top-drawer museums and galleries abound. The sublime works of Charles Rennie Mackintosh dot the town,

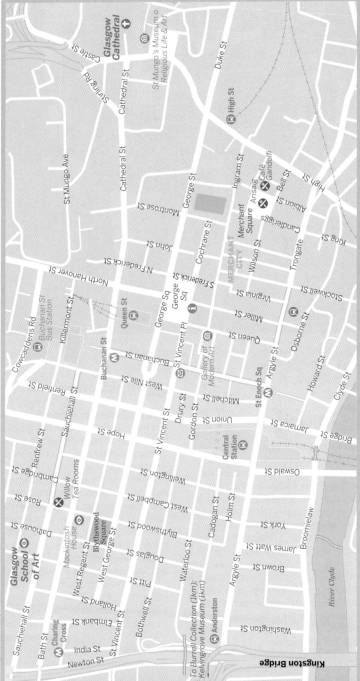

Glasgow City Centre

500 m
0.25 miles

Glasgow Cathedral

St Mungo's Museum o
Religious Life & Art

Castle St
Stirling Rd
Cathedral St
Duke St
High St

St Mungo Ave
Cathedral St
George St
Montrose St
Ingram St
Café
Gandolfi
Arisaig
Bell St
High St

John St
Cochrane St
MERCHANT
CITY
Merchant
Square
Candleriggs
Albion St
King St

North Hanover St
N Frederick St
Wilson St
Trongate
Stockwell St

Cowcaddens Rd
Buchanan St
Bus Station
Killermont St
George Sq
George
Sq
S Frederick St
Virginia St
Osborne St

Queen St
George Sq
St Vincent Pl
Miller St
Queen St
Argyle St
Howard St

Buchanan St
St Enoch Sq
Gallery of
Modern Art

Renfield St
West Nile St
Mitchell St
Argyle St
Clyde St

Cowcaddens
Sauchiehall St
Drury St
Gordon St
Union St
Jamaica St
Bridge St

Renfrew St
Hope St
St Vincent St
Central
Station
Oswald St

Cambridge St
Rose St
Dalhousie St
Willow
Tea Rooms
Wellington St
West Campbell St
Holm St
York St
Broomielaw

Glasgow
School
of Art
Mackintosh
House
Blythswood
Square
Blythswood St
Cadogan St
James Watt St
River Clyde

Sauchiehall St
West Regent St
West George St
Douglas St
Waterloo St
Argyle St
Brown St

Charing
Cross
Bath St
Holland St
Elmbank St
St Vincent St
Pitt St
Bothwell St
To Burrell Collection (1km);
Kelvingrove Museum (1km)
Anderston
Washington St

India St
Newton St
Kingston Bridge

Renfield St

311

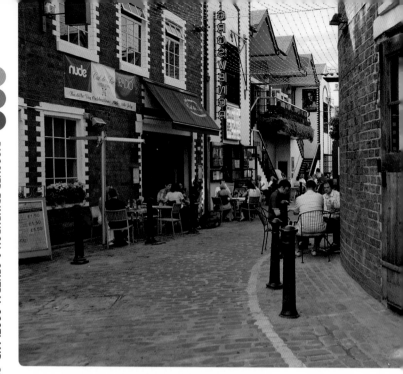

while the River Clyde, traditionally associated with Glasgow's earthier side, is now a symbol of the city's renaissance.

Sights

GLASGOW CATHEDRAL
Church

(HS; www.historic-scotland.gov.uk; Cathedral Sq; 9.30am-5.30pm Mon-Sat, 1-5pm Sun Apr-Sep, 9.30am-4.30pm Mon-Sat, 1-4.30pm Sun Oct-Mar) An attraction that shouldn't be missed, Glasgow Cathedral has a rare timelessness. The dark, imposing interior conjures up medieval might and can send a shiver down the spine. It's a shining example of Gothic architecture, and the only mainland Scottish cathedral to have survived the Reformation. The most interesting part of the cathedral, the **lower church**, is reached by a stairway. Its forest of pillars creates a powerful atmosphere around St Mungo's tomb (St Mungo founded a monastic community here in the 5th century), the focus of a famous medieval pilgrimage

that was believed to be as meritorious as a visit to Rome.

FREE KELVINGROVE MUSEUM
Museum, Gallery

(www.glasgowmuseums.com; Argyle St; 10am-5pm Mon-Thu & Sat, 11am-5pm Fri & Sun) In a magnificent stone building, this grand Victorian cathedral of culture has been revamped into a fascinating and unusual museum, with a bewildering variety of exhibits, but not too tightly packed to overwhelm. Here you'll find fine art alongside stuffed animals, and Micronesian shark tooth swords alongside a Spitfire plane, but it's not mix 'n' match: rooms are carefully and thoughtfully themed, and the collection is a manageable size. There's an excellent room of Scottish art, and a room of fine French Impressionist works, alongside quality Renaissance paintings from Italy and Flanders. You can learn a lot about art and more here, and it's excellent for the children with plenty for them to do, and displays aimed at a variety of ages.

Left: Diners in Glasgow; **Below:** Glasgow School of Art (p314)

PHOTOGRAPHERS: (LEFT) & (BELOW) MARGIE POLITZER / LONELY PLANET IMAGES ©

MACKINTOSH HOUSE

Mackintosh building

(www.hunterian.gla.ac.uk; 82 Hillhead St; admission £3, after 2pm Wed free; ⏰9.30am-5pm Mon-Sat) Attached to the Hunterian Art Gallery, this is a reconstruction of the first home that Charles Rennie Mackintosh bought with his wife, noted artist Mary Macdonald. The quiet elegance of the hall and dining room on the ground floor give way to a stunning drawing room. There's something otherworldly about the very mannered style of the beaten silver panels, the long-backed chairs and the surface decorations echoing Celtic manuscript illuminations.

FREE BURRELL COLLECTION

Gallery

(www.glasgowmuseums.com; Pollok Country Park; ⏰10am-5pm Mon-Thu & Sat, 11am-5pm Fri & Sun) One of Glasgow's top attractions is the Burrell Collection. Amassed by wealthy industrialist Sir William Burrell before being donated to the city,

it is housed in an outstanding museum, located 3 miles south of the city centre. This idiosyncratic collection of treasure includes everything from Chinese porcelain and medieval furniture to paintings by Renoir and Cézanne. It's not so big as to be overwhelming and the stamp of the collector lends an intriguing coherence.

 Eating

CAFÉ GANDOLFI　　Cafe, Bistro　££
(☎0141-552 6813; 64 Albion St; mains £8-14; ⏰9am-11.30pm Mon-Sat, noon-11.30pm Sun) In the fashionable Merchant City, this cafe was once part of the old cheese market. It's an excellent, friendly bistro and upmarket coffee shop – very much the place to be seen.

The Genius of Charles Rennie Mackintosh

Great cities have great artists, designers and architects contributing to the cultural and historical roots of their urban environment while expressing its soul and individuality. Charles Rennie Mackintosh was all of these. His quirky, linear and geometric designs have had almost as much influence on the city as have Gaudí's on Barcelona. Many of the buildings Mackintosh designed in Glasgow are open to the public, and you'll see his tall, thin, art nouveau typeface repeatedly reproduced.

Born in 1868, Mackintosh studied at the **Glasgow School of Art**. In 1896, when he was aged only 27, he won a competition for his design of the School of Art's new building. The first section was opened in 1899 and is considered to be the earliest example of art nouveau in Britain, as well as Mackintosh's supreme architectural achievement.

WILLOW TEA ROOMS　　　　Cafe　£
(www.willowtearooms.co.uk; light meals £4-8; ◷9am-5pm Mon-Sat, 11am-5pm Sun) Sauchiehall St **(217 Sauchiehall St)**; Buchanan St **(97 Buchanan St)** These re-creations of tearooms designed by Charles Rennie Mackintosh in 1904 – there are others cropping up around town – back up the design with excellent bagels, pastries, and, more splendidly, champagne afternoon teas (£17).

ARISAIG　　　　　　　　Scottish　££
(☏0141-553 1010; www.arisaigrestaurant.co.uk; 1 Merchant Sq; mains £11-17) Relocated into the Merchant Square building, a historical location converted into an echoing food court, Arisaig offers a good chance to try well-prepared Scottish cuisine at a fair price, with friendly service to boot.

ℹ Information

Tourist office (☏0141-204 4400; www.seeglasgow.com; 11 George Sq; ◷9am-5pm Mon-Sat)

ℹ Getting There & Away

Air

Ten miles west of the city, **Glasgow International Airport** (www.glasgowairport.com) handles domestic traffic and international flights. **Glasgow Prestwick Airport** (www.gpia.co.uk), 30 miles southwest of Glasgow, is used by **Ryanair** (www.ryanair.com) and some other budget airlines, with many connections to Britain and Europe.

Bus

Scottish Citylink (☏0870 550 5050; www.citylink.co.uk) Buses to most major towns in Scotland, including: **Edinburgh** (£6.30, 1¼ hours, every 15 minutes) and **Stirling** (£6.60, 45 minutes, at least hourly).

Train

As a general rule, Glasgow Central station serves southern Scotland, England and Wales, and Queen St station serves the north and east. There are buses every 10 minutes between them. **First ScotRail** (☏08457 55 00 33; www.scotrail.co.uk) runs Scottish trains. Destinations include: **Edinburgh** (£11.50, 50 minutes, every 15 minutes), **Oban** (£19.30, three hours, three to four daily), **Fort William** (£23.40, 3¾ hours, four to five daily) and **Inverness** (£70.40, 3½ hours, 10 daily, four on Sunday).

SOUTH OF GLASGOW
Alloway

The pretty, lush town of Alloway (38 miles south of Glasgow) should be on the itinerary of every Robert Burns fan – he was born here on 25 January 1759. The brand new **Robert Burns Birthplace**

Museum (NTS; www.nts.org.uk; adult/child £8; ⏰10am-5pm Oct-Mar, 10am-5.30pm Apr-Sep) displays a solid collection of Burnsiana, including manuscripts and possessions of the poet like the pistols he packed in order to carry out his daily work – as a taxman. A Burns jukebox allows you to select readings of your favourite verses, and there are other entertaining audio and visual performances.

Culzean Castle & Country Park

The Scottish National Trust's flagship property, magnificent **Culzean Castle** (NTS; cull-ane; www.culzeanexperience.org; adult/child/family £13/9/32, park only adult/child £8.50/5.50; ⏰castle 10.30am-5pm Apr-Oct, park 9.30am-sunset year-round) is one of the most impressive of Scotland's great stately homes. Designed by Robert Adam, who was encouraged to exercise his romantic genius in its design, this 18th-century mansion is perched dramatically on the edge of the cliffs.

The beautiful oval staircase here is regarded as one of his finest achievements. On the 1st floor, the opulence of the circular saloon contrasts violently with the views of the wild sea below. Even the bathrooms are palatial, the dressing room beside the state bedroom being equipped with a Victorian state-of-the-art shower.

Culzean is 49 miles south of Glasgow.

LOCH LOMOND

The 'bonnie banks' and 'bonnie braes' of Loch Lomond have long been Glasgow's rural retreat – a scenic region of hills, lochs and healthy fresh air within easy reach of Scotland's largest city Since the 1930s Glaswegians have made a regular weekend exodus to the hills – by car, by bike and on foot – and today the loch's popularity shows no sign of decreasing. (Loch Lomond is within an hour's drive of 70% of Scotland's population.)

The region's importance was recognised when it became the heart of **Loch Lomond & the Trossachs National Park** (www.lochlomond-trossachs.org) – Scotland's first national park, created in 2002. The national park falls into two distinct areas (virtually unconnected by

National Wallace Monument, Stirling (p320)

William Wallace, Scottish Patriot

William Wallace is one of Scotland's greatest heroes: a patriot whose exploits helped revive interest in Scottish history. In the wake of his victory over the English at Stirling Bridge in 1297, Wallace was knighted by Robert the Bruce and proclaimed Guardian of Scotland. However, it was only a short time before English military superiority and the fickle nature of the nobility's loyalties would turn against the defender of Scottish independence.

Disaster struck in July 1298 when King Edward's force defeated the Scots at the Battle of Falkirk. Many of the Scots nobility were prepared to side with Edward, and Wallace was betrayed after his return to Scotland in 1305, tried for treason at Westminster, and hanged, beheaded and disembowelled at Smithfield, London.

road): Loch Lomond and the surrounding hills in the centre and west, most easily reached from Glasgow; and the Trossachs in the east, most easily reached from Stirling.

Loch Lomond is the largest lake in mainland Britain and, after Loch Ness, perhaps the most famous of Scotland's lochs. Its proximity to Glasgow (20 miles away) means that the tourist honeypots of **Balloch**, **Loch Lomond Shores** and **Luss** get pretty crowded in summer. The main tourist focus is on the loch's western shore, along the A82, and at the southern end, around Balloch, which can occasionally be a nightmare of jet skis and motorboats. The eastern shore, which is followed by the West Highland Way long-distance footpath, is a little quieter.

ℹ️ Information

Balloch tourist office (☎0870 720 0607; Balloch Rd; ⏰9.30am-6pm Jun-Aug, 10am-6pm Apr & Sep)

Balmaha National Park Centre (☎01389-722100; Balmaha; ⏰9.30am-4.15pm Apr-Sep)

National Park Gateway Centre (☎01389-751035; www.lochlomondshores.com; Loch Lomond Shores, Balloch; ⏰10am-6pm Apr-Sep, 10am-5pm Oct-Mar; @ 🛜)

ℹ️ Getting There & Away

BUS First (www.firstgroup.com) Glasgow buses 204 and 215 run from Argyle St in central Glasgow to **Balloch** and **Loch Lomond Shores** (1½ hours, at least two per hour).

TRAIN There are frequent trains from Glasgow to **Balloch** (£4.15, 45 minutes, every 30 minutes).

STIRLING

POP 32,670

With an utterly impregnable position atop a mighty wooded crag (the plug of an extinct volcano), Stirling's beautifully preserved Old Town is a treasure-trove of noble buildings and cobbled streets winding up to the ramparts of its dominant castle, which offer views for miles around.

The castle makes a fascinating visit, but make sure you spend time exploring the Old Town and the picturesque path that circles it. Near the castle are a couple of snug pubs in which to toast Scotland's hoary heroes. Below the Old Town, retail-minded modern Stirling doesn't offer the same appeal; stick to the high ground as much as possible and you'll love the place.

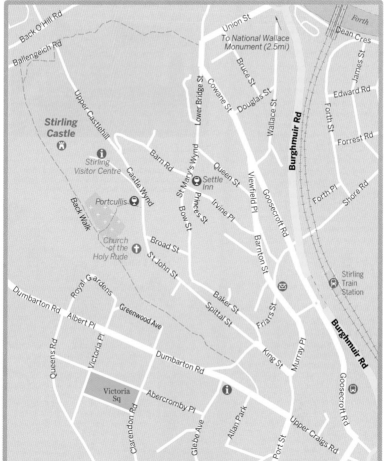

◉ Sights

STIRLING CASTLE   Castle
(HS; www.stirlingcastle.gov.uk; adult/child £7/4;
☺9.30am-6pm Apr-Sep, to 5pm Oct-Mar) Hold
Stirling and you control Scotland. This
maxim has ensured that a fortress of
some kind has existed here since prehistoric times. Commanding superb views,
you cannot help drawing parallels with
Edinburgh castle – but many find Stirling's
fortress more atmospheric; the location,

architecture and historical significance
combine to make it a grand and memorable visit. The **Great Hall** and **Gatehouse**
were built by James IV; observe the
hammer-beam roof and huge fireplaces in
the largest medieval hall in Scotland – the
result of 35 years of restoration.

After a long restoration project, the
Royal Palace is scheduled to re-open
as this book hits the shelves. It'll be
a sumptuous recreation of how this
luxurious Renaissance palace would have
looked when it was constructed by French

Stirling Castle

Planning Your Attack

Stirling's a sizeable fortress, but not so huge that you'll have to decide what to leave out – there's time to see it all. Unless you've got a working knowledge of Scottish monarchs, head to the Castle Exhibition ❶ first: it'll help you sort one James from another. That done, take on the sights at leisure. First, stop and look around you from the ramparts ❷; the views high over this flat valley, a key strategic point in Scotland's history, are magnificent.

Next, head through to the back of the castle to the Tapestry Studio ❸, which is open for shorter hours; seeing these skilful weavers at work is a highlight.

Track back towards the citadel's heart, stopping for a quick tour through the Great Kitchens ❹; looking at all that fake food might make you seriously hungry, though. Then enter the main courtyard. Around you are the principal castle buildings. During summer there are events (such as Renaissance dancing) in the Great Hall ❺ – get details at the entrance. The Museum of the Argyll & Sutherland Highlanders ❻ is a treasure trove if you're interested in regimental history, but missable if you're not. Leave the best for last – crowds thin in the afternoon – and enter the sumptuous Royal Palace ❼.

The Way Up & Down

If you have time, take the atmospheric Back Walk, a peaceful, shady stroll around the Old Town's fortifications and up to the castle's imposing crag-top position. Afterwards, wander down through the Old Town to admire its facades.

TOP TIPS

Admission Entrance is free for Historic Scotland members. If you'll be visiting several Scottish castles and ruins, a membership will save you plenty.

Vital Statistics First constructed: before 1110. Number of sieges: at least 9. Last besieger: Bonnie Prince Charlie (unsuccessful). Cost of refurbishing the Royal Palace: £12 million.

Museum of the Argyll & Sutherland Highlanders
The history of one of Scotland's legendary regiments – now subsumed into the Royal Regiment of Scotland – is on display here, featuring memorabilia, weapons and uniforms.

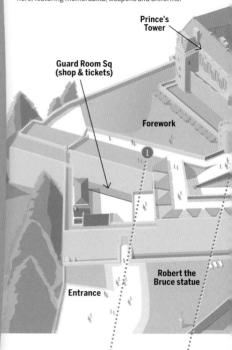

Prince's Tower

Guard Room Sq (shop & tickets)

Forework

Robert the Bruce statue

Entrance

Castle Exhibition
A great overview of the Stewart dynasty here will get your facts straight, and also offers the latest archaeological titbits from the ongoing excavations under the citadel. Analysis of skeletons has revealed surprising amounts of biographical data.

Royal Palace
The impressive new highlight of a visit to the castle is this recreation of the royal lodgings originally built by James V. The finely worked ceiling, ornate furniture and sumptuous unicorn tapestries dazzle.

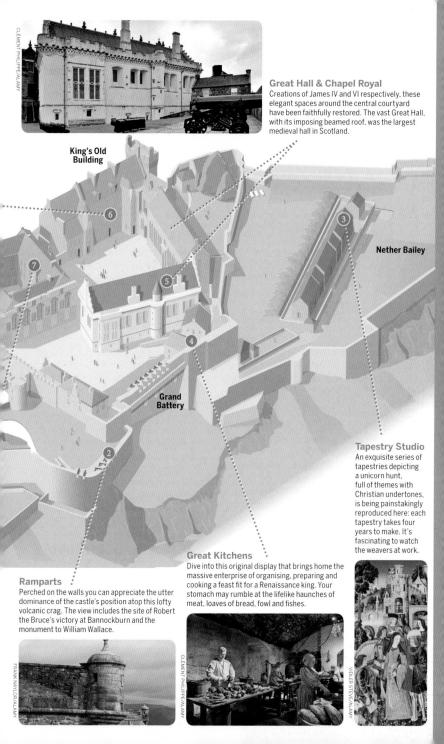

Great Hall & Chapel Royal
Creations of James IV and VI respectively, these elegant spaces around the central courtyard have been faithfully restored. The vast Great Hall, with its imposing beamed roof, was the largest medieval hall in Scotland.

King's Old Building

Nether Bailey

Grand Battery

Tapestry Studio
An exquisite series of tapestries depicting a unicorn hunt, full of themes with Christian undertones, is being painstakingly reproduced here: each tapestry takes four years to make. It's fascinating to watch the weavers at work.

Great Kitchens
Dive into this original display that brings home the massive enterprise of organising, preparing and cooking a feast fit for a Renaissance king. Your stomach may rumble at the lifelike haunches of meat, loaves of bread, fowl and fishes.

Ramparts
Perched on the walls you can appreciate the utter dominance of the castle's position atop this lofty volcanic crag. The view includes the site of Robert the Bruce's victory at Bannockburn and the monument to William Wallace.

Braemar & the Highland Games

Braemar is a pretty little village with a grand location on a broad plain ringed by mountains where the Dee valley and Glen Clunie meet. Just north of the village, turreted **Braemar Castle** (www.braemarcastle.co.uk; adult/child £5/3; ⊙11am-6pm Sat & Sun, also Wed Jul & Aug) dates from 1628 and served as a government garrison after the 1745 Jacobite rebellion.

There are Highland games in many towns and villages throughout the summer, but the best known is the **Braemar Gathering** (www.braemargathering.org), which takes place on the first Saturday in September. It's a major occasion, organised every year since 1817 by the Braemar Royal Highland Society. Events include highland dancing, pipers, tug-of-war, a hill race up Morrone, tossing the caber, hammer- and stone-throwing and the long jump. International athletes are among those who take part.

These kinds of events took place informally in the Highlands for many centuries as tests of skill and strength, but they were formalised around 1820 as part of the rise of Highland romanticism initiated by Sir Walter Scott and King George IV. Queen Victoria attended the Braemar Gathering in 1848, starting a tradition of royal patronage that continues to this day.

masons under the orders of James V (in the early 16th century) to impress his (also French) bride and other crowned heads of Europe.

OLD TOWN District

Below the castle, the steep Old Town has a remarkably different feel to modern Stirling, its cobblestone streets packed with 15th- to 17th-century architectural gems. Stirling has the best surviving **town wall** in Scotland. It was built around 1547 when Henry VIII of England began the 'Rough Wooing' – attacking the town in order to force Mary, Queen of Scots to marry his son so that the two kingdoms could be united. The wall can be explored on the **Back Walk**, which follows the line of the wall from Dumbarton Rd (near the tourist office) to the castle.

NATIONAL WALLACE MONUMENT
Monument

(www.nationalwallacemonument.com; adult/child £7.50/4.50; ⊙10am-5pm Apr-Oct, to 6pm Jul & Aug, 10.30am-4pm Nov-Mar) Towering over Scotland's narrow waist, this nationalist memorial is so Victorian Gothic it deserves circling bats and ravens. It commemorates the bid for Scottish independence depicted in the film *Braveheart*. From the visitors centre, walk or shuttle-bus up the hill to the building itself. Once there, break the climb up the narrow staircase inside to admire Wallace's 66 inches of broadsword and see the man himself recreated in a 3D audiovisual display.

Buses 62 and 63 run from Murray Place in Stirling to the visitors centre, otherwise it's a half-hour walk from central Stirling.

Eating & Drinking

PORTCULLIS Pub £

(☎01786-472290; www.theportcullishotel.com; Castle Wynd; bar meals £8-12; ⊙lunch & dinner) Built in stone as solid as the castle that it stands below, this former school is just the spot for a pint and a pub lunch after your visit.

SETTLE INN Pub

(91 St Mary's Wynd) A warm welcome is guaranteed at Stirling's oldest pub (1733),

a spot redolent with atmosphere, what with its log fire, vaulted back room, and low-slung ceilings.

ℹ Information

Stirling Visitor Centre (☏ 01786-450000; ⏱ 9.30am-6pm Apr-Sep, to 5pm Oct-Mar) Near the castle entrance.

Tourist office (☏ 01786-475019; www.visit scottishheartlands.com; 41 Dumbarton Rd; ⏱ 10am-5pm Mon-Sat year-round, plus Sun Jun–mid-Sep; @)

ℹ Getting There & Away

BUS Citylink (www.citylink.co.uk) offers a number of services to/from Stirling:

Edinburgh £6.70, one hour, hourly

Glasgow £6.60, 45 minutes, hourly

TRAIN First ScotRail (www.scotrail.co.uk) has services to/from a number of destinations:

Edinburgh £6.90, 55 minutes, twice hourly Monday to Saturday, hourly Sunday

Glasgow £7.10, 40 minutes, twice hourly Monday to Saturday, hourly Sunday

THE TROSSACHS

The Trossachs region has long been a favourite weekend getaway, offering outstanding natural beauty and excellent walking and cycling routes within easy reach of the southern population centres. With thickly forested hills, romantic lochs and an increasingly interesting selection of places to stay and eat, its popularity is sure to continue, protected by its status as part of Loch Lomond & the Trossachs National Park (p315).

Lochs Katrine & Achray

This rugged area, 6 miles north of Aberfoyle and 10 miles west of Callander, is the heart of the Trossachs. From April to October two **boats** (☏ 01877-332000; www.lochkatrine.com) run cruises from Trossachs Pier at the eastern tip of the loch. A one-hour cruise costs £10/7 per adult/child.

There are two good **walks** starting from nearby Loch Achray. The path to the rocky cone called **Ben A'an** (460m) begins at a car park near the old Trossachs Hotel. It's easy to follow, and the return trip is just under 4 miles. A tougher walk is up rugged **Ben Venue** (727m) – there is a path all the

Old Town, Stirling

way to the summit. There are great views of the Highlands and the Lowlands from the top. The return trip is about 5.5 miles – allow around four to five hours.

ST ANDREWS
POP 14,210

For a small place, St Andrews made a big name for itself, firstly as religious centre, then as Scotland's oldest university town. But its status as the home of golf has propelled it to even greater fame, and today's pilgrims arrive with a set of clubs. But it's a lovely place to visit even if you've no interest in the game, with impressive medieval ruins, stately university buildings, idyllic white sands and excellent accommodation and eating options.

 Sights

ST ANDREWS CATHEDRAL
Cathedral Ruins

(HS; www.historic-scotland.gov.uk; The Pends; adult/child £4.20/2.50, incl castle £7.20/4.30; ⊘9.30am-5.30pm Apr-Sep, to 4.30pm Oct-Mar) The ruins of this cathedral are all that's left of one of Britain's most magnificent medieval buildings. You can appreciate the scale and majesty of the edifice from the small sections that remain standing.

ST ANDREWS CASTLE
Castle

(HS; www.historic-scotland.gov.uk; The Scores; adult/child £5.20/3.10, with cathedral £7.20/4.30; ⊘9.30am-5.30pm Apr-Sep, to 4.30pm Oct-Mar) Not far from the cathedral and with dramatic coastline views, the castle is mainly in ruins, but the site itself is evocative.

 Sleeping

ABBEY COTTAGE
B&B ££

(☎01334-473727; www.abbeycottage.co.uk; Abbey Walk; s £40, d £59-64; P) This engaging spot sits below the town, surrounded by stone walls which enclose a rambling garden; it feels like you are staying in the country.

HAZELBANK HOTEL
Hotel £££

(☎01334-472466; www.hazelbank.com; 28 The Scores; s/d £90/151; @ 🛜) The front rooms have marvellous views along the beach and out to sea; those at the back are somewhat cheaper and more spacious.

OLD FISHERGATE HOUSE
B&B ££

(☎01334-470874; www.oldfishergatehouse. co.uk; North Castle St; s/d £75/100; 🛜) This historic 17th-century town house, furnished with period pieces, is in a great location – the oldest part of town, close to the cathedral and castle.

Playing the Old Course

Golf has been played at St Andrews since the 15th century and by 1457 was so popular that James II placed a ban on it because it interfered with his troops' archery practice. Although it lies beside the exclusive, all-male (female bartenders, unsurprisingly, allowed) Royal & Ancient Golf Club, the Old Course is public. Book in advance to play via **St Andrews Links Trust** (☎01334-466666; www.standrews.org.uk). You must reserve on or after the first Wednesday in September the year before you wish to play. No bookings are taken for Saturdays or the month of September. Unless you've booked months in advance, getting a tee-off time is literally a lottery; enter the ballot at the **caddie office** (☎01334-466666) before 2pm on the day before you wish to play (there's no Sunday play). Be warned that applications by ballot are normally heavily oversubscribed, and green fees are £130 in summer.

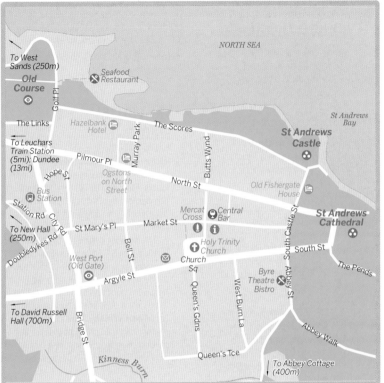

OGSTONS ON NORTH STREET

Hotel £££

(01334-473387; www.ogstonsonnorthst.com; 127 North St; s/d £100-120, d £120-160;) If you want to eat, drink and sleep in the same stylish place then this classy inn could be for you. Smartened-up rooms feature elegant contemporary styling and coolly beautiful bathrooms, some with jacuzzi.

Eating & Drinking

SEAFOOD RESTAURANT

Restaurant £££

(01334-479475; www.theseafoodrestaurant. com; The Scores; lunch/dinner £22/45; lunch & dinner) The Seafood Restaurant occupies a stylish glass-walled room, built out over the sea, with plush navy carpet, crisp white linen, an open kitchen and panoramic views of St Andrews Bay.

BYRE THEATRE BISTRO

Bistro ££

(www.byretheatre.com; Abbey St; mains £9-15; breakfast, lunch & dinner Tue-Sat;) A happy, buzzy spot with comfy couches, works of art on the wall and a well-developed menu that encompasses some delicious fusion cooking.

CENTRAL BAR

Pub

(77 Market St) Rather staid compared to some of the wilder student-driven drinking options, this likeable pub keeps it real with traditional features, an island bar, lots of Scottish beers, decent service and filling (if uninspiring) pub grub.

If You Like...
Whisky Distilleries

If you like a tipple, you may want to check out the home of your favourite whisky. Only hard-core malthounds will want to go to more than two or three distilleries.

1 ABERLOUR
(01340-881249; www.aberlour.com; tours £10; 10.30am & 2pm daily Easter-Oct, Mon-Fri by appointment Nov-Mar) This distillery has an excellent, detailed tour with a proper tasting session.

2 GLENFARCLAS
(01807-500257; www.glenfarclas.co.uk; admission £3.50; 10am-4pm Mon-Fri Oct-Mar, 10am-5pm Mon-Fri Apr-Sep, plus 10am-4pm Sat Jul-Sep) Small, friendly and independent, Glenfarclas is 5 miles south of Aberlour on the Grantown road. The in-depth Ambassador's Tour (Fridays only) is £15.

3 GLENFIDDICH
(01340-820373; www.glenfiddich.com; admission free; 9.30am-4.30pm Mon-Fri year-round, 9.30am-4.30pm Sat & noon-4.30pm Sun Easter–mid-Oct) Glenfiddich is big and busy, but handiest for Dufftown and foreign language tours are available. The standard tour starts with an overblown video, but it's fun, informative and free. An in-depth Connoisseur's Tour (£20) must be prebooked.

4 MACALLAN
(01340-872280; www.themacallan.com; standard tours £5; 9.30am-4.30pm Mon-Sat Apr-Oct, ring for winter hours) Excellent sherry-casked malt. Several small-group tours are available (last tour at 3.30pm), including an expert one (£15); all should be prebooked. Lovely location 2 miles northwest of Craigellachie.

Information

Tourist office (01334-472021; www.visit-standrews.co.uk; 70 Market St; 9.15am-6.30pm Mon-Sat & 9.30am-5pm Sun Jul-Sep, 9.15am-5pm Mon-Sat mid-Oct–Jun, plus 11am-4pm Sun Apr-Jun; @)

Getting There & Away

BUS There are frequent services to the following:

Edinburgh £9.40, two hours, hourly

Glasgow £9.40, 2 ½ hours, hourly

Stirling £7.30, two hours, six to seven Monday to Saturday

SPEYSIDE
Dufftown
POP 1450

Rome may be built on seven hills, but Dufftown's built on seven stills, say the locals. Founded in 1817 by James Duff, 4th earl of Fife, Dufftown is 17 miles south of Elgin and lies at the heart of the Speyside whisky-distilling region.

The **tourist office** (01340-820501; 10am-1pm & 2-5.30pm Mon-Sat, 11am-3pm Sun Easter-Oct) is in the clock tower in the main square; the adjoining museum contains some interesting local items. Ask at the tourist office for a **Malt Whisky Trail** (www.maltwhiskytrail.com) booklet, a self-guided tour around the seven stills plus the Speyside Cooperage.

 Sights

WHISKY MUSEUM Museum
(www.dufftown.co.uk; The Hub, 12 Conval St; 1-4pm Mon-Fri May-Sep) As well as housing a selection of distillery memorabilia (try saying that after a few drams), the Whisky Museum holds 'nosing and tasting evenings' where you can learn how to judge a fine single malt (£8 per person; 8pm Wednesday in July and August).

 Sleeping & Eating

DAVAAR B&B B&B ££
(01340-820464; www.davaardufftown.co.uk; 17 Church St; s/d from £40/60) Just along the street opposite the tourist office, Davaar is a sturdy Victorian villa with three small-ish but comfy rooms; the breakfast menu

Detour: Balmoral Castle

South of Dufftown and eight miles west of Ballater lies **Balmoral Castle** (www. balmoralcastle.com; adult/child £8.70/4.60; 10am-5pm Apr-Jul, last admission 4pm), the Queen's Highland holiday home, screened from the road by a thick curtain of trees. Built for Queen Victoria in 1855 as a private residence for the royal family, it kicked off the revival of the Scottish Baronial style of architecture that characterises so many of Scotland's 19th-century country houses.

The admission fee includes an interesting and well thought out audioguide, but the tour is very much an outdoor one through garden and grounds; as for the castle itself, only the ballroom, which displays a collection of Landseer paintings and royal silver, is open to the public. Don't expect to see the Queen's private quarters! The main attraction is learning about Highland estate management, rather than royal revelations.

is superb, offering the option of Portsoy kippers instead of the traditional fry-up (using eggs from the owners' chickens).

FIFE ARMS HOTEL Hotel ££
(01340-820220; www.fifearmsdufftown.co.uk; 2 The Square; s/d from £35/60; P) This welcoming hotel offers slightly cramped but comfortable accommodation in a modern block around the back; its bar is stocked with a wide range of single malts, and the restaurant (mains £9 to £16) dishes up sizzling steaks, homemade steak pies and locally farmed ostrich steaks.

A TASTE OF SPEYSIDE Scottish ££
(01340-820860; 10 Balvenie St; mains £16-20; noon-9pm Tue-Sun Easter-Sep, noon-2pm & 6-9pm Tue-Sun Oct-Easter) This upmarket restaurant prepares traditional Scottish dishes using local produce, including a platter of smoked salmon, smoked venison, brandied chicken liver pâté, cured herring, a selection of Scottish cheeses and homemade bread (phew!).

Getting There & Away

Buses link Dufftown to Inverness. On summer weekends, you can take a train from Inverness to Keith, then ride the Keith and Dufftown Railway to Dufftown.

Interior of the Glenfiddich distillery
PHOTOGRAPHER: ROCCO FASANO / LONELY PLANET IMAGES ©

Scotland's Highlands & Islands

The Highlands are clear testimony to the sculpting power of ice and weather. From the subarctic plateau of the Cairngorms to the rocky summit of Ben Nevis, here the Scottish landscape is at its grandest, with high peaks bounded by wooded glens, deep lochs and rushing waterfalls.

Glen Coe and Fort William draw hordes of hill walkers in summer and skiers in winter, while Inverness, the Highland capital, provides urban rest and relaxation. Not far away, Loch Ness and its elusive monster add a hint of mystery.

To the west are Scotland's many off-shore islands, including major highlights such as Skye and Mull. Even further off the track, beyond the mainland to the north sits another island group, the Orkneys, where intrepid travellers can admire some of the finest prehistoric sites in the whole of Britain.

Eilean Donan Castle (p350)

Scotland's Highlands & Islands

1 Loch Ness
2 Ben Nevis
3 Isle of Skye
4 Isle of Mull
5 Glen Coe
6 Eilean Donan Castle

SHETLAND ISLANDS

Herma Ness
Sand Wick
Housay
North Sea
Ronies Hill
Ulsta
Bard Head
Lerwick
ATLANTIC OCEAN
Fitful Head
Sumburgh Head

1°W
2°W
60°N

0 40 km
0 20 miles

ATLANTIC OCEAN

60 km
30 miles

ORKNEY ISLANDS

Northwall
Whitehall
To Shetland Islands
North Ronaldsay Firth
The North Sound
Balfour
Skaill
Mainland
Rousay
Burwick
Duncansby Head
Birsay
Hoy
Rackwick
Dunnet Head
Castletown
John O'Groats
Wick
Scrabster
Thurso
Achavanich
Lybster
Dunbeath
Melvich
Bettyhill
Sutherland Mountains
Kinbrace
Helmsdale
Melness
Ben Hope (927m)
Lairg
Brora
Dunrobin Castle
Dornoch
Portmahomack
Durness
Ben More Assynt (998m)
Croick
Bonar Bridge
Tain
Moray Firth
Lossiemouth
Elgin
Tarbet
Inchnadamph
Dundonell
HIGHLAND
Dingwall
Cromarty
Findhorn
Portknockie
Banff
Point of Stoer
Clachtoll
Achiltibuie
Garve
Black Isle
Fort George
Culloden
Inverness
Aberchirder
Keith
Dufftown
Fraserburgh
Boddam
Pennan
Maud
The Minch
Ruadh Reidh
Drumchork
Gairloch
Lower Diabaig
Achnasheen
Muir of Ord
Beauly
Aberlour
Port of Ness
Port nan Gizran
Redpoint
Torridon
Strathcarran
Portnahomack
Leumrabhagh
Stornoway
Brochel
Uig
Dunvegan 3
Portree
Garenin
Lewis
The Little Minch
ATLANTIC OCEAN
Husinish
Dirinishader
Harris
Rodel
Carnach
Boreraig
OUTER HEBRIDES
Port nan Long
North Uist
Cladach
Balivanich (Baile a'Mhanaich)
Geirinnis

59°N
58°N
8°W
4°W
3°W
2°W

Scotland's Highlands & Islands Highlights

1 Loch Ness

Stretching along the glacier-gouged trench of the Great Glen, 23-mile-long Loch Ness (p340) contains more water than all the lakes in England and Wales combined. Its peaty depths conceal the mystery of its legendary monster, and thousands flock here each year in hope of catching a glimpse. Top right: Likeness of Nessie, Fort Augustus

Need to Know
BEST TIME TO VISIT A calm, windless day **TOP TIP** Drive the minor road on the loch's east side to avoid crowds **BEST PHOTO OP** View from Urquhart Castle **For more, see p340**

Loch Ness Don't Miss List

ADRIAN SHINE, LEADER OF THE
LOCH NESS PROJECT

1 LOCH NESS EXHIBITION CENTRE

I designed this exhibition (p340) myself, presenting the results of eight decades of research. The collection has everything from one-man submarines to the ROSETTA apparatus that opened the 10,000-year-old time capsule concealed within the loch's sediment layers. The exhibition does not have all the answers and it will certainly not try to sell you a monster. Instead, it places the mystery in its proper context, which is the environment of Loch Ness.

2 URQUHART CASTLE

If, having learned some of the inner secrets of the loch, you want to see it through new eyes, you cannot do better than visit Urquhart Castle (pictured bottom left; p341). Perched on a rocky promontory jutting into Loch Ness, its exhibits recount the castle's history from a vitrified Pictish fort to its role in the Scottish Wars of Independence. The view from the Grant Tower is truly breathtaking.

3 FORT AUGUSTUS LOCKS

At the southern end of the loch there is a flight of locks on the Caledonian Canal, built by the great engineer Thomas Telford. It is always interesting to watch vessels being worked up this 'staircase' of water. British Waterways have a fascinating exhibition halfway up.

4 CRUISING THE LOCH

Venturing onto the water puts the seemingly tiny trunk road and Urquhart Castle into a new perspective. The Deepscan cruise boat runs from the Loch Ness Centre; I use this boat for my research and the skipper will tell you about his experiences. There are other cruise boats operating from Drumnadrochit, and the larger Jacobite vessels depart from Inverness.

5 WATERFALL WALKS

Starting from the car park at Invermoriston, cross the road to find the magnificent waterfall, then go back to take the path down the river through a mature beech wood to the shores of the loch. There is another famous waterfall at Foyers on the southeastern shore of Loch Ness, and Divach Falls up Balmacaan Rd at Drumnadrochit.

Ben Nevis

The highest summit in all of Britain and Ireland, Ben Nevis (p344) can be admired from below (it's just a few miles outside Fort William) or experienced to the full with a hike to the summit. Don't take it lightly – it's a strenuous outing and the weather can deteriorate rapidly. But treat Britain's tallest peak with respect and your reward (weather permitting) is a truly magnificent view and a great sense of achievement.

Isle of Mull

From the rugged ridges in the centre of the island, to the blinding white sand on the coast, Mull (p351) can lay claim to some of the finest and most varied scenery of all Scotland's islands. Add impressive castles, wildlife cruises, pretty harbourside houses, the sacred island of Iona and easy access from Oban and you can see why it's one of the most popular of all Scotland's islands. Tobermory harbour, Isle of Mull (p352)

FEARGUS COONEY / LONELY PLANET IMAGES ©

Isle of Skye

Taking its name from the old Norse *sky-a,* meaning 'cloud island' (a Viking reference to the often mist-enshrouded Cuillin Hills), this is the largest of Scotland's islands (p345), a 50-mile-long smorgasbord of velvet moors, jagged mountains, sparkling lochs and towering sea cliffs. The stunning scenery is the main attraction, but when the mist closes in there are plenty of castles and cosy pubs to retire to.

Glen Coe

One of Scotland's wildest, most scenic and most famous glens, the peacefulness and beauty of Glen Coe (p341) today belie the fact that it was the scene of a ruthless 17th-century massacre in which the local MacDonalds were murdered by soldiers of the Campbell clan. As well as history, there are many fine walks both easy and difficult, and enough photo opportunities to keep keen snappers happy.

Eilean Donan Castle

Perched on a tiny island linked to the shore by a picturesque arched bridge, Eilean Donan (p350) is the most iconic of Scottish castles. Its image has graced everything from postcards to shortbread tins, and has appeared in many movies including *Highlander* and *The World Is Not Enough.* Despite its venerable appearance, it is actually a relatively modern restoration, dating from the early 20th century.

Scotland's Highlands & Islands' Best…

Natural Beauty

o **Loch Ness** (p340) Classic loch views from Fort Augustus and Urquhart Castle

o **Glen Coe** (p341) Brooding mountain scenery looms over narrow glen

o **Cuillin Hills of Skye** (p347) Taking its name from 'keel' (of a boat), this razor-sharp ridge dominates the island

o **The Road to the Isles** (p343) From Fort William to Mallaig

Historic Sites

o **Glen Coe** (p341) Site of the Glencoe Massacre, one of Scottish history's most tragic episodes

o **Urquhart Castle** (p341) Impressive medieval castle overlooking Loch Ness

o **Eilean Donan Castle** (p350) Castle against backdrop of sea and mountains – star of a million shortbread tins

o **McCaig's Tower** (p348) Panorama over Oban Bay to the Isle of Mull

Waterfronts

o **Inverness** (p338) The main base for the Highlands has lovely riverside walks

o **Tobermory** (p352) Classic harbourside street with brightly painted houses

o **Portree** (p347) Main town on the Isle of Skye with a pretty harbour

o **Oban** (p348) The 'gateway to the isles' is a busy working port always with something interesting going on

Islands

- **Mull** (p351) This large island boasts mountains, beaches, castles and even a railway

- **Skye** (p345) Sail over the sea to the best known of all Scottish islands

- **Iona** (p353) Tiny sacred island still with a spiritual atmosphere

- **Orkney Islands** (p344) Rocky archipelago off Scotland's north coast, with astounding prehistoric remains

Need to Know

ADVANCE PLANNING

- **One month before** Book accommodation if visiting in summer, especially popular spots such as Mull and Skye

- **Two weeks before** If travelling by car, make reservations for any ferry crossings, especially in summer

- **One week before** Make bookings for wildlife-spotting boat trips

RESOURCES

Major tourist information websites for the region:

- **Highlands** (www.visithighlands.com)

- **Loch Ness** (www.visitlochness.com)

- **Cairngorms National Park** (www.visitcairngorms.com)

- **Fort William** (www.visit-fortwilliam.co.uk)

- **Skye** (www.skye.co.uk)

- **Iona** (www.isle-of-iona.com)

- **Oban and Mull** (www. visitscottishheartlands.com)

- **Caledonian Macbrayne** (www.calmac.co.uk)

GETTING AROUND

- **Bus** Long-distance buses between the main centres; reasonable network of local buses on islands

- **Car** The most time-efficient way to get around the Highlands; for island trips, if vehicle ferries are booked up, leave your car on the mainland for a day or two, jump aboard as a foot passenger and explore the islands by bus or taxi

- **Ferry** Frequent services from Oban to Mull year-round; for Skye there's a ferry from Mallaig and a bridge at Kyle of Lochalsh

- **Train** Scenic lines from Edinburgh or Glasgow to Inverness, Fort William, Oban, Mallaig or Kyle of Lochalsh

BE FOREWARNED

- **Midges** These tiny biting flies are a pest from June to September, especially in still weather around dawn and dusk; bring insect repellent and wear long-sleeved clothing

- **Weather** Always unpredictable on the west coast; be prepared for wet and windy days, even in the middle of summer

Left: Hiker, Glen Coe (p341); **Above:** McCaig's Tower, behind George St, Oban (p348)

OGRAPHERS: (LEFT) GARETH MCCORMACK / LONELY PLANET IMAGES ©; (ABOVE) DAVID ELSE / LONELY PLANET IMAGES ©

Scotland's Highlands & Islands Itineraries

The three-day trip takes in some big-name locations, while the five-day trip combines highlands with islands. The routes intersect at Fort William.

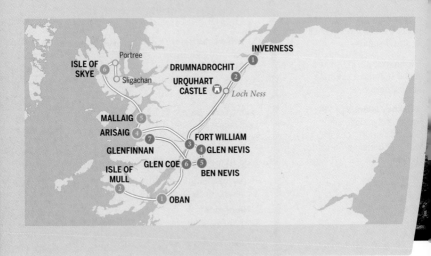

3 DAYS

INVERNESS TO GLENFINNAN
Scottish Icons

Start your tour in **(1) Inverness**, capital of the Highlands, then head south on the A82 along the west bank of legendary Loch Ness. Stop at **(2) Drumnadrochit** to visit the monster exhibitions and **Urquhart Castle**, and perhaps take a cruise on the **loch**. In the afternoon, continue south via **(3) Fort William**, the self-proclaimed 'Outdoor Capital of the UK'.

Depending on the weather, day two might start with a walk or drive along **(4) Glen Nevis**, which curls around the foot of **(5) Ben Nevis**. If you're active, you could hike to the summit. If you're more into

history, drive south from Fort William to the great valley of **(6) Glen Coe**.

Spend day three tootling westwards along the A830, the famous Road to the Isles, enjoying the spectacular scenery. Turn around at **(7) Glenfinnan**, where you can visit the monument to Bonnie Prince Charlie, or walk along the glen to view the railway viaduct that features in Harry Potter films. Or go as far as **Arisaig** or all the way to **Mallaig**, where ferries depart for the Isle of Skye.

OBAN TO SKYE
Highland & Island Hopping

Start your tour in **(1) Oban**, the 'gateway to the isles'. Take a day trip out to the smaller islands of Lismore or Kerrera, and in the evening walk up to McCaig's Tower.

The second day begins with the ferry ride across to the **(2) Isle of Mull**. Spend a day or two here, touring the island; options include the holy islet of Iona and the colourful island capital of Tobermory. The roads are narrow and the scenery stunning at every turn – two good reasons for allowing plenty of time.

Return to Oban and travel up the A828 towards Fort William. If time allows, at Ballachulish, divert east to the valley of **Glen Coe**.

In **(3) Fort William**, enjoy the views of Ben Nevis then aim west along the A830, the famous Road to the Isles. Leave the main road at **(4) Arisaig**, signposted 'Alternative Coastal Route' for the best views. In the work-a-day fishing harbour of **(5) Mallaig** take the ferry across to Armadale on the **(6) Isle of Skye**.

Spend the final day or two on Skye. Follow the scenic roads to **Portree**, the capital, via a stop at **Sligachan** for views of the Cuillin ridge. Return to the mainland (no more ferries) via the sweeping Skye Bridge.

Viaduct, Glenfinnan, the Road to the Isles (p343)
PHOTOGRAPHER: PATRICK HORTON / LONELY PLANET IMAGES ©

Discover Scotland's Highlands & Islands

THE HIGHLANDS
Inverness

POP 55,000

Inverness, the primary city and shopping centre of the Highlands, has a great location astride the River Ness at the northern end of the Great Glen. In summer it overflows with visitors intent on monster hunting at nearby Loch Ness, but it's worth a visit in its own right for a stroll along the picturesque River Ness and a cruise on the Moray Firth in search of its famous bottlenose dolphins.

◉ Sights & Activities

NESS ISLANDS   Park

Save the indoor sights for a rainy day – the main attraction in Inverness is a leisurely stroll along the river to the Ness Islands. Planted with mature Scots pine, fir, beech and sycamore, and linked to the river banks and each other by elegant Victorian footbridges, the islands make an appealing picnic spot. They're a 20-minute walk south of the castle – head upstream on either side of the river, and return on the opposite bank.

INVERNESS CASTLE   Castle

The hill above the city centre is topped by the picturesque Baronial turrets of Inverness Castle, a pink-sandstone confection dating from 1847 that replaced a medieval castle blown up by the Jacobites in 1746; it serves today as the Sheriff's Court. It's not open to the public, but there are good views from the surrounding gardens.

Waterfall at Glen Nevis (p336)
PHOTOGRAPHER: DAVID TOMLINSON / LONELY PLANET IMAGES ©

Sleeping

TRAFFORD BANK
B&B ££

(01463-241414; www.traffordbankguesthouse.
co.uk; 96 Fairfield Rd; s/d from £85/110; P 🛜)
Lots of word-of-mouth rave reviews for
Trafford Bank, an elegant Victorian villa
that was once home to a bishop, just a
mitre-toss from the Caledonian Canal
and only 10 minutes' walk from the city
centre. The luxurious rooms include fresh
flowers and fruit, bathrobes and fluffy
towels – ask for the Tartan Room, with its
wrought-iron king-size bed and Victorian
roll-top bath.

ARDCONNEL HOUSE
B&B ££

(01463-240455; www.ardconnel-inverness.
co.uk; 21 Ardconnel St; per person from £35; 🛜)
The six-room Ardconnel is another of our
favourites – a terraced Victorian house
with comfortable en-suite rooms, a dining
room with crisp white table linen, and a
breakfast menu that includes Vegemite
for homesick Antipodeans. Kids under 10
not allowed.

ACH ALUINN
B&B ££

(01463-230127; www.achaluinn.com; 27
Fairfield Rd; per person £25-35; P) This large,
detached Victorian house is bright and
homely, and offers all you might want
from a guest house – private bathroom,
TV, reading lights, comfy beds with two
pillows each, and an excellent breakfast.
Five minutes' walk from city centre.

Eating & Drinking

CONTRAST BRASSERIE
Brasserie ££

(01463-227889; www.glenmoristontownhouse.
com/contrast; 22 Ness Bank; mains £10-19;
noon-2.30pm & 5-10pm) Book early for
what we think is the best restaurant in
Inverness – a dining room that drips designer style, smiling professional staff, a
jug of water brought to your table without
asking, and truly delicious food. Try mussels with Thai red curry, wild mushroom
risotto, or pork belly with glazed walnuts
and watercress; 10 out of 10.

CAFÉ 1
Bistro ££

(01463-226200; www.cafe1.net; 75 Castle
St; mains £10-20; noon-2pm & 5.30-9.30pm
Mon-Sat) Café 1 is a friendly and appealing
little bistro with candle-lit tables amid
elegant blond-wood and wrought-iron
decor. There is an international menu
based on quality Scottish produce, from
succulent Aberdeen Angus steaks to crisp
sea bass with chilli, lime and soy sauce.

MUSTARD SEED
Modern Scottish ££

(01463-220220; www.mustardseedrestaurant.
co.uk; 16 Fraser St; mains £12-16; noon-10pm)
This bright and bustling bistro brings a
dash of big-city style to Inverness. The
menu changes weekly, but focuses on
Scottish and French cuisine with a modern twist. Grab a table on the upstairs
balcony if you can – it's the best outdoor
lunch spot in Inverness, with a great view
across the river.

PHOENIX
Pub

(108 Academy St) This is the best of the
traditional pubs in the city centre, with a
mahogany horseshoe bar, a comfortable,
family-friendly lounge, and good food at
both lunchtime and in the evening.

ℹ Information

Tourist office (01436-234353; www.
visithighlands.com; Castle Wynd; 9am-6pm
Mon-Sat & 9.30am-5pm Sun Jul & Aug, 9am-5pm
Mon-Sat & 10am-4pm Sun Jun, Sep & Oct, 9am-
5pm Mon-Sat Apr & May; limited hrs Nov-Mar)

ℹ Getting There & Away

AIR Inverness airport (www.hial.co.uk/
inverness-airport) At Dalcross, 10 miles east of
the city on the A96 towards Aberdeen. There are
scheduled flights to **London**, **Manchester** and
several other British airports.

BUS Scottish Citylink (www.citylink.co.uk)
Connections to **Glasgow** (£26, 3½ to 4½ hours,
hourly), **Edinburgh** (£26, 3½ to 4½ hours,
hourly), **Fort William** (£11, two hours, five daily)
and Portree on the **Isle of Skye** (£17, 3½ hours,
five daily).

TRAIN There are several direct trains a day from **Glasgow** (£55, 3½ hours) and **Edinburgh** (£55, 3¼ hours). The line from Inverness to **Kyle of Lochalsh** (£18, 2½ hours, four daily Monday to Saturday, two Sunday), the nearest train to the Isle of Skye, provides one of Britain's great scenic train journeys.

Loch Ness

Deep, dark and narrow, Loch Ness stretches for 23 miles between Inverness and Fort Augustus. Its bitterly cold waters have been extensively explored in search of Nessie, the elusive Loch Ness monster, but most visitors see her only in cardboard-cutout form at the monster exhibitions. The busy A82 road runs along the northwestern shore, while the more tranquil and picturesque B862 follows the southeastern shore. A complete circuit of the loch is about 70 miles – travel anticlockwise for the best views.

Drumnadrochit

POP 800

Seized by monster madness, its gift shops bulging with Nessie cuddly toys, Drumnadrochit is a hotbed of beastie fever, with two monster exhibitions battling it out for the tourist dollar.

The **Loch Ness Exhibition Centre** (www.loch-ness-scotland.com; adult/child £6.50/4.50; ⊘9am-6.30pm Jul & Aug, to 6pm Jun & Sep, 9.30am-5pm Feb-May & Oct, 10am-3.30pm Nov-Jan) is the better of the two Nessie-themed attractions, with a scientific approach that allows you to weigh the evidence for yourself, and featuring original footage of monster sightings plus exhibits of equipment used in the various underwater monster hunts.

The more homely **Nessieland Castle Monster Centre** (www.lochness-hotel.com; adult/child £5.50/4; ⊘9am-8pm Jul & Aug, 10am-5.30pm Apr-Jun, Sep & Oct, 10am-4pm Nov-Mar) is more of a miniature theme park aimed squarely at the kids, but its main function is to sell you Loch Ness monster souvenirs.

One-hour monster-hunting cruises complete with sonar and underwater cameras aboard the **Nessie Hunter** (☎01456-450395; www.lochness-cruises.com; adult/child £10/8) operate from Drumnadrochit. Cruises depart hourly from 9am to 6pm daily from Easter to December.

The Three Sisters, Glen Coe

FEARGUS COONEY / LONELY PLANET IMAGES ©

Loch Ness Monster

Highland folklore is filled with tales of strange creatures living in lochs and rivers, notably the kelpie (water horse) that lures unwary travellers to their doom. The use of the term 'monster' is a relatively recent phenomenon whose origins lie in an article published in the *Inverness Courier* on 2 May 1933, entitled 'Strange Spectacle on Loch Ness'.

The article recounted the sighting of a disturbance in the loch by Mrs Aldie Mackay and her husband. 'There the creature disported itself, rolling and plunging for fully a minute, its body resembling that of a whale, and the water cascading and churning like a simmering cauldron. In December 1933 the *Daily Mail* sent Marmaduke Wetherall, a film director and big-game hunter, to Loch Ness to track down the beast. Then in April 1934 came the famous 'long-necked monster' photograph taken by the seemingly reputable Harley St surgeon, Colonel Kenneth Wilson. The press went mad and the rest, as they say, is history.

Hoax or not, there's no denying that the bizarre mini-industry that has grown up around Loch Ness and its mysterious monster since that eventful summer over 75 years ago is the strangest spectacle of all.

Urquhart Castle

Commanding a brilliant location with outstanding views (on a clear day), **Urquhart Castle** (HS; adult/child £7/4.20; ⊙9.30am-6pm Apr-Sep, to 5pm Oct, to 4.30pm Nov-Mar) is a popular Nessie-watching hot spot. A huge visitor centre (most of which is beneath ground level) includes a video theatre (with a dramatic 'unveiling' of the castle at the end of the film), displays of medieval items discovered in the castle, a huge gift shop and a restaurant. The site is often very crowded in summer.

The castle was repeatedly sacked and rebuilt over the centuries, but was finally blown up in 1692 to prevent the Jacobites from using it. The five-storey tower house at the northern point is the most impressive remaining fragment and offers wonderful views across the water.

ⓘ Getting There & Away

Scottish Citylink and Stagecoach buses from Inverness to Fort William run along the shores of Loch Ness (six to eight daily, five on Sunday). There are bus stops at **Drumnadrochit** (£6.20, 30 minutes) and **Urquhart Castle** car park (£6.60, 35 minutes).

Glen Coe

Scotland's most famous glen is also one of the grandest and, in bad weather, the grimmest. The approach to the glen from the east, watched over by the rocky pyramid of **Buachaille Etive Mor** – the Great Shepherd of Etive – leads over the Pass of Glencoe and into the narrow upper valley. The southern side is dominated by three massive, brooding spurs, known as the **Three Sisters**, while the northern side is enclosed by the continuous steep wall of the knife-edged Aonach Eagach ridge. The main road threads its lonely way through the middle of all this mountain grandeur, past deep gorges and crashing waterfalls, to the more pastoral lower reaches of the glen around Loch Achtriochtan and Glencoe village.

Glencoe village was written into the history books in 1692 when the resident MacDonalds were murdered by Campbell soldiers in what became known as the Glencoe Massacre.

The remote **King's House Hotel** (☏01855-851259; www.kingy.com; Glencoe; bar meals £8-12; s/d £30/65; Ⓟ) claims to be one of Scotland's oldest licenced inns,

If You Like...
Scenic Glens

If you like the grand scenery of Glen Coe (p341), seek out some of Scotland's other stunning glens.

1 GLEN ETIVE
At the eastern end of Glen Coe a minor road leads south along this peaceful and beautiful glen. On a hot summer's day the River Etive contains many tempting pools for swimming in and there are lots of good picnic sites.

2 GLEN ROY
Near Spean Bridge, 10 miles north of Fort William, this glen is noted for its intriguing, so-called 'parallel roads'. These prominent horizontal terraces are actually ancient shorelines formed during the last ice age by the waters of an ice-dammed glacial lake.

3 GLEN FESHIE
Tranquil Glen Feshie extends south from Kincraig, deep into the Cairngorms, with Scots pine woods in its upper reaches surrounded by big, heathery hills. The 4WD track to the head of the glen makes a great mountain-bike excursion (25-mile round-trip).

4 GLEN LYON
This remote and stunningly beautiful glen runs for some 34 unforgettable miles of rickety stone bridges, Caledonian pine forest and sheer heather-splashed peaks poking through swirling clouds. It's reached via from the A9 via Aberfeldy.

dating from the 17th century. The hotel serves good pub grub and has long been a meeting place for climbers, skiers and hill walkers – the rustic **Climbers Bar** is round the back.

Getting There & Away

Scottish Citylink buses run between Fort William and **Glencoe village** (£7, 30 minutes, eight daily). Stagecoach bus 44 links Glencoe village with **Fort William** (35 minutes, hourly Monday to Saturday, three on Sunday).

Fort William
POP 9910

Basking on the shores of Loch Linnhe amid magnificent mountain scenery, Fort William has one of the most enviable settings in the whole of Scotland. If it weren't for the busy dual carriageway crammed between the town centre and the loch, and one of the highest rainfall records in the country, it would be almost idyllic. Even so, the Fort has carved out a reputation as 'Outdoor Capital of the UK' (www.outdoor capital.co.uk), and its easy accessability by rail and bus makes it a good place to base yourself for exploring the surrounding mountains and glens.

 Sleeping

LIME TREE   Hotel ££
(☎01397-701806; www.limetreefortwilliam. co.uk; Achintore Rd; s/d from £70/100; P) Much more interesting than your average guest house, this former Victorian manse overlooking Loch Linnhe is an 'art gallery with rooms', decorated throughout with the artist-owner's atmospheric Highland landscapes. Foodies rave about the **restaurant** and the gallery space – a triumph of sensitive design – stages everything from serious exhibitions (David Hockney in summer 2010) to folk concerts.

GRANGE   B&B ££
(☎01397-705516; www.grangefortwilliam. com; Grange Rd; r per person £56-59; P) An exceptional 19th-century villa set in its own landscaped grounds, the Grange is crammed with antiques and fitted with log fires, chaise lounges and Victorian roll-top baths.

CROLINNHE   B&B ££
(☎01397-702709; www.crolinnhe.co.uk; Grange Rd; r per person £56-64; P) If you can't get into the Grange try the neighbouring Crolinnhe, another grand 19th-century villa, with loch-side location, beautiful gardens and sumptuous accommodation.

Road to the Isles

The 46-mile A830 from Fort William to Mallaig is traditionally known as the Road to the Isles, as it leads to the jumping-off point for ferries to the Small Isles and Skye, itself a stepping stone to the Outer Hebrides. The final section of this scenic route, between Arisaig and Mallaig, has recently been upgraded to a fast straight road. Unless you're in a hurry, opt for the old coastal road (signposted 'Alternative Coastal Route').

 ## Eating & Drinking

CRANNOG SEAFOOD RESTAURANT
Seafood ££

(☏ 01397-705589; www.crannog.net; Town Pier; mains £14-20; ⊙ lunch & dinner) The Crannog easily wins the prize for the best location in town – it's perched on the Town Pier, giving window-table diners an uninterrupted view down Loch Linnhe.

BEN NEVIS BAR
Pub

(105 High St) The Ben Nevis, whose lounge bar enjoys a good view over the loch, exudes a relaxed, jovial atmosphere where climbers and tourists can work off leftover energy jigging to live music (Thursday and Friday nights).

❶ Information

Tourist office (☏ 01397-703781; www.visithighlands.com; 15 High St; ⊙ 9am-6pm Mon-Sat, 10am-5pm Sun Apr-Sep, limited hr Oct-Mar)

❶ Getting There & Away

BUS Scottish Citylink buses link Fort William with **Glasgow** (£21, three hours, eight daily) and **Edinburgh** (£30, 4½ hours, one daily direct, seven with a change at Glasgow) via **Glencoe**, as well as

Oban (£9, 1½ hours, three daily), **Inverness** (£11, two hours, five daily) and Portree on the **Isle of Skye** (£28, three hours, four daily).

TRAIN The spectacular West Highland line runs from Glasgow to Mallaig via Fort William. There are three trains daily (two on Sunday) from **Glasgow** to Fort William (£24, 3¾ hours), and four daily (three on Sunday) between Fort William and **Mallaig** (£10, 1½ hours). Travelling from **Edinburgh** (£40, five hours), you have to change at Glasgow's Queen St station. There's no direct rail connection between Oban and Fort William – you have to change at Crianlarich, so it's faster to use the bus.

Highland cow
PHOTOGRAPHER: KRISTIN PILJAY / LONELY PLANET IMAGES ©

Climbing Ben Nevis

As the highest peak in the British Isles, Ben Nevis (1344m) attracts many would-be ascensionists who would not normally think of climbing a Scottish mountain – a staggering (often literally) 100,000 people reach the summit each year.

Although anyone who is reasonably fit should have no problem climbing Ben Nevis on a fine summer's day, an ascent should not be undertaken lightly. Every year people have to be rescued from the mountain. You will need proper walking boots (the path is rough and stony, and there may be soft, wet snowfields on the summit), warm clothing, waterproofs, a map and compass, and plenty of food and water. And don't forget to check the weather forecast (see www.bennevisweather.co.uk).

Here are a few facts to mull over before you go racing up the tourist track: the summit plateau is bounded by 700m-high cliffs and has a sub-Arctic climate; at the summit it can snow on any day of the year; the summit is wrapped in cloud nine days out of 10; in thick cloud, visibility at the summit can be 10m or less; and in such conditions the only safe way off the mountain requires careful use of a map and compass to avoid walking over those 700m cliffs.

The total distance to the summit and back is 8 miles; allow at least four or five hours to reach the top, and another 2½ to three hours for the descent.

Mallaig

POP 800

If you're travelling between Fort William and Skye, you may find yourself over-nighting in the bustling fishing and ferry port of Mallaig.

 Sleeping

SEAVIEW GUEST HOUSE   B&B ££

(☏ 01687-462059; www.seaviewguesthousemallaig.com; Main St; r per person £28-35; ☺ Mar-Nov; P) Just beyond the tourist office, this comfortable three-bedroom B&B has grand views over the harbour, not only from the upstairs bedrooms but also from the breakfast room.

SPRINGBANK GUEST HOUSE   B&B £

(☏ 01687-462459; www.springbank-mallaig.co.uk; East Bay; r per person £25; P ☎) A little further around the bay than the Seaview, the Springbank is a traditional West Highland house with seven homely guest bedrooms, again with superb views across the harbour to the Cuillin of Skye.

. . . .

ℹ Getting There & Away

BOAT Ferries run from Mallaig to the **Isle of Skye**; see the transport information in that section for more details.

TRAIN The West Highland line runs between **Fort William** and Mallaig (£10, 1½ hours) four times a day (three on Sunday).

ORKNEY ISLANDS

The Orkney Islands are an archipelago of old-style hospitality and Viking heritage, with a special magic that you'll begin to feel as soon as the mainland slips away. Above all they are famous for a series of magnificent prehistoric monuments.

Situated off the northeast coast of Scotland, the islands may be off the beaten track for most visitors, but they can be enjoyed as a long day trip from Inverness.

Sights

Egypt has the pyramids, Scotland has **Maes Howe** (HS; 01856-761606; www. historic-scotland.gov.uk; adult/child £5.20/3.10; tours hourly 10am-3pm Oct-Mar, also 4pm Apr-Sep), a Stone Age tomb built about 5000 years ago from enormous sandstone blocks.

Idyllically situated by a sandy bay 8 miles north of Stromness, and predating Stonehenge, **Skara Brae** (HS; www.historic-scotland.gov.uk; Bay of Skaill; adult/child £6.70/4; 9.30am-5.30pm Apr-Sep, to 4.30pm Oct-Mar) is another of Scotland's most evocative ancient sites, and northern Europe's best-preserved prehistoric village.

The atmospheric **Ring of Brodgar** (HS; www.historic-scotland.gov.uk; 24hr) is a circle of standing stones built around 2500–2000 BC, their curious shapes created by centuries of erosion.

 Tours

Discover Orkney (01856-872865; www.discoverorkney.com) runs guided tours and walks with a qualified guide, **Orkney Archaeology Tours** (01856-721217; www.orkneyarchaeologytours.co.uk) offers half- or full-day tours (£160/£240) for up to four people, and **Wildabout Orkney** (01856-851011; www.wildaboutorkney.com) operates history, ecology, folklore and wildlife tours year-round from £49.

● **Getting There & Away**

The ferry to the Orkneys departs from **John O'Groats**, best known as the endpoint of the 874-mile trek from Land's End in Cornwall (Britain's southwest extremity), a popular if arduous route for cyclists and walkers. From May to September, **John O'Groats Ferries** (01955-611353; www.jogferry.co.uk; departs 7.30am, 13½ hour tours adult/child £57/28.50) runs daily tours by bus and ferry from **Inverness** to **Orkney** via John O'Groats. If you drive your own car to John O'Groats, you can take a one-day tour of the main sites for £46, including the ferry.

ISLE OF SKYE

POP 9900

The Isle of Skye (an t-Eilean Sgiathanach in Gaelic) takes its name from the old Norse *sky-a*, meaning 'cloud island', a Viking reference to the often mist-enshrouded Cuillin Hills. It's the biggest of Scotland's islands, a 50-mile-long smorgasbord of velvet moors, jagged mountains, sparkling lochs and towering sea cliffs. The stunning scenery is the main attraction, but when the mist closes in there are plenty of castles, crofting museums and cosy pubs and restaurants to retire to. Come prepared for changeable weather: when it's fine it's very fine indeed, but all too often it isn't.

 Tours

There are several operators who offer guided tours of Skye, covering history, culture and wildlife. Rates are from £140 for a six-hour tour for up to six people.

Red Deer Travel (01478-612142) Historical and cultural tours by minibus.

Isle of Skye

Isle of Skye Tour Guide Co (☎01471-844440; www.isle-of-skye-tour-guide.co.uk) Geology, history and wildlife by car.

ℹ️ Information

Portree and Broadford are the main population centres on Skye.

Broadford tourist office (☎01471-822361; The Car Park, Broadford; ⏰9.30am-5pm Mon-Sat, 10am-4pm Sun Apr-Oct)

Portree tourist office (☎01478-612137; Bayfield Rd, Portree; ⏰9am-6pm Mon-Sat & 10am-4pm Sun Jun-Aug, 9am-5pm Mon-Fri & 10am-4pm Sat Apr, May & Sep, limited opening Oct-Mar)

ℹ️ Getting There & Away

Boat

MALLAIG–ARMADALE CalMac (www.calmac.co.uk) operates the Mallaig to Armadale ferry (driver or passenger £3.85, car £20.30, 30 minutes, eight daily Monday to Saturday, five to seven on Sunday). It's very popular in July and August, so book ahead if you're travelling by car.

GLENELG–KYLERHEA Skye Ferry (www.skyeferry.co.uk) runs a tiny vessel (six cars only) on the short Glenelg to Kylerhea crossing (car and up to four passengers £12, five minutes, every 20 minutes). The ferry operates from 10am to 6pm daily from Easter to October only, till 7pm June to August.

Bus

Scottish Citylink runs buses from **Glasgow** to Portree (£38, seven hours, four daily) and Uig via Crianlarich, Fort William and Kyle of Lochalsh. Buses also run from **Inverness** to Portree (£17, 3½ hours, five daily).

Car & Motorcycle

The Isle of Skye became permanently tethered to the Scottish mainland when the Skye Bridge opened in 1995.

ℹ️ Getting Around

BUS Stagecoach (www.stagecoachbus.com) operates the main bus routes on the island, linking all the main villages and towns. Its Skye Dayrider ticket gives unlimited bus travel for one day for £6.70.

TAXI You can order a taxi or rent a car from Kyle Taxi Company (☎01599-534323). Rentals cost from around £38 a day, and you can arrange for the car to be waiting at Kyle of Lochalsh train station.

Ring of Brodgar, Orkney Islands (p345)

Detour: Cuillin Hills

The Cuillin Hills are Britain's most spectacular mountain range. Though small in stature (**Sgurr Alasdair**, the highest summit, is only 993m), the peaks are near-alpine in character, with knife-edge ridges, jagged pinnacles, scree-filled gullies and acres of naked rock. While they are a paradise for experienced mountaineers, the higher reaches of the Cuillin are off limits to the majority of walkers. But there are also plenty of good, low-level hikes within the ability of most walkers. One of the best is the steep climb from Glenbrittle camping ground to **Coire Lagan** (6 miles round trip; allow at least three hours).

DISCOVER SCOTLAND'S HIGHLANDS & ISLANDS   PORTREE (PORT RIGH)

Portree (Port Righ)

POP 1920

Portree is Skye's largest and liveliest town. It has a pretty harbour lined with brightly painted houses, and there are great views of the surrounding hills

 ## Sights & Activities

AROS EXPERIENCE   Visitor Centre
(www.aros.co.uk; Viewfield Rd; ⊙9am-5.30pm; ⚐) On the southern edge of Portree, the Aros Experience is a combined visitor centre, book and gift shop, restaurant, theatre and cinema.

MV STARDUST   Boat Trips
(☎07798-743858; www.skyeboat-trips.co.uk; Portree Harbour) Offers one- to two-hour boat excursions to the Sound of Raasay (£12 to £15 per person) with the chance to see seals, porpoises and – if you're lucky – white-tailed sea eagles.

 ## Sleeping

BEN TIANAVAIG B&B   B&B ££
(☎01478-612152; www.ben-tianavaig.co.uk; 5 Bosville Tce; r £65-75; P⚐) A warm welcome awaits from the Aussie/Brit couple who run this appealing B&B bang in the centre of town.

BOSVILLE HOTEL   Hotel ££
(☎01478-612846; www.bosvillehotel.co.uk; 9-11 Bosville Tce; s/d from £120/128; ⚐) The Bosville brings a little bit of metropolitan style to Portree with its designer fabrics and furniture, flatscreen TVs, fluffy bathrobes and bright, spacious bathrooms.

ROSEDALE HOTEL   Hotel ££
(☎01478-613131; www.rosedalehotelskye.co.uk; Beaumont Cres; s/d from £60/90; ⊙Mar-Nov) The Rosedale is a cosy, old-fashioned hotel – you'll be welcomed with a glass of whisky or sherry when you check in – delightfully situated down by the waterfront.

WOODLANDS   B&B £
(☎01478-612980; www.woodlands-portree.co.uk; Viewfield Rd; r per person £32-34; P) A great location, with views across the bay, and unstinting hospitality make this modern B&B, a half-mile south of the town centre, a good choice.

 ## Eating & Drinking

CAFÉ ARRIBA   Cafe £
(www.cafearriba.co.uk; Quay Brae; light meals £5-8, dinner mains £10-13; ⊙7am-10pm May-Sep, 8am-5.30pm Oct-Apr) This funky little cafe, brightly decked out in primary colours has the best choice of vegetarian grub on the island, ranging from a veggie breakfast fry-up to Indian-spiced bean cakes with mint yoghurt, as well as carnivorous treats such as slow-cooked haunch of venison with red wine and beetroot gravy.

SEA BREEZES — Seafood ££

(☎ 01478-612016; 2 Marine Buildings, Quay St; mains £10-20; ☺ noon-2.30pm & 5.30-10pm Tue-Sun, closed Nov, Jan & Feb) Sea Breezes is an informal, no-frills restaurant specialising in local fish and shellfish fresh from the boat – try the impressive seafood platter, a small mountain of langoustines, crab, oysters and lobster.

ℹ️ Getting There & Around

BUS There are seven Scottish Citylink buses a day from **Kyle of Lochalsh** to Portree (£13, one hour) and on to Uig. Stagecoach services (Monday to Saturday) run from Portree to **Broadford** (40 minutes, at least hourly) via Sligachan (15 minutes).

OBAN

POP 8120

Oban is a peaceful mainland town on a delightful bay, with sweeping views to Kerrera and Mull. OK, that first bit about peaceful is true only in winter; in summer the town centre is a heaving mass of humanity, its streets jammed with traffic and crowded with holidaymakers, day trippers and travellers headed for the islands. But the setting is still lovely.

Sights

MCCAIG'S TOWER — Historic Building

(admission free; ☺ 24hr) Crowning the hill above the town centre is the Victorian folly known as McCaig's Tower. To reach it on foot, make the steep climb up **Jacob's Ladder** (a flight of stairs) from Argyll St and then follow the signs. The views over the bay are worth the effort.

Tours

Bowman's Tours (☎ 01631-563221; www.bowmanstours.co.uk; Railway Pier & Queens Park) From April to October Bowman's Tours offers a **Three Isles day-trip** from Oban that visits Mull, Iona and Staffa (adult/child £49/24.50, 10 hours, daily). The crossing to Staffa is weather dependent.

 Sleeping

BARRIEMORE HOTEL — B&B ££

(☎ 01631-566356; www.barriemore-hotel.co.uk; Corran Esplanade; s/d from £65/92; P) The Barriemore enjoys a grand location, overlooking the entrance to Oban Bay. There are 13 spacious rooms (ask for one with a sea view), a guest lounge with magazines and newspapers, and plump Loch Fyne kippers on the breakfast menu.

HEATHERFIELD HOUSE — B&B ££

(☎ 01631-562681; www.heatherfieldhouse.co.uk; Albert Rd; s/d from £35/70; P @ 🛜) The welcoming Heatherfield House occupies a converted 1870s rectory set in extensive grounds and has six spacious rooms. If possible, ask for Room 1, complete with fireplace, sofa and a view over the garden to the harbour.

OLD MANSE GUEST HOUSE — B&B ££

(☎ 01631-564886; www.obanguesthouse.co.uk; Dalriach Rd; s/d from £62/74; P 🛜 👶) Set on a hillside above the town, the Old Manse commands great views over to Kerrera and Mull. The sunny, brightly decorated bedrooms have some nice touches (a couple of wine glasses and a corkscrew), and kids are made welcome with Balamory books, toys and DVDs.

Map with scale: 0 — 200 m / 0 — 0.1 miles

Oban Bay

To Barriemore Hotel (150m)

Dunollie Rd

To Connel Bridge (5mi)

Corran Esp

Dunollie Tce

Breadalbane St

Dalriach Rd

Ardconnel Rd

Albert Rd

War & Peace Museum

McCaig's Tower

Duncraggan Rd

North Pier

Stafford St

Oban Distillery

Ardconnel Rd

George St

Argyll St

Ardconnel Tce

Jacob's Ladder

Tweeddale St

To Isle of Mull, Coll, Tiree, Barra, Colonsay

Railway Pier

Train Station

Airds Cres

Stevenson St

Hill St

Rockfield Rd

CalMac Ferry Terminal

Argyll Sq

Combie St

Shore St

High St

Soroba Rd

To Manor House (200m)

Albany St

Creag An Airm

Glenshellach Tce

Lochside St

Black Lynn

Alma Cres

MANOR HOUSE Hotel £££
(☎ 01631-562087; www.manorhouseoban.com; Gallanach Rd; r £154-199; P) Built in 1780 for the duke of Argyll as part of his Oban estates, the Manor House is now one of Oban's finest hotels. It has small but elegant rooms in Georgian style, a posh bar frequented by local and visiting yachties, and a fine **restaurant** serving Scottish and French cuisine.

IZZET KERIBAR / LONELY PLANET IMAGES ©

Don't Miss **Eilean Donan Castle**

Photogenically sited at the entrance to Loch Duich, near Dornie village, Eilean Donan Castle is one of Scotland's most evocative castles, and must be represented in millions of photo albums. It's on an offshore islet, magically linked to the mainland by an elegant, stone-arched bridge. It's very much a re-creation inside with an excellent introductory exhibition. Keep an eye out for the photos of castle scenes from the movie Highlander. The castle is 8 miles east of Kyle of Lochalsh and the Skye Bridge.

THINGS YOU NEED TO KNOW

www.eileandonancastle.com; Dornie; adult/child/family £5.50/4.50/13.50; ⏰9.30am-6pm mid-Mar–mid-Nov

  Eating & Drinking

WATERFRONT RESTAURANT
Seafood ££

(☎01631-563110; www.waterfrontoban.co.uk; Waterfront Centre, Railway Pier; mains £10-18; ⏰noon-2.15pm & 5.30-9.30pm) Housed on the top floor of a converted seamen's mission, the Waterfront's stylish, unfussy decor – dusky pink and carmine with pine tables and local art on the walls – does little to distract from the superb seafood freshly landed at the quay just a few metres away.

CUAN MOR
Bistro ££

(www.cuanmor.co.uk; 60 George St; mains £8-16; ⏰lunch & dinner) This always-busy bar and bistro sports a no-nonsense menu of old favourites – from haddock and chips to sausage and mash with onion gravy – spiced with a few more sophisticated dishes such as scallops with black pudding, and a decent range of vegetarian dishes.

LORNE BAR
Pub

(www.thelornebar.co.uk; Stevenson St; 📶) A traditional pub with a lovely old island bar, the Lorne serves Deuchars IPA and local Oban Brewery real ales, as well as above-average pub grub. Food is served from noon to 9pm, and there's a trad music session every Wednesday from 10pm.

AULAY'S BAR
Pub

(8 Airds Cres) An authentic Scottish pub, Aulay's is cosy and low-ceilinged, its walls covered with old photographs of Oban ferries and other ships. It pulls in a mixed crowd of locals and visitors with its warm atmosphere and wide range of malt whiskies.

ℹ Information

Tourist office (☎ 01631-563122; www.oban.org. uk; Argyll Sq; ☉ 9am-7pm daily Jul & Aug, 9am-5.30pm Mon-Sat & 10am-5pm Sun May, Jun & Sep, 9am-5.30pm Mon-Sat Oct-Apr; @)

ℹ Getting There & Away

The bus, train and ferry terminals are all grouped conveniently together next to the harbour on the southern edge of the bay.

BOAT CalMac (www.calmac.co.uk) ferries link Oban with the islands of Kerrera, Mull, Coll, Tiree, Lismore, Colonsay, Barra and Lochboisdale.

BUS Scottish Citylink buses run to Oban from **Glasgow** (£17, three hours, four daily). West Coast Motors bus 918 goes to **Fort William** (£9, 1½ hours, three daily Monday to Saturday).

TRAIN Oban is at the terminus of a scenic route that branches off the West Highland line at **Crianlarich**. There are up to three trains daily from **Glasgow** to Oban (£19, three hours).

ISLE OF MULL
POP 2600

From the rugged ridges of Ben More and the black basalt crags of Burg to the blinding white sand, rose-pink granite and emerald waters that fringe the Ross, Mull can lay claim to some of the finest and most varied scenery in the Inner Hebrides. And with two impressive **castles** (Duart and Torosay), a **narrow-gauge railway**, the sacred island of Iona and easy access from Oban, you can see why it's sometimes impossible to find a spare bed here.

The waters to the west of Mull provide some of the best whale-spotting opportunities in Scotland, with several operators offering **whale-watching cruises**.

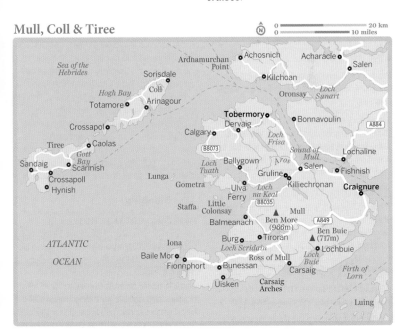

Mull, Coll & Tiree

Watching Wildlife on Mull

Mull's varied landscapes and habitats, from high mountains and wild moorland to wave-lashed sea cliffs, sandy beaches and seaweed-fringed skerries, offer the chance to spot some of Scotland's rarest and most dramatic wildlife, including eagles, otters, dolphins and whales.

Mull Wildlife Expeditions (☎01688-500121; www.torrbuan.com; Ulva Ferry) offers full-day Land Rover tours of the island with the chance of spotting red deer, golden eagles, peregrine falcons, white-tailed sea eagles, hen harriers, otters and perhaps dolphins and porpoises. The cost (adult/child £43/40) includes pick-up from your accommodation or from any of the ferry terminals, a picnic lunch and use of binoculars.

Sea Life Surveys (☎01688-302916; www.sealifesurveys.com) runs whale-watching trips from Tobermory harbour to the waters north and west of Mull. An all-day whale watch (£60 per person) gives up to seven hours at sea (not recommended for kids under 14), and has a 95% success rate for sightings. The four-hour family whale-watch is geared more towards children (£39/35 per adult/child).

About two-thirds of Mull's population lives in and around Tobermory, the island's capital, in the north. Craignure, at the southeastern corner, has the main ferry terminal and is where most people arrive. Fionnphort is at the far-western end of the long Ross of Mull peninsula, and is where the ferry to Iona departs.

❶ Information

Craignure tourist office (☎01680-812377; Craignure; ⊙8.30am-5pm Mon-Sat, 10.30am-5pm Sun)

Tobermory tourist office (☎01688-302182; The Pier, Tobermory; ⊙9am-6pm Mon-Sat & 10am-5pm Sun Jul & Aug, 9am-5pm Mon-Sat & 11am-5pm Sun May & Jun, shorter hrs rest of year)

❶ Getting There & Away

There are frequent CalMac car ferries from **Oban** to Craignure (passenger/car £4.65/41.50, 40 minutes, every two hours). There's another car-ferry link from **Lochaline** to Fishnish, on the east coast of Mull (£2.80/12.55, 15 minutes, at least hourly).

❶ Getting Around

BUS Bowman's Tours (☎01680-812313; www.bowmanstours.co.uk) The main operator, connecting the ferry ports and the island's main villages.

TAXI Mull Taxi (☎07760 426351; www.mulltaxi.co.uk) Based in Tobermory, and has a vehicle that is wheelchair accessible.

Tobermory

POP 750

Tobermory, the island's main town, is a picturesque little fishing port and yachting centre with brightly painted houses arranged around a sheltered harbour, with a grid-patterned 'upper town'. The village was the setting for the children's TV program *Balamory*, and while the series stopped filming in 2005 regular repeats mean that the town still swarms in summer with toddlers towing parents around looking for their favourite TV characters.

🛏 Sleeping

HIGHLAND COTTAGE HOTEL

Boutique Hotel £££

(☎01688-302030; www.highlandcottage.co.uk; Breadalbane St; d £155-190; ⊙mid-Mar–Oct; P ☎) Antique furniture, four-poster beds, embroidered bedspreads and fresh flowers and candlelight lend this small hotel (only six rooms) an appealingly old-fashioned cottage atmosphere, but with all mod cons including cable TV, full-size baths and room service. There's also an excellent fine-dining **restaurant**.

CUIDHE LEATHAIN
B&B ££

(☎ 01688-302504; www.cuidhe-leathain.co.uk; Salen Rd; r per person £35; 🛜) A handsome 19th-century house in the upper town, Cuidhe Leathain (pronounced 'coo lane'), which means Maclean's Corner, exudes a cosily cluttered Victorian atmosphere. The breakfasts will set you up for the rest of the day, and the owners are a fount of knowledge about Mull and its wildlife.

Eating & Drinking

CAFÉ FISH
Seafood ££

(☎ 01688-301253; www.thecafefish.com; The Pier; mains £10-16; ⏱ lunch & dinner) Seafood doesn't come much fresher than the stuff served at this warm and welcoming little restaurant overlooking Tobermory harbour – as their motto says, 'The only thing frozen here is the fisherman'!

MACGOCHAN'S
Pub ££

(Ledaig; mains £9-15; ⏱ lunch & dinner) A lively pub beside the car park at the southern end of the waterfront, MacGochan's does good bar meals (haddock and chips, steak pie, vegetable lasagne) and often has outdoor barbecues on summer evenings. There's a more formal **restaurant** upstairs, and live music in the bar on weekends.

ISLE OF IONA

There are few more uplifting sights on Scotland's west coast than the view of Iona from Mull on a sunny day – an emerald island set in a sparkling turquoise sea. From the moment you step off the ferry you begin to appreciate the hushed, spiritual atmosphere that pervades this sacred island.

St Columba sailed from Ireland and landed on Iona in 563 before setting out to spread Christianity throughout Scotland. He established a monastery on the island and it was here that the *Book of Kells* is believed to have been transcribed. It was taken to Kells in Ireland when Viking raids drove the monks from Iona.

The monks returned and the monastery prospered until its destruction during the Reformation. The ruins were given to the Church of Scotland in 1899, and by 1910 a group of enthusiasts called the **Iona Community** (www.iona.org.uk) had reconstructed the abbey. It's still a flourishing spiritual community that holds regular courses and retreats.

The **passenger ferry** from Fionnphort to Iona (£4.30 return, five minutes, hourly) runs daily. There are also various day trips available from Oban to Iona (see p348).

Duart Castle, Isle of Mull (p351)
PHOTOGRAPHER: PATRICK HORTON / LONELY PLANET IMAGES ©

Great Britain
In Focus

Man eating fish and chips, the Devon coast
HOLGER LEUE / LONELY PLANET IMAGES ©

Great Britain Today

Bagpipe-playing busker, Edinburgh (p294)

> the first decade of
> the 21st century
> has been a time of
> significant change
> and national soul-
> searching

belief systems
(% of population)

87	1	2	10
Christian	Hindu	Muslim	Other

if Britain were 100 people

85 would be Caucasian
4 would be South Asian
2 would be African & Afro Caribbean
9 would be other

population per sq km

🚶 ≈ 30 people

Britain   USA   France

All Change Please

For Britain and the British, the first decade of the 21st century has been a time of significant change and national soul-searching. The year 2010 was especially pivotal, thanks to two major events (and yes, they are listed in order of importance): a World Cup tournament where the England football squad floundered, while Wales and Scotland didn't even make it through the qualifying rounds; and a general election that saw the end of 13 years of Labour government.

The Odd Couple

The Labour government was replaced by a seminal coalition between the centre-right Conservatives and the centre-left Liberal-Democrats – a result that very few political pundits would have ever predicted. Unexpected or not, the new government got straight down to work and, despite coming from opposite sides of the centre ground, impressed most observers with laudable displays of collaboration. Key policies were based around

WILL SALTER / LONELY PLANET IMAGES ©

next few years will be dealing with the after-effects of the global financial crisis. Speeches from newly installed ministers promised 'straight talking', but in reality they refrained from too much detail. Most commentators – from all sides of politics – agree that the government will reduce spending and raise taxes more than it has so far admitted. For the people of Britain, it remains to be seen exactly what gets cut, and what gets spared.

Rule Britannia

Meanwhile, away from political battles, there are deeper schisms at work. Where once the state of Great Britain was a single entity, the process of devolution has seen the constituent countries of Scotland and Wales get their own independent ruling bodies based in their own capital cities: the Welsh Assembly in Cardiff, and the Scottish Parliament in Edinburgh. This has led to a reassessment by the people of England on what it actually means to be English, rather than British (the difference has been hazy for centuries), while the broader cultural vagaries of Britishness have also become a subject of fierce debate, with the English, Welsh and Scots forced to reflect on the values and institutions that bind their countries together – and keep them apart.

But, while the debates rumble on, if there's one thing this plucky little nation has proven down the centuries, it's resilience – as long as there's a nice hot mug of tea to hand, of course. Even though the wars are still raging, the economy is looking dicey and the national identity is under the glass, one thing's for certain: Britain's days are far from over yet.

the tenets of 'fairness' and 'choice' – aspects applauded as progressive by supporters and mocked as hopelessly woolly by opponents. Among these policies were, most notably, a major reform of National Health Service funding to give more flexibility to doctors and patients, and new laws allowing parents to set up their own schools. Both were the cause of much debate in Britain, where health and education are always two of the biggest political hot potatoes.

Home & Away

On the international front, the new government remained committed to keeping Britain's armed forces in Iraq and Afghanistan, arguing that the threat of terrorism at home needs to be tackled at the source, although public sympathy for UK involvement in what are perceived as 'foreign wars' is increasingly waning. It's likely, however, that the biggest single issue in British politics for the

History

Cerne Abbas Giant chalk figure (p372)

It may be a small island on the edge of Europe, but Britain was never on the sidelines of history. For centuries, invaders and incomers have made their mark: Neolithic peoples about 5000 years ago followed by Celts around 500 BC, then the Romans, the Vikings, the Anglo-Saxons and Normans. The result is a fascinating mix of culture and language – a dynamic pattern that shaped the nation and continues to evolve today.

First Arrivals

Stone tools discovered in eastern England show that human habitation in Britain stretches back at least 700,000 years. But for today's visitors things get interesting around 4000 BC, when early peoples used rocks and turf to build massive burial mounds and stone circles, most famously at Stonehenge.

3500 BC
First period of construction at Stonehenge begins.

Celts & Romans

By around 500 BC, the Celts had settled across much of the island of Britain, absorbing the indigenous people, and a Celtic-British population – sometimes known as the 'ancient Britons' – developed. The next arrivals were the Romans, colonising the island they called Britannia from around AD 43.

Early England, Wales & Scotland

When the power of the Romans faded around AD 410, the province of Britannia went into decline, and a new wave of invaders – Angles and Saxons – crossed from the European mainland, setting the foundation for the English language and culture.

Meanwhile the Celts on the outer fringes of Britain – today's Wales and Scotland – kept alive their own distinct culture. Under pressure from the Anglo-Saxons, by the 8th century the disparate tribes of Wales had started to band together and sow the seeds of nationhood.

Similar events were taking place to the north: the Picts were the region's dominant indigenous tribe, and named their kingdom Alba, which today is still the Gaelic word for Scotland.

The Viking Era

Just as the new territories of England, Wales and Scotland were becoming established, Britain was again invaded by a bunch of pesky Continentals. This time, the Vikings appeared on the scene from Scandinavia. The main wave conquered northeast England and by the 9th century started to expand southward into central England. However, blocking their route were the Anglo-Saxon armies, led by Alfred the Great. By 886, Alfred had pushed the Vikings back to the north, and was hailed as king of the English – the first time the Anglo-Saxons regarded themselves as a truly united people.

1066 & All That

The next major landmark in Britain's history was the 1066 Battle of Hastings, when the Norman king William led an invading army into southern England. The Saxons were defeated, and William became king of England, earning himself the prestigious epithet of Conqueror.

AD 43
Emperor Claudius orders the Roman invasion of province of Britannia.

5th–7th centuries
Anglo-Saxons migrate to England and expand across the country.

850
Vikings from today's Denmark invade northern England.

Royal & Holy Squabbling

By the 12th century, England was ruled by Henry I and then Henry II, who infamously had 'turbulent priest' Thomas Becket murdered in Canterbury in 1170. The beautiful cathedral is still a major attraction for pilgrims and visitors today.

Perhaps the next king, Richard I, wanted to make amends for his forebear's unholy actions by heading off on crusades. In his absence, England was ruled by his brother John. According to legend, it was during this time that Robert of Loxley, better known as Robin Hood, hid in Sherwood Forest and engaged in a spot of wealth redistribution.

Edward I in Wales & Scotland

By 1272 England was ruled by Edward I, a skilled king and ambitious general. First he invaded Wales, building massive castles at places like Caernarfon and Conwy that are still impressive today. Then he looked north, travelling through Scotland, forcing clan leaders to swear allegiance. In a final blow to Scottish pride, Edward removed the Stone of Scone, on which the kings of Scotland had been crowned for centuries.

In response, the Scots got in touch with Edward's old enemy, France, and arranged an anti-English partnership – the 'Auld Alliance' – that was to last for many centuries (and to the present day when it comes to rugby and football).

Edward wasn't the type to brook opposition. In 1296 his ruthless retaliation earned him the title 'Hammer of the Scots'. But in 1297, at the Battle of Stirling Bridge, the English were defeated by a Scots army under William Wallace. More than 700 years later, Wallace is still remembered as the epitome of Scottish patriotism.

Robert the Bruce

Back in England, Edward II came to the throne, but the new model lacked the military success of his forebear. Meanwhile, Robert the Bruce had crowned himself King of Scotland, been beaten in battle, gone on the run, and, while hiding in a cave, been inspired to renew his efforts by a spider persistently spinning its web. Bruce's army went on to defeat the English at the Battle of Bannockburn in 1314, another milestone in Scotland's long fight to remain independent.

The Best Historic Sites

1 Chester City Walls (p233)

2 Glencoe (p341)

3 Hadrian's Wall (p241)

4 Stonehenge (p178)

5 Westminster Abbey (p65)

6 Canterbury Cathedral (p109)

1066
Norman French armies defeat the English at the Battle of Hastings.

1272
Edward I invades Wales and makes his own son Prince of Wales.

1314
English army defeated by the Scots at the Battle of Bannockburn.

Houses of York & Lancaster

The year 1399 was another major milestone in Britain's history: King Richard II was ousted by a powerful baron called Henry Bolingbroke, who became Henry IV – the first monarch of the House of Lancaster.

Less than a year later, his rule was disrupted by a final cry of resistance from the downtrodden Welsh, led by Owain Glyndŵr, but the rebellion was crushed, Glyndŵr died an outlaw and the Welsh elite were barred from public life for many years.

Henry IV was followed, neatly, by Henry V. His defeat of France at the Battle of Agincourt and the patriotic tear-jerker speech he was given by Shakespeare ('cry God for Harry, England and St George') ensured his position among the most famous English kings of all time.

Still keeping things neat, Henry V was followed by Henry VI, whose main claim to fame was overseeing the building of great places of worship, including King's College Chapel in Cambridge, and Eton Chapel near Windsor – which can both still be admired today.

Henry VIII vs the Church

Of all England's kings called Henry, perhaps the best known is Henry VIII. Fathering a male heir was his problem – hence the famous six wives – but the pope's disapproval of divorce and remarriage led to Henry's split with the Roman Catholic Church, and the start of a period known as the English Reformation. This was the beginning of a pivotal division between Catholics and Protestants that still exists in some areas of Britain. As part of the process, in 1536 Henry 'dissolved' many monasteries in Britain and Ireland, and the ruined abbeys that dot the British landscape today are a legacy of that time.

Early Unions

Henry VIII's other great significant move for British history, was signing the Acts of Union (1536 and 1543), formally uniting England and Wales for the first time. This was welcomed by the aspiring Welsh gentry, as it meant English law and parliamentary representation for Wales, plus plenty of trade opportunities. The Welsh language, however, ceased to be recognised in the law courts.

Rough Wooing

Meanwhile, in Scotland, King James V had died in 1542, and his daughter Mary became queen. From his throne in England Henry VIII sent a proposal that Mary should marry his son. But the offer was rejected and – not forgetting the Auld Alliance – Mary was sent to France instead. Henry was furious and sent his armies to ravage southern Scotland and sack Edinburgh in an (unsuccessful) attempt to force agreement to the wedding – the Rough Wooing, as it was called with typical Scottish irony and understatement.

1400
Owain Glyndŵr leads Welsh rebels against the English army.

1415
The English army under Henry V defeats the French at the Battle of Agincourt.

1459–87
The Wars of the Roses between the Houses of Lancaster and York.

The Elizabethan Age

Henry VIII died in 1547 and, shortly after, his daughter Elizabeth came to the throne.

As Elizabeth I, she inherited a nasty mess of religious strife and divided loyalties, but after an uncertain start she gained confidence and turned the country around. Refusing marriage, she borrowed biblical imagery and became known as the Virgin Queen – perhaps the first English monarch to create a cult image.

Highlights of her 45-year reign included the naval defeat of the Spanish Armada, the far-flung explorations of English seafarers Walter Raleigh and Francis Drake and the expansion of England's increasingly global trading network – not to mention a cultural flourishing thanks to writers such as William Shakespeare and Christopher Marlowe.

Mary, Queen of Scots

Meanwhile, the Scottish queen (and Elizabeth's cousin) Mary had stayed in France and married the French prince, thereby also becoming queen of France. After her husband's death, Mary returned to Scotland, and from there ambitiously claimed the English throne as well – on the grounds that Elizabeth was illegitimate.

Mary's plans failed. She was forced to abdicate from the Scottish throne, but then escaped to England and appealed to Elizabeth for help. In an uncharacteristic display of indecision, Elizabeth held Mary under arrest for 19 years, moving her frequently from house to house, so that today England has many stately homes (and even a few pubs) claiming 'Mary, Queen of Scots, slept here'. Eventually, though, Elizabeth ordered her cousin's execution.

United Britain

When Elizabeth died in 1603, despite a bountiful reign, the Virgin Queen had failed to provide an heir. She was succeeded by her closest relative, the Scottish King James, the safely Protestant son of the executed Mary. He became James I of England and VI of Scotland, the first English monarch of the House of Stuart (Mary's time in France had Gallicised the Stewart name). Most importantly, James united England, Wales and Scotland into one kingdom for the first time in history – another step towards British unity, at least on paper – although the terms 'Britain' and 'British' were still not yet widely used in this context.

The Best Castles

1 Conwy Castle (p272)

2 Harlech Castle (p273)

3 Stirling Castle (p317)

4 Tower of London (p71)

5 Windsor Castle (p106)

6 Edinburgh Castle (p294)

IN FOCUS HISTORY

1536 & 1543
Henry VIII signs the Acts of Union, formally uniting England and Wales.

1642–49
English Civil War results in the execution of Charles I, and exile of Charles II.

1666
Great Fire of London burns much of the city to the ground.

English Civil War

During the reign of Charles I, a power struggle between king and parliament eventually degenerated into the English Civil War. The antiroyalist forces were led by Oliver Cromwell, a Puritan who preached against the excesses of the monarch and established church, and his parliamentarian (or Roundhead) army was pitched against the king's forces (the Cavaliers). It ended with victory for the Roundheads, the king executed, and England declared a republic – with Cromwell hailed as 'Protector'.

Return of the King

By 1653 Cromwell was finding parliament too restricting and assumed dictatorial powers, much to his supporters' dismay. On his death in 1658, he was followed half-heartedly by his son, but in 1660 parliament decided to re-establish the monarchy – as republican alternatives were proving far worse.

Charles II (the exiled son of Charles I) came to the throne, and his rule – known as the Restoration – saw scientific and cultural activity bursting forth after the strait-laced ethics of Cromwell's time.

Town of Conwy and Conwy Castle (p272).
PHOTOGRAPHER: MICAH WRIGHT / LONELY PLANET IMAGES ©

1707
The Act of Union links England, Wales and Scotland under one parliament.

1799–1815
Napoleon threatens invasion but is defeated at Trafalgar and Waterloo.

1837–1901
Under the reign of Queen Victoria, the British Empire expands its influence across the globe.

Age of Empire

In 1707, during Queen Anne's reign, the Act of Union was passed, bringing an end to the independent Scottish Parliament, and finally linking the countries of England, Wales and Scotland under one parliament (based in London) for the first time in history.

Stronger control over the British Isles was mirrored by even greater expansion abroad. The British Empire – which, despite its official title, was predominantly an *English* entity – continued to grow in America, Canada and India. The first claims were made to Australia after Captain James Cook's epic voyage in 1768.

The empire's first major reverse came when the American colonies won the War of Independence (1776–83). This setback forced Britain to withdraw from the world stage for a while, a gap not missed by French ruler Napoleon. He threatened to invade Britain and hinder the power of the British overseas, before his ambitions were curtailed by navy hero Viscount Horatio Nelson and military hero the Duke of Wellington, at the famous Battles of Trafalgar (1805) and Waterloo (1815).

The Industrial Age

While the empire expanded abroad, at home Britain had become the crucible of the Industrial Revolution. Steam power (patented by James Watt in 1781) and steam trains (launched by George Stephenson in 1825) transformed methods of production and transport, and the towns of the English Midlands became the first industrial cities.

This population shift in England was mirrored in Scotland. From about 1750 onwards, much of the Highlands region had been emptied of people, as landowners casually expelled entire farms and villages to make way for more-profitable sheep farming, a seminal event in Scotland's history known as the Clearances.

The same happened in Wales. By the early 19th century, copper, iron and slate were being extracted in South Wales, followed in the 1860s by coal mining. Wales soon became a major exporter of coal, as well as the world's leading producer of tin plate.

Three in One

The countries of England, Wales and Scotland make up the state of Great Britain. Three countries in one might seem a strange set-up, and visitors are sometimes confused about the difference between England and Britain – as are a lot of English people (although the Welsh and Scots are clear on the distinction). But getting a grip on this basic principle will ease your understanding of British history and culture.

1914
The assassination of Archduke Franz Ferdinand of Austria leads to the outbreak of WWI.

1926
Millions of workers down tools during the General Strike.

1939–45
WWII: Britain, with allies from America and the Commonwealth, defeats Germany.

When Queen Victoria took the throne in 1837, Britain's factories dominated world trade and Britain's fleets dominated the oceans. The times were optimistic, but it wasn't all tub-thumping jingoism. The British Prime Minister Benjamin Disraeli and his successor William Gladstone introduced many social reforms to address the worst excesses of the Industrial Revolution. Education became universal, trade unions were legalised and the right to vote was extended to commoners. Well, to male commoners – women didn't get the vote for another few decades, and only then thanks to a pioneering group of female protestors known as the suffragettes.

WWI

When Queen Victoria died in 1901, it seemed that Britain's energy fizzled out, and the country entered a period of decline. In continental Europe, other states were more active: the military powers of Russia, Austro-Hungary, Turkey and Germany were sabre-rattling in the Balkan states, a dispute that eventually culminated in WWI. When German forces entered Belgium on their way to invade France, Britain and the Allied countries were drawn in and the Great War became a vicious conflict of stalemate and slaughter – most infamously on the fields of Flanders and the beaches of Gallipoli. By the war's weary end in 1918 over a million Britons had died, not to mention millions more from the Commonwealth.

Disillusion & Depression

For soldiers who did return from WWI, disillusion led to questioning of the social order. Many supported the ideals of a new political force – the Labour Party, representing the working class – upsetting the balance long enjoyed by the Liberal and Conservative Parties.

The Labour Party was elected to government for the first time in 1923, in coalition with the Liberals, with James Ramsay MacDonald as prime minister. In the 1930s the world economy slumped and the Great Depression took hold. Even the royal family took a knock when Edward VIII abdicated in 1936 so he could marry a woman who was twice divorced and – horror of horrors – American.

The throne was taken by Edward's less-than-charismatic brother George VI and Britain dithered through the rest of the decade, with mediocre government failing to confront the country's deep-set social and economic problems.

The Best Historic Cities

1 London (p64)

2 York (p212)

3 Edinburgh (p294)

4 Oxford (p134)

5 Bath (p181)

6 Carlisle (p239)

1953

The coronation of Queen Elizabeth II takes place in Westminster Abbey.

1960s

Many former colonies in Africa and the Caribbean declare independence from Britain.

1979

Margaret Thatcher's Conservative Party wins the general election.

WWII

Meanwhile, on mainland Europe, Germany saw the rise of Adolf Hitler, leader of the Nazi party. Many feared another Great War, but Prime Minister Neville Chamberlain met the German leader in 1938 and promised Britain 'peace for our time' (a phrase still remembered, although usually misquoted as 'peace in our time'). He was wrong. The following year Hitler invaded Poland. Two days later Britain was once again at war with Germany.

Chamberlain, reviled for his earlier 'appeasement', stood aside for a new prime minister, Winston Churchill. The war raged for six years. By 1945 Hitler was dead, and his country ruined. Two atomic bombs forced the surrender of Germany's ally Japan, and finally brought WWII to a close.

Swinging & Sliding

In Britain, despite the victory, there was an unexpected swing on the political front. An electorate tired of war tumbled Churchill's Conservatives and voted in the Labour Party. This was the dawn of the 'welfare state'; the National Health Service was founded, while key industries (such as steel, coal and railways) were nationalised and came under government control.

Despite the moves towards socialism, Britain's royal family was still going strong. In 1952 George VI was succeeded by his daughter Elizabeth II, who has remained on the throne for more than five decades, overseeing a period of massive social and economic change.

During the Swinging Sixties Britain became the centre of a new explosion in youth culture, but by the 1970s economic decline had set in once again, and the rest of the decade was marked by strikes and disputes. Then came another historical landmark: the elections of May 1979 returned the Conservatives, led by a little-known politician named Margaret Thatcher.

The Thatcher Years

Love her or hate her, no one could argue that Mrs Thatcher's methods weren't direct and dramatic. The industries nationalised in the late 1940s were now seen as inefficient, and sold off with a sense of purpose that made Henry VIII's dissolution of the monasteries seem like a Sunday-school picnic.

By 1988, the 'Iron lady' had become the longest-serving British prime minister of the 20th century, but she was finally ousted in the early 1990s when her introduction of the hugely unpopular 'poll tax' sparked nationwide riots and huge public discontent.

1997
The Labour Party wins the general election with a record-breaking majority.

1999
Devolution leads to the formation of the Scottish Parliament and Welsh Assembly.

2003–04
Britain joins the US-led invasion of Iraq.

New Labour, New Millennium

In the elections of 1997, the now rebranded 'New' Labour swept to power under fresh-faced leader Tony Blair. Among a host of other reforms, Mr Blair's government established devolved parliaments in Scotland and Wales, granting both countries limited control over their own taxation and public policy – something they hadn't enjoyed since the Act of Union in 1707.

Tony Blair and New Labour enjoyed an extended honeymoon period, and the next election (in 2001) was another walkover. The Conservative Party continued to struggle, allowing Labour to win a historic third term in 2005, and a year later Blair became the longest-serving Labour prime minister in British history. In June 2007 Tony Blair resigned as Labour leader, allowing Gordon Brown, the Chancellor of the Exchequer (the British term for Minister of Finance) and for so long the prime-minister-in-waiting, to finally get the top job.

In the general election of 2010, a record 14 years of Labour rule came to an end. A coalition between the Conservative Party and the Liberal-Democrats formed the new government, with David Cameron as Britain's new prime minister.

London Eye (p81) and Big Ben (p64)

2005

Labour is re-elected for a third term with Tony Blair still at the helm.

2007

Tony Blair resigns, and Gordon Brown takes over as Britain's prime minister.

2010

A coalition between Conservatives and Liberal-Democrats wins the election.

Family Travel

GLENN BEANLAND / LONELY PLANET IMAGES

Britain is great for travel with children because it's compact, with a lot of attractions in a small area. So when the kids in the back of the car say 'are we nearly there yet?', your answer can often be 'yes'. With a bit of planning ahead, and some online research to get the best bargains, having the kids on board can make a trip around Britain even more enjoyable.

Attractions

Many places of interest in Britain cater for kids as much as adults. At the country's historic castles, for example, mum and dad can admire the medieval architecture, while the kids will have great fun striding around the battlements. In the same way, many national parks and holiday resorts organise specific activities for children. It goes without saying that everything ramps up in the school holidays (see Holiday Times, p370).

Most visitor attractions offer family tickets – usually two adults plus two children, for less than the sum of the individual entrance charges. Most offer cheaper rates for solo parents and kids too. Be sure to ask, as these are not always clearly displayed.

On the Road

If you're going by public transport, trains are great for families: intercity services have plenty of room for luggage and extra stuff like buggies (pushers), and the kids can move about a bit when bored. In contrast, they need to stay in their seats on long-distance coaches.

If you're hiring a car, most (but not all) rental firms can provide child seats – but you'll need to check this in advance. Most will not actually fit the child seats; you need to do that yourself, for insurance reasons.

There are usually hefty child discounts available on public transport, so it's well worth doing a bit of pre-trip planning to make sure you make the most of your funds.

Sleep Spots

Some hotels welcome kids (with their parents) and provide cots, toys and babysitting services, while others (especially at the boutique end) maintain an adult atmosphere and don't accept kids. Many places also quote prices per person, so you might find yourself having to pay extra (albeit at a reduced rate) even if the kids share your room. Some B&Bs offer 'family suites' of two adjoining bedrooms with one bathroom.

Dining Out

When it comes to refuelling, most cafes and teashops are child friendly. Restaurants are mixed: some offer highchairs and kiddy portions; others firmly say 'no children after 6pm'.

Children under 18 are usually not allowed in pubs serving just alcohol. Pubs serving meals usually allow children of any age (with their parents) in England and Wales, but in Scotland they must be over 14 and must leave by 8pm. If in doubt, ask the bar staff.

Breastfeeding in public remains mildly controversial, but if done modestly is usually considered OK.

The Best
Children's Attractions

1 Warwick Castle (p149)

2 Science Museum, London (p83)

3 Enginuity, Ironbridge (p152)

4 Eden Project, Cornwall (p196)

5 Jorvik Viking Centre, York (p212)

6 Natural History Museum, London (p81)

Need to Know

o **Changing facilities** In most large shopping centres, museums and attractions

o **Cots** Usually available at hotels, less common in B&Bs – ask in advance

o **Health** Just do as you'd do back home

o **Highchairs** Common in specific family-friendly restaurants

o **Nappies (diapers)** Sold in every supermarket

o **Transport** Look out for kids' discounts on trains and long-distance buses. Children under five usually travel free (but must give up the seat to paying passengers if transport is full).

All Change

On the sticky topic of dealing with nappies (diapers), most museums and other attractions in Britain usually have good baby-changing facilities (cue old joke: 'I swapped mine for a nice souvenir'). Elsewhere, some city-centre public toilets have baby-changing areas, although these can be a bit grimy; your best bet for clean facilities is an upmarket department store. On the road, baby-changing facilities are usually bearable at motorway service stations and OK at out-of-town supermarkets.

Holiday Times

The best time for families to visit Britain is pretty much the best time for everyone else – from April/May to the end of September. It's worth avoiding August – the heart of school summer holidays – when prices go up and roads are busy, especially near the coast. Other school holidays are two weeks around Easter Sunday, and mid-December to early January, plus three week-long 'half-term' breaks – usually late February (or early March), late May and late October.

Information

Tourist offices are a great source of information – the shelves are usually loaded with leaflets advertising kid-friendly attractions in the local area. Ask at national park information centres too about activities for children. Many holiday resort towns also organise activities for children, especially during school-holiday periods.

Some handy websites:

Baby Goes 2 (www.babygoes2.com) Advice, tips and encouragement (and a stack of adverts).

Mums Net (www.mumsnet.com) No-nonsense advice on travel and more from a gang of UK mothers.

Travel for Kids (www.travelforkids.com) Straightforward advice on kid-friendly places to visit.

Children playing in Piccadilly Gardens, Manchester (p226).
PHOTOGRAPHER: MARK DAFFEY / LONELY PLANET IMAGES ©

Architecture

Thatched cottage

ROCCO FASANO / LONELY PLANET IMAGES ©

One of the highlights of visiting Britain is the chance to explore its architectural heritage – encompassing everything from 5000-year-old stone circles to medieval cathedrals, thatched cottages and stunning stately homes. But don't make the mistake of thinking Britain is just one big museum piece. Landmark new buildings have sprung up in many major cities in recent years, demonstrating that Britain is still capable of mustering up a spirit of architectural adventure.

Early Foundations

The oldest buildings in the country are the grass-covered earth-mounds called 'barrows' (or 'tumuli') used as burial sites by Britain's prehistoric residents. These mounds measure anything from a rough semi-sphere just 2m high to much larger oval constructions 5m high and 10m long, dotted across the countryside. These are especially common in chalk areas such as Salisbury Plain and the Wiltshire Downs in southern England.

Perhaps the most famous earth-mound – and certainly the largest and most mysterious – is Silbury Hill, near Marlborough. Historians are not sure exactly why this huge conical mound was built – there's no evidence of it actually being used for burial. Theories include the possibility of it being used at cultural ceremonies or as part of the worship of deities in the style of South American pyramids. Whatever its original purpose, it's still very impressive today, many centuries after it was built.

Even more impressive than giant earth-mounds are another legacy of the Neolithic era: menhirs, or standing stones, especially well known when they're set out in rings. These include the iconic stone circle of Stonehenge, and the even larger Avebury Stone Circle, both in Wiltshire – although the Callanish Standing Stones on Scotland's Isle of Lewis are even older.

Bronze Age & Iron Age

After the large stone circles of the Neolithic era, the architecture of the Bronze Age that we can see today is on a more domestic scale. Hut circles from this period can still be seen in several parts of Britain, most notably on Dartmoor in Devon, while the Scottish islands also hold many of Europe's best surviving remains of Bronze Age and Iron Age times, such as the stone villages of Skara Brae on the Orkney Islands, off the north coast of Scotland.

Also during the Iron Age, the early peoples of Britain were organising themselves into clans or tribes. Their legacy includes the forts they built to defend territory and protect themselves from rival tribes or other invaders. Most forts consisted of a large circular or oval ditch, with a steep mound of earth behind. Famous examples include Maiden Castle in Dorset and Barbury Castle in Wiltshire, about 10 miles from Avebury.

The Roman Era

Roman remains are found in many towns and cities, mostly in England and Wales, as the Romans never colonised Scotland. There are impressive remains in Chester, Exeter and St Albans, and some in York, as well as the lavish Roman spa and bathing complex in Bath. But Britain's largest and most impressive Roman relic is the 73-mile sweep of Hadrian's Wall, built in the 2nd century AD as a defensive line stretching coast-to-coast across the country, for over 300 years marking the northern limit of the Roman Empire.

Medieval Cathedrals & Castles

In the centuries following the Norman invasion of 1066, Britain saw an explosion of architecture inspired by the two most pressing concerns of the day: worship and defence. Many landmark cathedrals were constructed during the early Middle Ages, including Salisbury, Winchester, Wells, Glasgow, St David's and Canterbury, plus York Minster, one of the finest cathedrals in all of Europe.

Chalk Figures

As you travel around Britain, look out for the chalk figures gracing many of the country's hilltops. They're made by cutting through the turf to reveal the white chalk soil below, so obviously are found in chalk areas – most notably in southwest England, especially the counties of Dorset and Wiltshire. Some figures, such as the Uffington White Horse, date from the Bronze Age, but most are more recent; the formidably endowed Cerne Abbas Giant is often thought to be an ancient pagan figure, although recent research suggests it was etched sometime in the 17th century.

As well as many grand cathedrals, a huge number of churches were built during this period too. Many remain intact today, and are of historical and architectural significance, especially in rural areas.

Alongside the churches and cathedrals, many abbeys and monasteries were built in Britain during the medieval period – and a large number of these were destroyed under the orders of Henry VIII between 1536 and 1540 as part of his dispute with the Catholic Church. The period is now known as the 'dissolution of the monasteries' and the legacy today are picturesque ruins such as Melrose, Tintern, Fountains, Glastonbury, St Andrews and Rievaulx.

As for castles in Britain, you're spoilt for choice, ranging from the atmospheric ruins like Tintagel and Dunstanburgh to relatively well-preserved structures like Warwick and Skipton and the sturdy ramparts of Conwy and Beaumaris, to the stunning crag-top fortresses of Stirling and Edinburgh. And then there's the most impressive of them all – the Tower of London, guardian of the capital for more than 2000 years.

IN FOCUS ARCHITECTURE

Stately Homes

The medieval period was tumultuous, but by the 17th century life became more settled, and the nobility had less need for their castles. While they were excellent for keeping out rivals or the common riff-raff, they were often too cold and draughty to be comfortable. So many castles saw the home improvements of the day – the installation of larger windows, wider staircases, better drainage – while others were simply demolished to provide building stone for a brand new dwelling next door. A classic example of 'knock down the old to build the new' is Hardwick Hall in Derbyshire.

Following the Civil War, the trend away from castles gathered pace, and through the late 17th and 18th centuries the landed gentry developed a taste for fine country houses designed by the most famous architects of the day. Many became the stately homes that are a major feature of the British landscape, and a major attraction for visitors today. Among the most extravagant are Chatsworth House and Blenheim Palace in England, Powis Castle in Wales and Hopetoun House in Scotland.

The great stately homes all display the proportion, symmetry and architectural harmony so in vogue during the 17th and 18th centuries, styles later reflected in the fashionable town houses of the Georgian era – most notably in the city of Bath, where Royal Crescent, with its stunning curved facade of about 30 houses, with a perfect harmonious design, is the epitome of the genre.

Victoriana

The Victorian era – mainly the 19th century – was a time of great national confidence in Britain, reflected in a period of great building. A style called Victorian-Gothic developed, echoing the towers and spires that were such a feature of the original Gothic cathedrals. The best-known example of this style is the Palace of Westminster, better known as the Houses of Parliament and the tower of Big Ben, in London. Other highlights in the capital include London's Natural History Museum and St Pancras Train Station. The style was copied around the country, especially for civic buildings – the finest examples including Manchester Town Hall and Glasgow City Chambers.

The Industrial Era

Through the late 19th and early 20th century, as Britain's cities grew in size and stature, the newly moneyed middle classes built streets and squares of smart town houses. In other areas the first town planners oversaw the construction of endless terraces of 'back-to-back' and 'two-up-two-down' houses to accommodate the massive influx of workers required to fuel the country's factories. In South Wales, similar houses – though often single storey – were built for the burgeoning numbers of coal miners, while the industrial areas of Scotland saw the rise of tenements, usually three or four storeys high, with a central communal staircase and two dwellings on each floor. In many cases the terraced houses and basic tenements are not especially scenic, but are perhaps the most enduring mark of all on the British architectural landscape today.

Postwar

During WWII many of Britain's cities were damaged by bombing, and the rebuilding that followed showed scant regard for the overall aesthetic of the cities, or for the lives of the people who lived in them. The rows of terraces were swept away in favour of high-rise tower blocks, while the 'brutalist' architects of the 1950s and '60s employed the modern and efficient materials of steel and concrete, leaving legacies such as London's South Bank Centre.

Perhaps this is why, on the whole, the British people are conservative in their architectural tastes, and often unhappy with experimental designs, especially when they're applied to public buildings, or when form appears more important than function. But a familiar pattern often unfolds: after a few years of resentment, first comes a nickname, then grudging acceptance, and finally – once the locals have become used to it – comes pride and affection for the new building. The Brits just don't like to be rushed, that's all.

Exterior of the Scottish Parliament Building (p295).
BETHUNE CARMICHAEL / LONELY PLANET IMAGES ©

House & Home

It's not all about big houses. Alongside the stately homes, ordinary domestic architecture can also still be seen in Britain's rural areas: black-and-white 'half-timbered' houses still characterise counties such as Worcestershire, honey-coloured stone and thatch are a feature of the Cotswolds, while brick-and-flint buildings pepper Suffolk and Sussex, and hardy centuries-old cottages and farms built with slate and local stone are seen all over Wales. In northern Scotland, a classic basic dwelling is the blackhouse – with walls of dry stone (no mortar) packed with earth and a roof of straw and turf.

21st Century

Over the last couple of decades, British architecture has started to redeem itself, and many big cities now have contemporary buildings their residents can enjoy and be proud of. Highlights in London's financial district include the bulging cone of the SwissRE building (inevitably dubbed 'The Gherkin'). Top examples around the country include Manchester's Imperial War Museum North, Birmingham's chic Bullring shopping centre, the Welsh National Assembly building and the Wales Millennium Centre (both on the Cardiff waterfront), and the interlocking arches of the Glasgow's Scottish Exhibition & Conference Centre (affectionately called 'The Armadillo').

Skyscrapers are back in fashion again in many of Britain's cities: in the past few years Leeds, Manchester, Brighton and Birmingham all announced plans for new buildings over 200m high. Top of the heap, however, is the London Bridge Tower (thanks to its shape it was quickly nicknamed 'The Shard'), which, at 306m, is set to become one of Europe's tallest buildings when it's completed in around 2012.

And on the drawing board are two more skyscrapers, which (if they go ahead) are set to dominate the capital's skyline – and, yes, they already have nicknames: 'The Walkie-Talkie' and 'The Cheese Grater'. As London continues to grow upwards, and British architecture continues to push new boundaries of style and technology, we look forward to seeing these new marvels for real some time in the next decade.

Writers & Artists

Loch Achray, the Trossachs (p321)

DAVID TOMLINSON / LONELY PLANET IMAGES

The roots of Britain's literary heritage stretch back to Early English epics such as Beowulf. As the English language spread around the world, so too did English literature, such that writers like Shakespeare and Austen are well known far from their homeland. Britain's visual art scene is equally rich, and as you travel around the region you'll see vistas you may recognise from classic paintings.

Literature
First Stars

Modern English literature starts around 1387 (a period considered 'modern' in history-soaked Britain), when the nation's first literary giant, Geoffrey Chaucer, produced *The Canterbury Tales*. Still a classic today, this mammoth poem is a collection of fables, stories and morality tales using travelling pilgrims as a narrative hook.

The next big name came two centuries later, when William Shakespeare entered the scene. His comedies and histories – such as *All's Well that Ends Well* and *Henry V* – are well known. Visitors to Britain today can see various houses associated with the Bard at Stratford-upon-Avon, as well as his plays. You can also see his works performed at a remarkably faithful replica of the original Globe Theatre on London's South Bank.

17th & 18th Centuries

The early 17th century saw the rise of the metaphysical poets, including John Donne and Andrew Marvell. Their vivid imagery and far-fetched 'conceits', or comparisons, daringly pushed the boundaries. In 'A Valediction: Forbidding Mourning', for instance, Donne compares the points of a compass with a pair of conjoined lovers. Racy stuff in its day.

Perhaps you're more familiar with 'Auld Lang Syne', traditionally sung at New Year throughout Britain. It was one of many songs and poems penned by prolific 18th-century lyricist – and Scottish icon – Robert Burns. His more unusual 'Address to a Haggis' plays an important part of Burns' Night, a Scottish celebration held on 25 January every year.

The Romantics

As the Industrial Revolution began to take hold in the late 18th and early 19th century, the response from a new generation of writers was to draw inspiration from the natural world and human imagination (in many cases helped along by a healthy dose of laudanum). Leading lights of the movement were William Blake, John Keats, Percy Bysshe Shelley, Lord Byron and Samuel Taylor Coleridge. Perhaps the best known of all was William Wordsworth, a resident of the English Lake District, where his famous lines from *Daffodils*, 'I wandered lonely as a cloud', were inspired by a hike in the hills.

At around the same time, Sir Walter Scott produced his well-known novels such as *Waverley* and *Rob Roy*, both partly set in the Scottish Highlands. Also popular during this period were two other Scottish novelists: Robert Louis Stevenson, best known for his children's book *Treasure Island*; and Sir Arthur Conan Doyle, inventor of detective Sherlock Holmes, who, with sidekick Watson, starred in a string of murder mysteries.

The Best Literary Locations

1 Canterbury (p109)

2 Stratford-upon-Avon (p145)

3 Lake District (p233)

4 The Trossachs (p321)

5 Bath (p181)

6 Laugharne (p264)

Jane Austen

Almost two centuries after her death in 1817, Jane Austen is still one of Britain's best-known novelists, thanks to exquisite observations of class, society, love, friendship, intrigues and passions boiling under the stilted preserve of provincial middle-class social convention – and in no small part to an endless stream of movies and TV costume dramas based on her works, including *Pride and Prejudice* and *Sense and Sensibility*. For visitors today, the location most associated with Jane Austen is the city of Bath, where many of the streets and squares are virtually unchanged since Austen's day, and society landmarks such as the Pump Rooms and Assembly Rooms can still be visited. The whole central area of Bath is a beautiful place even without the literary link.

Victoriana

Next came the reign of Queen Victoria and the era of industrial expansion, so key novels of the time explored social and political themes. Charles Dickens especially tackled many prevailing issues of his day: in *Oliver Twist*, he captures the lives of young thieves in the London slums; *Bleak House* is a critique of the English legal system and *Hard Times* criticises the excesses of capitalism.

Meanwhile, Thomas Hardy's classic *Tess of the D'Urbervilles* deals with the peasantry's decline, and *The Trumpet Major* paints a picture of idyllic English country life interrupted by war and encroaching modernity. Many of Hardy's works are based in the fictionalised county of Wessex, largely based on today's Dorset and surrounding counties, where towns such as Dorchester are popular stops on tourist itineraries.

20th Century

The ideological chaos and social disruption of the postwar period fed into the fractured narratives of modernism. Perhaps the greatest British novelist of the interwar period is DH Lawrence, particularly known for *Sons and Lovers,* following the lives and loves of generations in the English Midlands as the country changes from rural idyll to an increasingly industrial landscape, and his controversial exploration of sexuality in *Lady Chatterley's Lover,* originally banned as 'obscene'.

Other highlights of the interwar years included EM Forster's *A Passage to India*, about the hopelessness of British colonial rule, and Daphne du Maurier's romantic suspense novel *Rebecca*, set on the Cornish coast. Evelyn Waugh tackled the themes

National Gallery (p70), at London's Trafalgar Square

CHRISTOPHER GROENHOUT / LONELY PLANET IMAGE

The Brontë Sisters

Of the Brontë family's prodigious output in the first half of the 19th century, Emily Brontë's *Wuthering Heights* is the best known – an epic tale of obsession and revenge, where the dark and moody landscape plays a role as great as any human character. Charlotte Brontë's *Jane Eyre* and Anne Brontë's *The Tennant of Wildfell Hall* are classics of passion, mystery and love. Fans still flock to their former home in the Yorkshire town of Haworth, perched on the edge of the wild Pennine moors, that inspired so many of their novels.

of moral and social disintegration in *Brideshead Revisited*, and Richard Llewellyn wrote the Welsh classic *How Green Was My Valley*.

After WWII, Compton Mackenzie lifted postwar spirits with *Whisky Galore*, a comic novel about a cargo of booze washed up from a sinking ship onto a Scottish island. The Cold War was the setting for Ian Fleming's full-blooded British hero James Bond – today better known as a movie franchise. He first appeared in 1953 in the book *Casino Royale*, then swashbuckled through numerous thrillers for another decade.

Alongside the novelists, the first half of the 20th century was a great time for poets. Big names include WH Auden's *Funeral Blues* and TS Eliot's epic *The Waste Land*, although he is better known for *Old Possum's Book of Practical Cats* – turned into the musical *Cats* by Andrew Lloyd Webber.

Dylan Thomas, also known for his energetic social diary, came to the fore with *Portrait of the Artist as a Young Dog*, although his most celebrated work is a radio play *Under Milk Wood* (1954), exposing the tensions of small-town Wales.

New Millennium

As the 20th century came to a close, the nature of multicultural Britain proved a rich inspiration for contemporary novelists. Hanif Kurieshi sowed the seeds with his ground-breaking 1990 novel *The Buddha of Suburbia,* examining the hopes and fears of a group of suburban Anglo-Asians in London. Other star novelists covering (loosely defined) 'multicultural Britain' themes include Zadie Smith, who published her acclaimed debut *White Teeth* in 2000 followed by a string of literary best sellers including *The Autograph Man*; Monica Ali, whose *Brick Lane* was short-listed for the 2003 Man Booker Prize; Hari Kunzru, who received one of the largest advances in publishing history in 2002 for his debut *The Impressionist*; and Andrea Levy, winner of the 2004 Orange Prize for her novel *Small Island,* about a Jamaican couple settled in postwar London.

Alongside the work of British poets and novelists, it's impossible to overlook the recent trend for scurrilous celebrity autobiographies – penned by everyone from footballers to pop idol also-rans – a reminder of the increasing importance of hype over merit in the modern book market. But whatever you make of the literary qualities of these memoirs, it's hard to argue with the figures – the British public buys them by the bucket load.

Painting & Sculpture

Early Days

For many centuries, continental Europe – especially Holland, Spain, France and Italy – set the artistic agenda. The first artist with a truly British style and sensibility was arguably William Hogarth, whose riotous canvases exposed the vice and corruption of 18th-century London. His most celebrated work is *A Rake's Progress*.

While Hogarth was busy satirising society, other artists were hard at work showing it in its best light. The leading figures of 18th-century British portraiture were Sir Joshua Reynolds, Thomas Gainsborough and George Stubbs, the latter known for his intricate studies of animals (particularly horses). Most of these artists are represented at Tate Britain or the National Gallery in London.

19th Century

In the 19th century, leading painters favoured images of the landscape. John Constable's idyllic depictions of the Suffolk countryside are summed up in *The Haywain* (National Gallery), while JMW Turner was fascinated by the effects of light and colour, with his works becoming almost entirely abstract by the 1840s.

The Pre-Raphaelite movement of the mid- to late 19th century harked back to the figurative style of classical Italian and Flemish art, tying in with Victorian taste for myths and fairy tales. Key members of the movement included John Everett Millais; his *Ophelia*, showing the damsel picturesquely drowned in a pool, is an excellent example of their style, and can be seen the Tate Britain gallery.

A good friend of the Pre-Raphaelites was William Morris; he saw late 19th-century furniture and interior design as increasingly vulgar, and with Dante Gabriel Rossetti

Sculpture *Luci di Nara* (Hollow Face), by Igor Mitoraj, outside the British Museum, London (p84)

and Edward Burne-Jones founded the Arts and Crafts movement to encourage the revival of a decorative approach to features such as tapestries and windows.

North of the border, Charles Rennie Mackintosh, fresh from the Glasgow School of Art, fast became a renowned artist, designer and architect. He is still Scotland's greatest art nouveau exponent, and much of his work remains in this city.

Early 20th Century

In the tumultuous 20th century, British art became increasingly experimental. Its place on the international stage was ensured by the monumental sculptures of Henry Moore and Barbara Hepworth (whose work can be seen at St Ives in Cornwall), the contorted paintings of Francis Bacon and the works of the Scottish Colourists – Francis Cadell, SJ Peploe, Leslie Hunter and JD Ferguson – many turned into the type of prints and postcards favoured by souvenir shops.

Postwar

The mid-1950s and early '60s saw an explosion of British artists plundering television, music, advertising and popular culture for inspiration. Leaders of this new 'pop-art' movement included David Hockney, who used bold colours and simple lines to depict his dachshunds and swimming pools; and Peter Blake, who designed the collage cover for The Beatles' landmark *Sergeant Pepper* album.

The 1990s

The next big explosion in British art came in the 1990s; it was called 'Britart', and key figures included Damien Hirst and Tracy Emin. Another key artist of the period – and still going strong today – is the sculptor Antony Gormley, whose *Angel of the North*, a massive steel human figure with outstretched wings, was initially derided by the locals but is now an instantly recognised symbol of northeast England.

New Millennium

In 2008 a contest was announced to create a huge outdoor sculpture in Kent to counterbalance the *Angel of the North*. The final selection went to Mark Wallinger, winner of the 2007 Turner Prize, for his *White Horse of Ebbsfleet*. Due for completion by 2012, it will be over 50m high, so it should be clearly seen from the nearby A2 main road and the train line between London and Paris – a 'Welcome to Britain' sign for the 21st century.

Burning Bright

While some British artists fitted neatly into specific genres, the painter, writer, poet and visionary William Blake (1757-1827) occupied a world of his own, mixing fantastical landscapes and mythological scenes with motifs drawn from classical art, religious iconography and legend.

Music

Piping band on George Square, Glasgow (p310)

NEIL SETCHFIELD / LONELY PLANET IMAGES

Britain has a long heritage of traditional folk music, and classical music enjoys a strong following. But the British musical genre best known around the world is pop and rock, in all its many variations. Even in the days of falling CD sales, digital downloads and Myspace demos, British bands still seem hell bent on remaining top of the global charts.

Traditional & Folk Music

Scotland, England and Wales all have long histories of traditional folk music, each with its own distinctive styles and melodies. Well-known native instruments include the bagpipes in Scotland and the harp in Wales, while Wales also has a strong tradition of poetry and song (although perhaps the best-known genre – male voice choirs – is a relatively recent phenomenon). These days, the term 'folk music' generally refers to singers and musicians performing traditional (or traditional-style) songs accompanied by instruments such as guitar, fiddle and penny whistle.

British folk music mines a rich seam of regional culture, from the rhythmic 'waulking songs' of the tweed weavers of the Outer Hebrides to the jaunty melodies that accompany England's morris dancers. Local history plays its part too – many Welsh folk songs recall Owain Glyndŵr's battles against English domination, while English folk lyrics range from memories of the Tolpuddle Martyrs to sea shanties sung by Liverpool sailors. In Scotland, the Jacobite rebellion of 1745 was a rich source of traditional songs, while *Flower of Scotland* – written in 1967 by popular folk duo the Corries, and today the unofficial Scottish national anthem – harks back to the Battle of Bannockburn in 1314.

In the last decade or so, thanks largely to the rise in interest in world music, the folk music of Britain has enjoyed its biggest revival since the 1960s (and been rebranded as 'roots' music in some places). Leading exponents include Eliza Carthy, Kate Rusby and Bellowhead.

You can see traditional and folk music run at informal gigs or jam sessions in pubs (notably in Edinburgh), or at larger concerts and events such as Sidmouth Folk Festival in England, and cultural festivals such as the National Eisteddfod in Wales and the Mòd in Scotland.

Classical Music

The country that gave the world The Beatles, the Sex Pistols and Oasis is also fond of classical music, with 13 symphony orchestras, dozens of amateur orchestras, an active National Association of Youth Orchestras and concert halls in most major towns. Each year in July The Proms, one of the world's greatest music festivals, takes place in London's Royal Albert Hall.

Such enthusiasm is all the more remarkable given Britain's limited achievements in classical music. The only significant British composer before the 20th century was Henry Purcell. Since then, there has been a handful: Edward Elgar, famous for his *Enigma Variations*; Gustav Holtz, who wrote *The Planets*; Benjamin Britten, particularly known for his two operas *Peter Grimes* and *The Turn of the Screw*; and Vaughan Williams whose well-known *A London Symphony* ends with chimes of Big Ben.

Pop & Rock
Pioneers

Britain's been bringing pop to the world ever since The Beatles, The Rolling Stones, The Who, Cream, and The Kinks spearheaded the 'British Invasion' of the 1960s.

Glam rock swaggered in to replace peace and love in the early 1970s, with Marc Bolan and David Bowie donning spandex and glittery guitars in a variety of chameleonic guises, succeeded by art-rockers Roxy Music and anthemic popsters Queen and Elton John. Meanwhile Led Zeppelin laid down the blueprint for heavy metal and hard rock, and 1960s psychedelia morphed into the spacey noodlings of prog rock, epitomised by Pink Floyd, Genesis and Yes.

By the late '70s the prog bands were looking out of touch and punk exploded onto the scene, with nihilistic lyrics and short, sharp, three-chord tunes. The Sex Pistols produced one landmark album (*Never Mind the Bollocks: Here's the Sex Pistols*), a clutch of (mostly banned) singles and a storm of controversy, ably assisted by other punk pioneers such as The Clash, The Damned, The Buzzcocks and The Stranglers.

While punk burned itself out in a blaze of squealing guitars and earsplitting feedback, New Wave musicians including The Jam and Elvis Costello took up the torch, blending spiky tunes and sharp lyrics into a poppier, more radio-friendly sound.

IN FOCUS MUSIC

Madchester

The beats and bleeps of 1980s electronica fuelled the burgeoning dance-music scene of the early '90s. Pioneering artists such as New Order (risen from the ashes of Joy Division) used synthesised sounds to inspire the soundtrack for the ecstasy-fuelled rave culture, centred on famous clubs like Manchester's Haçienda and London's Ministry of Sound.

By the mid-1990s, Manchester was a focus for the burgeoning British indie scene, driven by guitar-based bands such as the Charlatans, the Stone Roses, James, Happy Mondays and Manchester's most famous musical export, Oasis. Such was the atmosphere and energy that the city was dubbed 'Madchester', and the whole world, it seemed, was 'up for it'. In the late 1990s indie segued into Britpop, a catch-all term covering bands Pulp and Blur (much to their distain, Oasis came under the banner too), all part of the short-lived phenomenon of 'Cool Britannia'.

New Millennium

The new millennium saw no let-up in the British music scene's continual shifting and reinventing. Jazz, soul, R&B and hip-hop beats fused into a new 'urban' sound epitomised by artists like Jamelia, The Streets and Dizzee Rascal.

On the pop side, singer-songwriters made a comeback, with artists such as Damien Rice, Ed Harcourt, James Blunt, Katie Mellua, Duffy and the famously self-destructive Amy Winehouse, while the spirit of shoe-gazing British indie was kept alive by Keane,

Balcony seats at Royal Albert Hall , London (p99)

CHRISTER FREDRIKSSON / LONELY PLANET IMAG

Live & Kicking

If you want to see live pop and rock music in Britain, most cities have at least one concert hall regularly hosting big names, and across the country there's a huge choice of smaller venues where the latest acts strut their stuff. Bands large and small are pretty much guaranteed to play in London, but often tour extensively so a night out in Cardiff, Liverpool or Glasgow is just as likely to land you a decent gig. For tickets and listings, agencies include **See** (www.seetickets.com) and **Ticketmaster** (www.ticketmaster.co.uk), or **Gigs in Scotland** (www.gigsinscotland.com) for info north of the border.

Foals, Editors and world-conquering Coldplay. At the same time, traces of punk and postpunk survived thanks to Franz Ferdinand, Razorlight, Babyshambles, Muse, The Klaxons, Dirty Pretty Things and The Arctic Monkeys.

Pop Today, Gone Tomorrow

Today's music scene is as fast-moving and varied as ever. Big names like Muse, Dizzee Rascal and Franz Ferdinand continue to headline summer festivals, backed up by current favourites like Mumford & Sons, Bombay Bicycle Club, Foals and The XX. Beyond the festivals, Britain's live music scene continues to thrive; a vital opportunity for bands to make money in a business squeezed by free file-sharing. Meanwhile, commercial pop acts like Leona Lewis and Diana Vickers are produced by endless – and obsessively followed – reality TV talent shows like *The X-Factor*.

By the time you read this book, half of the 'great new bands' of last year will have sunk without trace, and a fresh batch of unknowns will have risen to dominate the airwaves and download sites. One thing's for sure, the British music scene has never stood still.

Local football game

DOUG MCKINLAY / LONELY PLANET IMAGES

If you want a short cut into the heart of British culture, watch the British at play. They're passionate about their sport – as participants or spectators. Every weekend thousands of people turn out to cheer their favourite team, and sporting highlights such as Wimbledon keep the entire nation enthralled. The biggest sporting event of all – the Olympic Games – is coming to London in 2012.

Football (Soccer)

Despite what the fans may say in Madrid or Milan, the English football league has some of the finest – and richest – teams and players in the world. The Premier League is for the country's top 20 clubs, including internationally famous Arsenal, Liverpool and Manchester United, while 72 other teams from England and Wales play in the three divisions called the Championship, League One and League Two. The Scottish Premier League is dominated by Glasgow Rangers and Glasgow Celtic.

The football season lasts from August to May, but tickets for the big games in the upper division are like gold dust, and cost £20 to £50, even if you're lucky enough to find one.

Rugby

A popular witticism holds that football is a gentlemen's game played by hooligans, while rugby is the other way around. There are two variants of the game: rugby union is played in southern England, Wales and Scotland; rugby league is the main sport in northern England, although there is crossover. Many rules and tactics of both codes are similar, but in league there are 13 players in each team (ostensibly making the game faster), while rugby union sides have 15 players each.

The main season for club matches is roughly September to Easter, while the international rugby union calendar is dominated by the annual Six Nations Championship (England, Scotland, Wales, Ireland, France and Italy) between January and April. It's usual for the Scots to support Wales, or vice versa, when either team is playing the 'old enemy' England.

The Best Sporting Locations

Cricket

Cricket has its origins in southeast England, with the earliest written record dating to 1598. It became an international game during Britain's colonial era, when it was exported to the countries of the Commonwealth.

County cricket is the mainstay of the domestic game, while international one-day games and five-day test matches are played against sides such as Australia and the West Indies at landmark grounds like Lords in London and Headingley in Leeds. Test match tickets cost £25 to £100 and tend to sell fast. County championships usually charge £10 to £15, and rarely sell out. Twenty20 cricket is a TV-friendly short form of the game encouraging big scores; it's more interesting to watch, but decried by purists.

To catch a game, the easiest option of all – and often the most enjoyable – is stumbling across a local match on a village green as you travel around the country. There's no charge for spectators, and no one will mind if you nip to the pub during a quiet period.

London's Olympic Stardom

London will feature even more highly on the global stage in 2012, when the Olympic Games come to town. The key dates are 27 July to 12 August 2012 for the Olympics, and 29 August to 9 September for the Paralympics. To provide facilities for the athletes, a vast (and formerly neglected) area of East London has been regenerated, with the construction of new stadiums and an Olympic Village – which will become affordable housing for locals after the event.

Although London grabs the limelight, some events will be held across Britain, from sailing at Weymouth, to football qualifying rounds in Glasgow.

For information and tickets, see www.london2012.com.

Playing Golf

If you fancy a round as part of your visit to Britain, there are around 2000 private and public golf courses to choose from, with 500 in Scotland alone. (There are more golf courses per capita in Scotland than in any other country in the world.) Some private clubs admit only members or golfers with a handicap certificate, but most welcome visitors. Public golf courses are open to anyone. A round costs around £10 to £20 on a public course, and up to £50 on private courses.

Golf

Golf is a very popular sport in Britain, with millions taking to the fairways every week. The main golfing tournament for spectators is the Open Championship, often referred to simply as The Open (or the 'British Open' outside the UK). It's the oldest of professional golf's major championships (dating back to 1860) and the only one held outside the USA. It is usually played over the third weekend in July and the location changes each year, using nine courses around the country. Recent and future tournaments include 2009 Turnberry, 2010 St Andrews (the home of golf), 2011 Royal St George in Kent, 2012 Royal Lytham & St Annes in Lancashire, and 2013 Muirfield.

The Old Course, St Andrews (p322)

© IAIN MASTERTON / A

Other important competitions include the British Amateur Championship and the Welsh Open at Celtic Manor Hotel near Newport, South Wales – the course for 2010's Ryder Cup. Spectator tickets start at about £10, going up to £75 for a good position at the major events.

Tennis

Tennis is widely played in Britain, but the most famous tournament is the All England Lawn Tennis Championships – more commonly known as Wimbledon – when tennis fever sweeps through the country for the last week of June and the first week of July. In between matches, the crowds traditionally feast on strawberries and cream; that's 28 tonnes of strawberries and 7000L of cream annually, to be precise.

Demand for seats at Wimbledon (www.wimbledon.org) always outstrips supply, but to give everyone an equal chance the tickets are sold through a public ballot. You can also take your chance on the spot: about 6000 tickets are sold each day (but not on the last four days) and queuing at dawn should get you into the ground.

Cricket match

PHOTOGRAPHER: DAVID WALL / LONELY PLANET IMAGES ©

Food & Drink

Haggis, a Scottish speciality

BETHUNE CARMICHAEL / LONELY PLANET IMAGE

Britain once had a reputation for bad food, but the nation has enjoyed something of a culinary revolution over the last few years. London is recognised as having one of the best collections of restaurants in the world, while all across the country stylish eateries and gourmet gastropubs are springing up practically everywhere you look.

British Classics

As you're travelling around Britain, at hotels and B&Bs you'll notice the phenomenon of the Full English Breakfast (just Full Breakfast in Wales and Scotland), more colloquially known as a 'fry-up', consisting of bacon, sausage, egg, mushrooms, baked beans and fried bread. Other additions may include tomatoes (also fried, of course) and black pudding – known in other countries as 'blood sausage'.

The same dish will often be preceded by cereal and followed by toast and marmalade. If you don't feel like eating half a farmyard it's quite OK to ask for just the egg and tomatoes, for example. Some B&Bs offer other alternatives, such as kippers (smoked fish) – especially in Scotland – or a 'continental breakfast', which omits the cooked stuff and may even add something exotic like croissants.

Moving on to lunch, one of the many great inventions that Britain gave the world is the sandwich, supposedly invented in the 18th century by the aristocratic Earl of Sandwich. Another classic – especially in pubs – is the ploughman's lunch. Basically it's bread and cheese, usually accompanied by a spicy pickle, salad and some onions, although you'll also find other variations, such as farmer's lunch (bread and chicken), stockman's lunch (bread and ham) and so on.

For cheese and bread in a different combination, try Welsh rarebit – a sophisticated variation of cheese on toast, seasoned and flavoured with butter, milk and sometimes a little beer. Or sample Scotch broth, a thick soup of barley, lentils and mutton stock.

When it comes to main meals, a classic British dinner is roast beef. The most famous beef comes from Scotland's Aberdeen Angus cattle, while the best-known food from Wales is lamb. Venison – usually from red deer – is readily available in Scotland, as well as in parts of Wales and England, most notably in the New Forest.

The traditional accompaniment for British beef is Yorkshire pudding. It's simply roasted batter, but very tasty when properly cooked. Bring sausages and Yorkshire 'pud' together and you have another favourite dish: toad-in-the-hole.

But perhaps the best-known classic British staple is fish and chips, often bought as a takeaway. Sometimes the fish can be tasteless (especially when eaten far from the sea), but in towns with salt in the air this deep-fried delight is always worth trying.

The Best Local Classics

- Fish and chips
- Yorkshire pudding
- Welsh rarebit
- A pint of ale
- A dram of whisky
- Tea and cake

Regional Specialities

As befitting an island, many restaurants conjure up oysters, scallops, prawns, lobster and mussels – especially in Scotland, West Wales and southwest England. Scottish salmon is also well known, and available everywhere in Britain smoked or poached, but there's a big difference between the fatty version from fish farms and the tastier wild variety. Other British seafood includes herring, trout and haddock; in Scotland the latter is best enjoyed with potato and cream in the old-style soup called Cullen skink.

Treats in northern England include Cumberland sausage, a tasty mix of minced pork and herbs so large it has to be spiralled to fit on your plate. In Scotland, the most famous meaty speciality is haggis, a large sausage made from a sheep's stomach filled with minced meat and oatmeal.

For a snack in central England, try Melton Mowbray pork pies, cooked ham compressed in a casing of pastry. A legal victory in 2005 ensured that only pies made in the eponymous Midlands town could carry the Melton Mowbray moniker – in the same way that fizzy wine from regions outside Champagne can't claim that name.

Another British speciality that enjoys the same protection is Stilton – a strong white cheese, either plain or in a blue-vein variety. Only five dairies in the country are allowed to produce cheese with this name.

British Beer

Among alcoholic drinks, Britain is best known for its beer. Typically ranging from dark brown to bright orange in colour, technically it's called 'ale' and is more commonly called 'bitter' in England and Wales. Traditionally made and stored beer is called 'real ale' and, for the unwary, the first sip may come as a shock – a warm, flat and expensive shock. But focus on the flavour: this beer doesn't need to be chilled or fizzed to make it palatable.

Whisky

The spirit most visitors associate with Britain – and especially Scotland – is whisky. (Note the spelling – it's *Irish* whiskey that has an 'e'.) More than 2000 brands are produced, but the two main kinds are single malt, made from malted barley, and blended whisky, made from unmalted grain blended with malts. Single malts are rarer and more expensive. When ordering a 'dram' in Scotland remember to ask for whisky – only the English and other foreigners say 'Scotch'.

Enjoying a pint at a British pub

Survival
Guide

Cycling the Royal Mile, Edinburgh (p300)
PHOTOGRAPHER: IZZET KERIBAR / LONELY PLANET IMAGES ©

Directory

Price Ranges

Throughout this book, reviews of places to stay use the following price ranges, all based on double room with private bathroom, in high season. Hotels in London are more expensive than the rest of the country.

CATEGORY	LONDON	ELSEWHERE
budget (£)	<£80	<£50
midrange (££)	£80-180	£50–130
top end (£££)	>£180	>£130

Accommodation

Accommodation in Britain is as varied as the sights you visit. From hip hotels to basic barns, the wide choice is all part of the attraction.

B&BS & GUEST HOUSES

The B&B ('bed and breakfast') is a great British institution. At smaller places it's pretty much a room in somebody's house, and you'll really feel part of the family. Larger B&Bs may have around 10 rooms and more facilities. Sometimes a larger B&B may call itself a 'guest house'. Facilities usually reflect price: for around £20 per person you get a simple bedroom and share the bathroom; for around £25 to £30 you get a private bathroom – either down the hall or en suite.

B&B prices are usually quoted per person, based on two people sharing a room. Single rooms for solo travellers are harder to find, and attract a 20% to 50% premium. Some B&Bs simply won't take single people (unless you pay the full double-room price), especially in summer.

○ In country areas, B&Bs might be in the heart of a village or an isolated farm; in cities it's usually a suburban house.

○ Advance reservations are always preferred at B&Bs, and essential during popular periods. Many require a minimum two nights at weekends.

○ If a B&B is full, owners may recommend another place nearby (possibly a private house taking occasional guests, not in tourist listings).

○ In cities, some B&Bs are for long-term residents or people on welfare; they don't take passing tourists.

○ In country areas, most B&Bs cater for walkers and cyclists, but some don't, so let them know if you'll be turning up with dirty boots or wheels.

○ Some places reduce rates for longer stays (two or three nights).

○ Most B&Bs serve enormous breakfasts; some offer packed lunches (around £5) and evening meals (around £12 to £15).

○ If you're on a flexible itinerary and haven't booked in advance, most towns have a main drag of B&Bs; those with spare rooms hang up a 'Vacancies' sign.

○ When booking, check where your B&B actually is. In country areas, postal addresses include the nearest town, which may be 20 miles away – important if you're walking! Some B&B owners will pick you up by car for a small charge.

Book Your Stay Online

For more accommodation reviews by Lonely Planet authors, check out hotels.lonelyplanet.com/Great Britain. You'll find independent reviews, as well as recommendations on the best places to stay. Best of all, you can book online.

HOTELS

A hotel in Britain might be a small and simple place, perhaps a former farmhouse now stylishly converted, where peace and quiet – along with luxury – are guaranteed. Or it might be a huge country house with fancy facilities, acres of grounds and lines of stag-heads on the wall.

Charges vary. At the bargain end, you can find singles/doubles costing £30/40. Move up the scale and you'll pay £100/150 or beyond. More money doesn't always mean a better hotel though – some are excellent value, while others overcharge.

If all you want is a place to put your head down, budget chain hotels can be a good option. Most are totally lacking in style or ambience, but who cares? You'll only be there for eight hours, and six of them you'll be asleep. Most offer rooms at variable prices based on demand; on a quiet night in November twin-bed rooms with private bathroom start at around £20, and at the height of the tourist season you'll pay £45 or more. Options include:

Etap Hotels
(www.etaphotel.com)

Hotel Formule 1
(www.hotelformule1.com)

Premier Inn
(www.premierinn.com)

Travelodge
(www.travelodge.co.uk)

PUBS & INNS

As well as selling drinks, many pubs and inns offer lodging, particularly in country areas. Staying in a pub can be good fun – you're automatically at the centre of the community – although accommodation varies enormously.

Expect to pay around £20 per person at the cheap end, and around £30 to £35 for something better. An advantage for solo tourists is that pubs are more likely to have single rooms.

If a pub does B&B, it normally does evening meals, served in the bar or an adjoining restaurant.

●●●●

Activities

Walking and cycling are the most popular of all outdoor activities in Britain – for locals and visitors alike – because they open up some beautiful corners of the country and can be done virtually on a whim.

WALKING

Although you can walk pretty much anywhere in Britain, some areas are better than others. Some highlights of the different regions:

A day trip from London
The chalky hills of the South Downs, across the counties of West and East Sussex.

Southwest Favourite areas include Dartmoor and Exmoor; the entire coast offers dramatic walking conditions – especially along the beautiful cliff-lined shore of Cornwall.

Central England Cotswold Hills; for something higher, aim for the Peak District.

Northern England Lake District and the rolling hills of the Yorkshire Dales.

Wales The hills of the Brecon Beacons, the coast of Pembrokeshire and the mountains of Snowdonia.

Scotland The Loch Lomond and the Trossachs National Park; further north, serious hikers head to Glen Coe, Ben Nevis and the Isle of Skye.

Hotel Rates

You'll notice as you're travelling through Britain that there's often no such thing as a 'standard' hotel rate. Many hotels, especially larger places or chains, vary prices according to demand – or have different rates for online, phone or walk-in bookings – just like airlines and train operators. So if you book early for a night when the hotel is likely to be quiet, rates are cheap. If you book late, or aim for a public holiday weekend, you'll pay a lot. However, if you're prepared to be flexible and leave booking to the very last minute you can sometimes get a bargain as rates drop again. The end result: you can pay anything from £19 to £190 for the very same hotel room. With that in mind, the hotel rates we quote throughout this book are often guide prices only (B&B prices tend to be much more consistent).

Practicalities

o **Newspapers** Tabloids include the *Sun, Mail, Mirror* and *Daily Record* in Scotland; quality 'broadsheets' include (from right to left, politically) the *Telegraph, Times, Independent* and *Guardian*.

o **TV** Leading free-to-air options include BBC 1 and BBC 2, closely followed by ITV and Channel 4. Satellite and cable TV is dominated by Sky.

o **Weights & Measures** Britain uses a bizarre mix of metric and imperial measures; for example, petrol sold by the litre, but beer by the pint, mountain-heights in metres but road distances in miles.

o **Radio** Main BBC stations and wavelengths are Radio 1 (98-99.6MHz FM); Radio 2 (88-92MHz FM); Radio 3 (90–92.2 MHz FM); Radio 4 (92–94.4MHz FM); Radio 5Live (909 or 693 AM). National commercial stations include Virgin Radio (1215Hz MW) and non-highbrow classical specialist Classic FM (100–102MHz FM). All available on digital.

o **Video & DVD** PAL format (incompatible with NTSC/Secam).

o **Discount Card** No specific discount card for visitors to Britain, although travel cards are discounted for younger and older people – see p405.

CYCLING

A bike is the perfect mode of transport for exploring back-road Britain. A vast network of quiet country lanes winds through fields and peaceful villages, ideal for cycle-touring.

Mountain-bikers can go further into the wilds on the tracks and bridleways that cross Britain's hills and high moors, or head for dedicated mountain-bike centres where specially built trails wind through the forests, with options of varying difficulty – all indicated green to black in ski-resort style.

Southwest England
Cornwall and Devon are beautiful but the rugged landscape can make it tough for cycling. The neighbouring counties of Somerset and Wiltshire have more gentle hills and a network of quiet lanes perfect for leisurely touring.

Central England
The Cotswolds offer good cycling options, while the Peak District is very popular for mountain-biking and road cycling.

Northern England
Top spots include the Yorkshire Dales.

Wales
Brecon Beacons National Park is popular for cycle-tourists and off-roaders, while the Snowdonia region offers several dedicated mountain-bike areas – Coed-y-Brenin being one of the favourites.

Scottish islands For a true touch of the wild, bikes can be hired on some of the Scottish islands, such as Mull and Skye.

WEBSITES

Cyclists' Touring Club (www.ctc.org.uk) The UK's recreational cycling and campaigning body, includes a cycle-hire directory and mail-order service for maps and books.

National Trails (www.nationaltrail.co.uk) Great for specifics on longer routes.

Mountain Bike Britain (www.mtbbritain.co.uk) Good for off-road rides.

Ramblers' Association (www.ramblers.org.uk) The country's leading organisation for walkers.

Business Hours

Throughout this book we work on the basis that most restaurants and cafes are open for lunch or dinner or both, so precise opening times and days are given for individual places only if they differ markedly from the pattern outlined here.

BANKS

o Monday to Friday, open at 9.30am until 4pm or 5pm.

o Saturday, main branches open 9.30am to 1pm.

o Sunday closed.

Opening Hours

London and other cities have 24/7 convenience stores. In smaller towns and in country areas, shops often shut for lunch (normally 1pm to 2pm) and on Wednesday or Thursday afternoon too.

BARS & CLUBS

○ In cities, bars (and some pubs) open until midnight or later, especially at weekends.

CAFES

○ In cities, many cafes open from 7am to 6pm, sometimes later.

○ In country areas, teashops open for lunch, and stay open all afternoon until 5pm (often later in summer).

○ In winter months, country cafe hours are reduced; some close completely October to April.

MUSEUMS & SIGHTS

○ Large museums and sights usually open virtually every day of the year.

○ Some smaller places open Saturday and Sunday but are closed Monday and/or Tuesday.

○ Smaller places open daily in high season; but on weekends only or are completely closed in low season.

POST OFFICES

○ Monday to Friday, post offices keep same hours as shops.

○ Saturday 9am to 12.30. Main branches to 5pm.

○ Sunday closed.

PUBS

○ Pubs open daily 11am to 11pm Sunday to Thursday, sometimes to midnight or 1am Friday and Saturday.

○ Some pubs shut from 3pm to 6pm.

RESTAURANTS

○ Most restaurants open Mon to Sunday; some close Sunday evening, or all day Monday.

○ Most open for lunch (about noon to 3pm) *and* dinner (about 6pm to 11pm, to midnight or later in cities). Some restaurants open only for lunch *or* dinner.

○ A few restaurants open at around 7am and serve breakfast, but mainly cafes do this.

SHOPS

○ Monday to Friday, 9am to 5pm (5.30pm or 6pm in cities).

○ Saturday, 9am to 5pm.

○ Sunday, larger shops open 10am to 4pm.

Climate

London

°C/°F **Temp**
30/86 —
20/68 —
10/50 —
0/32 —

Rainfall inches/mm
— 4.9/125
— 3.9/100
— 2.9/75
— 2/50
— 1/25
— 0

J F M A M J J A S O N D

Edinburgh

°C/°F **Temp**
30/86 —
20/68 —
10/50 —
0/32 —
-10/-50 —

Rainfall inches/mm
— 6/150
— 4/100
— 2/50
— 0

J F M A M J J A S O N D

Cardiff

°C/°F **Temp**
30/86 —
20/68 —
10/50 —
0/32 —
-10/-50 —

Rainfall inches/mm
— 6/150
— 4/100
— 2/50
— 0

J F M A M J J A S O N D

Customs Regulations

Britain has a two-tier customs system: one for goods bought duty-free outside the EU; the other for goods bought in another European Union (EU) country where tax and duty is paid. Below is a summary of the rules; for more details go to www.hmce.gov.uk and search for 'Customs Allowances'.

DUTY FREE

For duty-free goods from outside the EU, the limits include 200 cigarettes, 2L of still wine, plus 1L of spirits or another 2L of wine, 60cc of perfume, and other duty-free goods (including beer) to the value of £300.

TAX & DUTY PAID

There is no limit to the goods you can bring from within the EU (if taxes have been paid), but customs officials use the following guidelines to distinguish personal use from commercial imports: 3200 cigarettes, 200 cigars, 10L of spirits, 20L of fortified wine, 90L of wine and 110L of beer. Still enough to have one hell of a party.

Local Water

Tap water in Britain is safe unless there's a sign to the contrary (eg on trains). Don't drink from streams in the countryside – you never know if there's a dead sheep upstream.

Electricity

230V/50Hz

Food

Throughout this book, reviews of eateries use the following price ranges:

budget (£)	<£9
midrange (££)	£9–18
top end (£££)	>£18

Gay & Lesbian Travellers

Britain is a generally tolerant place for gays and lesbians. London, Manchester and Brighton have flourishing gay scenes, and in other sizeable cities (even some small towns) you'll find communities not entirely in the closet. That said, you'll still find pockets of homophobic hostility in some areas. Resources include:

Diva (www.divamag.co.uk)

Gay Times (www.gaytimes.co.uk)

London Lesbian & Gay Switchboard (020-7837 7324; www.llgs.org.uk, www.queery.org.uk)

Pink Paper (www.pinkpaper.com)

Health

No immunisations are mandatory for visiting Britain. Regardless of nationality, everyone receives free emergency treatment at accident and emergency (A&E) departments of state-run NHS hospitals. European Economic Area (EEA) nationals get free nonemergency treatment (ie the same service British citizens receive) with a European Health Insurance Card (EHIC) validated in their home country. Reciprocal arrangements between Britain and some other countries (including Australia) allow free medical treatment at hospitals and surgeries, and subsidised dental care.

If you don't need full-on hospital treatment, chemists (pharmacies) can advise on minor ailments such as sore throats and earaches. In large cities, there's always at least one 24/7 chemist.

For more details see the **Department of Health** (www.doh.gov.uk) website and follow the links to 'Health care', 'Entitlements' and 'Overseas Visitors'.

Heritage Organisations

A highlight of a journey through Britain is visiting the numerous castles and historic sites that pepper the country. Membership of a heritage organisation gets you free admission (usually a good saving) as well as information handbooks and so on. If you join an English heritage organisation, it covers you for Wales and Scotland, and vice versa.

The **National Trust** (NT; www.nationaltrust.org.uk) protects hundreds of historic buildings plus vast tracts of land with scenic importance across England and Wales. Annual membership costs £49 (with discounts for under-26s and families). A Touring Pass allows free entry to NT properties for one/two weeks (£21/26 per person); families and couples get cheaper rates. The **National Trust for Scotland** (NTS; www.nts.org.uk) is similar.

English Heritage (EH; www.english-heritage.org.uk) is a state-funded organisation responsible for numerous historic sites. Annual membership costs £44 (couples and seniors get discounts). An Overseas Visitors Pass allows free entry to most sites for seven/14 days for £20/25 (with cheaper rates for couples and families). In Wales and Scotland the equivalent organisations are: **Cadw** (www.cadw.wales.gov.uk) and **Historic Scotland** (HS; www.historic-scotland.gov.uk).

We have included the relevant acronym (NT, NTS, EH etc) in the information brackets after properties listed throughout this book. You can join at the first NT/NTS/EH/HS/Cadw site you visit.

Insurance

Although everyone receives free emergency treatment, regardless of nationality, travel insurance is still highly recommended. It will usually cover medical consultation and treatment at private clinics, which can be quicker than National Health Service (NHS) places, and emergency dental care – as well as loss of baggage or valuable items and, most importantly, the cost of any emergency flights home. For car insurance see p405. Worldwide travel insurance is available at www.lonelyplanet.com/travel_services. You can buy, extend and claim online anytime, even if you're already on the road.

Internet Access

Internet cafes are surprisingly rare in Britain, especially away from big cities and tourist spots. Most charge from £1 per hour, and out in the sticks you can pay up to £5 per hour.

Public libraries often have computers with free internet access, but only for 30-minute slots, and demand is high. All the usual warnings apply about keystroke-capturing software and other security risks.

If you'll be using your laptop to get online, you'll be pleased to know that an increasing number of hotels, hostels, stations and coffee shops (even some trains) have wi-fi access, charging anything from nothing to £5 per hour. Wi-fi is often free, but some places (typically, upmarket hotels) charge.

Legal Matters

The age of consent is 16 (gay or straight). Travellers should note that they can be prosecuted under the law of their home country regarding age of consent, even when abroad.

You must be over 18 to buy alcohol and cigarettes. You usually have to be 18 to enter a pub or bar, although rules are different for under-18s if eating. Some bars and clubs are over-21 only.

Illegal drugs are widely available in Britain, especially in night clubs. Cannabis possession is a criminal offence; possible punishment for carrying a small amount may be a warning, a fine or imprisonment. Drug dealers face stiffer penalties, as do people caught with other drugs.

Drink-driving is a serious offence. See p406 for more information about speed limits.

On buses and trains (including the London Underground), people without a valid ticket are fined on the spot – usually around £20.

Money

The currency of Britain is the pound sterling (£). Paper money ('notes') comes in £5, £10, £20 and £50 denominations, although some shops don't accept £50 notes because fakes circulate. Scotland issues its own currency (including a £1 note), interchangeable with the money used in the rest of the UK.

Other currencies are rarely accepted, except by some gift shops in London, which may take euros, US dollars, yen and other major currencies.

For a rundown of exchange rates and costs, see p48.

ATMS

ATMs (often called 'cash machines') are easy to find in cities and even small towns. Watch out for ATMs which might have been tampered with; a common ruse is to attach a card-reader to the slot.

CHANGING MONEY

Cities and larger towns have banks and bureaus for changing your money (cash or travellers cheques) into pounds. Check rates first; some bureaus offer poor rates or levy outrageous commissions. You can also change money at some post offices – very handy in country areas, and exchange rates are fair.

Scottish Pounds

Although Scottish pounds are exactly the same value as (and freely interchangeable with) pounds in the rest of the UK, in reality you'll find shops more readily accept them in the north of England than in the south. Banks will always change them.

CREDIT & DEBIT CARDS

Visa and MasterCard credit and debit cards are widely accepted in Britain; good for larger hotels, restaurants, shopping, flights, long-distance travel, car hire etc. Smaller businesses, such as pubs or B&Bs, prefer debit cards (or charge a fee for credit cards), and some take cash or cheque only.

Nearly all credit and debit cards use a 'Chip and PIN' system (instead of signing). If your card isn't Chip and PIN enabled, you should be able to sign in the usual way, but some places may not accept your card.

TIPPING

In Britain, you're not obliged to tip if the service or food was unsatisfactory (even if it's been automatically added to your bill as a 'service charge').

○ Restaurants – around 10%. Also teashops and smarter cafes with full table service. At smarter restaurants waiters can get a bit sniffy if the tip isn't nearer 12% or even 15%.

○ Taxis – 10%, or rounded up to the nearest pound, especially in London. It's less usual to tip minicab drivers.

○ Toilet attendants – around 50p.

○ Pubs – around 10% if you order food at the table and your meal is brought to you. If you order and pay at the bar (food or drinks), tips are not expected.

TRAVELLERS CHEQUES

Travellers cheques are safer than cash, but are rarely used in Britain, as credit/debit cards and ATMs have become the method of choice. They are rarely accepted for purchases (except at large hotels), so for cash you'll still need to go to a bank or change bureau.

Public Holidays

Holidays for the whole of Britain are:

New Year's Day 1 January

Easter March/April (Good Friday to Easter Monday inclusive)

May Day First Monday in May

Spring Bank Holiday Last Monday in May

Summer Bank Holiday Last Monday in August

Christmas Day 25 December

Boxing Day 26 December

If a public holiday falls on a weekend, the nearest Monday is usually taken instead.

In England and Wales, most businesses and banks close on official public holidays (hence the quaint term 'bank holiday'). In Scotland, Bank Holidays are just for the banks, and many businesses stay open. Many Scottish

Public Holidays

Roads get busy and hotel prices go up during school holidays. Exact dates vary from year to year and region to region, but are roughly as follows:

Easter Holiday Week before and week after Easter

Summer Holiday Third week of July to first week of September

Christmas Holiday Mid-December to first week of January.

There are also three week-long 'half-term' school holidays – usually late February (or early March), late May and late October. These vary between Scotland, England and Wales.

towns normally have a spring and autumn holiday, but the dates vary.

On public holidays, some small museums and places of interest close, but larger attractions have their busiest times. If a place closes on Sunday, it'll probably be shut on bank holidays as well. Virtually everything – attractions, shops, banks, offices – closes on Christmas Day, although pubs are open at lunchtime.

There's usually no public transport on Christmas Day, and a very minimal service on Boxing Day.

Safe Travel

Britain is a remarkably safe country, but crime is not unknown in London and other cities. When travelling by tube, tram or urban train service at night, choose a carriage containing other people.

Unlicenced minicabs – a bloke with a car earning money on the side – operate in large cities, and are worth avoiding unless you know what you're doing. Annoyances include driving round in circles, then charging an enormous fare. Dangers include driving to a remote location then robbery or rape. To avoid this, use a metered taxi or phone a reputable minicab company and get an up-front quote for the ride.

Telephone
TELEPHONE CODES

In this book, area codes and individual numbers are listed together, separated by a hyphen.

Area codes in Britain do not have a standard format or length, eg it's ☎020 for London, ☎0161 for Manchester, ☎01225 for Bath, ☎029 for Cardiff, and ☎0131 for Edinburgh, followed as usual by the individual number.

Other codes:

- ☎0500 or ☎0800 – free calls

- ☎0845 – calls at local rate, wherever you're dialling from within the UK

- ☎087 – calls at national rate

- ☎089 or ☎09 – premium rate

- ☎07 – mobile phones, more expensive than calling a landline

To call outside the UK dial ☎00, then the country code (☎1 for USA, ☎61 for Australia etc), the area code (you usually drop the initial zero) and the number.

- operator ☎100

- international operator ☎155 – also for reverse-charge (collect) calls

For directory inquiries, a host of agencies compete for your business and charge from 10p to 40p; numbers include ☎118 192, ☎118 118, ☎118 500 and ☎118 811.

Important Numbers

Omit the area code if you're inside that area. Drop the initial 0 if you're calling from abroad.

Country code	☎+44
International access code	☎00
Emergency (police, fire, ambulance, mountain rescue or coastguard)	☎999

Tourist Information

All British cities and towns, and some villages, have a tourist information centre (TIC). Some TICs are run by national parks and often have small exhibits about the area. You'll also see 'visitor welcome centres' or 'visitor information centres' – for ease we've called all these places 'tourist offices' in this book.

Whatever the name, these places have helpful staff, books and maps for sale, leaflets to give away and loads of advice on things to see or do. They can also assist with booking accommodation. Most tourist offices keep regular business hours; in quiet areas they close from October to March, while in popular areas they open daily year-round.

For a list of all tourist offices around Britain see www.visitmap.info/tic. And before leaving home, check the informative, comprehensive and wide-ranging website of Britain's official tourist board, **VisitBritain** (www.visitbritain. com), covering all the angles of national tourism, with links to numerous other sites.

Travellers with Disabilities

New buildings have wheelchair access, and even hotels in old country houses often have lifts, ramps and other facilities. Smaller B&Bs are often harder to adapt, so you'll have less choice here. Many theatres, most banks and some public buildings have hearing loops, while the main public areas in cities and towns have some facilities for blind people, such as audible signals and special paving at crossings.

CITIES

Getting around in cities, new buses have low floors for easy access, but few have conductors who can lend a hand when you're getting on or off. Many taxis take wheelchairs, or just have more room in the back.

LONG-DISTANCE COACH

Coaches may present problems if you can't walk, but the main operator, **National Express** (www.nationalexpress. com) has wheelchair-friendly coaches on many routes. For details, ring their dedicated Disabled Passenger Travel Helpline on ☎ 0121-423 8479 or go to the website and follow links to 'Our Service' then 'Disabled Facilities'.

INTER-CITY TRAINS

On most inter-city trains there's more room and better facilities, compared to travel by coach, and usually station staff around; just have a word and they'll be happy to help.

ORGANISATIONS

Good Access Guide (www.goodaccessguide.co.uk)

Royal Association for Disability & Rehabilitation (RADAR; www.radar.org. uk) Published titles include *Holidays in Britain and Ireland*. Through RADAR you can get a key for 7000 public disabled toilets across the UK.

RNIB (www.rnib.org.uk)

RNID (www.rnid.org.uk)

Tourism for All (www. tourismforall.org.uk)

Visas

If you're a European Economic Area (EEA) national, you don't need a visa to visit (or work in) Britain. Citizens of Australia, Canada, New Zealand, South Africa and the USA are given leave to enter the UK at their point of arrival for up to six months (three months for some nationalities), but are prohibited from working. For more info see www.ukvisas. gov.uk or www.ukba.home office.gov.uk.

Transport

Getting There & Away

London is a global transport hub, so you can easily fly to Britain from just about anywhere. In recent years, the massive growth of budget ('no-frills') airlines has increased the number of routes – and reduced the fares – between Britain and other countries in Europe.

Your other main option for travel between Britain and mainland Europe is ferry, either port-to-port or combined with a long-distance bus trip, although journeys can be long and financial savings not huge compared with budget airfares. International trains are much more comfortable and a 'green' option; the Channel Tunnel allows direct rail services between Britain, France and Belgium, with onward connections to many other European destinations.

Flights, tours and rail tickets can be booked online at www.lonelyplanet.com/travel_services.

AIR

AIRPORTS

London's main airports:

Heathrow (LHR; www.heathrowairport.com) The world's busiest airport, and the UK's main airport for international flights, often chaotic and crowded. About 15 miles west of central London.

Gatwick (LGW; www.gatwickairport.com) The UK's number-two airport, also mainly for international flights, 30 miles south of central London.

Stansted (STN; www.stansted airport.com) About 35 miles northeast of central London, mainly handling charter and budget European flights.

Luton (LTN; www.london-luton.co.uk) Some 35 miles north of central London, especially well known as a holiday flight airport.

London City (LCY; www.londoncityairport.com) A few miles east of central London, specialising in flights to/from European and other UK airports. For details on getting between these airports and central London, see p102.

Some planes on European and long-haul routes go direct to major regional airports including Manchester and Glasgow, while smaller regional airports such as Southampton, Cardiff and Birmingham are served by flights to and from continental Europe and Ireland.

TRAIN

CHANNEL TUNNEL SERVICES

The Channel Tunnel makes direct train travel between Britain and continental Europe a fast and enjoyable option. High-speed **Eurostar** (www.eurostar.com) passenger services hurtle at least 10 times daily between London and Paris (journey time 2½ hours) and Brussels (two hours). You can buy tickets from travel agencies, major train stations or direct from the Eurostar website. The normal single fare between London and Paris/Brussels is around £150, but if you buy in advance and travel at a less busy period, deals drop to around £90 return or even less. You can also buy 'through fare' tickets from many cities in Britain – for example York to Paris, or Manchester to Brussels. You can also get very good train and hotel combination deals – bizarrely sometimes cheaper than train fare only.

Drivers use **Eurotunnel** (www.eurotunnel.com). At Folkestone in southern England or Calais in France, you drive onto a train, get carried through the tunnel and drive off at the other end. The trains run about four times an hour from 6am to 10pm, then hourly. Loading and unloading takes an hour; the journey takes 35 minutes. You can book in advance online or pay on the spot. The one-way cost for a car and passengers is around £90 to £150 depending on the time of day; promotional fares often bring it nearer to £50.

Climate Change & Travel

Every form of transport that relies on carbon-based fuel generates CO_2, the main cause of human-induced climate change. Modern travel is dependent on aeroplanes, which might use less fuel per kilometre per person than most cars but travel much greater distances. The altitude at which aircraft emit gases (including CO_2) and particles also contributes to their climate change impact. Many websites offer 'carbon calculators' that allow people to estimate the carbon emissions generated by their journey and, for those who wish to do so, to offset the impact of the greenhouse gases emitted with contributions to portfolios of climate-friendly initiatives throughout the world. Lonely Planet offsets the carbon footprint of all staff and author travel.

Getting Around

For getting around Britain your first main choice is going by car or public transport.

Your main public transport options are train and long-distance bus (called coach in Britain). Services between major towns and cities are generally good, although at 'peak' (busy) times you must book in advance to be sure of getting a ticket. Conversely, if you book ahead early or travel at 'off-peak' periods, ideally both, train and coach tickets can be very cheap.

✈ AIR

Britain's domestic air companies include British Airways, BMI, BMIbaby, EasyJet and Ryanair.

If you're really pushed for time, you'll find that flights on longer routes across Britain (eg Exeter or Southampton to Edinburgh or Inverness) can be handy, although you do miss seeing the glorious scenery in between. On some shorter routes, trains can compare favourably with planes on time, once airport downtime is factored in. On costs, you might get a bargain airfare, but trains can be cheaper if you buy tickets in advance.

Cycling – Road Rules

Bicycles aren't allowed on motorways, but you can ride on all other public roads, although main roads (A-roads) tend to be busy with cars and trucks, so should be avoided. Many B-roads suffer heavy motor traffic too, so the best places for cycling are the small C-roads and unclassified roads ('lanes') that cover rural Britain, especially in lowland areas, meandering through quiet countryside and linking small, picturesque villages.

For off-roaders, cycling is *not* allowed on footpaths in England and Wales, but it is allowed on unmade roads or bridleways (originally for horses but now for bikes too) that are a public right of way.

BICYCLE

Britain is a compact country, and getting around by bicycle is perfectly feasible – and a great way to really see the country.

Renting a bike is easy in London; the capital is dotted with automatic docking stations where bikes can be hired on the spot – and they're free for the first 30 minutes. For info go to the Transport for London site (www.tfl.gov.uk) and follow the links to Cycling. Other hire options are listed at www.lcc.org.uk.

Rental is also possible in tourist spots such as Oxford and Cambridge, and in country areas, especially at forestry sites and reservoirs now primarily used for leisure activities, eg Grizedale Forest in the Lake District. In some areas, disused railway lines are now bike routes, notably the Peak District in Derbyshire. The Great Glen Way in Scotland is another great option. Rates start at about £10 per day, £20 for something half decent.

For more on cycling areas and organisations, see p396.

🚌 BUS & COACH

If you're on a tight budget, long-distance buses (called coaches in Britain) are nearly always the cheapest way to get around, although they're also the slowest – sometimes by a considerable margin. Many towns have separate stations for local buses and long-distance coaches; make sure you go to the right one!

National Express (www.nationalexpress.com/coach) is the main coach operator, with a wide network and frequent services between main centres. North of the border, services tie in with those of **Scottish Citylink** (www.citylink.co.uk), Scotland's leading coach company. Fares vary: they're cheaper if you

Do I Need a Passport?

Getting between Britain's three nations of England, Scotland and Wales is easy. The bus and train systems are fully integrated and in most cases you won't even know you've crossed the border. Passports are not required – although some Scots and Welsh may think they should be!

book in advance and travel at quieter times, and more expensive if you buy your ticket on the spot and it's Friday afternoon. As a guide, a 200-mile trip (eg London to York) will cost around £15 to £20 if you book a few days in advance.

Megabus (www.megabus.com) operates a budget-airline-style coach service between about 30 destinations around the country. Go at a quiet time, book early, and your ticket will be very cheap. Book later, for a busy time and... You get the picture.

For information about short-distance and local bus services, see p406.

BUS PASSES & DISCOUNTS

National Express offers discount passes to full-time students and under-26s, called Young Persons Coachcards. They cost £10 and get you 30% off standard adult fares. Also available are coachcards for people over 60, families and disabled travellers.

For touring the country, National Express offers Brit Xplorer passes, allowing unlimited travel for seven days (£79), 14 days (£139) and 28 days (£219). You don't need to book journeys in advance; if the coach has a spare seat, you can take it.

🚗 CAR & MOTORCYCLE

Travelling by car or motorbike means you can be independent and flexible, and reach remote places. Downsides for drivers include traffic jams and high parking costs in cities.

Information Service

Traveline (☎ 0871 200 2233; www.traveline.org.uk) is a very useful information service covering bus, coach, taxi and train services nationwide, with numerous links to help plan your journey. By phone, you get transferred automatically to an adviser in the region you're phoning *from;* for details on another part of the country, you need to key in a code number (81 for London, 874 for Cumbria etc) – for a full list of codes, go to the Traveline website.

HIRE

Compared to many countries (especially the USA), hire rates are expensive in Britain; you should expect to pay around £250 per week for a small car (unlimited mileage) but rates rise at busy times and drop at quiet times. Some main players: **Avis** (www.avis.co.uk), **Budget** (www.budget.co.uk), **Europcar** (www.europcar.co.uk), **Sixt** (www.sixt.co.uk) and **Thrifty** (www.thrifty.co.uk).

Many international websites have separate web pages for customers in different countries, and the prices for a car in Britain on the UK webpages can differ from the same car's prices on the USA or Australia pages. You have to surf a lot of sites to find the best deals.

Another option is to look online for small local car-hire companies in Britain who can undercut the international franchises. Generally those in cities are cheaper than in rural areas. See a rental-broker site such as **UK Car Hire** (www.ukcarhire.net).

Yet another option is to hire a motorhome or campervan. It's more expensive than

hiring a car, but saves on accommodation costs, and gives almost unlimited freedom. Sites to check:

Cool Campervans (www.coolcampervans.com)

Just Go (www.justgo.uk.com)

Wild Horizon (www.wildhorizon.co.uk)

INSURANCE

Nearly all rental vehicles in Britain have insurance included in the price, although you may be liable for an 'excess' (ie paying for damage up to the value of anywhere between £200 and £500). This can be reduced to about £100 by paying a small extra fee.

PARKING

Many cities have short-stay and long-stay car parks; the latter are cheaper though maybe less convenient. 'Park & Ride' systems allow you to park on the edge of the city then ride to the centre on regular buses provided for an all-in-one price.

Yellow lines (single or double) along the edge of the road indicate restrictions.

Find the nearby sign that spells out when you can and can't park. In London and other big cities, traffic wardens operate with efficiency; if you park on the yellow lines at the wrong time, your car will be clamped or towed away, and it'll cost you £100 or more to get driving again. In some cities there are also red lines, which mean no stopping at all. Ever.

ROADS & RULES

Motorways and main A-roads are dual carriageways and deliver you quickly from one end of the country to another. Lesser A-roads, B-roads and minor roads are much more scenic and fun, as you wind through the countryside from village to village – ideal for car or motorcycle touring. You can't travel fast, but you won't care.

A foreign driving licence is valid in Britain for up to 12 months. If you plan to bring a car from Europe, it's illegal to drive without (at least) third-party insurance.

Some other important rules:

○ drive on the left (!)

○ wear fitted seat belts in cars

○ wear crash helmets on motorcycles

○ give way to your right at junctions and roundabouts

○ always use the left-side lane on motorways and dual-carriageways, unless overtaking (although so many people ignore this rule, you'd think it didn't exist)

○ don't use a mobile phone while driving unless it's fully hands-free (another rule frequently flouted)

Speed limits are 30mph (48km/h) in built-up areas, 60mph (96km/h) on main roads and 70mph (112km/h) on motorways and most (but not all) dual carriageways. Drinking and driving is taken very seriously; you're allowed a minimum blood-alcohol level of 80mg/100mL (0.08%) – campaigners want it reduced to 50mg/100mL.

LOCAL TRANSPORT

British cities usually have good local public transport systems – a combination of bus, train and tram – often run by a confusing number of separate companies. Tourist offices can provide maps and information. More details are given in the city sections throughout this book.

BUS

There are good local bus networks year-round in cities and towns. Buses also run in some rural areas year-round, although timetables are designed to serve schools and businesses, so there aren't many midday and weekend services (and they may stop running during school holidays), or buses may link local villages to a market town on only one day each week. In tourist spots (especially national parks) there are frequent services from Easter to September. It's always worth double-checking at a tourist office before planning your day's activities around a bus that may not actually be running.

In this book, along with the local bus route number, frequency and duration, we have provided indicative prices if the fare is over £5. If it's less than this, we have generally omitted the fare.

Bus passes

If you're taking a few local bus rides in a day of energetic sightseeing, day passes (with names like Day Rover, Wayfarer or Explorer) are cheaper than buying several single tickets. If you plan to linger longer in one area, three-day passes are also available; often they can be bought on your first bus, and may include local rail services. It's always worth asking ticket clerks or bus drivers about your options.

Motoring Organisations

Motoring organisations include the **Automobile Association** (www.theaa.com) and the **Royal Automobile Club** (www.rac.co.uk); annual membership starts at around £35, including 24-hour roadside breakdown assistance. A greener alternative is the **Environmental Transport Association** (www.eta.co.uk); it provides all the usual services (breakdown assistance, roadside rescue, vehicle inspections etc) but doesn't campaign for more roads.

Postbus Services

These are vans on usual mail services that also carries passengers, operating in some rural areas (often the most scenic and remote parts of the country) and especially useful for walkers and backpackers: www.royalmail.com/postbus.

FERRY

Local ferries, from the mainland to the Scottish islands for example, are covered in the relevant sections in the regional chapters.

TAXI

There are two sorts of taxi in Britain: the famous black cabs (some with advertising livery in other colours), which have meters and can be hailed in the street; and minicabs, which are cheaper but can only be called by phone. In London and other big cities, taxis cost £2 to £3 per mile. In rural areas it's about half that. The best place to find the local taxi's phone number is the local pub. Alternatively, call **National Cabline** (☎ 0800 123444) from a landline phone; the service pinpoints your location and transfers you to an approved local taxi company. Also useful is www.traintaxi.co.uk – designed to help you 'bridge the final gap' between the train station and your hotel or other final destination.

🚆 TRAIN

For long-distance travel around Britain, trains are generally faster and more comfortable than coaches but can be more expensive, although with discount tickets they're competitive – and often take you through beautiful countryside. The British like to moan about their trains, but around 85% run on time. The other 15% that get delayed or cancelled mostly affect commuters rather than long-distance services.

About 20 different companies operate train services in Britain (eg First Great Western runs from London to Bath, Cornwall and South Wales; National Express East Coast runs London to York and Scotland; Virgin Trains run the 'west coast' route from London to Carlisle and Scotland), while Network Rail operates track and stations. For some passengers this system can be confusing at first, but information and ticket-buying services are mostly centralised. If you have to change trains, or use two or more train operators, you still buy one ticket – valid for the whole of your journey. The main railcards are also accepted by all operators.

Your first stop should be **National Rail Enquiries** (☎ 08457-484950; www.nationalrail.co.uk), the nationwide timetable and fare information service. This site also advertises special offers, and has real-time links to station departure boards. Once you've found the journey you need, links take you to the relevant train operator or to centralised ticketing services (eg www.thetrainline.com, www.qjump.co.uk, www.raileasy.co.uk) to buy the ticket. To use these websites you always have to state a preferred time and day of travel, even if you don't mind when you go, but with a little delving around they can offer some real bargains.

You can also buy train tickets on the spot at stations, which is fine for short journeys, but discount tickets for longer trips are usually not available and must be bought in advance by phone or online.

For planning your trip, some very handy maps of the UK's rail network can be downloaded from the National Rail Enquiries website.

CLASSES

There are two classes of rail travel: first and standard. First class costs around 50% more than standard and, except on very crowded trains, is not really worth it. At weekends some train operators offer 'upgrades' for an extra £10 to £15 on top of your standard class fare.

COSTS & RESERVATIONS

For short journeys (under about 50 miles) it's usually best to buy tickets on the spot at rail stations. For longer journeys, on-the-spot fares are always available, but tickets are much cheaper if bought in advance. Essentially, the earlier you book, the cheaper it gets. You can also save if you travel 'off-peak' (ie the days and times that aren't busy). Advance purchase usually gets a reserved seat too. The cheapest fares are

Bikes on Trains

Bicycles can be taken free of charge on most local urban trains (although they may not be allowed at peak times when the trains are too crowded with commuters) and on shorter trips in rural areas, on a first-come, first-served basis – though there may be space limits. Bikes can be carried on long-distance train journeys free of charge as well, but advance booking is required for most conventional bikes. (Folding bikes can be carried on pretty much any train at any time.) In theory, this shouldn't be too much trouble as most long-distance rail trips are best bought in advance anyway, but you have to go a long way down the path of booking your seat before you start booking your bike – only to find space isn't available. A better course of action is to buy in advance at a major rail station, where the booking clerk can help you through the options, or phone the relevant operator's Customer Service department. Have a large cup of coffee and a stress-reliever handy. And a final warning: when railways are repaired, cancelled trains are replaced by buses – and they won't take bikes.

A very useful leaflet called 'Cycling by Train' is available at major stations or downloadable from www.nationalrail.co.uk/passenger_services/cyclists.html.

TRAIN PASSES

Discount Passes

Local train passes usually cover rail networks around a city (many include bus travel too), and are mentioned in the individual city sections throughout this book. If you're staying in Britain for a while, passes known as 'railcards' are available:

16-25 Railcard – for those aged 16 to 25, or a full-time UK student

Senior Railcard – for anyone over 60

Family & Friends Railcard – covers up to four adults and four children travelling together.

These railcards cost around £26 (valid for one year, available from major stations or online) and get you a 33% discount on most train fares, except those already heavily discounted. With the Family card, adults get 33% and children get 60% discounts, so the fee is easily repaid in a couple of journeys.

A **Disabled Person's Railcard** costs £18. You can get an application from stations or from the railcard website.

For full details on all discount passes see www.railcard.co.uk.

Regional Passes

If you're concentrating your travels on southeast England (eg London to Cambridge or Oxford) a **Network Railcard** covers up to four adults and

nonrefundable, so if you miss your train you'll have to buy a new ticket.

If you buy online, you can have the ticket posted (UK addresses only), or collect it at the station on the day of travel from automatic machines.

Whichever operator you travel with and wherever you buy tickets, these are the three main fare types:

○ **Anytime** Buy anytime, travel anytime – usually the most expensive option

○ **Off-peak** Buy ticket any time, travel off-peak

○ **Advance** Buy ticket in advance, travel only on specific trains – usually the cheapest option

For an idea of the price difference, an Anytime single ticket from London to York will cost around £100 or more, an Off-peak around £80, while an Advance is around £20, and even less if you book early enough or don't mind arriving at midnight.

If the train doesn't get you all the way to your destination, a **PlusBus** (www.plusbus.info) supplement (usually around £2) validates your train ticket for onward travel by bus – more convenient, and usually cheaper, than buying a separate bus ticket. For details, see the website.

How Much To…?

When travelling long distances by train or bus/coach in Britain, it's important to realise that there's no such thing as a standard fare. Prices vary according to demand and when you buy your ticket. Book long in advance and travel on Tuesday mid-morning, and it's cheap. Buy your ticket on the spot late Friday afternoon, and it'll be a lot more expensive. Ferries use similar systems. Throughout this book, we have generally quoted sample fares somewhere in between the very cheapest and most expensive options. The price you pay will almost certainly be different.

up to four children travelling together outside peak times.

National Passes

For country-wide travel, **BritRail** (www.britrail.com) passes are available for visitors from overseas. They must be bought in your country of origin (not in Britain) from a specialist travel agency. They're available in three different versions (England only; all Britain; UK and Ireland) and for periods from four to 30 days.

Behind the Scenes

Author Thanks

DAVID ELSE

As always, massive appreciation goes to my wife, Corinne, for joining me on many of my research trips around Britain. Thanks also to my co-author colleagues for providing the original material used in this book – my name goes down as coordinating author, but I couldn't have done it without this team. And finally, thanks to all the friendly faces in the commissioning, editing and production departments at Lonely Planet Melbourne for bringing this book to final fruition.

Acknowledgments

Climate map data adapted from Peel MC, Finlayson BL & McMahon TA (2007) 'Updated World Map of the Köppen-Geiger Climate Classification', *Hydrology and Earth System Sciences*, 11, 163344.

Illustrations: p72-3, p86-7 and p242-3 by Javier Zarracina; and p300-1, p304-5 and p318-19 by Michael Ruff.

Cover photographs: Front: Typical Cotswolds cottage, Chipping Campden (p141), © Olaf Protze / Photolibrary; Back: South bank of the River Thames near Tower Bridge, London (p76), Jane Sweeney / Lonely Planet Images. Many of the images in this guide are available for licensing from Lonely Planet Images: www.lonelyplanetimages.com.

This Book

This 2nd edition of *Discover Great Britain* was coordinated by David Else, and draws on the on-the-ground research and writing of David Atkinson, Oliver Berry, Joe Bindloss, Fionn Davenport, Marc Di Duca, Belinda Dixon, Peter Dragicevich, Etain O'Carroll, Andy Symington and Neil Wilson. The 1st edition was coordinated by Oliver Berry. This guidebook was commissioned in Lonely Planet's London office, and produced by the following:

Commissioning Editors Glenn van der Knijff, Clifton Wilkinson

Coordinating Editor Laura Crawford

Coordinating Cartographer Mark Griffiths

Coordinating Layout Designer Jessica Rose

Managing Editors Annelies Mertens, Kirsten Rawlings

Managing Cartographer Alison Lyall

Managing Layout Designers Jane Hart, Celia Wood

Assisting Editors Judith Bamber, Andi Lien, Martine Power, Helen Yeates

Assisting Cartographers Katalin Dadi-Racz, Xavier Di Toro

Cover Research Naomi Parker

Internal Image Research Aude Vauconsant

Thanks to Shahara Ahmed, Melanie Dankel, Janine Eberle, Ryan Evans, Chris Girdler, Laura Jane, Yvonne Kirk, Nic Lehman, John Mazzocchi, Wayne Murphy, Piers Pickard, Malisa Plesa, Averil Robertson, Lachlan Ross, Mik Ruff, Laura Stansfeld, Gerard Walker, Juan Winata

SEND US YOUR FEEDBACK

We love to hear from travellers – your comments keep us on our toes and help make our books better. Our well-travelled team reads every word on what you loved or loathed about this book. Although we cannot reply individually to postal submissions, we always guarantee that your feedback goes straight to the appropriate authors, in time for the next edition. Each person who sends us information is thanked in the next edition, and the most useful submissions are rewarded with a free book.

Visit **lonelyplanet.com/contact** to submit your updates and suggestions or to ask for help. Our award-winning website also features inspirational travel stories, news and discussions.

Note: We may edit, reproduce and incorporate your comments in Lonely Planet products such as guidebooks, websites and digital products, so let us know if you don't want your comments reproduced or your name acknowledged. For a copy of our privacy policy visit lonelyplanet.com/privacy.

Index

000 Map pages

How to Use This Book

These symbols will help you find the listings you want:

- ⊙ Sights
- 🍥 Festivals & Events
- ⭐ Entertainment
- 🏃 Activities
- 🛏 Sleeping
- 🛍 Shopping
- ☕ Courses
- 🍴 Eating
- ℹ Information/Transport
- 🚩 Tours
- 🍷 Drinking

Look out for these icons:

- **FREE** No payment required
- 🌱 A green or sustainable option

Our authors have nominated these places as demonstrating a strong commitment to sustainability – for example by supporting local communities and producers, operating in an environmentally friendly way, or supporting conservation projects.

These symbols give you the vital information for each listing:

- ☏ Telephone Numbers
- ⊙ Opening Hours
- Ⓟ Parking
- ⊜ Nonsmoking
- ✳ Air-Conditioning
- @ Internet Access
- 🛜 Wi-Fi Access
- 🏊 Swimming Pool
- 🍃 Vegetarian Selection
- 📖 English-Language Menu
- 👪 Family-Friendly
- 🐾 Pet-Friendly
- 🚌 Bus
- ⛴ Ferry
- Ⓜ Metro
- Ⓢ Subway
- ⊖ London Tube
- 🚊 Tram
- 🚆 Train

Reviews are organised by author preference.

Map Legend

Sights
- ⊙ Beach
- ⊛ Buddhist
- ⊙ Castle
- ⊕ Christian
- ⊙ Hindu
- ⊙ Islamic
- ⊙ Jewish
- ⊙ Monument
- ⊜ Museum/Gallery
- ⊙ Ruin
- ⊙ Winery/Vineyard
- ⊛ Zoo
- ⊙ Other Sight

Activities, Courses & Tours
- ☺ Diving/Snorkelling
- ☺ Canoeing/Kayaking
- ⊙ Skiing
- ⊙ Surfing
- ☺ Swimming/Pool
- ⊙ Walking
- ⊛ Windsurfing
- • Other Activity/Course/Tour

Sleeping
- ⊜ Sleeping
- ⌂ Camping

Eating
- ⊗ Eating

Drinking
- ⊙ Drinking
- ○ Cafe

Entertainment
- ⊙ Entertainment

Shopping
- ⊙ Shopping

Information
- ◉ Post Office
- ❶ Tourist Information

Transport
- ⊙ Airport
- ⊗ Border Crossing
- ⊜ Bus
- ⊕ Cable Car/Funicular
- ⊖ Cycling
- ⊖ Ferry
- Ⓜ Metro
- ⊗ Monorail
- Ⓟ Parking
- Ⓢ S-Bahn
- Ⓣ Taxi
- Train/Railway
- Tram
- ⊙ Tube Station
- Ⓤ U-Bahn
- • Other Transport

Routes
- Tollway
- Freeway
- Primary
- Secondary
- Tertiary
- Lane
- Unsealed Road
- Plaza/Mall
- Steps
-)=(Tunnel
- Pedestrian Overpass
- Walking Tour
- Walking Tour Detour
- Path

Boundaries
- International
- State/Province
- Disputed
- Regional/Suburb
- Marine Park
- Cliff
- Wall

Population
- ◎ Capital (National)
- ◉ Capital (State/Province)
- ● City/Large Town
- ● Town/Village

Geographic
- ⊙ Hut/Shelter
- ⊛ Lighthouse
- ⊙ Lookout
- ▲ Mountain/Volcano
- ⊙ Oasis
- ⊙ Park
-)(Pass
- ⊕ Picnic Area
- ⊙ Waterfall

Hydrography
- River/Creek
- Intermittent River
- Swamp/Mangrove
- Reef
- Canal
- Water
- Dry/Salt/Intermittent Lake
- Glacier

Areas
- Beach/Desert
- Cemetery (Christian)
- Cemetery (Other)
- Park/Forest
- Sportsground
- Sight (Building)
- Top Sight (Building)

FIONN DAVENPORT

York & Northern England Dublin-born and -bred, Fionn has been traipsing about his favourite bits of England (north of the Watford Gap) for more than a decade, all the while falling in love with a country so near to his own yet so utterly unknown to most who assume that England is just one giant suburb dotted with roundabouts. His favourite place is his beloved Anfield in Liverpool, but he'd also settle for the streets of Manchester's Northern Quarter and the fine restaurants of West Didsbury.

MARC DI DUCA

York & Northern England, Day Trips from London From Farnham to the Farne Islands, Marc topped and tailed his native land for this guidebook. Born a mile from the Stockton & Darlington railway, Marc spent a decade in central Europe before becoming a full-time travel-guide author based in the southeast. Chilling extremities in the nippy River Tees, sinking ale in Cinque Ports, scrambling along Hadrian's Wall and stalking Dickens across six counties all formed part of his research for this guide.

Read more about Marc at:
lonelyplanet.com/members/madidu

BELINDA DIXON

Bath & Southwest England Belinda made a gleeful bolt for the southwest 17 years ago and has worked as a writer, journalist and local radio broadcaster there ever since. This is her sixth mission for Lonely Planet in the region, and it's seen her hugging sarsens in the stone circle at Avebury, rummaging for fossils at Lyme, and cresting tor tops on Dartmoor. All that and rigorously (very rigorously) testing all the food and drink she can manage.

Read more about Belinda at:
lonelyplanet.com/members/belindadixon

PETER DRAGICEVICH

London; Snowdonia & Wales After a dozen years reviewing music and restaurants for publications in New Zealand and Australia, London's bright lights and loud guitars could no longer be resisted. And maybe it's because he's got half a dragon in his surname, but Wales has held a fascination ever since Peter was sent there to write about castles for one of his first ever travel features. He has contributed to 20 Lonely Planet titles, including *Wales*, *England*, *Walking in Britain* and the last edition of this book.

Read more about Peter at:
lonelyplanet.com/members/peterdragicevich

ETAIN O'CARROLL

Oxford & Central England, Day Trips from London Travel writer and photographer Etain grew up in rural Ireland but now calls Oxford home. She has worked on more than 20 Lonely Planet books including numerous *England* and *Great Britain* guides as well as *Cycling Britain*. Her top tip? Oxford and the Cotswolds are expensive to live in but great places to visit on a budget. There are world-class museums, stunning architecture, gorgeous villages and ancient pubs – most of them free to visit.

Read more about Etain at:
lonelyplanet.com/members/etainocarroll

ANDY SYMINGTON

Edinburgh & Central Scotland, Scotland's Highlands & Islands Andy's Scottish forebears make their presence felt in his love of malt, a debatable ginger colour to his facial hair and a love of wild places. From childhood slogs up the M1 he graduated to making dubious road trips around the firths in a disintegrating Mini Metro and thence to peddling whisky in darkest Leith. Whilst living there, he travelled widely around the country in search of the perfect dram; now resident in Spain, he continues to visit very regularly.

Read more about Andy at:
lonelyplanet.com/members/andy_symington

NEIL WILSON

York & Northern England, Edinburgh & Central Scotland, Scotland's Highlands & Islands Neil has made many cross-border forays into 'God's own country' from his home in Edinburgh, as well as regular expeditions around Scotland. Good weather on this research trip allowed for a memorable ascent of Ingleborough hill, a knee-trashing mountain-bike descent of the Pennine Way into Hawes, and a sunset panorama of the Applecross hills from a campsite on Skye's Trotternish Ridge. Neil has written more than 50 guidebooks for various publishers, including Lonely Planet's *Scotland* and *England* guides.

Read more about Neil at:
lonelyplanet.com/members/neilwilson

Our Story

A beat-up old car, a few dollars in the pocket and a sense of adventure. In 1972 that's all Tony and Maureen Wheeler needed for the trip of a lifetime – across Europe and Asia overland to Australia. It took several months, and at the end – broke but inspired – they sat at their kitchen table writing and stapling together their first travel guide, *Across Asia on the Cheap*. Within a week they'd sold 1500 copies. Lonely Planet was born.

Today, Lonely Planet has offices in Melbourne, London and Oakland, with more than 600 staff and writers. We share Tony's belief that 'a great guidebook should do three things: inform, educate and amuse'.

Our Writers

DAVID ELSE

Coordinating Author David is a professional travel writer and the author of more than 40 books, including numerous editions of Lonely Planet's *Great Britain*, *England* and *Walking in Britain*. His knowledge comes from a lifetime of travel around the country, a passion dating from university years, when heading for the hills was always more attractive than visiting the library. Originally from London, David has lived in Yorkshire, Wales and Derbyshire, and is currently based on the southern edge of the Cotswolds. As well as guidebooks, David writes on travel for magazines and websites, and broadcasts regularly on BBC radio.

Read more about David at:
lonelyplanet.com/members/davidelse

DAVID ATKINSON

Snowdonia & Wales Lapsed Welshman David Atkinson has been chasing the call of hiraeth for two editions of Lonely Planet's *Great Britain* guide, focusing this time exclusively on the green, green grass of north Wales. David writes widely for newspapers and magazines, and blogs about travel around northwest England and Wales at Hit the North (nowhitthenorth.wordpress.com).

OLIVER BERRY

Bath & Southwest England, York & Northern England Oliver is a writer and photographer based in Cornwall. Among many other projects for Lonely Planet, Oliver has written the first editions of *Devon, Cornwall & Southwest England* and *The Lake District*, and worked on several editions of the *England* and *Great Britain* guides. Research highlights for this edition were sampling some traditional 'scrumpy' on a Somerset cider farm and watching the sun rise over Glastonbury Tor. You can see some of his latest work at his website www.oliverberry.com.

Read more about Oliver at:
lonelyplanet.com/members/oliverberry

JOE BINDLOSS

Oxford & Central England Born of English stock, albeit in Cyprus, Joe spends a lot of time in the Marches, not least because his parents and brothers live in the sleepy village of Clun (hell, they even go Morris dancing). For this book, Joe juggled exploring rugged uplands and picturesque medieval villages with writing for newspapers and magazines and being a full-time dad in London. Joe has been writing guidebooks for Lonely Planet since 1999, covering everywhere from rural England to the high reaches of the Himalaya.

Read more about Joe at:
lonelyplanet.com/members/bindibhaji

 More Writers . . . .

Published by Lonely Planet Publications Pty Ltd
ABN 36 005 607 983
2nd edition – July 2011
ISBN 978 1 74220 113 9
© Lonely Planet 2011   Photographs © as indicated 2011
10 9 8 7 6 5 4 3 2 1
Printed in China